CITE THIS BOOK

THUS:

first tuesday

Landlords, Tenants and Property Management

Second Edition

Cutoff Dates:
Legal editing of this book was
completed January 2003

Second Edition
1st printing June 2003

Editorial Staff

Legal Editor/Publisher:
Fred Crane

Managing Editor:
Brandi Ortega

Editorial Assistant:
Joseph Duong

Senior Editor:
Ai M. Kelley

Contributing Editor:
Jenice Tam

Comments or suggestions to:
first tuesday, P.O. Box 20069, Riverside, CA 92516
e-mail: ftuesday@pe.net
www.firsttuesdayonline.com

Table Of Contents

SECTION A

**Ownership &
Possession**

SECTION B

**Agency &
Property
Management**

SECTION C

**Deposits &
Rents**

SECTION G

SECTION H

Table of Forms

INTRODUCTION

This book is entitled *Landlords, Tenants and Property Management* and is written exclusively for California brokers, agents, landlords, attorneys and resident managers. The book is designed as a technical desk reference and educational tool on landlord/tenant relationships in income properties located in California.

The goal in of this book is to fully inform the reader of federal, state and local landlord/tenant rights and obligations, and the well-developed nature of interests held in real estate by landlords and tenants. The content of this book enables the reader to reach well beyond a minimum acceptable level of awareness of landlord/tenant real estate issues.

Landlords, Tenants and Property Management examines and applies the detailed and exacting rules of leasing and renting to both residential and nonresidential income properties. Hundreds of examples vividly present and resolve landlord/tenant situations encountered by owners and real estate licensees who manage income property or perform services as leasing agents.

Included are forms and notices required to establish leasing agencies, to create, manage and terminate tenancies and to preserve enforcement of rent obligations. These forms fully reflect relevant codes, judicial decisions and practices in effect on the date of this publication. Forms referenced are **first tuesday** published forms.

SECTION A

Ownership and Possession

Chapter 1

Fee vs. leasehold

This chapter examines the entitlement to possession of real estate held by owners of different interests in a parcel of real estate.

A matter of possession

A parcel of real estate is located by circumscribing its *legal description* on the "face of the earth." Based on the legal description, a surveyor locates and sets the corners and **surface boundaries** of the parcel.

The legal description is contained in deeds, subdivision maps or government surveys relating to the property.

However, a parcel of real estate is three dimensional, reaching beyond the surface boundaries.

In addition to the surface area within the boundaries, real estate consists of the soil below the surface to the core of the earth as well as the air space above it to infinity.

All permanent structures, crops and timber within this *inverse pyramid* are also a part of the parcel of real estate.

A **parcel of real estate** is often mistakenly thought of as a plot of unimproved land. Also mistaken is the notion any improvements can be treated as personal property, unless they are to be removed from the land.

Real estate, sometimes legally called *real property*, consists of:

- the land;

- the improvements and fixtures attached to the land; and

- all rights incidental or belonging to the property. [Calif. Civil Code §658]

Real estate includes buildings, fences, trees, watercourses and easements within the parcel's horizontal and vertical boundaries.

Anything below the surface, such as water and minerals, or above the surface in the air space, such as crops and timber, is part of the real estate.

The rental of a boat slip includes the water and the land below it, both of which comprise the real estate. Thus, landlord/tenant law controls the rental of the slip. [**Smith** v. **Municipal Court of San Mateo County** (1988) 202 CA3d 685]

In the case of a condominium unit, the air space enclosed within the walls is the real estate conveyed and held by the owner of the unit. The structure, land and air space outside the unit are the property of the homeowners' association, creating what is called a *common interest development (CID)*. [CC §1351(f)]

Possessing interests in real estate

The **ownership interests** a person may hold in real estate are called *estates*. Four kinds of estates exist in real estate:

- fee estates, sometimes referred to as inheritance or perpetual estates;

- life estates;

- leasehold estates, sometimes called estates for years; and

- estates at will. [CC §761]

In practice, these estates are separated into three categories: fee simple estates, leasehold estates and life estates. Estates at will are part of the leasehold estates controlled by landlord/tenant law.

A **life estate** terminates on the death of the owner of the life estate or the death of another person named in the deed conveying or reserving the life estate to the owner.

Leasehold interests in the real estate exist for a period of time. The interest will terminate when the period of time expires.

An **estate at will**, unlike a leasehold, is not conveyed in an exchange for value, called *consideration*. Estates at will terminate at the discretion of the fee owner, subject to proper notice.

Possession of real estate under leasehold interests and estates at will is controlled primarily by landlord/tenant law.

Fee ownership

A fee owner has the right to possess and control his property for an indefinite duration. A fee owner's possession is exclusive and absolute. The owner has the right to deny others permission to cross his boundaries. No one can be on the owner's property without his consent or they are trespassing. The owner may recover any money losses caused by the trespass.

A fee owner has the exclusive right to use and enjoy the property. As long as local ordinances such as building codes and zoning regulations are obeyed, a fee owner may do as he pleases with his property. A fee owner may build new buildings, tear down old ones, plant trees and shrubs, grow crops or simply leave the property unattended.

A fee owner may *occupy, sell, lease* or *encumber* his parcel of real estate, give it away or pass it on to his heirs or to anyone he chooses on his death. The fee estate is the interest in real estate transferred in a real estate sales transaction, unless a lesser interest is noted.

A fee owner is entitled to the land's surface and anything permanently located above or below it. [CC §829]

The ownership interests in one parcel may be separated into several fee interests. One person may own the mineral rights beneath the surface, another may own the surface rights, and yet another may own the rights to the air space. Each solely owned interest is held in fee in the same parcel.

Underground oil and gas reserves have a tendency to flow from one place to another. However, the right to extract oil and gas can be separately conveyed by the fee owner of the real estate. The drilling rights separated from the fee ownership are called *profit a prendre*. [**Gerhard** v. **Stephens** (1968) 68 C2d 864]

Profit a prendre is the right to remove profitable materials from property owned and possessed by another.

Consider a fee owner who grants separate fee interests in his property to two individuals. One individual receives the land's surface and air space rights. The other individual receives the subsurface oil and mineral rights.

The surface owner claims the title to the entire parcel of real estate should be vested — *quieted* — in his name.

The subsurface owner objects, claiming the surface owner's real estate interest is less than the entire fee estate in the property.

Here, the surface owner's fee interest in the parcel of real estate is separate from the subsurface ownership and possession of the oil and mineral rights. Also, they are not co-owners of the real estate. Both owners hold an individual fee estate in mutually exclusive and divided portions of the same parcel. [**In re Waltz** (1925) 197 C 263]

In most cases, one or more individuals own the entire fee and lease the subsurface rights to remove underground oil or minerals to others. Thus, the fee owner conveys a leasehold interest in the oil and minerals while retaining the fee interest.

Life estates and the life tenant

A life estate is an interest in a parcel of real estate lasting the lifetime of the *life tenant*. Life estates are granted by a deed entered into by the fee owner, an executor under a will or by a trustee under an inter vivos trust.

Life estates are commonly established by a fee owner who wishes to provide a home or financial security for another person during that person's lifetime, called the *controlling life*.

Life estates terminate on the death of the controlling life. Life estates may also be terminated by agreement or by merger of different ownership interests in the property.

For example, an owner of a vacation home has an elderly aunt who needs a place to live. The owner grants her a life estate in the vacation home for the duration of her lifetime. The aunt may live there for the rest of her life, even if she outlives the fee owner who granted her the life estate.

Although the aunt has the right to exclusive possession of the entire parcel of real estate, the owner retains title to the fee. Thus, the conveyance of a life estate transfers a right to possession which has been "carved out" of the fee, comparable to possession under a leasehold interest conveyed out of a fee. Unlike a lease, a life estate does not require rent to be paid to own the life estate.

On the aunt's death, possession of the property *reverts* to the fee owner or his heirs since the right to possession under the life estate is extinguished on the aunt's death.

The holder of a life estate based on his life has the right of possession until death, as if he were the owner in fee. The holder of a life estate is responsible for taxes, maintenance and a reasonable amount of property assessments. [CC §840]

However, the holder of a life estate *may not impair* the fee interest. [CC §818]

For instance, the holder of a life estate may not make alterations which decrease the property's value, such as removing or failing to care for valuable plants or demolishing portions of the improvements or land.

Conversely, the owner of the life estate has the right to lease the property to others and collect and retain all rents produced by the property during the term of the life estate. Profit on the sale of the life estate can be taken in addition to rental income.

For example, a life estate tenant enters into a lease with a logging company allowing him to remove trees from the property.

The property value increases after the trees are removed since the property's best use is as a farm. Additional crops can be planted on the cleared land, making the parcel more productive and able to generate greater rents.

The fee owner claims the life tenant did not have the right to remove the trees which were improvements.

However, the life tenant did not injure the fee interest by diminishing its value, called *impairment*. The life estate tenant is entitled to the profits from selling any timber located on the parcel, provided the property's value is not impaired by removal of the trees. [**Sallee** v. **Daneri** (1942) 49 CA2d 324]

Also, a life tenant is entitled to be reimbursed by the fee owner for the fee owner's share of the costs to improve the property.

For example, a city inspector notifies a life tenant the city will order the property demolished unless the property is renovated to bring it up to health and safety codes.

The life tenant has a duty, owed to the fee owner, not to impair the property's value. Thus, the life tenant must prevent the demolition of the property.

To do so, the life tenant improves the property, satisfying code requirements and increasing the property's value, all at considerable expense.

Here, the fee owner is liable to the life tenant for any increase in the value of the fee ownership in the property resulting from the improvements to the property made by the life tenant. [**Eastman** v. **Peterson** (1968) 268 CA2d 169]

The rights of a life tenant as against the fee owner are quite different from those of a leasehold tenant against the fee owner (landlord).

Leasehold interests held by tenants

Leaseholds are the result of rights *conveyed* to a tenant by the fee owner (or life estate tenant or master lessee) to possess a parcel of real estate. Leaseholds are created when the landlord and the tenant enter into a lease or a rental agreement which conveys a possessory interest in the real estate to the tenant.

The tenant is the owner of a leasehold with the right to possess and use the entire property until the lease expires. The title to the fee interest in the property remains with the landlord (or his successor) throughout the term of the leasehold, subject to the tenant's right to possession which is *carved out of the fee* on the fee owner's entry into the lease agreement.

In exchange for the right to occupy and use the property, the landlord is entitled to rental income from the tenant during the period of the tenancy.

Types of leaseholds

Four types of leasehold interests exist which can be held by tenants. The interests are classified by the length of their term:

- a fixed-term tenancy, simply known as a *lease* and legally called an *estate for years*;

- a periodic tenancy, usually referred to as a *rental*;

- a tenancy-at-will; and

- a tenancy-at-sufferance, commonly called a *holdover tenancy*.

A **fixed-term tenancy** lasts for a specific length of time agreed to in a lease between a landlord and tenant.

On expiration of the lease, the tenant's right to possession automatically terminates unless an agreement, such as an exercised option, extends the expiration date or renews or establishes an entirely new tenancy.

Periodic tenancies also last for a specific length of time, such as for a week or a month. However, in the creation of a periodic tenancy, the landlord and tenant agree to automatic successive rental periods of the same length of time, such as in a month-to-month tenancy.

A **tenant-at-will** has the right to possession of property with the consent of the owner. Tenancies-at-will can be terminated at any time by notice from either party or as set by agreement. Tenancies-at-will do not have a fixed duration, are usually not in writing and a rent obligation does not exist.

Leaseholds conveying special uses

In addition to the typical residential and nonresidential leases, leases exist which serve special purposes.

Oil, gas, water and **mineral leases** convey the right to use mineral deposits below the earth's surface to others.

The purpose of an oil lease is to discover and produce oil or gas. The lease is a tool used by the property owner to develop and realize the wealth of his land. The tenant provides the money and machinery for exploration and development.

The tenant pays the landlord rent, called a *royalty*, and keeps any profits from the sale of the oil or minerals he extracts from beneath the surface of the parcel.

A **ground lease** on a parcel of real estate is granted to a tenant in exchange for the payment of rent. Rent is based on the rental value of the portion of the parcel called land, whether the parcel is vacant or improved. The lease is a financing tool for fee owners of vacant unimproved land to induce others to acquire an interest in the property and develop the property.

Ground leases are common in more densely populated areas. Developers often need financial assistance from owners to avoid massive cash outlay to acquire unimproved parcels. Also, owners of developable property often refuse to sell, choosing to become landlords for the long-term rental income they will receive.

The original tenant under a ground lease constructs his own improvements. Typically, the ground lease is encumbered by a trust deed as security for the construction loan.

Master leases benefit owners who want the financial advantages of renting fully improved property, but do not want the day-to-day risks of managing the property.

For instance, an owner of a shopping center and a prospective owner-operator agree to a master lease.

As the master tenant, the owner-operator will collect rent from the many subtenants, address their needs and concerns and maintain the property. The master tenant is responsible for the rent due under the master lease, even if the subtenants do not pay their rents.

The master lease is sometimes called a *sandwich lease* since the master tenant is "sandwiched" between the fee owner (the landlord on the master lease) and the many subtenants and their possession under subleases.

The **master lease** is a regular nonresidential lease agreement form with the deletion of any clause prohibiting assignments and subletting. A **sublease** is also a regular nonresidential lease agreement with an additional clause referencing the attached master lease and declaring the sublease subject to the terms of the master lease. [See **first tuesday** Form 552]

Another type of special-use lease is the **farm lease**, sometimes called *cropping agreements* or *grazing leases*.

The tenant will operate the farm and pay the landlord either a flat fee for rent or a percentage of the value of the crops or livestock produced on the land.

Chapter 2

Types of tenancies

This chapter discusses the different types of tenancies and how each is established.

Know your tenancy or lose time

A landlord and tenant enter into a lease without provisions for an option to renew or extend the term of the lease on expiration.

Several months before the lease expires, they begin negotiations to enter into a new lease. An agreement is not reached before the original lease expires. The tenant remains in possession on expiration of the lease — an unlawful detainer of the premises — commonly called a *holdover*.

The landlord and tenant continue lease negotiations. Meanwhile, the tenant pays monthly rent based on the old lease amount, which the landlord accepts.

Ultimately, they fail to agree on the terms for a new lease.

The landlord then serves a notice on the tenant to either *stay and pay* a substantially higher monthly rent or vacate. [See **first tuesday** Forms 569, 571 or 579; see Chapter 21]

The tenant does neither; he remains in possession and does not pay the increased rent.

Can the landlord file an unlawful detainer (UD) action and proceed to evict the tenant without further notice?

Yes! The tenant went from a fixed-term tenancy (lease) to a tenancy-at-sufferance (holdover) to a periodic (month-to-month) tenancy on acceptance of rent during the holdover period. The right to possession under the periodic tenancy ended due to the notice and the tenant's failure to pay rent (set by the notice) or quit.

However, the type of notice to quit used when the landlord decides to terminate the tenant's right to possession will differ depending on the **type of tenancy** which exists and the purpose of the notice.

Tenancies as leasehold estates

Tenancies are possessory interests in real estate, called *leasehold estates*.

Four types of tenancies exist:

1. Fixed-term tenancies;

2. Periodic tenancies;

3. Tenancies-at-sufferance; and

4. Tenancies-at-will.

To initially establish a tenancy, a landlord must somehow transfer to the tenant — either in writing, orally or by his conduct — the right to occupy the real estate. If the landlord does not transfer the right to occupy, the occupant who takes possession is a *trespasser*.

All tenancies must have an agreed-to termination date or be capable of termination by notice. Termination of a fixed-term tenancy conveyed under a **lease** occurs on the expiration date stated in the lease, without further notice.

For a month-to-month rental agreement, the automatically renewable periodic tenancy it conveys is terminated by service of a 30/60-day notice to vacate at any time or a 3-day notice on a breach of the rental agreement. [See Chapters 19 and 21]

A tenant's possessory interest in real estate can shift from one type of tenancy to another due to notices, expiration of a lease or by conduct.

Thus, before a landlord can file a UD action and proceed with the eviction process based on an unlawful detainer by the tenant, the tenant's right to possession under his tenancy must be terminated by the proper notice to vacate (quit), unless the tenant holds possession under a lease which has expired.

In our opening example, the tenant traversed three different types of **tenancies**:

1. *Fixed-term* (lease);

2. *Sufferance* (no agreed-to holdover); and

3. *Month-to-month* (acceptance of monthly payments), also called a *periodic tenancy*.

The tenant started his occupancy under a fixed-term tenancy, commonly called a *lease*. During the term of the lease, the tenant can only be evicted for cause — and then only after service of a 3-day notice to cure the breach or vacate (quit) the property. [See **first tuesday** Form 576]

On expiration of a lease, the tenant who remains in possession without an agreement or acceptance of rent by the landlord becomes a holdover tenant, legally called a *tenant-at-sufferance*. The landlord does not have to give a notice to vacate before filing a UD action to evict the holdover tenant. [Calif. Code of Civil Procedure §1161(1)]

However, if the landlord accepts monthly rent from a tenant after expiration of the lease, a month-to-month tenancy is established on the terms and conditions of the expired lease agreement, unless a renewal or extension option exists. When these options exist, the lease is renewed or extended by the post-expiration acceptance of the rent called for in the option. [Calif. Civil Code §1945]

To terminate a month-to-month tenancy created by acceptance of monthly rent after expiration of a lease, the landlord must serve the tenant with a notice to vacate before filing a UD action. [**Colyear** v. **Tobriner** (1936) 7 C2d 735]

Fixed-term tenancy

A **fixed-term tenancy**, also known as an *estate for years* or *leasehold*, is an agreement between the landlord and the tenant for a fixed time period, typically called a *lease*. [CC §761]

A lease must have a beginning date, called the *commencement date*, and an ending date, called the *expiration date*. If the rental period is longer than one year, the lease must be in writing and signed by the landlord and tenant to be enforceable. [CC §1624]

In a fixed-term tenancy, the tenant has an exclusive right to possession of the premises for the term of the lease. On expiration of the lease, the tenancy automatically terminates. The tenant is not entitled to any notice to vacate other than the notice in the lease of the tenancy's expiration date. [CCP §1161(1)]

For example, a landlord and tenant orally agree to a six-month lease.

At the end of six months, the landlord and tenant orally agree to another six-month lease.

At the end of the second term, the tenant refuses to vacate. The tenant claims the landlord must first serve him with a notice to vacate.

However, the tenant is not entitled to any further notice beyond the agreed-to termination date.

The oral agreement was not a periodic tenancy, such as a month-to-month rental agreement, even though it contained monthly rent payments. Rather, the occupancy agreement was a fixed-term lease with a set expiration date.

Thus, the tenant's right to possession terminates on expiration of the orally agreed-to six-month period. The oral lease is enforceable since it was for a term of less than one year. [**Camp** v. **Matich** (1948) 87 CA2d 660]

A fixed-term tenancy provides a tenant with several advantages:

- the right to occupy for the fixed term;

- a predetermined rental amount; and

- limitations on termination or modification.

However, some disadvantages also exist for the fixed-term tenant:

- the tenant is liable for rent for the entire term (subject to the landlord's duty to mitigate losses); and

- the tenant may need to vacate prior to expiration of the leasing period and assign or sublet the premises to a new tenant to cover rent obligations, but cannot due to prohibitions in the lease, called *restraints on alienation*.

Periodic tenancy

If the landlord finds a fixed-term tenancy too restrictive or inflexible for his financial purposes or use requirements, a periodic tenancy may be more suitable.

A periodic tenancy automatically continues for **successive periods**, each for the same length of time, until terminated by a notice to vacate. The length of each successive period of time is determined by the interval between scheduled rental payments.

Examples of **periodic payment** intervals include:

- annual rental payments, indicating a year-to-year tenancy;

- monthly rental payments, indicating a month-to-month tenancy; and

- weekly rental payments, indicating a week-to-week tenancy.

Consider a property manager who rents an apartment to a tenant under a fixed-term lease. At the end of the leasing period, the tenant retains possession and continues to pay rent monthly, which the property manager accepts.

Later, the tenant is served with a notice to vacate.

On expiration of the notice, the tenant refuses to vacate. The tenant claims he is now a tenant-at-will and entitled to an additional 3-day notice to vacate before he is unlawfully detaining the property since the notice to vacate served on him merely terminated his right to possession, which was for an indefinite term, and made him a tenant-at-will on expiration of the notice.

However, an agreement for an **indefinite term** with a monthly rent schedule is a month-to-month tenancy. Thus, a tenant is only entitled to one notice to vacate before a UD action may be filed to evict him. [**Palmer** v. **Zeis** (1944) 65 CA2d Supp. 859]

The flexibility of a periodic tenancy allows the landlord and the tenant to terminate a month-to-month tenancy by giving the appropriate notice to vacate to the other party. [CC §1946; see Chapter 21]

Also, the operator of a **residential hotel** may not require a resident to change units, or to check out and re-register, to avoid creating a month-to-month tenancy and falling under landlord/tenant law. A residential hotel operator violating this rule is liable for a $500 civil penalty and attorney fees. [CC §1940.1]

Tenancy-at-sufferance

When a fixed-term (lease) or periodic (month-to-month) tenancy terminates by prior agreement or notice, the tenant who remains in possession — a *tenant-at-sufferance* — unlawfully detains the property from the landlord.

A tenant-at-sufferance is more commonly called a *holdover tenant*. A holdover tenant retains possession of the premises without any contractual right to do so, a situation called an *unlawful detainer (UD)*.

A holdover tenant no longer owes rent under the expired lease or terminated rental agreement. However, the lease or rental agreement usually calls for a penalty rate of daily rent owed for each day the tenant holds over. Without a holdover rent provision, the tenant owes the landlord the *reasonable rental value* of the property, a daily rate owed for each day the tenant holds over in possession after expiration of his tenancy.

Holdover rent is due **after** the tenant vacates or is evicted, when the holdover period is known and the amount owed can be determined.

Note — The landlord's acceptance of "hold- over" rent **prior** *to the tenant vacating or being evicted establishes a periodic tenancy on receipt of the rent.*

For example, a tenant with a fixed-term lease holds over after the lease expires. The lease contains no agreement for the amount of rent due during any holdover period.

On the tenant's failure to vacate, the landlord serves the tenant a notice to either pay a rent amount substantially higher than rental market rates or vacate. The tenant refuses to pay any rent or vacate.

The landlord files a UD action seeking payment of rent at the rate given in the notice to pay or quit since the tenant did not vacate.

At the UD hearing, the landlord is awarded the reasonable market rental value for the entire time the tenant held over, not the higher rent demanded in the notice to pay or quit. The tenant never agreed to any amount of rent after the lease expired. Thus, a periodic tenancy was not established.

The higher rental amount demanded in the notice to pay or quit was not accepted by the holdover tenant since he refused to pay it.

Thus, a UD court will only award a reasonable rental value for the time period the tenant held over since he is a tenant-at-sufferance in unlawful possession of the property. Also, the notice to pay or quit was not needed to evict the tenant on expiration of the lease. [**Shenson** v. **Shenson** (1954) 124 CA2d 747]

Now consider a tenant who enters into a fixed-term lease for the second floor of a building.

Without a charge for additional rent, the tenant will also take and retain possession of the third floor until the landlord secures a bona fide tenant. The tenant has the right of first refusal to rent the third floor should the landlord find a tenant. If the tenant does not exercise his right of first refusal to rent the third floor, his right to possession of the third floor ends.

The tenant moves into the second and third floors of the building. Later, the landlord locates a prospective tenant to rent the third floor.

The landlord notifies the tenant he must immediately exercise his right of first refusal or vacate the third floor.

The tenant does not exercise his right of first refusal and refuses to move. The tenant claims he is a tenant-at-will with the right to receive a notice to vacate before his right to occupancy can be terminated.

However, the tenant's lease agreement for the third floor did have a *specific termination date*, i.e., the date the tenant fails to exercise his right of first refusal to remain in possession. Thus, he is a tenant for a fixed-term and not a tenant-at-will since his occupancy ended on expiration of his right of first refusal.

The tenant, now a holdover, became a tenant-at-sufferance on expiration of his right of first refusal. Thus, the tenant is not entitled to any further notice to quit to establish his unlawful detainer of the premises. The tenant's notice of the date of termination of the occupancy was his refusal to rent under his right of first refusal. [**Vandenbergh** v. **Davis** (1961) 190 CA2d 694]

For the tenant with a right of first refusal to be entitled to a notice to vacate and any additional period of lawful occupancy after expiration of a lease, a provision so stating must be included in the lease or the right of first refusal agreement.

A tenancy-at-sufferance also arises when a resident manager's compensation includes the right to occupy a unit rent-free, and then the landlord terminates the employment and the resident manager fails to vacate.

For example, a landlord hires a caretaker to do general maintenance work around an apartment complex in exchange for rent-free possession of a unit in the complex.

Several months later, during a dispute with the landlord, the tenant refuses to work.

The landlord delivers a notice to the tenant to immediately pay rent (as demanded in the notice) or quit. The tenant does neither and the landlord files a UD action.

The tenant contends he is a tenant-at-will, entitled to a notice to vacate before the landlord can establish an unlawful detainer and file his UD action.

However, the tenant's right to occupancy ended when his employment ended, a fixed term. Thus, the tenant became a holdover tenant who was not entitled to notice, other than the notice from the landlord terminating the employment, before the landlord could commence a UD action to evict him. [**Karz** v. **Mecham** (1981) 120 CA3d Supp. 1]

If the employee is to receive notice and time to pay or vacate on termination of his employment (and right to occupancy), his employment agreement must provide for it.

Under rent control ordinances, a tenant-at-sufferance must receive a notice to vacate. However, courts in rent-controlled areas have exempted employee-tenants from rent control protection by classifying them, for purposes of rent control, as licensees rather than tenants.

Yet, employee-tenants clearly are not licensees (for any other purpose) since they have exclusive rights to occupy the unit assigned to them. [**Chan** v. **Antepenko** (1988) 203 CA3d Supp. 21]

Tenancy-at-will

The characteristics of a tenancy-at-will include:

- possession delivered to the tenant with the landlord's knowledge and consent;

- possession for an indefinite and unspecified period; and

- no provision for the payment of rent.

For a tenancy-at-will, a written notice to vacate or set a rental rate is required to make any change in the right to occupy the premises. However, the parties can always agree to a shorter or longer notice period. [CC §§789; 1946]

For example, an owner-occupant agrees to sell his office building under a purchase agreement providing for the seller to retain the **free use and possession** of the property after closing until he can occupy an office building he is constructing. Thus, a tenancy-at-will is created.

The buyer agrees in the purchase agreement to give the seller a 90-day written notice to either vacate the property or pay rent.

The buyer resells the property to a new owner.

The new owner demands the tenant-seller pay rent or vacate immediately. The new owner claims he is not subject to the prior owner's **unrecorded agreement** to give a 90-day notice.

However, the new owner acquired the property subject to the rights held by the **tenant in possession**. Thus, the new owner is charged with *constructive knowledge* of the unrecorded agreement regarding notices and took title *subject to* the terms of the agreement.

Until the tenant-at-will receives the appropriate notice to vacate, he is not unlawfully detaining the property and the owner/landlord cannot proceed with a UD action to recover possession. [**First & C. Corporation** v. **Wencke** (1967) 253 CA2d 719]

A tenancy-at-will is terminated automatically should the tenant **assign or sublet** his right to occupy the property to another tenant. The new tenant becomes a tenant-at-sufferance or a trespasser. [**McLeran** v. **Benton** (1887) 73 C 329]

Also, the tenancy-at-will terminates on the **death** of either the landlord or tenant, unless an agreement to the contrary exists. [**Dugand** v. **Magnus** (1930) 107 CA 243]

Other situations giving rise to a tenancy-at-will include:

- when a tenant with the right to indefinitely occupy the property in exchange for making improvements fails to make the improvements [**Carteri** v. **Roberts** (1903) 140 C 164];

- when a tenant takes possession of the property under an unenforceable lease (e.g., the written lease was never signed by any of the parties) — unless a periodic rent is accepted which establishes a periodic tenancy [**Psihozios** v. **Humberg** (1947) 80 CA2d 215]; or

- when a tenant takes possession of the property without the payment of rent while negotiations on the lease are still in progress. [**Miller** v. **Smith** (1960) 179 CA2d 114]

Terminating a tenancy

A landlord's primary concern when terminating a tenancy is the type of notice to vacate to be delivered to establish an unlawful detainer under the different **types of tenancies**, including:

- a *tenancy for a fixed-term* — the landlord does not need to deliver any notice to vacate prior to commencing a UD action against a holdover tenant since the tenancy automatically expires by the terms of the lease [CCP §1161(1)];

- a *periodic tenancy* — the notice must be for a period at least as long as the interval between scheduled rental payments, but need not exceed 30/60 days depending on the length of the occupancy and whether the property is residential or nonresidential [CC §1946; see Chapter 21];

- a *tenancy-at-sufferance* — the holdover tenant is not entitled to any further notice prior to commencing eviction proceedings since a lease has expired or a periodic tenancy has been terminated [CCP §1161];

- a *tenancy-at-will* — a 30/60-day notice to vacate or otherwise alter the tenancy-at-will is required [CC §789; see Chapter 29];

- a *residential property in a rent control area* — termination of the right to possession is restricted by local ordinances; and

- a *tenancy-at-will in a mobilehome park* — a 60-day written notice is required to be delivered to the tenant. [CC §798.55(b)]

Further, a landlord and tenant by agreement can establish a shorter or lengthier notice period. Industrial and commercial tenants typically require three months minimum notice due to the time lost receiving and responding to a notice since it must first go through multiple tiers of corporate management. However, the notice-to-vacate period must be at least seven days. [CC §1946]

Changing the type of tenancy

A landlord, by using an improper notice, can end up with a different tenancy relationship from the one he had with a tenant to begin with.

When a tenancy is altered, in writing or by conduct, one type of tenancy can be converted into another.

A classic example involving a change in the type of tenancy arises when a holdover tenant (a tenancy-at-sufferance) becomes a month-to-month tenant (a periodic tenancy).

A landlord who accepts monthly rent from a holdover tenant under an expired lease has elected to treat the continuing tenancy as periodic. [**Peter Kiewit Sons Co.** v. **Richmond Redevelopment Agency** (1986) 178 CA3d 435]

Thus, a proper notice to vacate, a requisite to a UD eviction, must be served on the holdover tenant who paid rent accepted by the landlord. [Colyear, *supra*]

When the tenant holds over after a fixed-term tenancy expires or a periodic tenancy is terminated and the landlord accepts rent, the prior agreement is *renewed* on the same terms except for the period of occupancy, which is now periodic. [CC §1945]

On expiration of a fixed-term lease, the landlord's continued acceptance of rental payments does not renew the tenancy for another term equal to the term of the original lease. Rather, the tenancy is extended as a periodic tenancy for consecutive periods equal to the interval between rent payments — being one month if rent is paid monthly. [CC §1945]

For example, a landlord and tenant agree in writing to a three-year lease with rent paid annually in advance.

At the end of the three-year lease, the tenant holds over without further agreement. The tenant tenders an annual rent payment which the landlord accepts.

The acceptance of rent by the landlord extends the expired three-year lease for a period of one year since the rent paid was for an annual period. Without a written agreement to the contrary, the tenancy is extended only for the period of the prepaid rent even though the term of the original lease, the terms of which control the extended one-year occupancy, was for a three-year period. [**Hagenbuch** v. **Kosky** (1956) 142 CA2d 296]

Tenancy under a defective lease

A periodic tenancy arises when:

- a written lease is void or an agreement was never signed by either party;

- the tenant is in possession; and

- the landlord has accepted rent.

For example, a landlord and tenant orally agree to enter into a written five-year lease. The tenant moves into the building and begins paying monthly rent.

Ultimately, the lease is signed by the parties, but it is defectively prepared and unenforceable. One year later, the tenant sends the landlord a notice of his decision to vacate the building.

Can the landlord hold the tenant liable for the rent remaining for the full term of the five-year lease since both parties have been performing based on the terms of the unenforceable lease?

No! When a tenant enters into possession under an unenforceable lease and pays rent in monthly intervals, he is a month-to-month tenant. The tenancy can be terminated by either party by delivering a notice to vacate (quit) the premises. [**Kingston** v. **Colburn** (1956) 139 CA2d 623]

Transient occupancies and removals

An occupant of a vacation property, hotel, motel, inn, boardinghouse, lodginghouse, tourist home or similar sleeping accommodation for a period of 30 days or less is classified as a **guest**, also called a *transient occupant*.

The property occupied by the guest is called a *lodging, accommodation* or *unit* and not a rental which is a landlord/tenant characterization.

The guest's occupancy of the accommodations contracted for is labeled a *stay*, not possession, since the owner or manager of the property is entitled to enter the unit at check-out time even though the guest may not have departed yet.

The contract entered into for the lodging is usually called a *reservation agreement*, but never a rental agreement or lease.

Also, guests pay a daily *rate*, not a daily or weekly rent, and they *arrive* at a time on a date for *check-in*, not for commencement of possession. Likewise, guests *depart* at an hour on a date agreed to as the *check-out time*. Unlike a tenant, a guest does not vacate the premises, they check out.

When a guest fails to depart at the scheduled check-out hour on the date agreed, no holdover tenancy is created as occurs under a tenancy for occupancy conveyed by a rental agreement or lease. Thus, a UD action or court involvement is not required to evict the guest. [CC §1940(b)]

However, for the owner or manager to avoid the UD eviction process, the guest, when checking in, must have signed a notice stating:

- the unit is needed at check-out time for another guest who has been promised the unit; and

- if he has not departed at check-out time, the owner or manager may enter, take possession of the guest's property, re-key the doors and clean up the unit for the next guest. [CC §1865; see **first tuesday** Form 593]

To remove a guest who fails to timely depart the unit and remains in the unit after a demand has been made to leave, the police can be called in by the manager if self-help might cause a breach of the peace. The police or the sheriff will assist, without the need for a court order, in the removal of the guest to prevent a danger to persons or property during the re-keying, removal of possessions and clean-up for the arrival of the next guest. [Calif. Penal Code §§602(r); 803.1(a)(3)]

Transient occupancies include all occupancies which are taxed by local ordinance as transient occupancies or could be taxed as such by the city or by the county. Taxwise, the occupancy is considered a *personal privilege*, not a tenancy. Time share units, when occupied by their owners, are not transient occupancies and are not subject to these ordinances and taxes. [Calif. Revenue and Taxation Code §7280]

Transient units do not include *residential hotels* since the occupants of residential hotels treat the dwelling they occupy as their *primary residence*. Also, the occupancy of most individuals in residential hotels is more than 30 days.

A broker or any other person or entity who manages "vacation rental" occupancies for owners of single-family homes, units in a common interest development (condominium project), a unit in an apartment complex or any other residence subject to a local transient occupancy tax, must maintain **accounting records**.

Also, the property manager must send a monthly accounting to each owner he represents and make the records available for inspection and reproduction by the owner, as well as comply with the transient occupancy tax regarding collection, payment and record keeping. [CC §1864]

Chapter 3

Landlord's right to enter

This chapter addresses resolutions to conflicts between a tenant's right to privacy within his rented space and the landlord's need to access the space.

Conflict with tenant's right to privacy

Unknown to a residential landlord, a tenant changes the locks on the door to his unit.

Several months later, the tenant is arrested by law enforcement officers as he steps out of his apartment. The tenant is hastily escorted away. He leaves the light on and his pet inside, but locks the door.

The landlord becomes aware of the tenant's dilemma. Fearful the gas stove was also left on, he attempts, but is unable to enter with his passkey.

The landlord **calls the police** to witness the entry to make sure the apartment is in a safe and secure condition. The landlord then enters the apartment through a window. The police are let in to observe the landlord's conduct. They proceed to check out the apartment.

Unfortunately for the tenant, the police find illegal possessions in plain view casually lying around the apartment.

Did the landlord have the right to enter the apartment?

And did he have the right to allow the police to come in?

Yes to both! The landlord had the right to enter. The landlord reasonably believed the safety of his other tenants and the building might have been in jeopardy.

Also, the officer was present at the landlord's request to act as an eyewitness, so the tenant could not legitimately claim the landlord removed any of his possessions. [**People** v. **Plane** (1969) 274 CA2d 1]

In contrast, consider the landlord who permits the police to search a tenant's garage at the **request of the police,** but without a warrant. The police suspect the tenant is manufacturing drugs.

May a landlord consent and allow the police to enter a tenant's garage?

No! The landlord has no right to possession while the premises is occupied by the tenant. Thus, the landlord has no possessory right which allows him to let the police enter the premises once he has leased it to the tenant, even if he suspects the tenant of committing a crime. The police must first obtain a search warrant to legally authorize them to come onto the premises occupied by the tenant. [**United States** v. **Warner** (9th Cir. 1988) 843 F2d 401]

However, a landlord *does* have the right to allow police to enter a unit abandoned by the tenant under state law rules of abandonment or surrender. [**United States** v. **Sledge** (9th Cir. 1981) 650 F2d 1075]

Also, "lock-box" entry by the police with the assistance of a multiple-listing service (MLS) member to check out a crime is prohibited without a warrant. The entry violates the purpose of a listing broker's agency and his lock-box authority. The broker may enter only to show the premises to prospective tenants who accompany him (or other authorized agents), not to the police. The police are not prospective tenants. [**People** v. **Jaquez** (1985) 163 CA3d 918]

Landlord's right to enter

A landlord's right to enter a residential or nonresidential unit during the period of the tenant's occupancy is severely limited since the possessory rights to the property have been conveyed to the tenant and are no longer held by the landlord until *reversion*.

For instance, a residential landlord may enter the tenant's actual dwelling space during the lease or rental term only in limited circumstances, namely:

- in an emergency;

- to make repairs, alterations, improvements, or supply services which are either necessary or previously agreed to by the tenant;

- to complete a pre-termination inspection for deficiencies which may possibly be deducted from the security deposit [See Chapter 13];

- to show the unit to prospective or actual buyers, lenders, tenants or repairmen and contractors;

- when the tenant has vacated the premises by *surrender* or *abandonment*; or

- under a court order allowing entry. [Calif. Civil Code §1954]

A property manager's entry into a tenant's unit out of concern for the safety of the property or his other tenants constitutes an *emergency* allowing entry without the tenant's knowledge and permission. The property manager may properly enter the unit for the limited purpose of dealing with the emergency. [Plane, *supra*]

Consider a nonresidential real estate lease which prohibits any tenant violations of government laws and regulations.

The landlord asks the tenant for permission to come onto the property to investigate whether the leased property contains any contamination from hazardous waste.

The tenant refuses to give the landlord permission to conduct the investigation, claiming the landlord does not have a right to determine whether contamination exists until the lease expires.

However, the landlord has the right to determine if contamination is occurring on the property since hazardous waste contamination is a **violation of the law** and is a breach of the lease provision prohibiting unlawful activities on the property. [**Sachs v. Exxon Company, U.S.A.** (1992) 9 CA4th 1491]

Notice of entry for repairs

Before a residential landlord proceeds with any maintenance or services which require entry into a tenant's unit, the tenant must be given a written notice of the landlord's intent to enter. Maintenance includes all routine or non-emergency repairs, decorations, alterations, improvements, replacements or services, whether or not agreed to by the tenant. [CC §1954; see Form 567 accompanying this chapter]

The written notice of the need to enter must be served on the tenant and give him a reasonable time period in which to prepare for the entry. A 24-hour notice is considered reasonable, unless extenuating circumstances indicate more time is needed to actually receive the notice or prepare for the entry.

Service of a 24-hour notice of entry in advance of the entry is accomplished by **any one** of the following methods:

- handing a written notice to the tenant personally;

- handing the notice to an occupant of the unit who appears of suitable age and discretion to relay the notice to the tenant; or

- posting the notice on or near the usual entry door or under the door so it will be discovered by the tenant.

RIGHT TO ENTER AND FOR SALE NOTICE

DATE:_____, 20_____, at _____, California

Items left blank or unchecked are not applicable.

FACTS:

You are a Tenant under a lease or rental agreement

Dated: _____, at

_____, California

entered into by _____, Tenant,

and _____, Landlord,

recorded _____, as Instrument No. _____,

in _____ County Records, California,

regarding real estate referred as: _____

_____

_____

_____

> **NOTICE:**
>
> By this notice, a landlord or his listing agent may enter a tenant's unit during normal business hours after giving as least twenty-four (24) hours telephonic notice of their intent to enter for the purpose of exhibiting the unit to the buyers. [Calif. Civil Code §1954]

NOTICE TO TENANT:

1. You are hereby advised the property containing your unit has been placed on the real estate market as "For Sale".

2. During the period of 120 days following the date of the notice the landlord or his listing agent for the sale of the property may need to enter your unit during normal business hours for the purpose of exhibiting the premise for review by prospective or actual buyers.

3. At lease 24 hours prior to entry for this purpose you will be given telephonic or persona; notice of our intent to enter.

4. You are not required to be present on the premise during the entry and review. A passkey will be used should you be absent.

5. On completing the exhibiting of the unit and departing the premises, the re0al estate agents will leave a written note indicating they have entered and completed their review of the unit.

Date: _____, 20_____

Landlord: _____

Listing Agent: _____

Signature: _____

Address: _____

_____

Phone: _____

Fax: _____

E-mail: _____

Alternatively, the notice may be mailed, but at least six days must pass after mailing before the intended entry can be scheduled to occur. [CC §1954]

The time of day for the entry must only be during normal business hours, emergencies excepted. If the entry is after business hours, the tenant's consent must be obtained "at the time of entry," even if previously arranged to occur after business hours.

The notice of entry procedures should never be used to harass a tenant in a retaliatory and abusive manner. [CC §1954]

A tenant in a community apartment project or a homeowner in a condominium project, collectively called *common interest developments* (CIDs), must receive no less than 15 days and no more than 30 days written notice when the management or association needs the occupants to vacate the project in order to treat termites. [CC §1364(d)(2)]

Entry for pre-termination inspection

A residential landlord may enter a tenant's unit when the tenant requests a joint pre-termination inspection of the premises. [See Chapter 13]

The purpose of the pre-termination inspection prior to expiration or termination of the tenancy is to advise the tenant of any deficiencies in the condition of the premises so the tenant can correct or eliminate them before vacating to avoid deductions from his security deposit.

Before the residential landlord may enter to conduct the pre-termination inspection, the tenant must be given a 48-hour written notice stating the date and time for the inspection. [CC §1950.5(f)(1)]

Service of the 48-hour notice of entry is accomplished in the same manner as for the 24-hour notice of advance entry to complete repairs.

However, the tenant may waive the 48-hour notice if both he and the landlord sign a written waiver. [CC §1950.5(f)(1)]

Entry during "For Sale" period

Real estate brokers who list property for sale which is **occupied by a tenant**, called a *rental*, need to inform the seller of the **agent's right** to coordinate inspections of the property by prospective buyers under one of two notice procedures. [CC §1954]

The purpose of the advance notice of entry is to eliminate the element of surprise which leaves the tenant unprepared to deal with the inspection and to prepare the unit for exhibition on a later 24-hour notice.

Once informed of the procedure for entry and inspection, some sellers, justifiably or not, may restrict inspections of the property to **qualified buyers** who have entered into a purchase agreement. Thus, sellers might not allow prospective buyers to preview the premises. Sellers often feel the tenant should remain uninvolved in the sales process. The weaker the sales market, with its lessened likelihood of a sale, the greater the seller's concern will be to keep the tenant uninvolved until the agents have a buyer who has entered into a purchase agreement with the seller.

To avoid surprises for all when the tenant is contacted to cooperate in exhibiting the premises to the buyer or the buyer's home inspector, two procedures exist for the **listing agent** to enter the unit with a buyer.

A **24-hour advance written notice** of the intended entry may be served on the tenant personally, or on an occupant of the unit of suitable age and ability to inform the tenant of the notice, or by posting the notice on or near the entrance to the unit or leaving it under the door. If instead it is mailed by regular or certified mail, six days must pass before the time for entry can occur. [CC §1954; see Form 567]

The alternative to the 24-hour written notice is a **120-day "For Sale" notice** which is given to the tenant personally or by regular mail during the listing period. The notice commences a 120-day period during which the landlord or the landlord's listing agent may, on a 24-hour notice by phone, enter the unit during normal business hours with a prospective or actual buyer or the buyer's home inspector to conduct an inspection of the unit.

At the time for entry, the tenant then receives no less than **24 hours advance notice by phone** (or orally if in person) of the actual entry. The actual entry is conditioned on leaving a written note in the unit regarding the entry and completion of the inspection. [CC §1954; see Form 116 accompanying this chapter]

Here, the 24-hour notice by phone given during the 120-day period following service of the written "For Sale" notice is unique to sellers and their listing agents. The selling agent representing a buyer must arrange for the listing agent to give the 24-hour advance telephonic notice. The selling agent may not be given this authority, unless he is also the listing agent.

Thus, on taking a listing to sell property occupied by tenants, the listing agent needs to inform the seller of the two notice procedures for entry to exhibit the unit. Once resolved as to which notice procedure the seller is willing to authorize, the information is shared with selling agents through the MLS printout on the listed property under "showing instructions," such as "call the listing office (LO) or listing agent (LA) to arrange for 24-hour telephonic (or written) notice of entry."

The selling agent should be reminded when the listing agent arranges for entry by telephone that on completion of the inspection he must leave his card or other document in the unit noting he has entered and shown the property.

Entry on surrender or abandonment

A residential landlord or his manager may enter a dwelling unit when the tenant has vacated the unit and his right to possession has been terminated by expiration of a lease, surrender, a declaration of forfeiture under a 3-day notice or a notice of abandonment.

Neither a surrender nor an abandonment of the tenant's right to possession takes place when the tenant merely vacates the unit. The landlord must react to the tenant's vacating to actually work a termination of the tenant's leasehold interest to possession, and thus establish a surrender or abandonment.

By a surrender, the tenant who has breached the lease vacates the premises and conducts himself in a manner which indicates to the landlord the tenant's desire to both:

- **terminate possession** by a return of the premises to the landlord; and

- **cancel the lease** or rental agreement obligations owed to the landlord.

If the landlord agrees to the termination of the tenant's possession and a cancellation of the lease/rental agreement, or if the landlord's conduct on taking possession constitutes his acceptance of the tenant's offer to vacate in exchange for cancelling the lease agreement, a *surrender* has occurred. Thus, the tenancy is terminated (as well as the lease) and the landlord is allowed to enter and take possession of the dwelling unit (by mutual agreement).

As an alternative to accepting possession and cancelling any right to collect future rents due under the lease/rental agreement by a surrender, the landlord may serve the tenant with a 3-day notice to pay or quit and include a declaration of forfeiture in the notice. Thus, on expiration of the 3-day notice, the tenant's right to possession has been eliminated and the landlord or his agents may enter and reoccupy or relet the premises since it is vacant. The lease agreement remains uncancelled.

An *abandonment* requires a **breach** of the lease/rental agreement and a **vacating** of the premises by the tenant. Like a surrender, an abandonment requires the tenant to never intend to return to the premises. Also, a tenant intending to abandon the leased premises cannot unilaterally terminate his leasehold right to possession. The transfer of possession to the landlord requires the landlord to act before the right to possession is terminated by abandonment.

However, unlike agreeing to a surrender, the lease agreement is *not cancelled* on the landlord's notice of abandonment. Only the leasehold interest in the real estate is terminated.

To establish an abandonment by a tenant who has breached his lease and vacated, the landlord must serve the tenant with a *notice of abandonment*. On expiration of the notice without the tenant denouncing the abandonment, the tenant's leasehold interest is automatically terminated. The landlord retains the right to collect future rents due under the unexpired (and uncancelled) lease/rental agreement.

Without proof of the termination of the tenancy by abandonment on expiration of the notice, the landlord taking possession could be faced with an angry tenant claiming *forcible entry* — and money damages — or a financially detrimental surrender and elimination of the lease agreement.

For example, a manager rents an apartment to a couple who are expecting a child.

The husband, needing further training for his job, moves to another county for several months. His wife stays in the apartment, intending to do so until her husband returns.

Later, the wife leaves the unit and travels to visit her husband. She posts a note on the unit's front door. It is addressed to her brother who checks in on her from time to time. The note states her destination, but makes no mention whether she will return. A delinquency in the payment of rent does not exist.

The manager reads the note, misconstrues the meaning and re-rents the unit.

On the wife's return she discovers new tenants living in the unit and confronts the manager.

The expectant mother is reduced to retrieving the family possessions from the storage unit where the resident manager placed them.

Shortly afterwards, the wife suffers medical complications from the physical and emotional stress of relocating.

Here, the property manager's entry into the unit and the subsequent re-renting was unjustified. Thus, the property manager, as well as the landlord, is liable for all losses caused by the property manager's actions. [**Richardson** v. **Pridmore** (1950) 97 CA2d 124]

Alternatives to abandonment include:

- acceptance of a surrender terminating the possession and cancelling the lease/rental agreement; or

- service of a 3-day notice to cure the breach (pay) or vacate which includes a declaration of forfeiture of the lease.

On expiration of the 3-day notice or the notice of abandonment, the landlord or his agents may enter and occupy or relet the premises while retaining the right to collect future rents due under the lease/rental agreement breached by the tenant.

Entry by court order

Even if a landlord has the right to possession of the premises due to a forfeiture or expiration of the lease, he may only enforce his possessory right to recover possession from the tenant who remains on the property by using legal means to evict the tenant — *self-help* is absolutely unacceptable.

For instance, in an unlawful detainer (UD) action, a landlord obtains a judgment against a tenant due to the tenant's failure to promptly

RIGHT TO ENTER AND EXHIBIT UNIT TO BUYERS
(For Residential and Nonresidential Rentals)

DATE:_____, 20_____, at _____, California

Items left blank or unchecked are not applicable.

FACTS:

You are a Tenant under a lease or rental agreement

Dated: _____, at

_____ , California

entered into by _____, Tenant,

and _____, Landlord,

recorded _____, as Instrument No. _____,

in _____ County Records, California, regarding real estate referred as:

_____

_____

_____

_____

> **NOTICE:**
>
> For 120 days after notice to a tenant, a landlord or his listing agent may enter the leased premises during normal business hours to exhibit the unit to buyers after giving the tenant at least twenty-four (24) hours telephonic notice of their intent to enter [Calif. Civil Code §1954]

NOTICE TO TENANT:

1. You are hereby advised the premises you occupy has been placed on the real estate market "For Sale".

2. During the period of 120 days following the date of this notice, the landlord or his authorized listing agent for the sale of the property may need to enter your unit during normal business hours for the purpose of exhibiting the premises for review by prospective or actual buyers.

3. At lease 24 hours prior to entry for this purpose, you will be given telephonic or personal notice of our intent to enter.

4. You are not required to be present on the premise during the entry and review. A passkey will be used should you be absent.

5. On departing the premises, the real estate agents will leave a written note indicating they have entered and completed their exhibiting of the unit to the buyers.

Date: _____, 20_____

Landlord: _____

Listing Agent: _____

Signature: _____

Address: _____

_____

Phone: _____

Fax: _____

E-mail: _____

FORM 116   09-02   ©2003 **first tuesday**, P.O. BOX 20069 RIVERSIDE, CA 92516 (800) 794-0494

answer the lawsuit. Before the eviction is carried out under the court order, the court "sets aside" the judgment. The court-ordered eviction is now invalid.

However, the landlord acts on the now *invalid* eviction order. The landlord enlists two uniformed county marshals who, without knowing the eviction order is invalid, appear at the tenant's door demanding the tenant vacate the unit.

The tenant leaves the unit immediately and the landlord takes possession. Later, the tenant seeks a money judgment against the landlord claiming the conduct of the landlord was a *forcible entry and detainer* of the premises.

The landlord claims his conduct cannot be considered a forcible entry and detainer since his method for evicting the tenant did not lie wholly outside the law. The landlord obtained a court order (although he knew it was invalid) and did not personally evict the tenant — he used law enforcement officers instead.

However, the landlord is liable for forcible entry and detainer. He evicted the tenant by relying on a judgment which he knew was no longer valid.

The landlord's use of uniformed law officials to carry out the forcible entry and removal of the tenant does not excuse his use of a known invalid eviction order. The landlord is still using forcible self-help methods. [**Bedi** v. **McMullan** (1984) 160 CA3d 272]

Now consider a nonresidential landlord who obtains a **money judgment** against his tenant for unpaid rent.

A *writ of possession* is erroneously issued and the tenant is evicted by the sheriff.

The tenant seeks to recover possession since the money judgment did not award the landlord possession of the premises or include an eviction order.

The court refuses to order the landlord to surrender possession of the property to the tenant, but recalls the writ as having been erroneously issued.

The tenant then seeks to recover his money losses for the eviction claiming the landlord is liable for forcible entry and detainer since the landlord had him involuntarily removed under an invalid writ of possession.

The landlord claims he is not liable for forcible entry or detainer since he relied on court authorization — the writ of possession — to evict the tenant and recover and retain possession of the premises.

Here, the landlord is not liable for the tenant's money losses since imposing liability on landlords who rely on a properly issued court order which is erroneous and later recalled, would undermine the *public policy* favoring orderly judicial process (instead of self-help) by opening up landlords to liability when acting under the authority of the court. [**Glass** v. **Najafi** (2000) 78 CA4th 45]

Tenant's right to privacy

Leases and rental agreements occasionally contain a provision giving the landlord the *right of re-entry* for the purpose of **retaking possession** of the premises should the tenant breach any performance called for in the lease or rental agreement.

However, these re-entry-on-breach provisions are unenforceable. A tenant's right to possession is a leasehold estate. A leasehold cannot be contracted away, released or waived based on the tenant's later breach of a provision in the lease or rental agreement. To be an enforceable transfer of possession, the tenant's possessory interest (leasehold) must be *conveyed* by the tenant at the time of the breach in exchange for cancellation of the lease (or some other consideration for conveyance), such as occurs under a deed-in-lieu of foreclosure. [CC §1953(a)(l)]

However, consider an owner who goes on an extended overseas vacation. He rents his home for the duration of his trip. The rental agreement acknowledges that the tenant will vacate immediately on the owner's return.

The owner returns from his trip, but the tenant refuses to immediately relinquish possession of the house. While the tenant is at work, the owner enters the house, moves the tenant's belongings and retakes possession of his residence.

Can the owner use self-help to dispossess the tenant?

No! The tenant's occupancy gives him the right to exclude others, including the owner, as it does for almost all occupancies under an exclusive right to possession, such as a lease or rental agreement.

An owner, even though entitled to possession, cannot automatically re-enter when the tenant denies the owner possession.

As a landlord, the owner must first serve the occupant with a notice to vacate (unless the occupancy follows expiration of a lease) and proceed with a UD action to regain possession.

The bottom line: the tenant's breach of the lease does not by itself work a **forfeiture** or **conveyance** of the leasehold to the landlord. Statutory notice requirements must be met to terminate a tenant's right to possession by establishing the tenant's unlawfully detainer of the premises (except on expiration of a lease). [**Lamey** v. **Masciotra** (1969) 273 CA2d 709]

Forcible entry

Forcible entry by a landlord or property manager is conduct consisting of:

- entry by open doors, windows or other parts of the premises *without permission*, *prior notice*, or *justification*;

- entry by any kind of *violence* or *threat of terror*; or

- entry by peaceable means, *after which threats, force* or *menacing conduct* is used to dispossess the tenant. [Calif. Code of Civil Procedure §1159]

Actions by a landlord, property manager or resident manager which are construed as forcible entry include:

- any physical acts of force or violence;

- entry through a window and removal of the tenant's belongings in the occupant's absence [**Bank of California** v. **Taaffe** (1888) 76 C 626];

- entry under the false pretense of making an inspection and then taking over possession from the tenant [**White** v. **Pfieffer** (1913) 165 C 740];

- entry by unlocking the door of the unit in the tenant's absence [**Winchester** v. **Becker** (1906) 4 CA 382];

- entry accomplished by a locksmith who opens the door during the tenant's absence [**Karp** v. **Margolis** (1958) 159 CA2d 69]; and

- entry by breaking locks. [**Pickens** v. **Johnson** (1951) 107 CA2d 778]

Tenant's possessions as security

Some leases contain a clause purporting to give the landlord the right to take or hold the tenant's **personal property as security** should the tenant default in the payment of money owed to the landlord under the lease.

For example, a tenant enters into a lease and occupies an apartment unit.

The lease provides the landlord with the right to re-enter the unit on the tenant's default in the payment of rent and take the tenant's personal possessions as security until the rent is paid.

The tenant fails to pay rent before it becomes delinquent. To enforce the security provision in the lease, the landlord uses his key to enter the unit in the tenant's absence and remove the tenant's possessions.

The landlord then refuses to allow the tenant to re-enter the unit until he is paid.

However, a landlord may not enter or interfere with a tenant's access to the premises based on the tenant's default on the lease, no matter how peaceably the entry is accomplished. [**Jordan v. Talbot** (1961) 55 C2d 597]

Forcible entry by others

Forcible entry onto the premises leased to a tenant occurs whenever **anyone** enters the tenant's premises without the tenant's *present consent.*

Consider a hotel operator who encumbers his interest in a hotel with a trust deed to provide security for a loan. The trust deed states the lender may appoint a trustee to take possession of the real estate and operate and manage the hotel should the hotel operator default on repayment of the loan.

The operator defaults on the loan. The lender appoints a trustee in compliance with the trust deed provision.

The trustee goes to the hotel to remove the hotel operator from the premises as agreed to in the trust deed provision.

The trustee, although not entering by force, breaks and replaces locks on the storage cabinets, raids cash registers and threatens to harm the hotel operator if he refuses to voluntarily relinquish possession of the hotel.

Is the trustee guilty of forcible entry onto the property even though the trustee was appointed under a trust deed provision agreed to by the operator and used non-violent means to enter onto the premises?

Yes! The trustee holds the same status as the secured lender and has no more right to possession than the lender. Thus, the trustee's right to possession could only be lawfully obtained by judicial process — a receivership or foreclosure (judicial or by trustee's sale) — against the interest in the property encumbered by the trust deed, and a UD action. [**Calidino Hotel Co. of San Bernardino** v. **Bank of America Nat. Trust & Savings Ass'n** (1939) 31 CA2d 295]

Forcible entry by the tenant

Even a tenant can be guilty of forcible entry.

Consider a prospective tenant who enters into a rental agreement without first inspecting the condition of the premises.

On inspecting the premises, the tenant discovers the physical condition of the premises is unacceptable. The tenant refuses to take possession. The tenant is not given a key or any other means of accessing the premises.

The landlord then renovates the improvements, realizing he will not be able to rent the premises until the premises is restored.

On the landlord's completion of the renovations, the would-be tenant climbs through an open window in the landlord's absence and takes possession of the premises.

Here, the tenant did not have authority from the landlord to occupy the premises since he refused to accept delivery of possession under the rental agreement and was not given further access to the premises. The tenant's occupancy was gained only by his unauthorized entry, legally called *forcible entry.* [**McNeil** v. **Higgins** (1948) 86 CA2d 723]

Landlord as co-tenant

Consider the owner of a single-family residence who rents rooms to individuals, called *roommates*.

Soon, the owner spends less and less time residing on the property. However, the owner continues to maintain his mailing address at the residence.

After a week-long absence, the owner returns and discovers the locks on all the doors have been changed. He breaks a window and enters the property. The roommates claim the owner is guilty of forcible entry since he broke into the property by using force.

Did the owner's roommates have the exclusive right to possession barring the owner from forcibly entering the property?

No! The owner was not attempting to regain possession. Rather, he was a co-occupant in **actual possession** of the premises at the time of entry.

The owner and his roommates had joint possession. No one roommate had been given exclusive possession as against any other roommate. As a joint possessor with the right to occupy the premises concurrently with others, the owner is not liable for forcible entry. [**Bittman** v. **Courington** (1948) 86 CA2d 213]

Losses due to wrongful dispossession

A tenant wrongfully removed from his premises by a landlord or property manager is entitled to be returned to possession of the premises, called *restitution*. The tenant also has additional remedies against the landlord and the property manager. [CCP §1174(a), (b)]

A tenant may recover all money losses caused by the wrongful entry by a landlord or his agent. However, the amount of money the tenant may collect is limited to losses incurred during the time period the tenant retained a legal right to possession prior to the expiration of his lease or termination of a rental agreement, but was dispossessed. [**Orly** v. **Russell** (1921) 53 CA 660]

For example, a nonresidential tenant is served a notice to vacate by the landlord to terminate his month-to-month tenancy.

Later, prior to the expiration of the notice to vacate, the tenant is barred from entry to his premises by the landlord. The tenant is unable to continue operating his business from the location of the property. The tenant's period of occupancy expires under the notice to vacate without his regaining possession of the premises.

The tenant wants to recover for the landlord's unlawful detention of the property and for loss of business income.

However, recovery of the tenant's losses is limited to the net operating income (NOI) which could have been earned during the balance of the unexpired term. [Orly, *supra*]

Damages to the *goodwill* of a tenant's business may also be considered. If the tenant has built up goodwill with the customers of his business, he may be able to use the remaining days of his final period of tenancy to advise customers of his expired lease and new location.

The landlord who forcibly enters the leased premises during the remaining period of the tenancy is liable for the tenant's losses due to lost earning power when the tenant is deprived of transferring customers to his new location, called *business goodwill*. [**Schuler** v. **Bordelon** (1947) 78 CA2d 581]

A tenant whose possession has been interfered with can recover his money losses due to:

- lost profits [**Stillwell Hotel Co.** v. **Anderson** (1935) 4 C2d 463];

- rental value of the lost use of the premises [Stillwell Hotel Co., *supra*];

- loss of goodwill (earning power) [Schuler, *supra*]; and

- emotional distress caused by the landlord or property manager's conduct towards the tenant. [**Newby** v. **Alto Riviera Apartments** (1976) 60 CA3d 288]

Also, the tenant may collect up to three times his actual money losses for the forcible entry as punishment judicially inflicted on the landlord if the landlord willfully or maliciously took possession from the tenant.

For example, a landlord seeking to collect a debt owed by his tenant ejects his tenant's employees from the leased premises, changes the locks and refuses to allow the tenant access to records and personal property.

Here, the landlord is acting with malice and the tenant has the right to recover trebled damages. [**Civic Western Corporation** v. **Zila Industries, Inc.** (1977) 66 CA3d 1]

Additionally, a landlord or property manager using actual force or violence to enter a leased unit is guilty of a misdemeanor. [Calif. Penal Code §418]

Chapter 4

Leasehold improvements

This chapter discusses improvements made by tenants on leased property and the landlord's rights to improvements.

Ownership rights

A retail business owner, as a tenant, enters into a nonresidential lease agreement for commercial space. The leased premises does not contain tenant improvements since the building is nothing more than a shell.

In the lease, the tenant agrees to make all the **tenant improvements** necessary for him to occupy the premises and operate his business (i.e., walls, flooring, carpeting, lighting, plumbing, telephone and electronic wiring, etc.). The tenant will also install trade fixtures on the premises.

The lease states the property will be delivered to the landlord on expiration of the lease "in the condition the tenant received it" less normal wear and tear.

However, no other provision addresses whether improvements made by the tenant will remain with the property or if the property will be restored when the lease expires.

On expiration of the lease, the tenant strips the premises of all the improvements he made and vacates. The building is returned to the landlord in the condition it was found by the tenant, a shell, less wear and tear. The landlord replaces nearly all the tenant improvements removed in order to relet the space.

Is the tenant liable for the landlord's costs to replace the tenant improvements for the next tenant?

Yes! Improvements made by a tenant which are **permanently affixed** to real estate become part of the real estate to which they are attached. Improvements become part of the real estate and are to remain with the property on expiration of the tenancy, unless the landlord and the tenant agree to the contrary in the lease agreement. [Calif. Civil Code §1013]

With the exception of *trade fixtures*, improvements attached to the building become part of the real estate. [CC §660]

However, the landlord's right to the improvements is conditioned on:

- the permanent or temporary nature of the improvements made by the tenant (i.e., built-in or free standing); and

- any lease provisions relating to the tenant removal of improvements or the restoration of the premises.

Examples of improvements which become part of the real estate include:

- built-ins (i.e., central air conditioning or heating, cabinets and stairwells);

- fixtures (i.e., electrical and plumbing);

- walls, doors and dropped ceilings; and

- flooring which is attached (i.e., carpeting, tile or linoleum).

On expiration of the lease, the landlord is entitled to property improvements and alterations made by the tenant, unless agreed to the contrary.

Leasehold improvement provisions

Nonresidential leases do or should contain a *further-improvement* provision allowing the landlord to either retain tenant improvements and alterations made by the tenant or require restoration of the property to its original condition on expiration of the lease. [See **first tuesday** Form 552 §9]

The **further-improvement** clause usually includes provisions which state:

- who will make the improvements (landlord or tenant);

- who will pay for the improvements (landlord or tenant);

- the landlord's consent is required before the tenant makes improvements;

- any mechanic's liens due to improvements contracted by the tenant will be removed;

- the condition of the premises on expiration; and

- whether the improvements are to remain or be removed on expiration of the lease.

Failure to make improvements

Consider a landlord who obligates himself under a lease to make improvements. Once agreed to, the landlord must complete the improvements in a *timely* manner so the tenant may use them or the lease may be terminated by the tenant.

For example, a landlord agrees to make all the improvements necessary to convert a ranch into a dairy farm for a tenant who operates a dairy.

The landlord is to construct a barn and several sheds which are essential to the operation of the tenant's dairy business.

The tenant moves into the property before the improvements begin. Several months pass and the landlord does not start construction on the promised improvements. The tenant vacates the property since it is impossible to conduct his dairy business without the dairy barn.

Here, the landlord's failure to make the promised improvements is a breach of the lease agreement.

Since the landlord has breached an essential provision of the lease, the tenant may vacate the property and terminate the lease without obligation to pay further rent. [**Souza** v. **Joseph** (1913) 22 CA 179]

Now consider a landlord who agrees to construct the shell of a building for a tenant.

The tenant agrees to install all other improvements and fixtures required to occupy and use the property.

However, before the building is completed by the landlord, the building code is changed to require the installation of a sprinkler system. The tenant demands the landlord pay the cost of installing the sprinkler system since he cannot occupy the premises without the sprinkler system.

The landlord refuses to pay the additional cost to install the sprinkler system claiming the lease agreement calls for him to build the structure, not to make it ready for occupancy.

Is the tenant responsible for the cost of the sprinkler system?

Yes! It is the tenant's responsibility to make the alterations or improvements required to bring the building into compliance with use (occupancy) ordinances since the tenant agreed to make all improvements to the structure needed to take occupancy. [**Wong** v. **DiGrazia** (1963) 60 C2d 525]

Alternatively, lease provisions can obligate a tenant to improve vacant, unimproved property, such as occurs with ground lease arrangements.

Improvements promised by the tenant

A tenant must complete the improvements he has agreed to construct or install on the leased premises within the time period agreed to in the lease or within a reasonable period of time if no commencement or completion date for construction is agreed to in the lease. [CC §1657]

However, if the tenant fails to make or complete mandated improvements prior to expiration of the lease and the improvements were to remain with the property on expiration of the lease, the tenant is liable to the landlord for the cost incurred to complete the agreed-to improvements.

For example, a tenant agrees to construct additional buildings on leased property in lieu of paying rent for a one-year period. When the lease expires, the improvements will remain with the property.

The tenant fails to construct the buildings during the term of the lease. The tenant claims the lease provision calling for construction is permissive, not mandatory, since he only had to build if he needed to do so for the operation of his business.

However, the improvements were agreed to in exchange for rent. The tenant is obligated to make the improvements since the landlord **bargained for them** in the lease agreement. Thus, the landlord is entitled to recover an amount equal to the cost of the improvements the tenant failed to construct. [**Simen** v. **Sam Aftergut Co.** (1915) 26 CA 361]

Additionally, if the tenant agrees to and does not complete the construction of improvements which are to remain with the property on expiration of the lease, the landlord may complete the improvements. The tenant is then responsible for the landlord's expenditures to construct the improvements he agreed to construct. [**Sprague** v. **Fauver** (1945) 71 CA2d 333]

The landlord is also entitled to recover lost rent and expenses incurred after the expiration of a lease resulting from the tenant's failure to construct the promised improvements.

Consider a landlord who enters into a lease and agrees to construct a building for the tenant.

However, after the foundation is laid, the landlord and tenant orally modify the construction arrangement. The tenant agrees to finish construction of the building in exchange for the landlord relinquishing his construction profit.

The tenant then breaches the *oral modification* of the written lease by failing to complete the construction of the building. The breach places the landlord in financial jeopardy as he now must complete the building himself and relet it. The landlord terminates the lease, evicts the tenant and completes the construction promised by the tenant.

Here, the tenant is not only responsible for the landlord's costs of construction, he is also liable for lost future rents and any expenses the landlord incurs to relet the property. [**Sanders Construction Company, Inc.** v. **San Joaquin First Federal Savings and Loan Association** (1982) 136 CA3d 387]

Landlord's consent to improvements

Lease provisions often allow a tenant to make improvements to the leased premises. However, further-improvement provisions typically call for the landlord to approve the planned improvements before construction is started.

For example, a tenant wishes to add a room to the premises he has leased to operate his business. The tenant begins construction without the landlord's prior approval as called for in the lease. The addition is located in space outside the area described in the lease as the leased premises, an encroachment on other land owned by the landlord.

In the past, the landlord has approved other improvements made by the tenant. This time, however, the landlord refuses to give consent and complains about the construction the tenant has begun and the encroachment.

The landlord continues to accept rent while he negotiates with the tenant regarding the approval of the addition and the modification of the lease to include the area subject to the encroachment.

Ultimately, after a few years of negotiations without resolution, the landlord declares a *forfeiture of the lease* based on both the breach of the provision requiring his prior consent to construction and the encroachment of the unapproved improvements.

The tenant now claims the landlord has *waived* his right to declare a forfeiture of the lease since the landlord continued to accept the rental payments after the breach and encroachment.

However, a landlord does not waive his right to consent to additional improvements by accepting rent from the tenant as long as negotiations to resolve the breach continue. [**Thriftimart, Inc.** v. **Me & Tex** (1981) 123 CA3d 751]

Likewise, when a tenant with an option to buy makes improvements with the expectation he will ultimately become the owner of the property, the landlord's consent to improvements called for in the lease is needed before any improvements can be made.

Further, the tenant is not entitled to reimbursement for the cost of improvements, whether or not the landlord consents to the improvements. The improvements will not become the tenant's unless he exercises his option to buy. [**Whipple** v. **Haberle** (1963) 223 CA2d 477]

Some lease provisions allow a tenant to make improvements, but do not specifically mandate that he do so. Here, the tenant is not obligated to make the improvements, but is merely authorized to do so without the need for further consent from the landlord.

For instance, a landlord and tenant sign a long-term lease. A lease provision authorizes the tenant to demolish an existing building located on the property and construct a new one in its place without first obtaining the landlord's consent. The rent is based on the current value of the premises.

However, the lease provision does not state a specific time period is not stated for demolition or construction.

The tenant does not make an effort to tear down the old building or erect a new one. Ultimately, the landlord claims the tenant has breached the lease for failure to demolish the existing building and construct a new building.

However, the tenant has not breached the lease. The tenant was not obligated to build since the lease contained **no promise** by the tenant to build. The tenant was merely authorized to build without the need for further consent.

Thus, the tenant was granted a privilege to make improvements. Further improvements on the tenant's part were not mandatory, they were permissive. [**Kusmark** v. **Montgomery Ward and Co.** (1967) 249 CA2d 585]

Now consider a lease provision requiring that a tenant construct improvements on a vacant parcel he has leased. A date is not specified for completion of the improvements. Since construction of improvements is mandated to occur, the tenant must complete construction within a reasonable period of time.

For example, a landlord leases unimproved land to a developer who is obligated to build improvements, contingent upon his ability to obtain a construction loan. A time period is not set for commencement or completion of the construction. Also, no provision authorizes the landlord to terminate the lease if the required construction is not completed.

However, the lease gives the tenant/developer the right to terminate the lease after one year if financing is not found to fund the construction.

The tenant does not find financing within the one-year period. However, the tenant does not exercise his right to cancel the lease and avoid the payment of future rents. Instead, the tenant continues his good faith effort to locate and qualify for construction financing. Ultimately, financing is not located and construction is not commenced.

A few years after commencement of the lease, the landlord claims the lease has been breached for lack of the promised construction.

The tenant claims the landlord cannot terminate the lease as long as the tenant continues his good faith effort to locate financing and remains solvent to qualify for the financing.

Here, the tenant has breached the lease. He failed to construct the intended improvements within a *reasonable period of time*. The original purpose of the lease was to have buildings erected without specifying a completion date. However, the landlord gave the tenant/developer a reasonable amount of time in which to procure financing for the transaction before terminating the lease — 40 months.

A landlord cannot be forced to leave the property unimproved forever when the original intention under the lease was to develop the land. [**City of Stockton** v. **Stockton Plaza Corporation** (1968) 261 CA2d 639]

Surrender of improvements

All tenant improvements and alterations are to remain with the leased property on expiration or other termination of the lease unless a lease, provision exists **permitting** or **mandating** removal by the tenant.

Most leases merely provide for the property to be returned in *good condition*, minus ordinary wear and tear for the years of the tenant's occupancy.

Thus, the tenant is not required, much less allowed, to *restore* the property to the actual condition he received it in when he took possession. The covenant for ordinary care of the premises during the lease does not mean removal of tenant improvements or renovation to eliminate deterioration, obsolescence or wear and tear due to the use permitted to the tenant. [**Kanner** v. **Globe Bottling Co.** (1969) 273 CA2d 559]

Now consider a landlord and tenant who enter into a lease of nonresidential property. The lease agreement contains a provision requiring the tenant, if the landlord at his option so demands, to **restore** the premises to the original condition received by the tenant, less normal wear and tear.

The tenant makes all the tenant improvements necessary to operate his business, such as installation of a concrete vault, the removal of partitions and a stairway, and the closing of two entrances into the premises.

On expiration of the lease, the tenant vacates the premises. The landlord exercises his right to require removal of tenant improvements by making a demand on the tenant to **restore** the premises, which the tenant rejects.

The landlord incurs costs to restore most of the premises to prepare it for reletting to a new tenant.

The landlord claims the tenant is liable for costs he incurred to restore the premises since the tenant's improvements radically altered the premises and made it unrentable to others.

The tenant claims he is not liable for the landlord's costs to remove the improvements and restore the premises to its original condition since the alterations are beneficial to the property.

Is the tenant liable for the landlord's costs to restore the premises to a rentable condition?

Yes! On expiration of the lease, the tenant is obligated to restore the premises to its original condition, less normal wear and tear, since the lease provides for restoration by the tenant on a demand from the landlord. The tenant improvements made the premises less desirable and unsuitable for other occupants. On the tenant's failure to restore the premises, the landlord was forced to incur restoration expenses to relet the premises. Thus, the tenant is liable for the landlord's expenditures to restore the premises to relet to a new tenant. [**Masonic Temple Ass'n. of Sacramento** v. **Stockholders Auxiliary Corporation** (1933) 130 CA 234]

In another example, a lease states a tenant will return the property in *good repair* and *restore* the premises to its original condition, less normal wear and tear.

The tenant modifies the premises to run his business. After the lease expires, the tenant moves out and leaves all his improvements and modifications on the property.

The landlord is unable to relet the premises in the condition left by the tenant.

Here, the tenant is liable for the reasonable costs incurred by the landlord to restore the premises to its original condition and for lost rental income for the period of time it takes to make the repairs.

Thus, lease provisions requiring **restoration** of the premises to its original condition require the tenant to restore the property to its original condition, minus any normal deterioration due to time and use of the premises as permitted. [**Iverson** v. **Spang Industries** (1975) 45 CA3d 303]

If a lease does not require the tenant to **restore the property** to the condition it was in when received, the tenant may only remove his personal improvements, called *trade improvements* or *trade fixtures*.

The tenant need only leave the property and tenant improvements in good condition. [**Formosa Corp.** v. **Rogers** (1951) 108 CA2d 397]

Reimbursement for tenant improvements on eviction

But what compensation may be due a tenant who has improved the property and is evicted prior to expiration of the lease?

A tenant who is evicted is entitled to the **rental value** of his improvements for the remainder of his unexpired lease term.

The tenant is not, however, entitled to reimbursement for the market value or cost of the improvements. Since reimbursement is not required, the landlord receives a windfall profit

for his use of the tenant's improvements until they revert to him on expiration of the original lease.

Thus, an evicted tenant is limited to collecting the reasonable value for the landlord's use of the improvements during the remainder of the term on the original lease. [**Asell** v. **Rodrigues** (1973) 32 CA3d 817]

Real estate fixtures vs. trade fixtures

Two types of fixtures exist to distinguish improvements installed on buildings located on a parcel of real estate:

- real estate fixtures; and

- trade fixtures.

A *real estate fixture* is personal property which has become **attached** to the real estate. It becomes part of the real estate it is attached to and is conveyed with the property. [CC §§660; 1013]

In other words, if a tenant rents an office and builds bookshelves into the wall rather than merely anchoring them to the wall, the bookshelves become part of the improvements located on the real estate.

When the lease expires, real estate fixtures are the property of the landlord. The landlord takes possession of the real estate fixtures as part of the real estate surrendered to the landlord, *unless the lease provides for restoration* or permits removal by the tenant. The passage of real estate fixtures from tenant to landlord on expiration of the lease is a conveyance called *reversion*. [**City of Beverly Hills** v. **Albright** (1960) 184 CA2d 562]

However, **trade fixtures** do not revert to the landlord on expiration of the lease.

A *trade fixture* is an improvement which is attached to the real estate by the tenant that is peculiar to the operation of his business.

For example, a tenant leases property to operate a beauty salon. The tenant moves in work-related furnishings (i.e., mirrors, salon chairs, wash stations and dryers) which are needed to run the business. The items are attached to the floor, walls, plumbing and electrical leads.

On expiration of the lease, the tenant removes the fixtures which were used to render the services offered by the business. The landlord claims the fixtures are improvements to his property and cannot be removed since they have become part of the real estate.

However, furnishings which are unique to the operation of the business are considered trade fixtures even though the furnishings are attached and built into the structure. Thus, they are removable by the tenant.

A tenant may, at the end of or anytime during the lease term, remove any fixture used for trade purposes if the removal can be done without damaging the premises. [**Beebe** v. **Richards** (1953) 115 CA2d 589]

Fixtures which have become an integral part of the building structure due to the way they are attached or the general purpose they serve cannot be removed. Examples of fixtures not used to render services include toilets, air conditioners, vent conduits, sprinkler systems and lowered ceilings. [CC §1019]

Trade fixtures as security

However, leases often contain a default provision prohibiting the tenant from removing the trade fixtures when he breaches the lease. The tenant (and a tenant's unsecured creditors) no longer have a right to the trade fixtures under a default provision.

Consider a tenant who signs a commercial lease agreeing to operate a frozen packaging plant on the premises.

The lease states all fixtures, trade or leasehold, will belong to the landlord should the lease be terminated due to a breach by the tenant.

The tenant later encumbers his trade fixtures by borrowing money against them. The tenant then defaults on his lease payments.

While in default on the lease, the tenant surrenders the property to the landlord, including all trade fixtures.

Does the lender secured by the trade fixtures have a right to repossess them?

No! The tenant lost his ownership right to remove the trade fixtures under the lease. Any right to the fixtures held by the secured lender is similarly lost since the lender is junior in time and thus subordinate to the landlord's interest in the fixtures under the lease.

If the trade fixtures installed by the tenant are owned by a third party, or if a third party had a lien on them at the time of their installation, the landlord has no more right to them than the tenant. [**Goldie** v. **Bauchet Properties** (1975) 15 C3d 307]

Notice of Nonresponsibility

A landlord may find himself paying for improvements made by the tenant if he does not **post** a notice on the premises of his intention not to be responsible for the improvements, called a *Notice of Nonresponsibility*, and **record** the notice with the county recorder. [See Form 597 accompanying this chapter]

Tenants occasionally contract for improvements to be constructed on the premises they have leased. Any mechanic's lien by a contractor for nonpayment initially attaches to the tenant's leasehold interest in the property. [CC §3128]

However, the mechanic's lien for unpaid labor and materials may also attach to the *fee simple* interest held by the landlord if:

- the landlord or his property manager acquires knowledge the construction is taking place; and

- fails to post and record a Notice of Nonresponsibility.

A **Notice of Nonresponsibility** is a written notice which must be:

- posted in a conspicuous place on the premises within ten days after the landlord (or his agent) first has knowledge of the construction; and

- recorded with the county recorder's office within the same 10-day period. [CC §3094]

However, the landlord who becomes aware of the construction and fails to post and record the nonresponsibility notice is not personally liable to the contractor. Rather, the contractor can only lien the landlord's interest in the real estate and then foreclose on his lien to collect for unpaid labor and materials delivered to improve the property under contract with the tenant. [**Peterson** v. **Freiermuth** (1911) 17 CA 609]

Further, a mechanic's lien can attach to the landlord's interest even when he has posted and recorded a Notice of Nonresponsibility if the lease requires the tenant to make improvements.

For example, a lease states the tenant is to make certain improvements as a condition of renting the property. Since the improvements are not permissive, the tenant is deemed to be the **landlord's agent** when he contracts for the construction of the mandated improvements.

Thus, the mechanic's lien incurred by the tenant will attach to both the tenant's and the landlord's interest in the property despite any posting and recording of a Notice of Nonresponsibility. The lease mandated the tenant to construct improvements. [**Los Banos Gravel Company** v. **Freeman** (1976) 58 CA3d 785]

Had the lease merely *authorized* the tenant to make nonmandatory (permissive) improvements or make improvements subject to or without the landlord's prior consent, the tenant is not then acting as an agent for the landlord. Thus, the landlord's interest in the property will not be subject to a mechanic's lien if the Notice of Nonresponsibility is timely posted and recorded on discovery of the tenant improvements. [**Baker** v. **Hubbard** (1980) 101 CA3d 226]

Also, a mechanic's lien cannot be recorded against the landlord if the improvements are removed by the contractor recording the lien.

For example, a tenant contracts to have air conditioning installed in the building. The contractor sells the equipment to the tenant on a conditional sales contract. The contractor retains title to the equipment as security until the sales contract debt is paid.

The landlord's consent to the improvements is not obtained by the tenant, but the landlord has knowledge the work has commenced. The landlord does not post a Notice of Nonresponsibility.

Later, after the air conditioning units are installed, the tenant vacates the property.

The contractor is not paid and files a mechanic's lien against the landlord's fee interest in the property. Further, the contractor repossesses the air conditioning units and resells them at a loss, which he now seeks to recover under his lien.

However, by his election to repossess the units, the contractor waived his right to pursue the mechanic's lien to foreclosure.

Whether the air conditioning units are considered a removable fixture due to the financing or a property improvement permitting the recording of a mechanic's lien is no longer an issue after their removal.

The contractor removed the air conditioning units (as authorized by the conditional sales contract) and chose to treat the units as personal property, not real estate fixtures. Thus, the contractor lost his lien rights for nonpayment. [**Cornell** v. **Sennes** (1971) 18 CA3d 126]

RECORDING REQUESTED BY

AND WHEN RECORDED MAIL TO

Name ⌈   ⌉

Street
Address

City &
State ⌊   ⌋

SPACE ABOVE THIS LINE FOR RECORDER'S USE

NOTICE OF NONRESPONSIBILITY
(Civil Code §3094)

DATE:_____, 20_____, at _____, California

NOTICE IS HEREBY GIVEN:

1. _____ is the vested and legal

   owner of real property located in the County of _____, State of California, identified as:

   1.1   Common address: _____

   1.2   Legal description:

2. _____ is:

   2.1   ☐ The buyer of the property under a purchase agreement, option or land sales contract, or

   2.2   ☐ The tenant under a lease of the property.

3. Within 10 days before the posting and recording of this notice, the undersigned owner or agent of the owner obtained knowledge that a work of improvement has commenced on the site of the property involving ☐ construction, ☐ alteration, or ☐ repair.

4. The owner will not be responsible for any claim arising out of this work of improvement.

5. I declare under penalty of perjury under the laws of the State of California that the foregoing is true and correct.

   Date:_____, 20_____   Signature: _____

                                         ☐ Owner, or ☐ Agent of the owner.

STATE OF CALIFORNIA   )
COUNTY OF_____)

On _____ before me,

_____
(name of notary public)

personally appeared _____

_____,
(name of principal)

personally known to me (or proved to me on the basis of satisfactory evidence) to be the person(s) whose name(s) is/are subscribed to the within instrument and acknowledged to me that he/she/they executed the same in his/her/their authorized capacity(ies), and that by his/her/their signature(s) on the instrument the person(s), or the entity upon behalf of which the person(s) acted, executed the instrument.

WITNESS my hand and official seal.

Signature: _____
           (Signature of notary public)

(This area for official notarial seal)

FORM 597   10-01   ©2003 **first tuesday**, P.O. BOX 20069 RIVERSIDE, CA 92516 (800) 794-0494

Consider the tenant who leases a property containing tanks for holding gasoline. The tenant negotiates a reduced rental payment in exchange for his installing fuel pumps free of any liens.

The tenant purchases the pumps on credit and the pumps are installed. The supplier of the pumps does not receive a UCC-1 financing statement from the tenant, and thus does not file a UCC-1 with the Secretary of State, a requisite to perfecting the supplier's lien on the pumps.

Later, the pump supplier claims title to the pumps due to the unpaid installation debt and seeks to repossess them.

However, the landlord owns the pumps as fixtures which became part of the real estate. He gave consideration in the form of reduced rent to acquire the pumps. More importantly, the pump supplier failed to perfect its lien on installation of the pumps. [**Southland Corp.** v. **Emerald Oil Company** (9th Cir. 1986) 789 F2d 1441]

Chapter 5

Options to buy and the right of first refusal

This chapter distinguishes the tenant's right to buy under an owner's irrevocable offer to sell from the tenant's preemptive right to buy should the owner decide to sell.

Purchase rights held by tenants

A prospective tenant is negotiating to lease a single-user property.

The offer to lease prepared by the leasing agent provides for the landlord to grant the tenant an **option to purchase** the property, an irrevocable right to later buy the property at the *tenant's discretion*. If the landlord accepts the offer to lease, he will be obligated to sell the property on the terms of the option should the tenant decide to buy.

However, the landlord rejects the offer to lease because he is not willing to sell the property.

While discussing a counteroffer with the landlord, the leasing agent discovers the landlord is willing to grant him a **right of first refusal** for the term of the lease, called a *preemptive right*. Thus, should the landlord decide to sell the leased premises before the lease expires, the tenant could then acquire the property.

To exercise the right of first refusal, the tenant must *accept* the terms of sale presented by the seller or match an offer made by a buyer.

However, the tenant will retain possession under the lease should he not exercise his right of first refusal. If the property is sold, ownership is transferred subject to the tenant's leasehold interest which no longer includes his preemptive right to acquire the property since the right of first refusal expired unexercised. [**Manasse v. Ford** (1922) 58 CA 312]

Option to buy vs. right of first refusal

A landlord and tenant can agree the tenant may later buy the property under provisions granting the tenant either:

- an **irrevocable right to purchase** the property within a specific time period, called an *option to buy*; or

- a **pre-emptive right to purchase** the property should the landlord later decide to sell the property, called a *right of first refusal*.

Typically, the option to buy is evidenced by an agreement separate from the lease due to its requirement to include all the terms of purchase. It is usually referenced in the lease and attached as an addendum. [See Form 161 accompanying this chapter]

Conversely, the right of first refusal is a provision included in the body of the lease agreement, or by an addendum, since the provision rarely contains any sales terms. [See Fig. 1]

Unlike the right of first refusal, an option to buy must contain all terms necessary to form an enforceable agreement to sell the real estate.

The tenant holding an option to buy has the discretionary right to buy or not to buy on the sales terms stated in the option, and to do so within an agreed-to time period. No variations are allowed.

To buy the property under an option, the tenant *exercises* his right to buy by accepting the *irrevocable offer to sell* granted by the option. Thus, the decision to buy or not to buy the property rests at all times with the tenant, the landlord having already agreed to sell.

Conversely, when a landlord grants his tenant a right of first refusal, the tenant only has a right to buy or not to buy the property if the landlord later decides to sell.

However, once the tenant is notified that the landlord intends to sell, the right of first refusal becomes an option to buy on the terms then offered by the landlord.

On presentation of the landlord's offer to sell, the tenant has the right to accept the offer and buy the property within the period of time fixed by the right of first refusal provision.

The landlord's motives

A landlord who desires to sell his property often uses the option to buy or a right of first refusal as a device to induce a tenant to buy the property, not just rent it.

The timing of a sale by the use of options and the right of first refusal provisions may reflect:

- the tenant's present inability to buy;

- the seller's inability to find a buyer;

- the landlord's desire to sell later, not now; and

- the buyer's desire to buy.

The landlord's motives for delaying the decision to sell the leased property when the prospective tenant would rather buy now include:

- tax benefits, such as the delaying of the sale and the reporting of profit until a year when profit taxes will be lower or the profit can be offset by losses on the sale or operations of other properties;

- financial incentives, such as delaying the sale to obtain the highest price possible in a rising market, the elimination of neighborhood obsolescence, the re-zoning of the property, or avoiding locked-in financing on property which prohibits a current sale;

- legal problems, such as a *lis pendens* or toxic cleanup hindering the sale (and value) of the property; and

- personal concerns, such as not being ready to sell the property due to health, estate planning or family considerations.

Also, a landlord may grant a right of first refusal even though he has no intention of ever selling the property. The tenant may request a right of first refusal on the theory the landlord may change his mind or die and the successor will sell.

The right of first refusal serves the same purpose for the landlord as an option serves for the tenant — to avoid entering into an enforceable commitment to, respectively, sell or buy real estate.

Consideration for granting an option

To create an enforceable option to buy or right of first refusal agreement, *mutuality of obligation* must exist between the landlord and the tenant. Accordingly, the landlord and the tenant must each commit themselves in some legally binding way before the tenant can enforce the agreement against the landlord. [**Kowal** v. **Day** (1971) 20 CA3d 720]

The **landlord commits** by *signing* a document granting the tenant the option to buy or the right of first refusal. To bind the landlord's offer to sell and create an enforceable option to buy or right of first refusal, the tenant must make a commitment in return. These commitments to one another are called *consideration*.

When the option or right of first refusal is negotiated concurrently as an addendum to the lease, the **tenant's commitment** is his promise to pay rent and perform under the lease he *signs* concurrent with receiving the option or right of first refusal.

However, if the option to buy or right of first refusal is later added to an existing lease, some additional consideration must be negotiated and delivered to the landlord since the tenant is not committing himself to do anything new or different. Here, the **tenant's commitment** could be agreeing to a modification of the terms in the existing lease or the payment of a sum of money, for example, $100.

The option agreement

Under an option agreement, the tenant has no obligation to buy the leased property. The tenant is merely given the right to buy if he so chooses, a type of *call option.*

For the option to be enforceable, the purchase price of the property and terms of payment on exercise of the option must be included in the option agreement.

The right to buy must be exercised by the tenant within a specified time period, called the *option period*. The option period often runs until the lease expires.

If the option is not exercised during the option period precisely as agreed, it will expire of its own accord. Thereafter, the option will be unenforceable by the tenant. [**Bekins Moving & Storage Co.** v. **Prudential Insurance Company of America** (1985) 176 CA3d 245]

When options to renew or extend are included in the lease, the **expiration** of the option to buy is tied to either:

the expiration of the initial lease term; or

- the expiration of any renewal or extension.

For example, a tenant rents space under a ten-year lease with an **option to extend** the term of the lease for additional years.

The tenant also holds an option to buy the leased property. The option references the lease term — until expiration — as the period for exercise of the option to buy.

STANDARD OPTION TO PURCHASE
Irrevocable Right-to-Buy

DATE:_____, 20_____, at _____, California

Items left blank or unchecked are not applicable.

1. OPTION MONEY:

Optionor herewith receives from Optionee option money in the amount of $_____ evidenced by ☐ cash, ☐ check, or ☐ _____, given in consideration for this option to purchase real property.

2. REAL PROPERTY UNDER OPTION:

Address: _____

_____

Legal description/Assessor's parcel number: _____

_____

_____

_____

3. ADDITIONAL CONSIDERATION:

As further consideration for this option, Optionee is to obtain at his expense and deliver to Optionor prior to expiration of this option the following checked items regarding the property:

☐ Property survey report by licensed California surveyors.   ☐ Off-site improvement plans.

☐ Architectural plans and specifications.   ☐ Soil engineer's report.

☐ Zoning ordinance request.   ☐ Land use study.

☐ On-site engineering plans.   ☐ Application for a conditional use permit.

☐ Application for a parcel map or waiver.   ☐ _____

4. OPTION PERIOD:

Optionor hereby grants to Optionee the irrevocable option to purchase the Optionor's rights, title and interest in the property on the terms stated, for a period commencing with the acceptance of this option and expiring _____, 20_____.

5. EXERCISE OF OPTION:

Optionee may exercise this option during the option period by:

5.1   Signing escrow instructions, identical in provisions to those attached as **Exhibit A**, and delivering the instructions to escrow [**first tuesday** Form 401]; and

5.2   Depositing cash in escrow of $_____; and

5.3   Delivering an escrow certified copy of the signed escrow instructions to Optionor, within the option period, in person or by both certified and regular mail.

6. ESCROW CONTRACT:

In the event this option is exercised, the transaction shall be escrowed with:

_____

Escrow shall close within _____ days after exercise.

7. DELIVERY OF TITLE:

Within _____ days after exercise, Optionor shall place all documents and instruments into escrow necessary to close within the escrow period.

8. BROKERAGE FEE:

Optionor agrees to pay a brokerage fee of _____ of the selling price IF:

8.1   This option is exercised;

8.2   Within one year after expiration of option period and any extension or renewal, Optionor enters into an agreement to option, sell, lease or exchange with Optionee, or their assigns; or

8.3   Optionor wrongfully prevents the exercise of this option,

To Broker: _____

Address: _____

Phone: _____   Fax: _____

— — — — — — — — — — — — — — *PAGE ONE OF TWO — FORM 161* — — — — — — — — — — — — — — —

9. **SALE TERMS:**

Price of $_____ payable as follows:

9.1 ☐ All cash.

9.2 Cash down payment in the amount of $_____.

9.3 Assume a trust deed note with a balance of $_____. Interest not to exceed _____%, ☐ VIR, payable approximately $_____ monthly over the loan's remaining life, impounds being $_____ monthly.

   a. Loan balance differences to be adjusted in _____.

9.4 Assume a trust deed note balance of $_____. Interest not to exceed _____%, payable approximately $_____ monthly, due and payable _____, 20_____.

9.5 A NOTE for the balance of the purchase price in the amount of $_____ to be executed by Optionee in favor of Optionor and secured by a trust deed on the property being purchased, payable $_____ monthly, or more, starting one month after closing, including interest at _____% from closing, due and payable _____ years after closing.

   a. This note and trust deed to contain provisions to be provided by Optionor for: ☐ due-on-sale, ☐ prepayment penalty, ☐ late charges, ☐ _____

   b. ☐ The attached Carryback Disclosure Statement is an addendum to this agreement (mandatory on four-or-less residential units). [ft Form 300]

   c. Optionee to provide a Request for Notice of Delinquency to senior encumbrancers. [ft Form 412]

10. **GENERAL PROVISIONS:**

10.1 ☐ **See addendum for additional provisions.** [ft Form 250]

10.2 Attached as addendums are the following checked provisions mandated on four-or-less residential units:

   a. ☐ Condition of Property (Transfer) Disclosure statement [ft Form 304]

   b. ☐ Natural Hazard Disclosure Statement [ft Form 314]

   c. ☐ Disclosure of sexual predator database [ft Form 250]

   d. ☐ Hazard Disclosure Booklet, and related Optionor disclosures, containing Environmental Hazards, Lead-based paint and Earthquake Safety. [ft Forms 313 and 315]

   e. ☐ Documentation from any Homeowners' Association involved.

10.3 Optionee has inspected the property and improvements.

10.4 Possession of the property to be delivered on: ☐ close of escrow, or ☐ see attached Occupancy Agreement. [ft Forms 271 and 272]

10.5 Both parties reserve their rights to assign, and agree to cooperate in effecting an Internal Revenue Code §1031 exchange prior to close of escrow, on either party's written notice.

10.6 **Expiration of Option:**

   This offer to sell shall be deemed expired if not accepted by exercise during the option period. This option contract shall automatically expire/terminate on _____, 20_____.

I hereby grant this option and agree to perform under its terms.	I hereby accept this option and agree to perform under its terms.
Date:_____, 20_____	Date:_____, 20_____
Optionor: _____	Optionee: _____
Signature: _____	Signature: _____
Address: _____	Address: _____
_____	_____
Phone: _____	Phone: _____
Fax: _____	Fax: _____
E-mail: _____	E-mail: _____

FORM 161   10-01   ©2003 **first tuesday**, P.O. BOX 20069 RIVERSIDE, CA 92516 (800) 794-0494

If the lease is later extended, the option period is automatically extended with the extension of the lease since the option to buy allows the tenant to exercise the option *during the lease term*. [**In re Marriage of Joaquin** (1987) 193 CA3d 1529]

Now consider a lease which contains an **option to renew**, not to extend. The option requires the preparation and signing of a new lease on *identical terms* to the initial lease. The initial lease, by way of a referenced attachment, also provides the tenant with an **option to buy** which can be exercised *prior* to the expiration of the lease.

On renewal of the lease, the tenant must ensure the option to buy does not expire at the end of the initial lease term. The new lease must also reference the option to buy (as part of the identical terms of the original lease) since a new lease is not an *extension* of the original lease. [In re Marriage of Joaquin, *supra*]

To avoid an expiration of the option to buy on an extension or renewal of a lease, the initial and renewal leases should make reference to the attached option to buy.

Right of first refusal

To trigger the tenant's right of first refusal, the landlord does not need to first agree to sell the leased property by entering into a purchase agreement with another person, "subject to the tenant's right of first refusal."

Any indication the landlord has decided to sell the property is sufficient to activate the right to buy, including:

- listing or advertising the property for sale;

- offering the property to a buyer;

- accepting an offer or making a counteroffer involving a buyer; and

- granting a purchase option to another person.

For example, a buyer of income property contacts the owner of leased commercial property to acquire it. The buyer is informed the major tenant holds the right to buy the property under a right of first refusal provision in the lease.

The buyer attempts to circumvent the right of first refusal by negotiating an option to buy the property, exerciseable only after the tenant's right of first refusal expires.

The landlord grants the buyer an option to buy the property. The granting of the option now binds the landlord unconditionally to sell the property should the option be exercised.

Here, the landlord's granting of the option to sell the property is a clear indication of his intention to sell. Thus, the right of first refusal is triggered allowing the tenant to now purchase the property on the same terms as contained in the option. [**Rollins** v. **Stokes** (1981) 123 CA3d 701]

Note — The right of first refusal is not triggered by conveyance of the property to the landlord's heirs on his death. The heirs take title subject to the right of first refusal. However, the right of first refusal is triggered by a sale of the property ordered by the probate court or entered into by the heirs. To exercise the right of first refusal, the tenant must match the highest offer submitted in open bidding and approved by the court, or the listing or sale of the property by the executor. [**Estate of Patterson** (1980) 108 CA3d 197]

Once the landlord's decision to sell is manifested, the right of first refusal becomes an option to buy. Control of the transaction then passes to the tenant holding the right of first refusal, converting the tenant to an optionee.

The landlord may not now retract his decision to sell the property without breaching the right of first refusal provision.

Matching the back-up offer

The landlord subject to a **right of first refusal** held by a tenant is obligated to notify the tenant of the terms of any sales listing, option to buy, offer to purchase, counteroffer or acceptance of an offer to purchase which triggers the tenant's right to buy under the right of first refusal provision.

The tenant must then agree to match the sales terms within the time period set in the right of first refusal provision or he has waived the right to buy for failure to *exercise* the right.

Consider a tenant who holds a right of first refusal on the industrial property he leases.

A buyer makes an offer to purchase the property. The terms for the payment of the price in the buyer's offer include cash and an assumption of the existing first trust deed on the property.

The property is also encumbered with a nonrecourse second trust deed (carried back by a prior owner) which will be paid off and reconveyed on closing.

The landlord accepts the offer and notifies the tenant, giving the tenant the opportunity to match the buyer's offer under his right of first refusal.

The tenant exercises his right of first refusal by agreeing to purchase the property at the same price, but by assuming both the existing first trust deed and nonrecourse second and paying the remainder of the price in cash.

The landlord rejects the tenant's conditions and refuses to sell to the tenant.

However, the landlord must accept the tenant's terms for payment of the price. The tenant need merely provide the **same net financial result** to the landlord as the offer being matched — a cash-out of the seller's equity in the property. The tenant's performance under the right of first refusal does not need to be identical in all aspects to the buyer's offer.

Thus, the landlord must sell under the tenant's exercise of his right of first refusal since the landlord's net proceeds, economic benefits and liabilities resulting from the sale on terms set by the tenant would be the same as those he would experience under the purchase offer which triggered the right of first refusal. [**C. Robert Nattress & Associates** v. **CIDCO** (1986) 184 CA3d 55]

Now consider a buyer who offers to purchase leased property with a cash down payment and a note for the balance of the landlord's equity secured by a trust deed on other property which has adequate value as security. The landlord accepts the offer and notifies the tenant who agrees to match the buyer's offer.

However, the value of the property offered by the tenant as security is inadequate, and the landlord refuses to accept it.

Here, due to the inadequate value of the security offered by the tenant for an identical note, the tenant's offer is not financially equivalent to the terms of the buyer's offer since the risk of loss on default has been increased. The landlord is not obligated to accept the tenant's offer and the tenant's deficient exercise of his preemptive right constitutes a waiver of his right to buy. The landlord may now sell the property to the buyer — on the same terms. [**McCulloch** v. **M & C Beauty Colleges** (1987) 194 CA3d 1338]

Reinstatement of the right of first refusal

A right of first refusal provision automatically carries with it the *reinstatement* of the right when:

- the landlord agrees to sell the property on terms different from the terms offered to the tenant; or

- the property remains unsold after the running of an agreed-to period of time following the tenant's waiver of the right to buy. [See Fig. 1]

Consider a landlord who, under a right of first refusal, notifies his tenant of the purchase terms on which he is willing to sell. The tenant chooses not to exercise his option to buy at the price and terms offered.

The landlord later lowers the sales price or alters the terms for payment of the price when listing or offering to sell the property.

Here, the price reduction or modification of terms **reinstates** the tenant's right of first refusal and the landlord becomes obligated to allow the tenant to purchase on these new terms. The tenant waived only his right of first refusal for a sale based on the terms originally given to him by the owner, not on the different price or set of terms.

Should a buyer purchase the property on terms other than those offered to the tenant, the buyer takes title subject to the tenant's preemptive right to purchase which is reinstated due to the sale on different terms. Thus, the buyer must sell to the tenant on the same price and terms he paid since the buyer is on notice of the tenant's rights in the property.

SECTION B

Agency and Property Management

Chapter 6

Property management agreement

This chapter discusses the function of a property management agreement and the landlord's and property manager's rights and responsibilities under the agreement.

Authority to operate the rental property

A property manager's authority to take control of income-producing real estate and manage its leases, rents and expenses in expectation of a fee is established in a property management agreement. [See Form 590 accompanying this chapter]

A property management agreement sets out the specific rights, responsibilities and expectations of both the property manager and the landlord, including expense limitations, performance standards and authorized activities.

Landlord responsibilities include handing the property manager the information and files needed to manage the property and its tenants, such as all lease/rental agreements, service and maintenance contracts and utilities. Also, information on hazard and worker's compensation insurance is needed to cover the activities of the property manager and his employees.

The management agreement also authorizes the property manager to locate tenants, enter into leases and rental agreements, collect rents, incur operating expenses and disburse funds to pay expenses, loan payments and management fees.

Further, the management agreement includes written authorization which is required for the property manager to enter into and sign leases and bind the landlord to leases for a term of over one year. [Calif. Civil Code §1624(a)(3)]

Short-form vs. long-form agreements

Brokers who manage property should enter into highly detailed property management agreements, not generalized "short-form" management agreements.

Short-form agreements do not specifically identify, much less clarify, the performance and expectations of both the property manager and the landlord. Instead, short-form agreements *imply industry customs* will be followed — whatever those customs might be or become.

These implied standards, while familiar to the broker, are often misunderstood or unknown to the landlord. Disputes usually result when landlords have high expectations and then receive less than they believe they bargained for when they employed the property manager.

Management obligations detailed in a long-form agreement, which spells out what conduct the landlord can expect from his broker, better insulate a broker from claims he has breached his duties to the landlord. Surprises are eliminated and client expectations are more realistic.

Property managed "as is"

Some landlords want their property maintained at a below-standard level. The broker taking on the management must document the "maintenance" he recommends by using either an addendum to the management agreement or estoppel letters sent from time to time stating the situation and his recommendations with a request for authority to act on the recommendations.

For example, a property manager should document a landlord's refusal to trim back overgrown and top-heavy landscaping needed to prevent damage from occurring to the structure or injury to the tenants.

Also, note any advice given and rejected by the landlord regarding the installation or maintenance of security systems, lighting or other maintenance or installation work needed to eliminate dangerous conditions.

Handling rents and expenses

Property management agreements authorize the broker to handle, on behalf of the landlord, all income received and expenses incurred in the operation of the property.

The property manager's responsibilities regarding the property's income and expenses include:

- collecting rents and other amounts due, such as common area maintenance charges (CAMs) and assessments for property insurance and real estate taxes;

- collecting, accounting for and refunding security deposits;

- paying expenses and loans owed by the landlord from rent paid by tenants; and

- complying with any local rent control ordinances.

A written management agreement spells out which expenses, insurance premiums, utilities, loan payments and taxes are to be paid by the property manager, and which are to be paid by the landlord.

Trust accounts

The receipt and accounting for cash reserves, security deposits, rent and other amounts received from tenants and coin-operated machines will be handled as trust funds owned by the landlord. Trust funds of this nature must be deposited into a trust account in the name of the broker.

Accounting provisions in the management agreement:

- authorize the property manager to pay, out of the income and reserve funds held in the trust account, obligations incurred in the management and ownership of the property;

- specify the bank to be used; and

- call for all remaining funds held on behalf of the landlord to be disbursed periodically and on termination of the property management agreement.

The management agreement sets the amount of cash reserves the landlord will deposit with the property manager to hold in the trust account as a minimum balance to cover operating expenses and fees.

Periodic accounting by the manager

The landlord is entitled to a statement of accounting at least once a quarter and when the property management agreement is terminated. [Calif. Business and Professions Code §10146]

The management agreement sets forth the time periods for the property manager's accounting to the landlord.

The accounting provision indicates the property manager will disburse to the landlord, with each accounting, any funds exceeding the minimum balance to be held for reserves.

The broker's authority to withdraw his management fee from the trust account is included.

Brokerage fee enforcement

Property managers cannot enforce collection of their management fees without a written agreement.

PROPERTY MANAGEMENT AGREEMENT

DATE:_____, 20_____, at _____, California

Items left blank and unchecked are not applicable.

1. RETAINER PERIOD:

1.1 Owner hereby retains and grants Broker the exclusive right to lease, rent, operate and maintain the property as property manager, commencing _____, 20_____, and continuing for one year and thereafter until terminated.

2. RECEIPT OF SECURITY DEPOSITS:

2.1 Owner hands $_____ to Broker for deposit into the trust account towards Owner's security deposit obligation to tenants.

3. RECEIPT OF CASH RESERVE:

3.1 Owner hands $_____ to Broker as a deposit towards Owner's obligation under the agreement.

3.2 Owner to maintain a minimum cash reserve, in addition to any security deposits in the amount of $_____. On request from Broker, Owner will advance additional funds to maintain this minimum balance.

3.3 The reserve deposit may be used to pay costs diligently incurred by Broker or due Broker in fulfilling Broker's obligations.

4. BROKERAGE FEE:

NOTICE: The amount or rate of real estate fees is not fixed by law. They are set by each broker individually and are negotiable between Owner and Broker.

4.1 Broker compensation to be:

1. _____% of all rents collected and deposited by Broker during the month, except for any first month's rent for brokerage compensation due under §2 following;

2. _____% of the first month's rent collected and deposited under ☐ rental agreements and ☐ leases; and

3. All sums remaining from credit check fees in excess of credit report expenses.

5. TRUST ACCOUNT:

5.1 Broker will place Owner's deposit for costs and security deposits into:
☐ Broker's trust account, or ☐ separate trust account for Owner, maintained with _____ at their _____ branch.

This account shall be: ☐ non-interest bearing, or ☐ interest bearing.

5.2 All funds received by Broker for the account of Owner will be placed in the trust account.

5.3 Amounts to pay and satisfy the obligations incurred by Broker may be disbursed from the account after payment is due.

5.4 On termination of this agreement, Broker will return to Owner all remaining trust funds belonging to Owner.

6. PERIODIC ACCOUNTING:

6.1 Within ten days after each calendar ☐ month, or ☐ quarter, and on termination of this agreement, Broker will deliver to Owner a Statement of Account for all receipts and expenditures, together with a check to Owner for any funds in excess of minimum reserves under §3.

6.2 Amounts to compensate Broker under §4 may be withdrawn from the trust account.

6.3 Each Statement of Account delivered by Broker shall include no less than the following information for the period:

1. Amount of security deposits received or refunded.

2. Amount of rent or receipts, itemized by unit.

3. An itemized description of disbursements.

4. End of month balance of the income, expense and security deposit trust accounts.

— — — — — — — — — — — *PAGE ONE OF THREE — FORM 590* — — — — — — — — — — — — — —

6.4 ☐ Reserve and disburse from the trust account any property and employee taxes, special assessments, insurance premiums, loan payments and other payments required to be made due to ownership.

6.5 Advertising costs incurred to locate new tenants to be: ☐ paid by Owner, or ☐ paid by Broker.

7. TITLE CONDITION AND LOANS:

7.1 The property is referred to as:_____

_____

_____

_____

7.2 Owner's interest in the property is:
☐ Fee simple ☐ Other

7.3 Loan payments to be timely disbursed by Broker to:

1. Lender: _____

   Address: _____

   _____

   _____

   Phone:_____

   Payment of $_____, due on the _____ day and delinquent on the _____ day of each month.

2. Lender: _____

   Address: _____

   _____

   _____

   Phone:_____

   Payment of $_____, due on the _____ day and delinquent on the _____ day of each month.

8. BROKER AGREES TO:

8.1 Use diligence in the performance of this employment.

8.2 Continuously maintain a California real estate broker's license.

8.3 Collect all rents, security deposits or other charges and expenses due Owner, and timely refund tenants' security deposits less allowable deductions.

8.4 Prepare and place advertisements for prospective tenants.

8.5 Show property to prospective tenants, obtain credit reports and confirm creditworthiness of tenants before executing leases or rental agreements.

8.6 Execute, renegotiate or cancel rental agreements or leases with tenants.
No lease to exceed _____ months.

8.7 Serve rent collection and other notices, file unlawful detainer and money damage actions, recover possession of premises or settle with delinquent tenants.

8.8 Inspect the property monthly and when tenants vacate.

8.9 Maintain and periodically confirm the inventory of personal property on premises.

8.10 Evaluate leases and rental agreements periodically for income, expense and provision updates.

8.11 Contract for utilities, services and equipment to operate and maintain the property and safeguard the tenants.

8.12 Contract for any repairs, maintenance or improvements needed to lease or rent the property. Owner to approve all repairs in excess of $_____.

8.13 Obligate Owner to no unauthorized agreement or liability.

8.14 Protect and enhance the goodwill of Owner's rental business and keep secure any knowledge of Owner's business activities acquired during this employment.

8.15 Hire, supervise and discharge: ☐ a resident manager, and ☐ an assistant resident manager.

8.16 Inspect and take any action necessary to comply with federal, state, county or municipal safety and building codes affecting the property.

8.17 Notify Owner of any potential hazards to the tenants or property, and Owner to respond within seven (7) days. Should an emergency situation arise placing the tenants or property in jeopardy, Broker may immediately remedy the situation without further authority from Owner.

9. OWNER AGREES TO:

9.1 Hand Broker all keys and entry codes to the property, and copies of leases and rental agreements with existing tenants.

9.2 Hand Broker (if Broker is to disburse) loan payment coupons/envelopes, property tax bills, insurance premium billings and _____.

9.3 Indemnify Broker for the expense of any legal action arising out of Broker's proper performance of this agreement.

9.4 Provide public liability, property damage and worker's compensation insurance sufficient in amount to protect Broker and Owner, naming Broker as an additional insured.

Owner's insurance agent is: _____

_____

9.5 _____

_____

10. TERMINATION:

10.1 This agreement shall continue until terminated by mutual written agreement or either party, for legally justifiable cause, serves written Notice of Termination.

10.2 Owner may terminate this agreement at any time during the initial one-year term by paying Broker a fee equal to three times Broker's management fee earned during the month preceding termination.

10.3 On termination, Owner will assume the obligation of any contract entered into by Broker under this agreement.

11. GENERAL PROVISIONS:

11.1 Broker is authorized to place a for rent/lease sign on the property and publish and disseminate property information.

11.2 Owner authorizes Broker to cooperate with other brokers and divide with them any compensation due.

11.3 The authorized agent-for-service is ☐ Broker; ☐ Owner; ☐ _____

11.4 If an action is instituted to enforce this agreement, the prevailing party shall receive reasonable attorney fees.

11.5 ☐ **See attached addendum(s) for additional terms.**

11.6 _____

_____

Broker:	**Owner:**
I agree to render services on the terms stated above.	I agree to employ Broker on the terms stated above.
Date:_____, 20_____	Date:_____, 20_____
Broker: _____	Owner: _____
Address: _____	Address: _____
_____	_____
Phone: _____	Phone: _____
Fax: _____	Fax: _____
E-mail: _____	E-mail: _____

FORM 590   10-00   ©2003 **first tuesday**, P.O. BOX 20069 RIVERSIDE, CA 92516 (800) 794-0494

If the landlord and property manager orally agree to management fees, the property manager will be unable to enforce collection of his fees for services rendered should the landlord fail to pay. [**Phillippe** v. **Shapell Industries, Inc.** (1987) 43 C3d 1247]

Thus, the property management agreement sets forth the fees due the property manager.

An accounting is provided at the end of the employment period, usually each month, since trust account balances for each client must be reconciled at least once a month. [Department of Real Estate Regulations §2831.2]

A property manager who fails to give the landlord a timely and accurate accounting faces loss of his real estate broker's license. [**Apollo Estates Inc.** v. **Department of Real Estate** (1985) 174 CA3d 625]

The property manager must also keep all documents connected with any transaction requiring a real estate broker's license for three years.

Thus, a property manager must retain his management and accounting files for each activity on the property for three years. [B & P C §10148]

Management of CIDs

Brokers often are retained by condominium homeowners' associations (HOAs) or other common interest developments (CIDs) to manage membership, exercise control over the common areas and structures, and account for assessment revenues, expenses and reserves. Brokers seeking such employment are called *prospective managing agents.*

Before a broker acting as a prospective managing agent enters into a management agreement with a CID, the broker must disclose:

- the names and addresses of the owners of the brokerage company if it is an entity;

- the relevant licensing of the owners, such as for architectural design, construction, engineering, real estate or accounting, and the effective dates of the licensees; and

- the relevant professional designations held by the owners, what organizations issued the designation, the issuance dates and any expiration dates. [CC §1363.1]

The benchmark professional certification is the Certified Community Association Manager and is issued by the California Association of Community Managers.

Funds received by the managing agent belong to the HOA. If the HOA does not have a bank account, the manager will maintain a separate trust fund account as trustee for the HOA. Extensive statutory controls are placed on the handling of the trust fund account. [CC §1363.2]

Chapter 7

Resident managers

This chapter discusses the hiring of a resident manager, the pay and reporting regulations, and the termination of the employment and occupancy.

Employees: not independent contractors, not tenants

A broker, retained as a property manager, hires an individual as an on-site resident manager to handle the daily operations of an apartment building comprised of 16 or more residential units. The resident manager enters into an employment contract with the property manager. [See Form 591 accompanying this chapter]

Under the employment contract, the resident manager:

- acknowledges he is an employee of the property manager; and

- agrees to vacate the property on termination of employment.

The resident manager's job is to show vacant units, run credit checks, negotiate and sign leases, collect rents, supervise repairs and maintenance, serve 3-day and 30/60-day notices, etc.

In exchange for his services, the resident manager receives the use of an apartment rent-free.

Later, the property manager terminates the resident manager's employment.

The landlord demands the resident manager immediately vacate the premises and relinquish possession of the unit to the property manager.

However, the resident manager claims he is a tenant and does not need to vacate until he is served a notice to vacate. [See Chapter 29]

Is a resident manager who holds the right to occupy and use a residential unit as compensation for managing an apartment complex entitled to a notice to vacate?

No! A resident manager who occupies a unit after termination of employment is a *tenant-at-sufferance* — a holdover tenant who does not have a right to a notice to vacate since the term of his occupancy was fixed in the resident manager agreement as the date of termination of employment. [**Roberts** v. **Casey** (1939) 36 CA2d Supp. 767]

On termination of employment, a resident manager is not entitled to retain possession of the unit since the term of the occupancy expires on termination of the employment. Possession of the unit is part of his compensation and the compensation ended, as agreed, with the employment.

Also, the resident manager who is being evicted by an unlawful detainer (UD) action cannot defend his possession by asserting a good cause must exist for terminating his employment or by relying on local rent control ordinances. [**Tappe** v. **Lieberman** (1983) 145 CA3d Supp. 19]

Unless the employment agreement provides for a tenancy following the termination of employment, such as a monthly rent payment after termination, the property manager may begin eviction proceedings against the resident manager on termination of the employment without serving any notices — other than the notice terminating the employment and the occupancy as agreed. [Calif. Code of Civil Procedure §1161(1)]

RESIDENT MANAGER AGREEMENT

DATE:_____, 20_____, at _____, California

Items left blank or unchecked are not applicable.

1. RETAINER PERIOD:

1.1 Employer hereby employs _____, Employee, as Resident Manager of the rental property referred to as:

_____

located at _____, California, commencing _____, 20_____ and continuing until terminated.

2. EMPLOYEE AGREES TO:

2.1 Collect all rents, security deposits or other charges due the Owner and maintain collection records.

2.2 Advertise available rental units.

2.3 Screen and select tenants.

2.4 Show rental units to prospective tenants.

2.5 Negotiate, execute or cancel lease/rental agreements with tenants. No lease is to exceed _____ months.

2.6 Serve three-day notices as needed.

2.7 Clean, repair and maintain the rental real estate, inside and outside, as needed to promote the occupancy of the units.

2.8 Inspect daily the structure, grounds, parking lots, garages, and vacant units of the rental property for cleanliness and repairs.

2.9 Maintain receipt books, key racks and petty cash records in good order.

2.10 Conduct all minor maintenance and repairs not exceeding $_____ in cost. All materials to be purchased out of petty cash.

2.11 Contact the material and labor suppliers retained by the Employer to conduct all major repairs and maintenance. Employer to approve all repairs in excess of $_____.

2.12 Notify Employer immediately of any potential hazards to the tenants or property. Should an emergency situation arise placing tenants or property in jeopardy, Employee may immediately take action without further authority from Employer.

2.13 Conduct no other business on the premises nor solicit the tenants for any business other than the rental of the property.

3. BANKING:

3.1 Employee will place all rents, security deposits, and other funds received for the benefit of the Owner into an account maintained by Employer with _____ at their _____ branch.

3.2 On depositing funds into the Employer's Account, Employee shall deliver to Employer a copy of the bank deposit identifying the itemized deposits by the unit from which they were collected.

4. COMPENSATION OF EMPLOYEE AND HOURS WORKED:

4.1 As compensation for services, Employee shall be paid a total monthly salary, from all sources, of $_____.

4.2 In part, Employee's salary shall be in the form of possession to rental unit _____, which must be occupied as a condition of employment. The rental credit is $_____. The fair monthly rental value of the unit is $_____.
The utilities including gas, electricity, and trash removal ☐ are, ☐ are not, included with the occupancy.

— — — — — — — — — — — — — *PAGE ONE OF TWO — FORM 591* — — — — — — — — — — — — — — —

4.3 The balance of the Employee's salary shall be paid ☐ monthly, ☐ semi-monthly, on the _____ of each calendar month.

4.4 Employee will not work more than _____ hours per day and _____ hours per week.

4.5 Employee to have _____ days off weekly being the weekdays of _____.

4.6 Employee agrees to obtain Employer's consent if the hours required to carry out duties exceeds the agreed-to hours.

4.7 Employee will notify Employer within 48 hours of additional hours worked in an emergency situation.

4.9 Employee acknowledges he is not a tenant, but is an employee for purpose of occupancy of the unit provided for his on-site residency.

4.10 _____
_____
_____
_____
_____
_____
_____

5. EMPLOYER AGREES TO:

5.1 Hand Employee all keys and entry codes to the property, and copies of leases/rental agreements with existing tenants.

5.2 Provide public liability, property damage and worker's compensation insurance sufficient in amount to protect the Employee and Employer.

5.3 Hand to Employee $_____ to be accounted for as petty cash to pay costs incurred in performing Employee's duties, and to replenish this amount on Employee's request.

5.4 Withhold all Employee's social security, federal and state income taxes, and disability insurance from cash salary paid.

5.5 Pay all federal and state unemployment insurance, worker's compensation and Employer's social security payments.

EMPLOYEE:	EMPLOYER:
I agree to perform on the terms stated above.	I agree to employ on the terms stated above.
Date:_____, 20_____	Date:_____, 20_____
Employee: _____	Employer: _____
Address: _____	Address: _____
_____	_____
Phone:_____	Phone: _____
Fax: _____	Fax: _____
E-mail: _____	E-mail: _____
By: _____	By: _____

FORM 591   10-01   ©2003 **first tuesday**, P.O. BOX 20069 RIVERSIDE, CA 92516 (800) 794-0494

Resident manager activities

A resident manager is a person who lives in a residential unit, on either residential rental property or nonresidential property, as an employee managing the daily operations of the property, including:

- screening tenants and negotiating leases;

- cleaning vacated units;

- supervising landscaping, maintenance and repairs;

- serving notices; or

- attending to tenant inquiries.

Apartment buildings with 16 or more units must have an owner, resident manager or responsible caretaker living on the premises to manage the property. [25 Calif. Code of Regulations §42]

Resident managers do not need to be licensed to negotiate leases or collect rents. However, the nonresident property manager, other than the landlord himself, must be a licensed real estate broker. [Calif. Business and Professions Code §10131.01]

Hiring a resident manager

Brokerage activities of concern to a property manager when employing an on-site resident manager include:

- selecting and hiring the resident manager;

- overseeing the resident manager; and

- terminating the resident manager.

The resident manager's status as an employee is established in the resident manager employment agreement.

Any family members of the resident manager should be listed in the employment agreement as living with the resident manager, noting they are not tenants. They are employees **required to reside** in a unit on site.

References to the parties in the employment agreement identify the property manager/landlord as "employer" and the resident manager as "employee." [See Form 591 §4.9]

Payment for services

Depending on the size of the complex, the resident manager may receive occupancy of a unit in the complex as compensation for his services based on:

- a reduced rent reflecting a reduction in exchange for the value of the resident manager's services;

- free rent for services; or

- free rent plus a monthly salary.

On the resident manager agreement, the **salary** paid to the resident manager is stated as a monthly amount. The fair rental value of the resident manager's unit is deducted from the salary. After the rent deduction, the resident manager is paid the balance of the salary remaining unpaid. Utilities may also be included as part payment for the resident manager's services and a deduction from the agreed-to salary. [See Form 591 §4]

As an **employer**, the property manager/landlord has the responsibility to withhold all proper federal and state income taxes, as well as make required payments for social security, unemployment insurance and disability insurance. [Calif. Unemployment Insurance Code §13020]

The property manager or landlord must carry workers' compensation insurance to cover resident manager injuries incurred while on the job.

Due to the degree of control the property manager retains over a resident manager, a resident manager does not qualify as an independent contractor to avoid tax withholding, employer contributions and workers' compensation premiums.

Rental value is not income

Consider the property manger who retains a resident manager to run a large apartment complex. As part of his salary, the resident manager receives a unit rent-free plus a fixed monthly salary.

Is the value of the unit occupied by the resident manager in exchange for services considered **income** which the resident manager must declare for state or federal tax reporting?

No! Taxwise, the value of the apartment is not income to the resident manager and is not declared as income when the unit occupied by the resident manager is:

- located on the premises managed;

- for the property manager's or landlord's convenience; and

- occupied by the resident manager as a condition of the employment. [Revenue Regulations §1.119-1(b)]

Minimum wage requirements

A resident manager's employment is subject to minimum wage laws even though the portion of the wages paid by a reduction in rent or free rent is not taxable as income. [Calif. Labor Code §1182.8]

Strict minimum wage requirements apply to resident managers since they **carry out the instructions** of the property manager or landlord rather than having authority to make their own independent decisions about management policies. [8 CCR §11050(1)(B)(1)]

A **rent credit** may be used as all or part of the wages received per hour of work performed by a resident manager to establish the amount earned per hour for minimum pay requirements. However, a cap exists limiting the rent credit toward hourly wages at two thirds of the fair rental value of the unit, but not to exceed $381.20 per month. Should a couple be employed as resident managers the rent credited toward hourly pay cannot exceed $563.90 per month. [8 CCR §11050(10)(C)]

Thus, the property manager should require the resident manager to prepare time cards, limit the number of hours per week the resident manager may work so wages per hour do not drop below the minimum, and make provisions for the payment of any overtime permitted. Weekly work reports by the resident manager and a review of the reports by the property manager or landlord are to confirm the total compensation exceeds the minimum wages for time spent on the job. These reports will help avoid any resident manager's claim he worked excessive hours in relation to his salary and maximum rent credit. [See Form 591 §4]

Thus, all work requiring additional hours, except emergency work, must be approved by the property manager prior to being performed by the resident manager.

For example, a resident manager who is provided with a base salary, plus a unit, is required to remain on the premises at all times, but only performs five hours of daily work as limited by the resident manager employment agreement.

The resident manager claims he is entitled to overtime pay for the hours he is required to be on the premises.

However, the resident manager is only entitled to receive compensation for the time he actually performed work agreed to in the resident manager employment agreement, not for the time he was required to remain on the premises doing no work at all. [**Brewer** v. **Patel** (1993) 20 CA4th 1017]

Mismanaged managers

A resident manager is an employee of the property manager or the landlord who employs him.

As an employer, it is the landlord or property manager who is liable to others who are injured due to the improper conduct (negligence) of the resident manager which occurs in the course and scope of the resident manager's employment. [Calif. Civil Code §2338]

To avoid liability for negligent violations of law or personal injuries to others, the conduct of resident managers must be **closely supervised** by the property manager or landlord.

Termination

A resident manager employment agreement creates an agency with the property manager or landlord which is an *at-will* relationship. Thus, the employment of the resident manager may be terminated at any time and without prior notice.

While a landlord or property manager does not need to have a good reason to terminate a resident manager, they cannot have an improper reason.

For instance, a resident manager has managed a large complex for many years as an agent for the property manager. The resident manager is over 62 years of age.

The property manager hires a new, younger resident manager and relegates the old resident manager to a lesser position.

The property manager constantly suggests to the older manager that he should retire and demotes him to even lesser positions while dramatically reducing his compensation.

Has the property manager discriminated against the older resident manager?

Yes! The property manager's basis for demotion was not substandard performance, but age.

As a result, the property manager is responsible for money damages for emotional distress and attorney fees. A property manager or landlord cannot terminate the resident manager or otherwise harass him because of race, creed, color, gender or age. [**Stephens** v. **Coldwell Banker Commercial Group, Inc.** (1988) 199 CA3d 1394]

Terminating the occupancy

Consider a resident manager employment agreement which provides for a property manager to receive immediate possession of the unit occupied by the resident manager on termination of the resident manager's employment.

The employment agreement should avoid creating any landlord/tenant relationship in the resident manager's occupancy of a unit or requiring prior notice to be given to the resident manager before his occupancy can be terminated.

For example, an owner of an apartment complex hires a resident manager to run the complex. In exchange for his services, the resident manager receives an apartment rent-free and a monthly salary.

Under the resident manager's employment agreement, he agrees to vacate the apartment unit on termination of employment. Thus, the right to possession is terminated on being fired.

The owner terminates the resident manager. The owner then serves the resident manager with notice to **immediately vacate** the premises and relinquish possession of the unit, or alternatively, **stay and pay** monthly rent.

The resident manager remains in possession of the apartment, but fails to pay the monthly rent called for in the notice to vacate. Without further notice, the owner begins UD proceedings to regain possession of the apartment from the fired resident manager.

The resident manager claims he is now a tenant and the owner must serve him with a notice to vacate to establish his unlawful detainer of the unit.

The landlord claims the resident manager is a holdover tenant-at-sufferance who has been unlawfully detaining the premises since the termination of the employment.

Is the resident manager entitled to a notice to vacate?

Yes! The resident manager's occupancy was converted to a month-to-month tenancy when the owner served the resident manager with a notice to vacate the apartment which included an offer to remain in possession, which the tenant did.

Here, the resident manager's continued occupancy of the apartment constituted acceptance of the new tenancy offered by the owner. Thus, the failure to pay rent is a breach of the new tenancy agreement noted in the notice to stay and pay. The owner's UD action cannot be filed until a 3-day notice to vacate is given to terminate the resident manager's new tenancy for failure to pay rent. [**Karz** v. **Mecham** (1981) 120 CA3d Supp. 1; CC §1946]

On termination, the resident manager should not have been served any notice to pay or vacate. On termination of employment, the manager is unlawfully detaining the property and can be evicted if he remains in possession.

Neither the landlord nor the property manager should at any time enter into a separate lease/rental agreement with a resident manager.

Rather, the occupancy arrangement should be written as part of the employment agreement — even if the management services do not equal the unit's rental value and the resident manager pays the difference as a reduced monthly rent charged for the unit. [Form 591 §4]

To avoid creating a tenancy which continues on termination of the resident manager, the resident manager employment agreement must state:

- possession is incidental to his employment;

- possession automatically terminates concurrent with termination of his employment; and

- failure to perform managerial duties constitutes a breach of the employment agreement and grounds for immediate termination and eviction.

Chapter 8

Identification of property manager or landlord

This chapter discusses the disclosure required to be given to residential tenants identifying the landlord or the landlord's agent-for-service, his property manager and the resident manager.

Notice to tenant of agent-for-service

A residential landlord turns over the management of his property to a broker employed under a property management agreement.

The broker will take control of the management and care of the property, as well as all contact with the tenants, including the decision to enter into all future lease and rental agreements.

One of the landlord's objectives is to become as anonymous as possible and avoid giving the tenants any information about himself.

The broker advises the landlord he can avoid being identified to the tenants when he appoints another individual to act as his *agent-for-service*, such as the broker or the landlord's attorney. The agent-for-service, acting on behalf of the landlord, will accept service of legal documents and notices initiated by tenants. [Calif. Civil Code §1962(a)(1)(B)]

Here, when the landlord appoints an agent-for-service, the landlord's name and address do not need to be disclosed to any tenant, even if the tenant is suing the landlord. Serving the agent-for-service with the lawsuit is the same as serving the landlord. [CC §1962(a)(1)(B)]

Note — The identity of a landlord may be easily located by a search of the county records. If title to the property is vested in the name of a limited liability company (LLC), corporation, etc., a review of other records with the Secretary of State might be required to locate the individual vested with title who manages the entity.

Appointing the agent-for-service

A landlord may accept service of tenant notices and legal documents himself.

However, a residential landlord may appoint any individual, including his property manager or his attorney, to be his agent-for-service.

The property manager may be appointed as a landlord's agent-for-service by including an **agent-for-service clause** in the property management agreement employing the broker. [See Fig.1]

As the landlord's *agent-for-service of process*, the broker accepts personal service of legal documents on behalf of the landlord, such as notices and lawsuits initiated by tenants.

Both the broker and the landlord should thoughtfully consider whether the broker should act as the landlord's agent-for-service.

Placing on the broker the additional responsibility of accepting service of tenant complaints on behalf of the landlord conflicts with the broker's main responsibilities of managing and caring for the landlord's property.

Litigation might result from the broker's purported mismanagement of the property. A landlord may prefer to appoint an attorney as his agent-for-service to avoid the potential conflict of interest.

Who is identified to the tenant?

The names and addresses of the following individuals must be disclosed to all residential tenants:

CHANGE OF OWNER OR PROPERTY MANAGER
Addendum To Lease or Rental Agreement

DATE:_____, 20_____, at _____, California

To Tenant: _____

Items left blank or unchecked are not applicable.

FACTS:

This is an addendum to the ☐ lease, ☐ rental agreement dated _____,

at _____, California, entered into by

_____, Landlord, and

Tenant(s) _____, and

_____, recorded _____,

as Instrument No. _____ in _____

County Records, California, regarding real estate referred to as: _____

_____

_____

AGREEMENT:

1. ☐ The ownership of the real estate you lease or rent has been transferred.

2. ☐ The new property management broker is:_____
   Address:_____
   Phone: _____

3. ☐ The new resident manager is: _____
   Address:_____
   Phone: _____

4. Beginning _____, 20_____, your monthly rent to be paid by ☐ cash, ☐ check, or ☐ cashier's check made payable to Landlord.

   4.1 Rent may be tendered by ☐ mail, or ☐ personal delivery to:
   _____ (Name)
   _____ (Address)
   _____
   _____ (Phone)

   a. Personal delivery of rent will be accepted during the hours of _____ am to _____ pm on the following days: _____

   4.2 Rent may also be paid by deposit into account number _____ at:
   _____ (Financial Institution)
   _____ (Address)
   _____

5. Your current monthly rent is $_____.

6. Your rent has been paid up to and including _____, 20_____.

– – – – – – – – – – – – – – *PAGE ONE OF TWO — FORM 554* – – – – – – – – – – – – – – –

7. Your security deposit of $_____

   ☐ has been transferred to the new owner.
   ☐ has been transferred to the new property manager.

8. No breach of your lease or rental agreement by Landlord or Tenant currently exists.

9. Any notices or demands on the owner by Tenant, including service of process, may be served on:

   Name: _____

   Address:_____

   Phone: _____

10. All terms and conditions of your lease and rental agreement remain in effect.

I agree to the terms stated above.	**I agree to the terms stated above.**
Date:_____, 20_____	Date:_____, 20_____
Landlord: _____	Tenant: _____
Agent: _____	Tenant: _____
Signature: _____	Signature: _____
Address: _____	Signature: _____
_____	Address: _____
Phone: _____	_____
Fax: _____	Phone: _____
E-mail: _____	Fax: _____
	E-mail: _____

FORM 554   02-02   ©2003 **first tuesday**, P.O. BOX 20069 RIVERSIDE, CA 92516 (800) 794-0494

- the landlord or other individual appointed by the landlord as his agent-for-service;

- any property managers; and

- any resident managers. [CC §1962(a)]

The addresses given for the manager and agent-for-service must be *street* addresses where legal notices can be **personally** served on the individual. A post office box will not suffice. [CC §1962(a)(1)]

The individual responsible for making the disclosures is:

- the landlord; or

- the individual authorized to enter into lease and rental agreements on behalf of the landlord, such as the property manager or resident manager. [CC §1962(a)]

Delivery of the notice

The names and addresses of the landlord's manager and agent-for-service may be disclosed in:

- the lease and rental agreements entered into with tenants; or

- a notice posted on the property. [CC §§1962(a); 1962.5(a)]

When the disclosure notice is posted, the notice must be posted in two conspicuous places on the property. [CC §1962.5(a)(2)]

If the rental property contains an elevator, the written notice must be posted in:

- every elevator in the building; and

- one other conspicuous place on the property. [CC §1962.5(a)(1)]

If the residential rental or lease agreement is oral, a written statement containing the name and address of the manager and agent-for-service must be provided. [CC §1962(b)]

Change in ownership and management

The landlord, property manager or resident manager responsible for entering into lease and rental agreements must notify all tenants of the name and address for service of notices or complaints initiated by the tenants within 15 calendar days after any change in:

- the manager(s) of the property;

- the owner(s), unless the owner has appointed an agent-for-service; or

- the landlord's agent-for-service. [CC §1962(c); see Form 554 accompanying this chapter *ante*]

To disclose a change in ownership or management, the broker or resident manager responsible for leasing should:

- prepare the notice of change of ownership or property manager as an addendum to each existing lease or rental agreement which is handed to each tenant for him to sign and return [See Form 554]; or

- post the property with the name and address of the manager and landlord's agent-for-service.

The notice must also include information regarding when and how rent will be paid.

Failure to give notice

The broker, acting as property manager for a residential landlord, or the landlord's resident manager responsible for leasing is to make the disclosures.

When the name and address of the landlord or agent-for-service is not disclosed, the individual who enters into rental agreements on behalf of the landlord:

- automatically becomes the landlord's agent-for-service of process and agent for receipt of all tenant notices and demands [CC §1962(d)(1)]; and

- will be treated as the landlord for the performance of all obligations arising under lease and rental agreements with tenants. [CC §1962(d)(2)]

When the person signing the lease or rental agreement for the landlord fails to make the disclosures, the tenant may have no indication the person signing is not the landlord.

However, the landlord is not relieved of any liability to tenants should the name and address of the owner or agent-for-service not be disclosed. [CC §1962(e)]

Chapter 9

Exclusive authorization to lease

This chapter discusses a broker's right to collect his fee from a nonresidential landlord who employs the broker as his exclusive leasing agent.

Leasing agent's bargain for fees

A nonresidential property is offered for lease by the owner, who is called a *landlord*. A broker makes an appointment with the landlord to discuss the possibility of becoming the landlord's *leasing agent*.

During the discussion, the broker explains he can best help lease the property if he is operating under a signed exclusive authorization to lease, also called a *listing*. Under the listing, the broker, on behalf of the landlord, will be able to:

- market the space and locate prospective tenants, called *users*, as the landlord's sole representative [See Form 110 §1 accompanying this chapter];

- disclose the terms under which a user can actually lease and occupy the space [See Form 110 §10];

- assure other brokers the landlord has agreed to pay a fee and the fee can be shared in cooperation with brokers who represent users [See Form 110 §5.2]; and

- conduct negotiations with users and their brokers, and accept deposits with offers to lease the space. [See Form 110 §5.3]

The broker will not be managing the property, only locating tenants and leasing space.

Right to compensation for services

The **exclusive authorization** listing assures the broker he will receive a fee for his efforts if *anyone* procures a tenant during the listing period, either on:

- the leasing terms sought in the listing; or

- other terms accepted by the landlord.

However, the landlord is reluctant to give up his ability to lease the property himself. Further, he would like to avoid employing the broker and paying a brokerage fee.

On the other hand, the landlord feels he has a better chance of finding a tenant on acceptable terms in the current market if he is represented by a member of the local brokerage community of leasing agents.

Ultimately, the landlord orally agrees to employ the broker. He confirms he will work exclusively with the broker to market the space and locate a user. However, the landlord does not believe it is necessary to have a written agreement — a handshake and his word should do the job.

The broker explains an exclusive authorization must be written and signed by the landlord for the broker to be entitled to collect a fee — no signed writing, no services.

Is the broker correct in his analysis?

Yes! An agreement in writing signed by the client is the only way a broker can protect his right to be compensated for work done — whether representing a tenant or a landlord.

An oral fee agreement between a broker and his client, be the client a tenant or a landlord, **without a later writing** signed by the client, is unenforceable against the person who orally agrees to pay the fee.

Oral fee agreements are unenforceable even when the broker documents the oral agreement by referencing the fee and terms of payment in written correspondence sent to and acted on by the client. [**Phillippe** v. **Shapell Industries, Inc.** (1987) 43 C3d 1247]

Thus, a broker best protects his right to collect a fee for acting on behalf of a landlord by entering into an exclusive authorization, signed by the landlord, before performing any services.

Note — If a broker is employed to renegotiate an existing lease (rather than originate one), his employment does not need to be in the form of a signed written agreement. Fees promised a broker for the negotiation of modifications, expansions, extensions or renewals of existing leases are not required to be written to be enforceable. [**Shell** v. **Darnell** (1984) 162 CA3d 957]

Exclusive authorization

An exclusive authorization to lease operates like an exclusive right-to-sell listing agreement.

The leasing agent is employed to "sell the use" by locating a user of the landlord's property, rather than "sell the ownership" by locating a buyer of the property.

Thus, the broker has the same obligations and duties to the client under an exclusive leasing authorization as are owed to a client under an exclusive right-to-sell listing. The primary obligation is the use of *due diligence* to continuously and conscientiously market the property and locate qualified tenants.

Conversely, a broker's performance under an **open listing** requires only his *best efforts*, not constant diligence in the search for a tenant as is required under an exclusive listing.

An open listing sets the leasing agent in competition with the landlord and other brokers to be the **first to locate** a tenant and be entitled to collect a fee.

To best secure his time, energy and money invested (and provide incentive) to locate a tenant and lease the premises on behalf of a landlord, a leasing agent uses an exclusive authorization to lease form. [See Form 110]

The exclusive authority authorization to lease form has a fee provision which calls for a fee schedule to be prepared and attached. The fee schedule references leasing situations which trigger the earning of formulated fees, such as 5% of the total rents for the first five years and 3% of the total rents for the balance of the lease. The schedule includes fees for extensions, renewals and other continuing leasehold and purchase arrangements which might be entered into in the future by the tenant and the landlord. [See **first tuesday** Form 113]

The fee amount established in the fee schedule is earned and due on the occurrence of the following events:

- an *exclusive right-to-collect clause* assures payment of the agreed-to fee if the broker, another broker, the landlord or anyone else procures a tenant on the terms stated in the listing or on any other terms accepted by the landlord [See Form 110 §4.1a];

- an *early-termination option* assures payment of the fee should the landlord withdraw the property from the rental market during the listing period [See Form §4.1b];

- a *termination-of-agency clause* assures payment of the fee if the landlord cancels the employment under the listing before it expires [See Form 110 §4.1c]; and

- a *safety clause* assures payment of the fee if, within a year after termination of the exclusive authorization, the landlord enters into negotiations which later result in the leasing or selling of the property to a prospective tenant with whom the broker negotiated with during the listing period. [See Form 110 §4.1d]

EXCLUSIVE AUTHORIZATION TO LEASE PROPERTY

DATE:_____, 20_____, at _____, California

Items left blank or unchecked are not applicable.

1. RETAINER PERIOD:

1.1 Landlord hereby retains and grants to Broker the exclusive and irrevocable right to solicit prospective tenants and negotiate for the lease of the property for the period:
beginning on _____, 20_____ and terminating on _____, 20_____.

1.2 Broker to use diligence in the performance of this agreement.

2. ADDENDUMS to this agreement:

a.. ☐ Title Report, or ☐ Title Policy

b. ☐ Work Authorization [**first tuesday** Form 108] (Also see §3.1b)

c. ☐ Property Operating Data [**ft** Form 562]

d. ☐ Agency Law Disclosure Addendum [**ft** Form 305]
(Mandated for one-to-four residential units if lease exceeds one year.)

e. ☐ Lead-based Paint Disclosure [**ft** Form 557]
(Mandated for one-to-four residential units constructed before 1978.)

f. ☐ _____

g. ☐ _____

h. ☐ _____

3. LANDLORD'S DEPOSIT:

3.1 Landlord hands $_____ to Broker for deposit into Broker's trust account for application to obligations under this agreement and the following attachments:

a. ☐ Advance Fee Addendum [**ft** Form 106]

b. ☐ Advance Cost Addendum [**ft** Form 107] (Also see §2b)

4. BROKERAGE FEE:

NOTICE: The amount or rate of real estate fees is not fixed by law. They are set by each Broker individually and may be negotiable between the Client and Broker.

4.1 Landlord agrees to pay Broker ☐ see attached fee schedule [**ft** Form 113], or
☐ _____ as compensation for services rendered, IF:

a. Anyone procures a tenant on the terms stated in this agreement, or any other terms acceptable to Landlord, during the period of this agreement.

b. The property is withdrawn from the rental market or made unmarketable by Landlord during the period of this agreement.

c. The Landlord terminates this employment of the Broker during the period of this agreement.

d. Within one year after termination of this agreement, Landlord or his agent commences negotiations which later result in a transaction contemplated by this agreement with a tenant with whom the Broker, or a cooperating broker, negotiated during the period of this agreement. Broker to identify prospective tenants by written notice to the Landlord within 21 days after termination of this agreement. [**ft** Form 122]

4.2 Should this agreement terminate without Landlord becoming obligated to pay Broker a fee, Landlord to pay Broker the sum of $_____ per hour of time accounted for by Broker, not to exceed $_____.

4.3 If Broker procures a tenant who purchases the property during the term of tenant's lease or any modification, extension or renewal of the lease or other continuing occupancy of leased property, Landlord agrees to pay Broker a fee of ☐ see attached fee schedule [**ft** Form 113], or
☐ _____.

— — — — — — — — — — — — — *PAGE ONE OF THREE — FORM 110* — — — — — — — — — — — — — —

5. GENERAL PROVISIONS:

5.1 Broker is authorized to place a For Lease sign on the property and publish and disseminate property information to meet the objectives of this employment.

5.2 Landlord authorizes Broker to cooperate with other agents and divide with them any compensation due.

5.3 Broker is authorized to receive, on behalf of any tenant, an offer and deposit.

5.4 The Landlord's acceptance of any tenant's offer to lease to be contingent on approval of the tenant's creditworthiness and management capabilities.

5.5 In any action to enforce this agreement, the prevailing party shall receive attorney fees.

5.6 This agreement will be governed by California law.

6. REAL ESTATE:

Type: _____

Address: _____

Described as: _____

_____

_____

_____

_____

Vesting: _____

7. ENCUMBRANCES OF RECORD:

7.1 A first loan in the amount of $_____ payable $_____ per month until paid, including interest at _____%, ☐ ARM, type _____, impounds being $_____ monthly.
Lender: _____

7.2 A second loan in the amount of $_____ payable $_____ per month, including interest at _____%, due_____, 20_____.
Lender: _____

7.3 Other encumbrance, bond, assessment or lien in the amount of $_____.

7.4 Any defaults:_____

8. PERSONAL PROPERTY INCLUDED:

Described as: _____

_____

_____

_____

9. CONDITION OF TITLE:

9.1 Landlord's interest in the property is:

☐ Fee simple

☐ Leasehold

☐ _____

☐ _____

9.2 Landlord warrants there are no unsatisfied judgments or actions pending against him, no condemnation/eminent domain proceedings or other actions against the property, and no unrecorded deeds or encumbrances against the property.

10. LEASE TERMS:

10.1 The lease term sought is for a period of _____.

10.2 Occupancy to be available _____, 20_____.

10.3 Initial rent shall be $_____ payable on the _____ day of each month, with adjustments annually based on _____.

10.4 A total deposit of $_____, being $_____ advance rents and $_____ security deposit.

10.5 A late charge of $_____ to be incurred _____ days after the rent is due, plus interest at _____% per annum beginning from the due date for the delinquent rent.

10.6 Tenant to pay for and maintain:

☐ Water

☐ Gas

☐ Electricity

☐ Heat/Air Conditioning

☐ Public liability insurance

☐ Property damage insurance

☐ Plate glass insurance

☐ Other:_____

10.7 Landlord to maintain:

_____

_____

10.8 Tenant may not assign, lease or sublet any portion of the property without written consent of the Landlord.

10.9 The lease form sought to be used by Landlord is form #_____ published or drafted by _____.

10.10 Other terms:

_____

_____

_____

_____

I agree to render services on the terms stated above.	I agree to employ Broker on the terms stated above.
Date:_____, 20_____	Date:_____, 20_____
Broker:_____	Landlord:_____
By: _____	Signature:_____
Signature: _____	Address: _____
Address: _____	_____
_____	Phone: _____
Phone: _____	Fax: _____
Fax: _____	E-mail: _____
E-mail: _____	

FORM 110   10-01   ©2003 **first tuesday**, P.O. BOX 20069 RIVERSIDE, CA 92516 (800) 794-0494

Ready, willing and able tenant

Now consider a broker who is employed by a landlord under an exclusive authorization to lease.

The authorization states the landlord will pay the broker a fee if the broker, or anyone else including the landlord, produces a tenant *ready, willing and able* to lease the property on the **same terms** specified in the exclusive authorization agreement. [See Form 110 §4.1a]

The broker produces a creditworthy tenant who is financially capable of leasing the premises on the terms set forth in the exclusive authorization agreement. [See Form 110 §10]

The broker prepares and submits the tenant's offer to lease on terms substantially identical to the leasing terms in the authorization, called a *full listing offer*. [See **first tuesday** Form 556]

The landlord refuses to accept the offer, disclosing to the broker he now wants a higher rental rate.

The broker claims he is entitled to his fee since he produced a tenant who is *ready, willing and able* to lease the property on the terms stated in the exclusive authorization agreement.

The landlord claims the broker is not entitled to a fee since the property was never leased.

Here, a written fee agreement exists under which the broker only needs to **locate a tenant** ready, willing and able to lease the landlord's property **on the terms listed** for the broker to earn and be entitled to immediate payment of his fee. [**Twogood** v. **Monnette** (1923) 191 C 103]

An exclusive right to collect

Now consider a broker whose exclusive authorization to lease contains a fee provision stating he is entitled to his fee if the landlord rents the space to any tenant during the listing period, called a *right-to-collect clause*. It is the right-to-collect clause which makes an exclu-sive listing exclusive. The clause states "a fee is due if anyone procures a tenant." [See Form 110 §4.1a]

The broker places a "For Lease" sign on the premises. The sign is seen by a prospective tenant.

Without contacting the broker, the prospective tenant locates and contacts the landlord of the premises.

Before the exclusive authorization period expires, the prospective tenant and landlord enter into a lease agreement on terms different from those specified in the broker's exclusive authorization.

Even though the landlord's broker had no contact with the prospective tenant (other than the sign exposure), the broker is entitled to his fee. A tenant's offer to lease was accepted by the landlord during the exclusive authorization period.

Further, the broker receives his fee even though the final terms agreed to by the landlord and the tenant differed from the terms of the listing since the tenant's terms were accepted by the landlord during the exclusive authorization period. [**Carlsen** v. **Zane** (1968) 261 CA2d 399]

Early termination by landlord

A typical exclusive authorization agreement also contains boilerplate wording in the fee provision stating the landlord will pay the broker the agreed-to fee if the property is:

- withdrawn from the rental market;

- transferred or conveyed;

- leased without the broker's consent; or

- made unrentable by the landlord, called an *early-termination clause*. [See Form 110 §4.1b]

This clause protects the broker from loss of his time and money expended in a *diligent effort* to locate a tenant should the landlord's conduct actually or effectively remove the property from the rental market before a suitable tenant is located. When the landlord **interferes with the objective** for employing the broker — to produce a ready, willing and able tenant under the terms of the employment — a fee has been earned and is immediately due.

Consider a broker and a landlord who enter into an exclusive authorization to lease which expires in six months. The agreement contains a fee provision with an early-termination clause.

The broker **diligently attempts** to locate a tenant for the landlord's property.

During the listing period, the landlord notifies the broker the property is no longer for lease. The broker is instructed to stop marketing the property. In compliance with his client's instructions, the broker takes the property off the market.

The broker then makes a demand on the landlord for a full listing fee. The early-termination clause provides for payment of the broker's fee by the landlord if the landlord withdraws the property from the rental market before expiration of the listing period.

The landlord claims the broker cannot collect a fee under the early-termination clause since it calls for a lump sum payment on the landlord's breach of the employment agreement, called a *liquidated damages* provision, a penalty courts abhor.

Is the broker entitled to his fee on the client's termination of the broker's employment?

Yes! The broker is entitled to his fee since the early-termination clause gives the landlord the **option to cancel** the exclusive authorization agreement in exchange for paying the broker a fee. The landlord exercises the right to cancel by his conduct which interferes with the broker's ability to lease the property, such as taking the property off the market.

The landlord does not breach the exclusive authorization to lease when he withdraws the property from the rental market. He merely exercises his option to do so. Thus, the amount due is not liquidated damages for a breach. [**Blank** v. **Borden** (1974) 11 C3d 963]

However, the landlord did ultimately breach the exclusive authorization agreement. The landlord failed to compensate the broker for the fee earned and due when he exercised his option to take the property off the market.

Note — See **first tuesday** *Form 121 for an agreement to cancel an exclusive authorization during the listing period.*

Safety clause covers prospects

A landlord's broker can further protect his time and effort spent during the listing period locating a tenant which later produces results by also including a *safety clause* in the fee provisions of an exclusive authorization to lease. [See Form 110 §4.1d]

The safety clause states the landlord will pay the broker the scheduled fee if, within **one year after** the exclusive authorization expires, the landlord enters into negotiations during the safety clause period (one year) which later result in a lease of the premises to a tenant who was located and exposed to the property by the broker or his agents during the listing period.

Consider a broker and a landlord who enter into an exclusive authorization to lease containing a fee provision with a safety clause.

On expiration of the listing period, the broker, as agreed to in the safety clause, supplies the landlord with the **names of tenants** he has had contact with and who received information regarding the property, called *negotiations* with the tenant.

Thus, the name of each prospective tenant the broker or a cooperating broker provided with information about the property is "registered" with the landlord. [See **first tuesday** Form 122]

After the listing expires, the landlord employs a second broker without discussing the terms of the prior listing.

Within the one-year period after expiration of the first broker's authorization, the second broker arranges a lease of the premises to a tenant registered by the first broker, but without the first broker's participation in negotiations or the fee.

Here, the landlord owes the first broker the entire amount of the agreed-to fee even though the property was leased while listed exclusively with another broker.

The exclusive authorization entered into by the landlord and the first broker promises the first broker his fee if, within one year after expiration of the listing, the landlord **enters into negotiations** which result in a lease with a prospective tenant located and registered by the first broker. [**Leonard** v. **Fallas** (1959) 51 C2d 649]

A safety clause is necessary for the preservation of the broker's time, effort and money expended in the exercise of his due diligence duty as the client's agent under a listing. As a "safety net" for brokerage services rendered, the clause discourages the landlord from attempting to avoid payment of the broker's fee by:

- waiting until the exclusive authorization agreement expires and then directly or indirectly approaching a prospective tenant located and solicited by the broker; or

- making special fee arrangements with another broker which re-ignite negotiations with a prospective tenant located and exposed to the property by the broker.

Contingency fees

Offer to lease forms typically contain a provision stating the broker's fee is payable on the transfer of possession to the tenant, called a *contingency fee clause*. [See Form 556 §15]

Sometimes, the lease agreed to in the offer to lease is never entered into by the landlord and prospective tenant. Without a lease, the agreed-to change of possession triggering payment of the fee the broker has earned — occupancy — does not occur due to a breach of the offer to lease. As a result, the brokerage fee which has been earned is not paid since the condition for payment of the fee — occupancy — did not occur.

Residential agency disclosures

Before a landlord enters into an exclusive authorization to lease residential property, a property manager or leasing agent is required to hand the landlord a Rules-of-Agency Disclosure if:

- the lease will be for a term of **more than one year**; and

- the premises is a one-to-four unit residential property or mobilehome. [Calif. Civil Code §§2079.13(j); 2079.14]

The rules-of-agency should be disclosed by attaching the Rules-of-Agency Disclosure to the exclusive authorization. [See **first tuesday** Form 305]

If the broker fails to deliver the rules-of-agency to the **residential landlord** prior to entering into the exclusive authorization:

- the fee agreement is unenforceable; and

- the broker is not entitled to a fee even if the agency disclosure is later delivered with the offer to lease or the lease itself. [**Huijers** v. **DeMarrais** (1992) 11 CA4th 676]

However, a broker may recover contingency fees contained in offers to lease even when, due to a breach by either the landlord or the tenant, the lease agreed to in the offer is not later entered into and possession is not transferred.

Consider a landlord who accepts an **offer to lease** submitted by a broker on behalf of a prospective tenant.

The signed offer to lease states the broker's fee is payable by the landlord on change of possession.

Later, the landlord wrongfully refuses to enter into a lease and convey the leasehold estate (occupancy) as agreed to in the offer to lease.

When the lease is not entered into with the prospective tenant, the broker makes a demand on the landlord for payment of a fee.

The landlord claims the broker is not entitled to receive a fee since the right to possession was never conveyed to the prospective tenant, i.e., the lease contracted for in the offer to lease was never entered into.

Is the broker entitled to his fee?

Yes! The landlord cannot avoid paying the fee the broker has already earned by claiming the transfer-of-possession contingency was not satisfied (no lease) since it is the **landlord's breach** of the offer to lease agreement which prevented the transfer of occupancy to the tenant. The landlord failed to deliver the lease and possession as agreed to in the offer to lease. The failure to enter into the lease now triggers payment of the fee previously earned by the broker when the landlord accepted the tenant's offer to lease.

The contingency fee provision included in the offer to lease merely **designates the time** for payment of a fee which was previously earned (on locating a tenant). The contingency fee provision in the offer does not defeat the broker's right to be compensated simply because the landlord later wrongfully refused to enter into the agreed-to lease. [**Steve Schmidt & Co.** v. **Berry** (1986) 183 CA3d 1299]

The contingency fee provision in an offer to lease, as under a purchase agreement, shifts the **time for payment** of the fee from the time the fee is earned (and due) under an exclusive authorization agreement to the time a lease is entered into under the offer to lease agreement.

Also, unless the listing broker approves, the landlord cannot include and enforce a fee provision in the offer to lease which is contrary to the fee schedule terms agreed to by the landlord and the broker in the exclusive authorization agreement.

For instance, the landlord cannot unilaterally insert and enforce a provision in a leasing document for the broker's fee to be paid in installments when the broker has only agreed under the exclusive authorization or offer to lease to accept payment of his fee at the time an offer or lease is entered into by the landlord. [**Seck** v. **Foulks** (1972) 25 CA3d 556]

Additional fees on extension of lease

Exclusive authorization agreements have fee schedules attached which contain formulas for calculating the brokerage fee earned based on the length of the lease negotiated with the tenant. Also, they usually state the broker will receive an **additional fee** for any extension, renewal or modification of the tenant's occupancy under the original lease. [See **first tuesday** Form 113]

For example, a broker operating under the authority of a written leasing agent listing procures a tenant who signs a ten-year lease. The broker is paid the fee called for in the listing agreement fee schedule.

The fee schedule also provides for a percentage fee to be paid on any future leasehold arrangements entered into between the landlord and the tenant for **continued occupancy** of the premises on the expiration of the original lease.

On expiration of the original lease, the landlord and tenant negotiate a new lease for the tenant's **continuing occupancy and use** of the premises. A brokerage fee is not paid for the tenant's continued occupancy.

The broker makes a demand for an additional fee under the original listing agreement claiming the new lease, which he did not negotiate, earned him a fee.

The landlord claims he does not owe the broker a fee since the new lease is a separate agreement, not an extension, renewal or modification of the original lease.

However, the landlord must pay the broker the additional fee agreed to in the original listing based on a percentage of the total rent due under the new lease since the new lease *constitutes an extension* of the original lease.

Here, the tenant located by the broker continued in possession and use of the premises on expiration of the original lease. The listing agreement stated the broker was to be paid a fee on this event, no matter what form of documentation (new lease agreement) was used to permit the continued occupancy of the premises. [**John B. Kilroy Company** v. **Douglas Furniture of California, Inc.** (1993) 21 CA4th 26]

Chapter 10

Exclusive authorization to locate space

This chapter discusses the benefits enjoyed by a broker and a prospective nonresidential tenant when the tenant employs the broker to locate space under an exclusive authorization listing.

A broker and his nonresidential tenant

An owner of nonresidential property holds an open house attended by brokers who are leasing agents to encourage them to locate tenants for his vacant space.

Leasing agents who are in attendance and represent tenants, typically called *users,* are handed the owner's brochure on available space. The information includes a schedule of broker fees the owner will pay if a tenant is procured for the property. The informational handout also includes a tenant registration form.

One of the brokers who received a brochure inspects the property with a prospective tenant.

The broker completes the tenant registration form which identifies the broker and the prospective tenant. The registration form does not reference the fee schedule or any amount payable to the broker as a fee.

The registration form is handed to the owner, or the owner's employee, who signs it and returns a copy to the broker.

Later, the broker prepares an **offer to lease** which is signed by the tenant and submitted to the landlord. The offer-to-lease form contains a provision which states the tenant will pay the brokerage fee in the event the landlord does not agree to pay the broker a fee. [See **first tuesday** Form 556 §15]

The offer to lease is not accepted by the landlord. The landlord does not make a counteroffer.

However, without contacting the broker, the landlord and the tenant engage directly in lease negotiations. Later, they enter into a lease which does not provide for a fee to be paid to the broker.

In the lease, the landlord agrees to be responsible for payment of any brokerage fee due as a result of the lease, called a *hold harmless provision.*

On discovering the tenant's occupancy, the broker seeks payment of his fee from the tenant.

The broker claims the tenant breached the brokerage fee provision in his offer to lease by failing to provide for payment of the fee he earned when the tenant leased the property.

The tenant claims he is not liable for payment of the brokerage fee since the landlord agreed to pay the brokerage fee under the hold harmless provision in the lease.

Can the broker recover his fee from the tenant?

Yes! The offer to lease **signed by the tenant** contains a fee provision which states the broker will receive compensation for his efforts should the tenant enter into a lease of the premises.

Thus, the broker is able to enforce collection of a fee from the tenant since the tenant signed an agreement regarding the leasing of the property which contained a provision calling for the broker to be paid a fee. [**Rader Company** v. **Stone** (1986) 178 CA3d 10]

Conversely, a broker who does not have an agreement signed by the tenant which contains provisions for the payment of a fee should the tenant lease property — such as a tenant listing agreement or offer to lease — will be unable to enforce collection of a fee from the tenant. An oral agreement to pay a brokerage fee is unenforceable against the client making the oral promise. [**Phillippe** v. **Shapell Industries, Inc.** (1987) 43 C3d 1247]

Written fee agreements

A leasing agent has the opportunity to enter into a written fee agreement on at least four occasions during leasing negotiations:

- when soliciting a **nonresidential landlord** for authorization to represent the landlord as his leasing agent to locate users and negotiate a lease acceptable to the landlord, called an *exclusive authorization to lease* [See **first tuesday** Form 110; see Chapter 9];

- when soliciting (or being solicited by) a **nonresidential tenant** for authorization to act as his leasing agent to locate suitable space and negotiate a lease acceptable to the tenant, called an *exclusive authorization to locate space* [See Form 111 accompanying this chapter];

- when preparing a **tenant's offer to lease** by including a brokerage fee provision in the offer; and

- when preparing **the lease** by including a fee provision in the lease.

These opportunities are listed in order of the leasing agent's declining ability to negotiate.

The employment agreement

A broker approached by a tenant to locate space should ask for and enter into an **employment agreement** with the tenant before analyzing the tenant's needs, locating space or exposing the tenant to available space not listed with the broker. [See Form 111]

The exclusive authorization assures the broker he will be paid for time and effort spent locating and analyzing available space should the tenant ultimately lease space of the type and in the area noted in the authorization. Through the exclusive authorization, the tenant commits himself to work with the broker to accomplish the objective of the employment — renting space.

The exclusive authorization form is similar in structure and purpose to a buyer's listing agreement and includes:

- the term of the retainer period;

- the formulation for calculating the broker's compensation [See **first tuesday** Form 113];

- a description of the type and location of space or property sought by the tenant; and

- identification of the broker as the agent and the tenant as the client.

The description of the property in the exclusive authorization specifies the space requirements, location, rental range, terms and other property conditions sought by the tenant.

Under an exclusive authorization to locate space, a fee is due if the tenant enters into a lease agreement for space similar to the space sought under the exclusive authorization, no matter who — the tenant's broker, another broker or the tenant himself — negotiates the lease, called the *exclusive clause* or *right-to-collect clause*.

Also, under a fee provision containing a *safety clause*, a brokerage fee is due if property located by the broker and disclosed to the tenant during the retainer period is later leased by the tenant due to negotiations commenced during the one-year period after the exclusive authorization expires.

EXCLUSIVE AUTHORIZATION TO LOCATE SPACE

DATE:_____, 20_____, at _____, California

Items left blank or unchecked are not applicable.

1. RETAINER PERIOD:

1.1 Tenant hereby retains and grants to Broker the exclusive right to locate space of the type described below and to negotiate terms and conditions for its rental acceptable to the Tenant, for a retainer period beginning on _____, 20_____ and terminating on _____, 20_____.

2. BROKER'S OBLIGATIONS:

2.1 Broker to use diligence in the performance of this employment.

2.2 ☐ Attached is the Agency Law Addendum.
　　　[**first tuesday** Form 305]

3. TENANT'S DEPOSIT:

3.1 Tenant hands $_____ to Broker for deposit into Broker's trust account for application to Tenant's obligations under this agreement and the following attachments:

　　a. ☐ Advance Fee Addendum [ft Form 106]

　　b. ☐ Advance Cost Addendum [ft Form 107]

4. GENERAL PROVISIONS:

4.1 In any action to enforce this agreement, the prevailing party shall receive attorney fees.

4.2 Tenant authorizes Broker to cooperate with other agents and divide with them any compensation due.

4.3 This agreement will be governed by California law.

5. BROKERAGE FEE:

NOTICE: The amount or rate of real estate commissions is not fixed by law. They are set by each broker individually and may be negotiable between the Tenant and the Broker.

5.1 Tenant agrees to pay Broker ☐ see attached fee schedule [ft Form 113], or ☐ _____ of the rental price of the space located, IF:

　　a. Tenant, or any person acting on Tenant's behalf, leases space located during the retainer period.

　　b. Tenant terminates this employment of the Broker during the retainer period.

　　c. Within one year after termination of this agreement, Tenant or his agent commences negotiations which later result in a transaction contemplated by this agreement with a landlord with whom the Broker, directly or indirectly, negotiated during the period of this agreement. Broker to identify prospective properties by written notice to Tenant within 21 days after termination of this agreement. [ft Form 123]

5.2 Should this agreement terminate without Tenant becoming obligated to pay Broker a fee, Tenant to pay Broker the sum of $_____ per hour of time accounted for by Broker, not to exceed $_____.

5.3 Should the Landlord of space leased to Tenant agree to pay a fee acceptable to the Broker, Tenant's obligation to pay a brokerage fee will be satisfied.

TYPE OF SPACE SOUGHT:

GENERAL DESCRIPTION: _____

SIZE: _____

LOCATION: _____

RENTAL AMOUNT AND TERMS: _____

_____

I agree to render services on the terms stated above.	I agree to employ Broker on the terms stated above.
Date:_____, 20_____	Date:_____, 20_____
Tenant's Broker: _____	Tenant: _____
By: _____	Signature: _____
Address: _____	Address: _____
_____	_____
Phone:_____ Fax: _____	Phone:_____ Fax: _____
E-mail: _____	E-mail: _____

FORM 111　　　　10-00　　　©2003 **first tuesday**, P.O. BOX 20069 RIVERSIDE, CA 92516 (800) 794-0494

Should the tenant decide not to lease space during the exclusive authorization period, the fee provision is structured so the broker can include payment of a fee on an hourly basis for the time spent locating rental property, called a *consultation fee*.

Benefits of exclusive authorization

An exclusive authorization to locate space is mutually beneficial since it commits a nonresidential tenant and broker to work together to accomplish a single objective — the leasing of space.

Typically, an unrepresented tenant is at the mercy of leasing agents employed by owner. Agents employed by owners owe the employing owners an agency duty to use diligence in seeking the most qualified tenant and negotiating lease terms most favorable to the owners in exchange for a fee. Their only agency duty to a non-client tenant is to avoid misleading the tenant when making disclosures.

The exclusive authorization to locate space is an *employment agreement*. It imposes on the broker an agency duty to use diligence in locating suitable space and negotiating the best leasing terms available for the tenant in exchange for a fee — even though the fee is paid by the owner.

The tenant who exclusively authorizes a competent broker to locate space is saving time and money and has retained a professional advisor to conduct the search and handle negotiations to lease property on his behalf.

With readily available information, the tenant's broker will be able to locate qualifying properties for the tenant's review.

Conversely, the tenant who works directly with the owner's broker will initially (and properly) see only the spaces that the broker has been employed to lease and will receive disclosures only when he asks for them.

In a rising market, landlords have superior negotiating power. Thus, it is in the tenant's best interest to employ a broker as his exclusive representative.

Curiously, when the market allows landlords and sellers to control negotiations in real estate transactions, brokers tend to disregard employment by tenants and buyers who then most need representation. It seems to be easier to list property and wait for the inevitable user to contact the listing broker, instead of the reverse activity.

However, in a falling market, when tenants and buyers have more negotiating power than landlords and owners due to the increasing availability of space and properties, brokers are naturally less able to obtain written employment agreements from prospective tenants.

Also, when the market position of landlords weakens, landlords become more flexible in lease negotiations and more apt to employ brokers to help fill vacant space by locating tenants.

Interference with the broker's economic advantage

Consider a nonresidential landlord who **orally promises** a broker he will pay a fee if the broker procures a tenant who leases space.

A prospective tenant for the landlord's space is located by the broker. The tenant is orally advised by the broker that the landlord has agreed to and will pay his fee.

The tenant, after seeing the property and before signing an offer, contacts the landlord directly to negotiate a lease.

Ultimately, the tenant and landlord enter into a lease. The transaction does not contain provisions for a brokerage fee.

Here, the broker cannot enforce collection of his fee from the landlord who orally promised to pay.

Thus, the broker makes a demand on the tenant for the brokerage fee claiming the tenant knew about the landlord's oral promise to pay him and interfered.

The tenant claims the broker is not entitled to recover anything from him since a written fee agreement does not exist to evidence the fee agreement with the landlord.

Is the tenant liable for payment of the broker's fee which was orally agreed to by the landlord?

Yes! The tenant is liable for the brokerage fee the landlord promised to pay since the tenant:

- was actually aware the landlord had promised to pay the broker a fee if the broker located a tenant; and

- excluded the broker from lease negotiations with the intent of avoiding payment of the fee. [**Buckaloo** v. **Johnson** (1975) 14 C3d 815; **Della Penna** v. **Toyota Motor Sales, U.S.A., Inc.** (1995) 11 C4th 376]

When a tenant (successfully) induces a landlord to not pay the brokerage fee agreed to by the landlord, the tenant becomes liable for the fee the landlord promised to pay the broker whether or not the employment agreement between the broker and the landlord is **oral or written**. The broker is not pursuing the person who agreed to pay the fee.

Understanding dual agency

Now consider a broker engaged in locating space for a tenant. The broker does not ask for and is not employed under an exclusive authorization to locate space. The broker extends his search to space which he does not have listed.

The broker locates space acceptable to the tenant, space the owner does not have listed with a broker.

Solely to assure payment of his fee, the broker enters into a so called "one-time" or "one-party" listing agreement with the owner.

The broker does not advise the owner about his agency relationship with the tenant which was established due to his efforts to locate suitable space on behalf of the tenant.

On listing the property, the broker presents the owner with the tenant's signed offer to lease. The owner rejects the offer by making a counteroffer. No disclosure or *confirmation* of the agency relationship with the tenant is made to the owner.

Negotiations conducted by the broker between the tenant and the owner ultimately result in an agreement to lease. The agreement contains a provision stating the brokerage fee will be paid by the owner.

The owner then discovers the broker was also acting as an agent on behalf of the tenant, a dual agency relationship which was not disclosed to the owner when he was induced to enter into the listing. The owner refuses to pay the broker his fee.

The broker makes a demand on the owner for payment of the agreed-to fee claiming he acted as the exclusive agent of the tenant at all times and undertook no agency duty to act on behalf of the owner by entering into the "one-party" listing.

The owner claims the broker is not entitled to his fee since the broker failed to disclose he was representing both parties as a *dual agent*.

Can the broker enforce collection of his fee?

No! The broker is not entitled to a fee. He was an **undisclosed dual agent** in the transaction.

The broker became the **tenant's agent** when he undertook the task of locating and submitting all available space including space not listed with the broker, which might be suitable for the tenant.

On entering into the listing agreement with the owner, the broker also became employed as the owner's agent. The result was a conflicting employment, i.e., control over the actions of both parties, which imposed a duty to disclose the resulting dual agency to both the landlord and tenant. [**L. Byron Culver & Associates** v. **Jaoudi Industrial & Trading Corporation** (1991) 1 CA4th 300]

Residential agency rules and confirmation of representation

A broker acting on behalf of a **residential tenant** is required to provide both the tenant and the landlord with a Rules-of-Agency Disclosure if:

- the lease will be for a term of more than one year; and

- the premises is a one-to-four unit residential property or a mobilehome. [Calif. Civil Code §§2079.13(j); 2079.14]

The rules-of-agency form is to be handed to the tenant prior to the tenant's signing of an offer to lease for more than one year by attaching a Rules-of-Agency Disclosure to an offer to lease residential property. [CC §2079.14(d); see **first tuesday** Form 305]

If the tenant's broker did not prepare the offer to lease himself, the broker should provide the tenant with the rules-of-agency no later than the next business day after the tenant hands him the signed offer to lease. [CC §2079.14(d)]

The landlord is to be provided with the rules-of-agency when the prospective tenant's offer to lease is presented. [CC §2079.14(b)]

If a residential landlord's broker fails to deliver the Rules-of-Agency Disclosure prior to or concurrent with signing the exclusive authorization to lease for more than one year:

- the authorization is unenforceable; and

- the broker is not entitled to a fee. [**Huijers** v. **DeMarrais** (1992) 11 CA4th 676]

Further, when a tenant signs an offer to lease a residence for a period exceeding one year, the broker must provide the tenant with an *Agency Confirmation Statement*. [See **first tuesday** Form 306]

The Agency Confirmation Statement discloses any agency relationships the broker may have with the landlord or the prospective tenant, disclosing whether the agency is exclusive, dual or nonexistent.

To avoid losing the right to collect a fee on the transaction, the broker should have asked the tenant, rather than the owner, to enter into a written employment agreement before undertaking the agency duty of locating space on behalf of the tenant.

Thus, an agency relationship with the owner would not have arisen as the tenant's offer to lease would have been submitted without first obtaining a listing from the owner, even though the owner may agree to pay the fee in an offer to lease or the lease itself.

No written authorization from tenant

Now consider a broker who represents a tenant without the tenant's written authorization. The broker locates space and prepares an offer to lease. The space is listed with another broker.

Here, the broker should first enter into a written or oral *cooperative fee-splitting agreement* with the owner's broker. [See **first tuesday** Form 105]

A cooperative fee-splitting agreement ensures payment of the broker's fee on any lease his tenant may enter into for the space listed with the other broker. **Oral agreements** between brokers to share fees are enforceable.

Brokers all too often undertake the agency duty to locate space on behalf of a nonresidential tenant without first asking for and obtaining a written authorization granting the broker the right to represent the prospective tenant.

However, without a signed written authorization to act as the agent for a tenant, the broker has no initial assurance he will be paid by the owner or the tenant for his services rendered on behalf of the tenant.

Chapter 11

Cost of operating leased space

This chapter analyzes the property operating cost approach used by leasing agents to assist prospective tenants in the selection of available space.

Disclosures by leasing agents

The availability of data and the advice given by brokers to assist prospective tenants, also called *users*, who are making major decisions about leasing property, has increased dramatically in the past decade.

In the 1960s and 1970s, brokers disclosed little more than what could be discovered about a property from a general walk-through by a user.

However, in recent years, consumer expectations when leasing property have risen. Unlike other industries, competition among brokers for clients has not been the primary impetus behind the rising consumer expectations. Consumers have taken hits and the legislature has taken action to pressure brokers into making disclosures. Brokers should know what it is they are marketing.

Today, a greater burden for investigation and advice is placed on those brokers who represent users as opposed to the lesser burden carried by the landlord's broker when dealing with perspective tenants. The user's broker must know his client's needs and capacities in order to locate space best suited to meet his client's needs and objectives. Then, on locating a qualifying property, disclosures and representations about the property must be based on investigations, not conjecture. [**Field** v. **Century 21 Klowden-Forness Realty** (1998) 63 CA4th 18]

As each new expectation placed on brokers by users of real estate surfaces, the issue as to whether brokers have a duty to respond to the consumer's expectations is judicially resolved. Resolution is based on the agency environment surrounding the demands of users for information and the availability to brokers of the information or the source of the information.

Also, as the expectations of real estate consumers are reviewed by the courts, the *level of competency* imposed on brokers and the extent to which landlords and brokers must disclose information (and its source) becomes clearer.

As couriers of information and the "gatekeepers" for almost all real estate transactions, brokers are retained by consumers to sort out and inform them about the relevant conditions surrounding a property, which include (for our purposes) the carrying costs of leasing and operating a space.

As for landlords and their brokers, their role in marketing a space has been reduced to avoiding misleading disclosures, which does not include enlightening users of facts that would assist them in making an intelligent decision on the selection among the available properties for the premises best suited for them.

It is the role and burden of the tenant's leasing agent to ferret out the facts about the properties (or advise the tenant on what they should do to get the facts), and make recommendations to assist the tenant to meet his goals.

The factual information available to brokers about properties and the assistance brokers can offer to users who are leasing space fall into three general categories for analysis:

1. The property's **physical aspects** (square footage, shipping facilities, utilities, tenant improvements, fixtures, condition of the structure, soil, geologic hazards, toxic or noise pollution, etc.);

2. The conditions affecting the **use and enjoyment** of the property, i.e., facts available from title companies (CC&Rs, trust deeds and vesting), planning, redevelopment and taxing agencies (permitted uses and business tax rates), natural hazards and the area surrounding the location; and

3. The **cost of operating** the leased premises when put to the expected use.

Additionally, the business tax local agencies charge a user for locating and conducting business in their jurisdiction weighs on the selection of available space. Business taxes vary greatly from city to city.

Operating costs disclosed

The listing of a property's operating costs is a part of the property's signature. Operating costs distinguish the property from other available properties. A property's operating costs are gathered and set forth on the *occupant's cost sheet* which is handed to perspective tenants to induce them to rent the space. [See Form 562 accompanying this chapter]

Property related expenditures which will be incurred by a user during the leasing period, other than the payment of rent and any debt secured by the leasehold, fall into two categories:

- recurring operating expenses; and

- nonrecurring deposits or charges.

Users, their leasing agents and property managers **compare the costs** a user will incur to occupy and operate in a particular space against the costs to operate in other available space, called a *comparative cost analysis*.

The user's cost analysis is made more relevant for negotiations during periods of economic slowdown due to the accompanying increase in vacancy levels from either overbuilding or a decline in the population of users within the age groups or businesses traditionally occupying this type of space.

When users search for space without the pressure of high occupancy levels (scarcity) experienced during periods of peak economic activity, they are more likely to compare properties based on operating costs or user improvements the owner will provide, rather than rent alone.

Thus, owners renting for less than the competition should be subjected to requests for information and history on the operating costs the user will incur in addition to the rent. The below-market rent may be suspect due to the excessive operating costs of the premises and local taxes.

The nondisclosure of a property's operating costs a user will incur under a net or modified *gross rent* lease leaves the perspective user to speculate on what will be the amount of monthly operating costs (in addition to rent) the property will generate.

The nondisclosure of operating costs is more likely to occur during tight rental markets when owners and their brokers are less responsive to (or downright uncooperative) in the release of information to users and their leasing agents.

At the very least, the user's leasing agent has the obligation to **bring the availability** of the data to the user's attention. Then, if the user wants the information, it can be obtained to clear contingencies in the process of negotiations. At his best, the user's leasing agent not only advises, but investigates and gets the data to his client with an analysis and recommendation.

OCCUPANT'S OPERATING EXPENSE SHEET

DATE:_____, 20_____, at _____, California

Occupant (Buyer or Tenant):_____

Property type: _____

Address:_____

Items left blank or unchecked are not applicable.

FACTS:

This cost sheet demonstrates the cash expenditures the Occupant should initially experience while owning or leasing the property.

These amounts are:

☐ figures currently experienced in operating the property.

☐ estimates and not amounts confirmed by the owner or former occupant.

OPERATING EXPENSES:

Electricity . . . . $_____

Gas . . . . $_____

Water . . . . $_____

CATV/Phone . . . . $_____

Rubbish . . . . $_____

Sewage . . . . $_____

Insurance . . . . $_____

Taxes . . . . $_____

General obligation bonds . . . . . . $_____

Lawn/Gardening . . . . $_____

Pool/Spa . . . . $_____

Janitorial/Maids . . . . $_____

Maintenance and repair . . . . $_____

Other . . . . $_____

    Total Operating Expenses . . . . $_____

    Monthly Loan or Lease Payments $_____

    TOTAL Monthly Expenditures . $_____

DEPOSITS:

Rental Security Deposit . . . . . $_____

Water Deposit . . . . $_____

Sewage and Rubbish Deposit $_____

Gas Service Deposit . . . . $_____

Phone Service Deposit . . . . . . $_____

Other:_____ . $_____

    TOTAL Deposits . . . . $_____

I have read and approve this information:

Date:_____, 20_____

Seller/
Landlord: _____

Seller/
Landlord: _____

Date Prepared: _____, 20_____

Broker:_____

Agent: _____

Address: _____

_____

Phone: _____

Fax: _____

I have read and received a copy of this estimate.

Date: _____, 20_____

Occupant's Signature: _____

Occupant's Signature: _____

FORM 562   10-00   ©2003 **first tuesday**, P.O. BOX 20069 RIVERSIDE, CA 92516 (800) 794-0494

The owner either knows, or can easily obtain from his property manager, the actual costs of operating his property for the use intended.

The property's operating data is readily available to the owner. If the owner or the owner's broker refuses to supply the data to the user, the user's broker can research the history of expenses the prior users have experienced.

Armed with knowledge of the costs, the user's broker can comfortably make an informed disclosure to his client.

Leases on nonresidential properties often include charges for common area maintenance (CAMs) — expenses incurred by the owner and paid by the user as rent, in addition to the base rent, adjustments and percentages. The prospective user and his agent should insist on an operating cost sheet estimating the monthly charge for the user's share of the CAMs he would incur in this space.

Since information about the amount of CAMs paid by the prior occupant of the space might affect the user's negotiations and rental commitment, it is a *material fact* essential to the user's decision-making process.

A broker has a duty to disclose all conditions or aspects of a property which might affect a user's decision to lease, called *material facts*. [**Ziswasser** v. **Cole & Cowan, Inc.** (1985) 164 CA3d 417]

Accurate estimates by brokers

Disclosing the costs the user will incur while occupying and operating the property imposes on the user's broker a duty to disclose the actual costs which have been incurred in the space. If not available and estimates are provided, they must state they are estimates and must be reasonably accurate.

Also, the user's broker must **identify the source** of the data provided to the user and the reliability of the source as known to the broker.

If a need exists for further confirmation of the data due to questionable reliability, the offer to lease, oral or written, needs to include a further-approval contingency so the user can check out and confirm his expectations or cancel the offer. [**Ford** v. **Cournale** (1973) 36 CA3d 172]

The proper brokerage activity for disclosing the operating costs and deposits incurred to occupy and operate leased space include:

- the preparation of an operating cost sheet by the owner (or property manager) of each available space, with or without the assistance of a leasing agent, which is **signed** by the owner;

- a comparison by the user and the user's broker of the costs to operate in this space against the cost of operating in other space; and

- a review of the economic (cost) impact of operating expenses when added to the rent to be paid for this space against rent and operating costs incurred in other qualifying space.

With documentation and a comparative analysis of operating costs and rent completed, the user and the user's broker can intelligently negotiate the best lease arrangements for the user.

Occasionally, a property owner may want to be "close-chested" about the operation data due to various different arrangements with numerous tenants. Thus, the owner (or his broker) will insist a **confidentiality agreement** be entered into with the prospective tenant before any data is released.

Should the user be unrepresented, he loses the benefit of a comparative analysis and the experienced advice available from a broker who could have been retained to represent his best interests.

Chapter 12

Offers to lease

This chapter discusses the importance of written negotiations before entering into a nonresidential lease.

Negotiating the nonresidential lease

Once a leasing agent locates a suitable premises for a prospective tenant, the agent must bring the landlord and tenant together through negotiations to develop the terms of a lease acceptable to all.

The role the broker plays in negotiations and his duties as a leasing agent depends on who he represents in the transaction: the landlord, the tenant or both.

When representing the tenant, the broker must initially determine his client's need for space and the rental amount he is willing and able to pay for the space. This information is gathered on the tenant lease worksheet prepared when first interviewing the tenant. [See **first tuesday** Form 555]

When representing the landlord, the broker must know the rental terms and leasing conditions sought by the landlord to rent the space. Usually, this data is set out in a property management agreement. [See **first tuesday** Forms 110 and 590]

The offer to lease

Whether a broker represents the tenant or the landlord, the broker initiates negotiations most efficiently by preparing an **offer to lease** form for the tenant to review and consider for signing. [See Form 556 accompanying this chapter]

The tenant enters into the offer to lease much like a buyer reviews and signs an offer to purchase real estate.

For example, a *tenant* under an offer to lease, which is accepted by a landlord, acquires a right to possession which the landlord agrees to *convey* to the tenant for a set period of time under the lease.

Likewise, a *buyer* of a real estate interest under a purchase agreement acquires either an existing leasehold (held by an existing tenant) or fee title (from the owner) which will be conveyed to the buyer by an assignment or deed.

Thus, like a sales transaction, the arranging of a lease transaction has two phases:

the offer and acceptance (agreement to lease); and

the drafting and signing of the lease agreement and delivery of funds and possession (the conveyance of the leasehold interest on closing).

In the leasing situation, the broker, the landlord or the landlord's attorney prepares and handles all the closing instruments, such as the lease and transfer of funds.

Leasing is usually accomplished without the benefit of a formal escrow. If documents are to be recorded, such as occurs in a long-term leasing transaction, a title officer and title insurance company become involved with a title search and issuance of a policy of leasehold title insurance.

Contents of the offer

An offer to lease sets forth the crucial elements of the leasing arrangements. [See Form 556]

OFFER TO LEASE
And Receipt of Deposit

DATE:_____, 20_____, at _____, California

Items left blank or unchecked are not applicable.

Received from _____, and

_____, the sum of $_____

evidenced by ☐ check, or ☐ _____,

payable to _____,

to be held undeposited until acceptance of this offer as a deposit toward the leasing of the following premises:

_____

The following checked addendums are part of this offer to lease:

☐ Plat of the premises   ☐ Tenant's credit application [ft Form 302]   ☐ Tenant's profit and loss statements

☐ Proposed lease form   ☐ Option to renew/extend [ft Form 565]   ☐ Option to buy [ft Form 161]

☐ _____

TERMS:

1. The commencement date of the lease to be _____, 20_____, and the expiration date to be _____, 20_____.

2. The monthly rent to be payable in advance as follows:

    2.1 ☐ Monthly rent to be fixed at $_____ until expiration of the lease. Holdover rent to be $_____ daily. On each anniversary of commencement, base rent to be increased an additional _____%.

    2.2 ☐ Monthly rent to be adjusted from a monthly base rent for the first year of $_____. On each anniversary date of the lease, the monthly base rent shall be adjusted upward only based on the annual increase in the Consumer Price Index for All Urban Consumers (CPI-U) for:

    ☐ Los Angeles-Anaheim-Riverside   ☐ San Diego   ☐ Other index _____

    ☐ San Francisco-San Jose-Oakland   ☐ National   ☐ Capped at a _____% annual increase

    2.3 ☐ Monthly rent to be graduated on each anniversary under the following schedule:

    a. Base year monthly rent of $_____, and on each anniversary month an upward adjustment to the monthly rent of _____% over the prior year's monthly rent; or

    b. Base Year: $_____   Second Year:$_____   Third Year: $_____

    Fourth Year:$_____   Fifth Year: $_____   Sixth Year: $_____

    2.4 ☐ Rent to be the greater of _____% of monthly gross sales/receipts or the total of other rents, taxes, insurance and common area maintenance (CAMs) checked in this offer.

    2.5 ☐ Monthly base rent to be adjusted upward to current market rental value every _____ years.

3. The utility expenses for the space leased to be paid as follows:

    Tenant to pay: _____

    Landlord to pay:_____

4. ☐ Common Area Maintenance (CAMs) costs for the maintaining and operating of the common areas are to be paid by Tenant based on his proportionate share of the total space leased on the premises, or _____% of the CAMs. The CAMs charge shall be assessed: ☐ monthly, or ☐ quarterly, and payable within 10 days.

5. Real estate taxes and assessments on the real estate shall be paid by ☐ Landlord, or ☐ Tenant.

    5.1 Any taxes and assessments paid by Tenant to be capped at a _____% annual increase.

6. A security deposit of $_____ to secure the performance under Tenant's lease to be paid on signing of the lease.

7. ☐ Tenant to have the option to renew or extend the lease as set forth in the attached option to renew/extend. [ft Form 565]

— — — — — — — — — — — — — — *PAGE ONE OF TWO — FORM 556* — — — — — — — — — — — — — — —

8. Tenant may assign, sublet or encumber the leasehold interest subject to Landlord's consent:
    _____

9. Landlord to make the following improvements prior to the time Tenant is to take possession:
    _____
    _____

10. Tenant's intended use of the premises is: _____
    _____

11. Tenant may alter the premises as follows, subject to Landlord's approval of plans: _____
    _____
    _____

12. Tenant may exercise the right to lease additional space from Landlord as follows (note the premises, rent,
    terms, and period): _____
    _____

13. Tenant to maintain insurance on the premises to cover any casualty loss in the amount of $_____

14. Landlord and Tenant to sign a lease to be prepared by ☐ Tenant, or ☐ Landlord on a form entitled
    _____ published by _____

15. Parties to pay Broker(s) a fee of ☐ see attached fee schedule [ft Form 113], or
    ☐ _____, as follows:
    Landlord to pay the brokerage fee on change of possession. The party wrongfully preventing a change of
    possession to pay the brokerage fee. Landlord's Broker and Tenant's Broker, respectively, to share the
    brokerage fee _____:_____.

16. This offer shall be deemed revoked unless accepted in writing and personally delivered to Tenant or
    Tenant's Broker on or before _____, 20_____.

17. _____
    _____
    _____
    _____

Tenant's/	Landlord's/
Selling Broker: _____	Listing Broker: _____
By: _____	By: _____
Is the agent of: ☐ Buyer exclusively, or	Is the agent of: ☐ Seller exclusively, or
☐ both Seller and Buyer.	☐ both Seller and Buyer.
I agree to the terms stated above.	**I agree to the terms stated above.**
Date:_____, 20_____	Date:_____, 20_____
Landlord: _____	Tenant: _____
Agent: _____	Tenant: _____
Signature: _____	Signature: _____
Address: _____	Signature: _____
_____	Address: _____
Phone: _____	_____
Fax: _____	Phone: _____
E-mail: _____	Fax: _____
	E-mail: _____

FORM 556   10-01   ©2003 first tuesday, P.O. Box 20069, RIVERSIDE, CA 92516 (800) 794-0494

An offer to lease, like an offer to purchase, contains four sections:

1. Identification of the parties and premises;

2. Rental payment schedules and period of occupancy;

3. Property maintenance and terms of possession (use); and

4. Signatures of the parties.

The identification section names the contracting parties, describes the premises and acknowledges receipt of any good faith deposit. A floor plan or common description of the premises is usually attached by a reference in the identification section.

The tenant should be asked to include a good faith deposit as would be asked of a fee simple buyer under a purchase agreement.

The section of the offer setting forth rental payment schedules is a checklist of various rental arrangements from which the tenant selects to pay rent, and includes:

- the duration/term of the initial leasing period;

- the monthly base rent for the first year;

- any rental adjustments during the leasing period for inflation and appreciation;

- responsibility for payment of utilities;

- any common area maintenance charges (CAMs);

- any assessment for insurance or taxes;

- the amount of the security deposit; and

- options to renew or extend the leasing period or to buy the property.

It is good brokerage practice to reference and attach a copy of the proposed lease form to the offer as it includes boilerplate provisions covering:

- the responsibility for property operating and maintenance expenses;

- the right to sell, sublet or encumber the lease; and

- default remedies.

In the offer's miscellaneous leasing terms section, the tenant and landlord further agree to other terms peculiar to leasing, including:

- the tenant's proposed use;

- the lease form to be used;

- responsibility for tenant improvements;

- any alterations by the tenant;

- brokerage fees; and

- the time and manner for accepting the offer to lease.

Some landlords initially present prospective tenants with fully prepared but unsigned leases, a condition which generally works to the landlord's advantage. The parties then orally negotiate the final terms. The technique is loose and works for or against the tenant or the landlord, depending on availability of space.

To better clarify negotiations, the broker should write up the offer to lease (and counteroffers) and, within the offer-counteroffer context, develop acceptable terms based on signed offers and counteroffers. Expectations are properly reached and negotiations are memorialized in writing to avoid later conjecture (and litigation).

The final section of the offer to lease is the signature section where the landlord and tenant sign and agree to the terms stated in the offer.

Offers to lease vs. proposals

By signing an offer to lease prepared by a broker, a prospective tenant initiates the negotiations. Acceptance by the landlord concludes the search for space.

The key difference between an offer and a **proposal to lease** is the offer can be *accepted* and the proposal is a mere *solicitation* and inquiry into the landlord's intentions.

Solicitations, such as proposals sent by leasing agents, require the landlord, should he respond, to "negotiate with himself" regarding his previously announced terms and conditions. No offer exists for the landlord to accept or counter. If the landlord responds, he should make an offer in writing which forces the leasing agent to submit the offer to lease to the tenant for consideration.

A proposal merely evidences a tenant's or landlord's intent to negotiate. The tenant and the landlord are not yet ready to make a binding commitment, otherwise an offer would be substituted by one or the other.

Brokers using their knowledge can and should do better than proposals, unless the tenant is not yet ready to be bound due to concurrent negotiations with other landlords.

Counteroffers focus negotiations

To form a binding agreement to lease, an offer or counteroffer must be accepted in its entirety and without qualification or alteration. [Calif. Civil Code §1582]

When the landlord or tenant conditions his acceptance of an offer to lease by changing or adding specific terms, acceptance does not occur and a binding agreement to lease is not formed. [CC §1585]

The added conditions or changes establishes a *counteroffer*. To avoid alteration of a signed document (the offer or lease), a counteroffer form referencing the signed document should be prepared, signed and submitted for the other party to then accept, reject or further counter.

Thus, if the offer to lease is not acceptable to the landlord (or the tenant), he can counter by using a counteroffer form to state terms which are acceptable. [See **first tuesday** Form 180]

As the negotiations in writing continue, an acceptable set of terms develops by the use of counteroffer forms. Written counteroffers keep the parties focused on the remaining unnegotiated details and demonstrate an intent to be seriously considered by all — as is indicated by a deposit with the offer.

After acceptance of the offer or counteroffer to lease, only the preparation of the lease (and other closing documents), transfer of possession, and payment of the security deposits and initial rent remain to close the lease transaction — tenant improvements notwithstanding.

Interference with negotiations

Consider a landlord who is currently negotiating with the CEO of a company to enter into a lease agreement. A competing landlord (or his broker) actively solicits officers and board members of the company to lease space from him instead.

Ultimately, the company enters into a lease agreement with the competing landlord.

The landlord who lost out seeks to recover lost rent from the competing landlord, claiming the competing landlord *intentionally interfered* with his prospective economic advantage. The landlord claims the competing landlord induced the officers and board members to consider and accept the competing landlord's proposal while he was **completing negotiations** with the company's CEO.

However, a competing landlord has a right to solicit a tenant who he knows is negotiating with another@ andlord as a *privilege of competition*. The competing landlord did not engage in unlawful interference since the tenant had not yet finalized negotiations by entering into an enforceable agreement to rent with another landlord.

A landlord who has not yet entered into a binding offer to lease or lease agreement cannot establish that he holds an economic advantage (a binding contract) with which a competing landlord can interfere. [**San Francisco Design Center Associates** v. **Portman Companies** (1995) 41 CA4th 29]

SECTION C

Deposits and Rents

Chapter 13

Security deposits and pre-termination inspections

This chapter discusses the different rules for residential and nonresidential landlords who receive and refund security deposits, and the residential tenant's right to a pre-termination inspection.

Requirements for residential and nonresidential landlords

An investor, primarily in nonresidential income-producing properties, is acquiring his first residential rental property.

The residential rental property is a large apartment complex consisting of furnished and unfurnished units.

The investor retains a property manager with experience in managing apartment buildings of comparable size and quality in the local rental market.

Initially, the property manager inspects the units and, with the investor, reviews the impact of the local residential rental market on rents and security deposits.

As a result, rents and security deposits to be charged are established based on the size of the units, the maximum number of occupants for the various sizes of units, amenities each unit offers, the unit's location within the complex and whether or not the units are furnished.

The investor is aware he must rent to families with children whose credit and background qualify them as tenants. However, the investor is concerned about the excessive wear and tear children might cause to the units. Excessive wear and tear brought on by a tenant and remaining unrepaired when the tenant vacates is a breach of the lease, called a *default*. As a result, the landlord will incur additional cleanup expenses.

If a unit will be occupied by a family with children whose background check indicates they will likely place an excessive burden on the unit, the broker can recommend the rent be adjusted upward to cover the additional wear and tear brought about by the increased number of occupants.

However, the investor would like to impose a larger security deposit equal to one-half month's rent for each child who will occupy a unit since the increased deposit would either discourage large families from renting or provide funds to restore the unit for re-renting when they vacate.

The property manager informs the investor security deposits charged to tenants of residential units are controlled by statute calling for *nondiscriminatory, equal treatment,* unlike security deposits negotiated by landlords and tenants of nonresidential property.

Thus, the investor is warned he cannot require higher security deposits for tenants with children than for tenants without children. Any increase in a security deposit for families is a prohibited discriminatory practice. [Calif. Government Code §12955(a); 24 Code of Federal Regulations §100.65; see Chapter 38]

Also, other limitations are placed on the upfront charges for rent and security deposits. In addition to the collection of one month's advance rent, the maximum amount which a residential tenant may be required to pay as a security deposit to cover defaults during the period of occupancy is limited to:

- two months' rent for unfurnished units; and

- three months' rent for furnished units. [Calif. Civil Code §1950.5(c)]

Thus, if supported by the local rental market, the investor may require of all tenants, an advance payment of the first month's rent and either:

- the last month's rent and a security deposit equal to one month's rent; or

- a security deposit equal to two months' rent.

The property manager informs the investor a security deposit equal to one month's rent, together with one month's advance rent, is all the market will currently bear for his units. If he demands more, the units will not readily rent.

Security against nonperformance

Both nonresidential and residential landlords traditionally require tenants to deposit money in addition to rent. [See **first tuesday** Forms 550 §1.1 and 552 §1.2]

The additional deposit is **security** for any default in the tenant's future performance of obligations the tenant agrees to in the lease or rental agreement. Tenant obligations include paying rent, reimbursing the landlord for expenses incurred due to the tenant's conduct, maintaining the premises during the occupancy and leaving the premises in the same level of cleanliness it was in when leased to the tenant, less ordinary wear and tear.

However, for residential rentals, all money paid to the landlord **in addition** to the first month's rent, screening fee and waterbed administrative fee is considered a security deposit. Security deposits include any funds received for the purpose of covering defaults by the tenant under the lease/rental agreement, no matter the name given to the funds by the landlord, such as a nonrefundable deposit or last month's rent. [CC §§1940.50; 1950.5(b), (c); 1950.6]

Thus, any funds legally recharacterized as a security deposit are refundable when the tenant vacates, less deductions for unpaid rent or

costs incurred by the landlord, such as for the repair of damages caused by the tenant or for the cleaning of the premises. [CC §§1950.5(b); 1950.7(c)]

The amount a nonresidential landlord will ask for as a security deposit should be based on the risk of loss the tenant's business success poses for the landlord.

For nonresidential tenancies, a small services firm may pay an amount equal to one month's rent as a security deposit, while a photography studio which uses chemicals in its film processing may be asked to pay an amount equal to two month's rent.

Note — A photography studio tenant or other users of chemicals may also be required to provide insurance coverage.

In a market downturn, aggressively competitive landlords are less likely to require a security deposit in exchange for maintaining current rental income (occupancy), and thus expose themselves to an increased risk of loss should the tenant default.

Like all other terms in a nonresidential lease, the security deposit is negotiated between the nonresidential landlord and the tenant prior to entering into the lease.

Unlike nonresidential tenants, residential tenants, as a matter of public policy, are perceived as lacking bargaining power when they negotiate a lease or rental agreement. Thus, limits are imposed by law on the amount of security deposit a residential landlord may require.

Last month's rent

When unfurnished residential vacancies are low, landlords often require the maximum permissible amount of advance payment, which includes the first and last month's rent, plus a security deposit equal to one month's rent to eliminate the less solvent tenants.

Note — Legally, this is recharacterized as one month's advance rent and a security deposit equal to two month's rent. [CC §1950.5(c)]

Nonresidential landlords also generally require an advance payment of both the first and last month's rent on a lease.

However, the local rental **market conditions** may prevent a residential or nonresidential landlord from requiring:

- a security deposit in addition to first and last months' rent; or

- a security deposit equal to two months' rent and advance payment of one month's rent.

Now consider a tenant who pays the first month's rent and a security deposit equal to one month's rent on entering into his lease.

When the last month's rent becomes due the tenant does not pay, knowing the defaulted payment of rent will be deducted from his security deposit, a permissible use of the security deposit by the landlord on the tenant's default in the last month's rent payment.

On expiration of the lease, the tenant vacates the unit. Due to excess wear and tear on the unit by the tenant, repairs and replacements are required before the unit can be re-rented.

However, after deducting the unpaid last month's rent from the security deposit, no security deposit remains to reimburse the landlord for the cost of the repairs.

Since the landlord did not require an advance payment of both the first and the last month's rent, as well as a security deposit (or a security deposit equal to two months' rent), his recovery of the repair costs is limited to a demand on the tenant, and if unpaid, a small claims court action to enforce collection.

A similar result may occur if the landlord requires advance payment of the first and last month's rent, but no security deposit.

Note — The landlord could promptly serve a 3-day notice to pay or vacate on expiration of the grace period before delinquency, and on expiration of the 3-day notice without payment or vacating, file an unlawful detainer (UD) action.

Residential deposits

A residential landlord must require the same security deposit for all units, such as an amount equal to one month's rent, or base the amount of security deposit on each tenant's creditworthiness.

Note — If a landlord sets the security deposit amount based on a tenant's creditworthiness — the greater or lesser risk of a loss due to a prospective tenant's failure to perform on lease provisions — he must establish clear and precise standards for his different levels of creditworthiness and apply each level's credit standards equally to all prospective tenants who fall into that level of credit. [24 CFR §100.60(b)(4)]

A residential landlord has limited authority to require an additional **pet deposit** if the tenant is permitted to keep one or more pets in the unit.

However, the total security deposit received from a tenant **with a pet** may not exceed the maximum security deposit allowed, such as an amount equal to two months' rent for an unfurnished unit or three months' rent for a furnished unit. [See Chapter 37]

However, these security deposit limitations may be exceeded when a tenant maintains a **waterbed on the premises**. The residential landlord may then require:

- an amount equal to one-half month's rent, in addition to the maximum security deposit; and

- a reasonable fee to cover administrative costs of processing the waterbed arrangements. [CC §1940.5(g); see Chapter 37]

Deferring the first month's rent

Consider a landlord who locates a creditworthy tenant for his residential property.

In addition to the advance payment of the first month's rent, the landlord requires a security deposit equal to one month's rent.

The tenant asks the landlord if he can pay half the security deposit in advance and the other half with the second month's rent. The tenant is unable to pay the security deposit in full until he receives his security deposit refund from his current landlord.

The landlord wants this applicant as a tenant and is willing to extend the credit.

To be cautious, the landlord structures receipt of the funds as payment of the entire security deposit and half of the first month's rent. The tenant will pay the remaining half of the first month's rent with payment of the second month's rent.

Thus, should the tenant fail to pay either the second month's rent or the remainder of the first month's rent when due:

- the landlord may serve a 3-day notice to pay rent or quit; and

- if not paid, deduct the amount from the security deposit as a last resort.

Conversely, consider a landlord who allows a tenant to allocate his initial payment on the lease to one full month's rent, with payment of the balance due on the security deposit spread over two or more months.

Here, should the tenant fail to pay the second installment of the security deposit, the default will not be a *material breach* of the lease or rental agreement. A material breach is necessary before a UD action based on service of a 3-day *notice to perform* can proceed to an eviction. A security deposit is not rent, although it is an amount "owed" to the landlord.

A tenant's breach must be material and go to the root of the lease or rental agreement, such as a failure to pay rent, before the landlord can justify service of a 3-day notice. **A minor breach** of the lease will not justify serving a 3-day notice to forfeit the tenant's right to possession. **[Baypoint Mortgage** v. **Crest Premium Real Estate Investments Retirement Trust** (1985) 168 CA3d 818]

Also, if the term of a residential lease is six months or more, the landlord and tenant may agree to the tenant's advance payment of six months' rent or more, instead of one month's rent. [CC §1950.5(c)]

Thus, advance payment of only two to five month's rent is prohibited.

Should the landlord and tenant agree to an advance payment of six months' rent on the lease of an unfurnished unit, the landlord may also require the maximum security deposit of two months' rent.

Any money handed to a residential landlord by a tenant on entering into a lease or rental agreement must be characterized as one of the following:

- a tenant screening fee for processing an application;

- a waterbed administrative fee;

- rent; or

- a security deposit. [CC §§1940.5(g); 1950.5(b); 1950.6(b)]

Holding security deposits

Funds held by residential and nonresidential landlords, which are intended to cover defaults in the tenant's performance of his obligations on the lease or rental agreement, are called security deposits. The funds belong to the tenant who deposited them. [CC §§1950.5(d); 1950.7(b)]

However, a landlord may **commingle** security deposits with other funds in a general business account. No trust relationship is established when a landlord holds a tenant's security deposit. [**Korens** v. **R.W. Zukin Corporation** (1989) 212 CA3d 1054]

Since no trust relationship exists, the landlord's receipt of a security deposit imposes no obligation on him to pay **interest** on the security deposit for the period held.

However, some local rent control ordinances require residential landlords to pay interest to tenants on their security deposits (and the legislature has been actively thinking about extending this to all residential landlords).

For example, the city of San Francisco requires residential landlords to pay simple interest to tenants on security deposits held by the landlord for one year or more as long as the rent is not subsidized by any government agency. [San Francisco Administrative Code §49.2]

Joint pre-termination inspection

A residential landlord must notify a tenant in writing of the tenant's **right to request** a joint inspection of his unit within two weeks prior to the date the tenancy terminates due to:

- expiration of the lease term; or

- a notice to vacate initiated by either the landlord or the tenant. [CC §1950.5(f)(1); see Form 567-1 accompanying this chapter]

The purpose for the joint pre-termination inspection, legally called an *initial inspection*, is to require the landlord to advise the tenant of the repairs or conditions he needs to correct to avoid deductions from the security deposit.

If a residential tenant requests the pre-termination inspection, the landlord or his agent must complete the inspection no earlier than two weeks before the tenant is to vacate the unit.

Ideally, the notice advising the tenant of his right to a joint inspection should be given to the tenant at least 30 days prior to the end of the lease term or, in the case of a rental agreement, immediately upon receiving or serving a notice to vacate. A period of 30 days will allow the tenant time to request the inspection and provide two full weeks in which to participate in the inspection and remedy any repairs or cleaning the landlord observes during the inspection which might constitute a deduction from the security deposit.

NOTICE OF RIGHT TO REQUEST
A JOINT PRE-TERMINATION INSPECTION

DATE:_____, 20_____, at _____, California

To Tenant: _____

Items left blank or unchecked are not applicable.

FACTS:

You are a Tenant under a rental agreement or lease

Dated _____, at

_____, California,

entered into by _____, Tenant,

and _____, Landlord,

regarding real estate referred to as: _____

_____,

which tenancy terminates or expires _____, 20_____.

> **NOTICE:**
> Residential tenants may request a joint pre-termination inspection of the premises they occupy and at the inspection receive a statement of deficiencies itemizing the repairs and cleaning necessary to be remedied or eliminated by the tenant to avoid a deduction of their costs from the security deposit. [Civil Code §1950.5(f)]

NOTICE:

1. You are hereby advised of your right to request and be present at a pre-termination inspection of the premises you occupy, and at the time of the inspection, be given the Landlord's itemized statement of deficiencies specifying repairs and cleaning which will be the basis for deduction from your security deposit.

    1.1 The purpose for the inspection and the statement of deficiencies is to give you the opportunity to remedy or eliminate the specified deficiencies before vacating to avoid a deduction of their cost from your security deposit.

    1.2 The inspection, if requested by you, may be scheduled no earlier than two weeks before the termination/expiration of your tenancy, and is separate from the Landlord's final inspection after you vacate.

    1.3 If you do not request a pre-termination inspection, no inspection will be made prior to the final inspection after you vacate.

2. You may request an inspection at any time after you are given this notice by preparing the form attached to this notice and giving it to the Landlord or his agent.

    2.1 On the Landlord's receipt of your request, the Landlord will attempt to set a mutually agreeable date and time for the inspection.

    2.2 On the Landlord's receipt of your request, you will be given a written 48-hour notice of entry advising you of the date and time scheduled by the Landlord for the inspection.

3. On completion of the scheduled inspection, whether or not you are present, the Landlord or his agent will hand you or leave on the premises a copy of an itemized statement of deficiencies specifying repairs and cleaning which will be the basis for deductions from your security deposit, unless you remedy or eliminate them prior to your vacating on or before your tenancy terminates or expires.

    3.1 Once you have requested an inspection you may withdraw the request at any time prior to the inspection.

Date:_____, 20_____

Landlord/Agent: _____

Signature:_____

Address:_____

_____

Phone: _____

Fax: _____

E-mail: _____

REQUEST FOR JOINT PRE-TERMINATION INSPECTION

DATE:_____, 20_____, at _____, California

To Landlord: _____

I, the Tenant, hereby request an inspection at the earliest possible date and time during the two-week period prior to the termination or expiration of my tenancy.

The dates I prefer for an inspection during normal business hours include:_____

I understand you will give me a 48-hour notice prior to the inspection.

Address of the premises: _____

Tenant's name: _____

Signature: _____

Daytime telephone number:_____

FORM 567-1   02-02   ©2003 **first tuesday**, P.O. BOX 20069 RIVERSIDE, CA 92516 (800) 794-0494

On the landlord's receipt of the tenant's request for an inspection, the landlord must serve a 48-hour written notice of entry on the tenant stating the date and time of the pre-termination inspection. If the date and time cannot be mutually agreed to, they are to be set by the landlord. [CC §1950.5(f)(1); see **first tuesday** Form 567-2]

However, if an acceptable time for the inspection is within 48 hours, a written waiver of the notice of entry must be signed by both the landlord and tenant. [CC §1950.5(f)(1); see **first tuesday** Form 567-2]

If the waiver is signed, the landlord may proceed with the inspection, whether or not the tenant is present at the premises, unless the tenant has previously withdrawn his request for the inspection.

On completion of the pre-termination inspection, the landlord must give the tenant an itemized statement of deficiencies specifying any repairs or cleaning necessary to be undertaken by the tenant to avoid deductions from his security deposit. The itemized statement of deficiencies must contain the contents of subdivisions (b) and (d) of Civil Code §1950.5. [See Form 567-3 accompanying this chapter]

The pre-termination inspection statement must be served by either:

- giving the statement directly to the tenant if he is present at the inspection; or

- leaving the statement inside the premises if the tenant is not present. [CC §1950.5(f)(2)]

The purpose for the inspection and statement of deficiencies in repairs or cleanliness is to give the tenant time in which to attempt to remedy the identified repairs before vacating the premises.

Alternatively, the tenant may choose not to request a pre-termination inspection, in which case the landlord or his agent will not have to conduct an inspection or prepare and give the tenant a statement of deficiencies.

However, the notice of the tenant's right to request a pre-termination inspection **must** be given to the tenant.

If the tenant chooses to withdraw after requesting an inspection, the landlord should send a memo to the tenant confirming the tenant's decision to withdraw. [See **first tuesday** Form 525]

Note — The completion of a pre-termination inspection by the landlord does not bar the landlord from deducting from the security deposit for the costs of:

- *any damages noted in the joint pre-termination inspection statement which are not cured;*

- *any damages which occurred between the pre-termination inspection and termination of the tenancy; or*

- *any damages not identified during the pre-termination inspection due to the tenant's possessions being in the way.* [CC §1950.5(f)]

Regardless of whether or not the tenant requests a pre-termination inspection, the final inspection after the tenant vacates and the itemized statement for the refund of the security deposit less any deductions must still be completed and mailed within three weeks after the tenant vacates the residential unit. [CC §1950.5(g)]

Residential refund requirements

Within **three weeks** after a residential tenant vacates, the residential landlord must:

- refund the security deposit, less reasonable deductions; and

- provide the tenant with an itemized statement for any deductions from the security deposit. [CC §1950.5(g); see Form 585 accompanying this chapter]

If the last month's rent on a lease is prepaid, it is considered a security deposit since it has not yet been earned. Prepaid rent must be accounted for as a security deposit if the tenant vacates before expiration of the lease (and the arrival of the month for which rent has been prepaid).

Reasonable deductions from a residential tenant's security deposit include:

- delinquent rent;

- costs to clean the premises after the tenant vacates, if the tenant agreed to and failed to leave the unit in the same level of cleanliness as when he took occupancy;

- costs of repairs for damages caused by the tenant, excluding ordinary wear and tear; and

- costs to replace or restore furnishings provided by the landlord if agreed to in the lease. [CC §1950.5(b)]

Unpaid late charges incurred on a proper demand may be deducted from the security deposit since they are a **form of rent** in that they are **amounts due** the landlord under the lease agreement.

The landlord may not deduct from a tenant's security deposit the costs he incurs to repair defects in the premises which existed prior to the tenant's occupancy. [CC §1950.5(e)]

Tenants seeking to recover security deposits retained by landlords may make unfounded claims that the excessive wear and tear existed when they took possession of the property. To best avoid claims of pre-existing defects, a joint inspection of the unit (landlord and tenant) and written documentation of any defects should be completed **before possession** is given to the tenant. [See **first tuesday** Form 560]

Itemized security deposit statements

When a residential tenant vacates, the landlord itemizes the deductions from the tenant's security deposit on a security deposit disposition. [See Form 585]

If a landlord is required by local rent control ordinances (or state law) to pay interest on security deposits, the landlord may also use the itemized statement to account for interest accrued on the security deposit. [See Form 585 §3.2]

A residential landlord who, in bad faith, fails to comply with security deposit refund requirements may be subjected to statutory penalties of up to twice the amount of the security deposit. [CC §1950.5(l)]

A residential or nonresidential landlord also delivers an itemized statement to tenants on the **sale of the property**, indicating the amount of the security deposits, any deductions and the name, address and telephone number of the buyer. [CC §§1950.5(h); 1950.7(d); see **first tuesday** Form 586]

Nonresidential refund requirements

A nonresidential lease does not need to set forth:

- the circumstance under which a tenant's security deposit will be refunded; and

- a time period within which a landlord will refund a tenant's security deposit.

Other than its receipt, a nonresidential lease does not even need to contain a provision addressing when the security deposit will be returned. [See **first tuesday** Form 552]

However, if **unpaid rent** is deducted from a security deposit after a nonresidential tenant vacates, the landlord is required to refund the security deposit within two weeks from the date he takes possession of the property.

Also, if a nonresidential landlord deducts amounts from a security deposit to cover the costs of cleaning or making repairs to the premises, any remaining portion must be refunded no more than 30 days from the date the landlord receives possession. [CC §1950.7(c)]

STATEMENT OF DEFICIENCIES
ON JOINT PRE-TERMINATION INSPECTION

DATE:_____, 20_____, at _____, California

To Tenant: _____

Items left blank or unchecked are not applicable.

FACTS:

1. On this date, a pre-termination inspection was conducted by the Landlord on the premises and appurtenances which are the subject of a rental agreement or lease

   Dated _____, at _____, California,

   entered into by _____, Tenant(s),

   and _____, Landlord,

   regarding real estate referred to as: _____

   _____

   1.1 ☐ The Tenant was present and given a copy of this statement prepared and signed by the Landlord or his agent.

   1.2 ☐ The Tenant was not present and a copy of this statement prepared and signed by the Landlord or his agent was left inside the premises.

2. The tenancy under the rental agreement or lease terminates or expires on _____, 20_____ by which date you are to vacate the premises.

3. **NOTICE TO TENANT:**

   3.1 You have until the date for termination or expiration of your tenancy to remedy or eliminate the repairs and cleaning specified in this statement of deficiencies to avoid the deduction from your security deposit of the cost to repair and clean the identified deficiencies.

   3.2 Unobservable conditions or conditions which occur after the pre-termination inspection requiring repair and cleaning will be deducted from your security deposit after the final inspection by the landlord or his agent.

STATEMENT OF DEFICIENCIES:

4. The following itemized list of identified deficiencies in repairs and cleaning will be the basis for deductions from your security deposit, unless remedied or eliminated by you prior to vacating and later confirmed by the Landlord or his agent during a final inspection.

   4.1 Damage to the premises and appurtenances caused by the Tenant or their guests, other than ordinary wear and tear, which needs to be repaired are listed as follows:

   _____

   _____

   _____

   _____

   _____

   4.2 Cleaning which needs to be performed to bring the premises up to the level of cleanliness which existed on commencement of the tenancy is listed as follows:

   _____

   _____

   _____

   _____

   _____

— — — — — — — — — — — — — — *PAGE ONE OF TWO — FORM 567-3* — — — — — — — — — — — — — —

5. The following recitals are excerpts from Civil Code §1950.5 regarding security deposits:

5.1 1950.5(b) As used in this section, "security" means any payment, fee, deposit or charge, including, but not limited to, any payment, fee, deposit, or charge, except as provided in Section 1950.6, that is imposed at the beginning of the tenancy to be used to reimburse the landlord for costs associated with processing a new tenant or that is imposed as an advance payment of rent, used or to be used for any purpose, including, but not limited to, any of the following:

(1) The compensation of a Landlord for a Tenant's default in the payment of rent.

(2) The repair of damages of the premises, exclusive of ordinary wear and tear, caused by the Tenant or by a guest or licensee of the tenant.

(3) The cleaning of the premises upon termination of the tenancy necessary to return the unit to the same level of cleanliness it was in at the inception of the tenancy. The amendments to this paragraph enacted by the act adding this sentence shall apply only to tenancies for which the Tenant's right to occupy begins after January 1, 2003.

(4) To remedy future defaults by the Tenant in any obligation under the rental agreement to restore, replace, or return personal property or appurtenances, exclusive of ordinary wear and tear, if the security deposit is authorized to be applied thereto by the rental agreement.

5.2 1950.5(d) Any security shall be held by the Landlord for the Tenant who is party to the lease or agreement. The claim of a Tenant to the security shall be prior to the claim of any creditor of the Landlord.

Date:_____, 20_____

Landlord/Agent: _____

Signature: _____

Address:_____

_____

Phone: _____

Fax: _____

FORM 567-3   02-02   ©2003 first tuesday, P.O. BOX 20069 RIVERSIDE, CA 92516 (800) 794-0494

SECURITY DEPOSIT DISPOSITION
ON VACATING RESIDENTIAL PREMISES

DATE:_____, 20_____, at _____, California

To Tenant: _____

Items left blank or unchecked are not applicable.

FACTS:
This is notice to the tenant of any Landlord deductions from the security deposit under the following agreement:

☐ Residential lease agreement
☐ Month-to-month residential rental agreement
☐ Occupancy agreement
☐ Other: _____

Dated _____, entered into by

_____ , Landlord,

and _____ , Tenant,

regarding residential premises referred to as: _____

_____

_____

> **NOTICE:**
> This itemized statement of the security deposit's disposition must be given to the tenants by the landlord within 21 days after a tenant vacates residential property. [California Civil Code §1950.5(f)]
>
> Use of this form in a timely and proper fashion avoids landlord liability for 2% monthly penalty on any portion of the security deposit wrongfully retained.

DISPOSITION OF DEPOSIT:

1. Under the above referenced agreement, Tenant handed Landlord a security deposit in the amount of . . . . $_____

2. The following deductions have been made by Landlord from the security deposit:

   2.1 Repair of damages   Cost
       a. _____ $_____
       b. _____ $_____

   2.2 Necessary cleaning of the premises   Cost
       a. _____ $_____
       b. _____ $_____

   2.3 Delinquent or holdover rent   Amount
       a. From:_____To:_____ $_____

   2.4 Replacement/repair of lost or damaged furnishings   Cost
       a. _____ $_____

   2.5   TOTAL deductions from security deposit . . . . $_____

3. ☐ **BALANCE DUE TENANT:**

   3.1   Balance of security deposit remaining after deductions . . . . $_____
   3.2   Interest on the security deposit from _____ to _____
       at _____% per annum . . . . $_____
   3.3   Balance due Tenant herewith refunded is the amount of . . . . $_____
       by Landlord/Agent's check #_____.

4. ☐ **BALANCE DUE LANDLORD:**

   4.1   Balance remaining due Landlord for costs in excess of the security deposit . . . . $_____
   4.2   Less interest on the security deposit from _____ to _____
       at _____% per annum . . . . $_____
   4.3   Tenant to hand or mail Landlord/Agent the balance due of . . . . $_____
       Landlord/Agent: _____
       Address: _____

This statement is true and correct:

Date:_____, 20_____

Landlord/Agent: _____

Signature: _____

Address: _____

_____

Phone:_____ Fax: _____

By: _____

FORM 585   10-01   ©2003 **first tuesday**, P.O. BOX 20069 RIVERSIDE, CA 92516 (800) 794-0494

If a refund period is not agreed to and the nonresidential landlord does not take any deductions from the security deposit, the landlord must refund the security deposit within a reasonable time period.

Thirty days from the date the nonresidential landlord receives possession is a reasonable refund period since the landlord is allotted 30 days to determine whether repairs are needed. After 30 days, no good reason exists to continue to hold the deposit.

Unlike the residential landlord, the nonresidential landlord is not required to provide tenants with an itemized statement of deductions when the security deposit is refunded.

However, a prudent nonresidential landlord provides tenants with an itemized statement when they vacate, unless a full refund is made.

An accounting avoids the inevitable demand for documentation which arises when a tenant does not receive a full refund of his security deposit.

A nonresidential landlord who, in bad faith, fails to comply with the refund requirements is liable to the tenant for up to $200 in statutory damages. [CC §1950.7(f)]

Chapter 14

Recovery of residential turnover costs

This chapter discusses how rent, not masked security deposits or other one-time fees, is a residential landlord's sole source for funds to pay for tenant turnover costs.

The security deposit plays no role

The landlord of an apartment complex is determined to reduce or offset the costs of tenant turnover by "shifting the costs" to the tenants.

An increasing number of his tenants are staying for shorter periods of time. On vacating, the units are re-renting quickly, keeping lost rent due to "turn-around" at a minimum.

However, each tenant turnover requires expenditures to:

- refurbish the unit to eliminate the cumulative effect of normal wear and tear, such as painting the walls, deep-cleaning the carpet and dry-cleaning the drapery;

- advertise the unit's availability to locate a tenant;

- pay for time and effort spent showing the unit and clearing prospective tenants; and

- pay the property manager's tenant-origination fee.

Since the rate of tenant turnovers is exceeding normal expectations, the landlord's *net operating income* (NOI) is being reduced by excessive refurbishing and reletting costs. [See **first tuesday** Form 352]

From the landlord's point of view, the NOI consists of amounts remaining from rental income generated by the property after deducting expenses incurred in operating the property — prior to deductions for interest paid on purchase and improvement loans and depreciation.

The landlord is concerned about the economics of the property since the *value* of the property for establishing its net worth (equity), maximum loan amount and sales price is based on the NOI. Also, *spendable income* slips due to increasing turnover costs.

To increase the property's NOI and net spendable income, the landlord chooses to add a *stay-or-pay* clause to his month-to-month rental agreements.

The stay-or-pay clause calls for the residential tenant to forego a return of his security deposit if he moves within six months after taking occupancy. [See Fig. 1]

The landlord believes the stay-or-pay clause will dissuade month-to-month tenants from moving for at least six months.

If a tenant is unpersuaded and vacates the premises within the first six months, the stay-or-pay clause states the landlord can recover his "prematurely incurred" turnover costs from the tenant's security deposit.

Can the landlord enforce the stay-or-pay clause in his rental agreements based on sound economic policies?

No! The stay-or-pay clause is unenforceable. It is an illegal forfeiture of the security deposit.

If the tenant has not breached the lease or rental agreement and on expiration of proper notice returns the unit in the condition it was received, normal wear and tear excepted for the use allowed, the security deposit must be fully refunded no matter how long the unit remains vacant.

The security deposit **may not** be used to cover rent lost for the period of the vacancy or costs incurred to eliminate normal wear and tear and refurbish the unit for the next tenant. [Calif. Civil Code §1950.5(e)]

Thus, the landlord cannot use the stay-or-pay clause in tandem with the security deposit to cut a better deal for himself in the form of more revenue (rent) to cover his operating costs. Revenue for operating expenses must come from rents, not a one-time lump sum advance payment.

Classifying the receipt of tenant funds

Funds received from a tenant by a **residential landlord** fall into only four classifications of receipts:

- tenant screening fees;

- waterbed administration fees;

- rent; and

- security deposits.

The amount of the **tenant screening fee** may not exceed $33.96 for 2002 as annually adjusted from an original statutory amount of $30 in 1997 based on the Consumer Price Index (CPI).

Further, the amount of the tenant screening fee is limited to:

- the out-of-pocket cost for gathering the information; and

- the cost of the landlord's or property manager's time spent obtaining the information and processing an application to rent. [CC §1950.6(b)]

Rent is compensation, usually periodic, received as revenue by a landlord in exchange for the tenant's use, possession and enjoyment of the property. [**Telegraph Ave. Corporation** v. **Raentsch** (1928) 205 C 93]

Rents also include any late charges agreed to and demanded on the delinquent payment of periodic rent. [**Canal-Randolph Anaheim, Inc.** v. **Moore** (1978) 78 CA3d 477]

A charge for any purpose other than rent, a tenant screening fee or a waterbed administration fee is a refundable security deposit, regardless of the name or form given to the funds received. [**Granberry** v. **Islay Investments** (1984) 161 CA3d 382]

A **security deposit** is any advance payment designed to be used as security for the tenant's future performance of his obligations agreed to in a rental agreement or lease.

Security deposit deductions

When one month's rent is collected in advance from a residential tenant, the **security deposit is limited** to an amount equal to:

Fig. 1   (*an unenforceable provision*)

A stay-or-pay minimum tenancy clause

If the tenancy is terminated during the six-month period following commencement of this agreement, tenant shall forfeit tenant's security deposit.

- two months' rent for an *unfurnished unit*; or

- three months' rent for a *furnished unit*. [CC §1950.5(c)]

A residential landlord may deduct from the security deposit those amounts reasonably necessary to:

- cure tenant defaults in the payment of rent;

- repair damages to the premises caused by the tenant;

- clean the premises except for normal wear and tear; and

- dispose of abandoned personal property. [CC §1950.5(b)]

Any amount of security deposit remaining after taking allowable deductions must be refunded to the residential tenant within three weeks after the tenant moves out. [CC §1950.5(f)]

A residential landlord's retention of any portion of a security deposit in violation of the deduction rules subjects the landlord to statutory penalties of up to twice the amount of the security deposit, in addition to actual damages. [CC §1950.5(l)]

Is it extra rent or a screening fee?

A landlord funds the care and maintenance expenses of property from rents, not from an initial lump sum amount paid in addition to rent.

Consider a residential landlord who requires new tenants to prepay one month's rent and make a refundable security deposit equal to one month's rent before entering into a lease or rental agreement.

In addition, the landlord charges a one-time, nonrefundable, new-tenant fee, membership fee or application expense reimbursement fee.

The purpose of the **nonrefundable fee** is to cover administrative expenses and services related to **processing** the tenant's application to rent the unit.

A tenant seeks to recover the one-time extra charge, claiming it is a nonrefundable security deposit since the lump sum charge covers expenses which must be recovered through amounts collected as rents and thus makes it a security deposit.

Can the tenant recover the one-time extra charge imposed by the landlord as a masked security deposit?

No, not as a security deposit! The one-time charge for administrative costs incurred by the landlord to process the tenant's rental application is not a security deposit. A security deposit is imposed and collected to secure the landlord against future tenant defaults under the lease or rental agreement by providing a source of recovery for any loss caused by the default. [**Krause** v. **Trinity Management Service, Inc.** (2000) 23 C4th 116; CC §§1950.5; 1950.6]

However, a "nonrefundable upfront fee" is controlled by the tenant screening fee statute which limits the amount of the application processing fee to $33.96 for 2002. Thus, the difference is refundable as an excess charge which is neither rent nor a security deposit.

Unenforceable liquidated damages

Consider a residential landlord who includes a *liquidated damages* provision in the rental agreement in an effort to reduce or offset his tenant turnover costs. [See Fig. 2]

In addition to the first month's rent, the landlord properly collects a security deposit from the tenant in an amount equal to one month's rent to cover any future breach of the rental agreement by the tenant.

Before six months runs, a tenant gives 30 days' notice to the landlord and vacates the unit.

Within 21 days of vacating, the landlord sends the tenant an itemized accounting of the security deposit, deducting one month's rent for the liquidated damages agreed to and owed due to the early (and proper) termination of the month-to-month rental agreement.

The tenant claims the security deposit must be refunded since a **liquidated damages** provision in a rental agreement or lease is unenforceable as a *forfeiture*.

Is the liquidated damages provision unenforceable?

Yes! A liquidated damages provision is unenforceable in residential rental agreements and leases. The amount of recoverable losses a residential landlord incurs when a tenant vacates a unit, such as the lost rent and the maintenance costs of labor and materials to cover excess wear and tear, is readily ascertainable. [CC §1671(d)]

A liquidated damages provision may only be enforced when conditions make it extremely difficult or impracticable to determine the amount of actual money losses. This is never the case in real estate rentals. [CC §1671(d)]

Further, liquidated damages do not represent a recovery of **actual money losses** incurred by the landlord, losses which without calling for a forfeiture could be deducted from the security deposit. The purpose of the landlord's liquidated damages provisions is not to recover money lost due to unpaid rent owed or excessive wear and tear.

Even if the landlord does not deduct the liquidated damages amount agreed to from the security deposit, he will not be able to recover the liquidated damages from the tenant in a civil action.

Covering tenant turnover costs

Recovery of a landlord's turnover costs must come from the periodic rents bargained for and received from his tenants — an expense of operations deducted from income.

The costs of refurbishing a unit to eliminate normal wear and tear so it can be re-rented in a "fresh" condition are known in advance. Further, the amount of the refurbishing costs must be amortized over the length of each tenant's probable occupancy period so the costs can be recovered as a component of the periodic rent charged to a tenant.

However, since the rental marketplace sets rent ceilings, a landlord is limited in the amount he can charge for rent and successfully compete for tenants.

Thus, a landlord's most logical cost recovery approach is to stretch out each tenant's term of occupancy to an optimal length of time which will reduce the frequency of tenant turnover and increase net spendable income.

The lease reduces costs

The landlord's best method for recovering turnover costs is to rent to creditworthy tenants on a lease with a term of more than one year, local rental market permitting. Rent may have to be adjusted.

Fig. 2　　　　　　*(an unenforceable provision)*

A liquidated damages minimum tenancy provision

Should the tenant choose to terminate this tenancy during the six-month period beginning on commencement of this tenancy, the tenant shall pay as *liquidated damages*, and not as a penalty or forfeiture, an amount equal to one month's rent in consideration for exercising the right to vacate prematurely.

A lease allows the landlord to amortize the anticipated costs of refurbishing the unit over the maximum term negotiable. Also, the lease of a unit reduces the frequency of vacancies and provides a schedule for turnover maintenance since tenants under a lease tend to remain in possession until the lease term expires.

Although the market limits the amount a landlord can charge for rent, different rental rates exist for leases and rental agreements in most local markets.

Month-to-month tenancies provide less time over which the landlord can amortize his turnover costs. Also, a landlord with month-to-month tenants must deal with the likelihood of frequent turnovers and the investment of time and money to constantly re-rent vacant units.

As compensation, a landlord is able to charge higher rents for month-to-month tenancies which reflects the cost-push of higher and more frequent turnover expenses than under a lease.

In contrast, a lease locks a tenant into a fixed period of occupancy, such as one year or more. Leases reduce the tenant turnover rate, and in turn, reduce operating costs and lost rent due to vacancies. Thus, the landlord amortizes his anticipated turnover costs over a greater period of time.

As a result, the lower rent usually received on leases is a reflection of lower overall refurbishing expenses, reduced annual vacancy rates, less management and usually less risk of lost rents.

Tiered rents for time in occupancy

A month-to-month rental agreement structured with tiered rents for future periods of occupancy provide for a slightly higher rent for months included in the first-tier period — such as the first six months of the periodic tenancy — than in the following months.

If the month-to-month tenant continues in occupancy after the first-tier period, the rental agreement calls for a lower rent during a second-tier period or for the remainder of the occupancy, both rates being consistent with the marketplace, of course.

Tiered rents which decrease after a period of time encourage tenants to stay longer since their rent will be lower.

Thus, the landlord's turnover costs are amortized and "reserved" through the higher periodic rent charged during the first tier.

If the month-to-month tenant does vacate on 30 days notice before the period of higher first-tier rent ends, less of the landlord's turnover costs prematurely incurred due to the early vacancy are left unamortized.

However, tiered rents will only avoid the security deposit limitations if:

- a security deposit of a customary amount is charged;

- the higher monthly rent is consistently charged over a long enough period so as not to be characterized as a disguised or delayed receipt of a security deposit, application processing (screening) fee, cleaning fee or forfeiture; and

- the tenancy is month-to-month.

It is not certain that tiered rents will never be construed as a disguise for a nonrefundable security deposit, but it has become far less likely. [Krause, *supra*]

The same amortization logic applies to the cost of tenant improvements (TIs) made by a nonresidential landlord. For example, if the TIs are recovered over the first four years of a lease as part of the rent amount, the rent thereafter (second tier) could be reduced to an amount which reflects the elimination of the TI charges in order to induce the tenant to stay for a greater period of time.

Chapter
15

Accepting
partial rent

This chapter distinguishes the differing rights held by residential and nonresidential landlords to file or continue an unlawful detainer (UD) action on receipt of partial rent.

Rights of residential and nonresidential landlords

A **nonresidential tenant**, also called a *commercial tenant*, experiences cash flow difficulties due to a business downturn. As a result, the tenant becomes delinquent in the payment of rent.

Discussions between the landlord and tenant follow. Eventually, to enforce collection of the rent, the landlord serves the tenant with a **3-day notice** to pay rent or quit the premises. [See **first tuesday** Form 575]

Prior to the filing of an unlawful detainer (UD) action, the tenant *offers* to hand the landlord a partial payment of the delinquent rent. However, the tenant wants to pay the balance of the rent by a specified date if the landlord will agree in writing to defer any filing of a UD action, called a **partial payment agreement**. [See Form 558 accompanying this chapter]

The partial payment agreement sets forth the amount of **deferred rent** remaining unpaid, the date for its payment and the consequences of nonpayment — eviction by a UD action without further notice.

Thus, if the deferred rent is not paid as rescheduled, the nonresidential landlord has the agreed-to **right to file** a UD action to evict the tenant without repeating the 3-day notice requirement for filing a UD action.

Here, the partial payment agreement has temporarily delayed the landlord from moving forward with the eviction process commenced by the service of the 3-day notice on the tenant.

Under the partial payment agreement, the nonresidential landlord has retained his right to proceed on the 3-day notice to evict by filing a UD action should the deferred payment for the balance of the delinquency not be received as rescheduled.

The tenant fails to pay the deferred remainder of the delinquent rent on the date scheduled for payment.

Without further notice to the tenant, the landlord files a UD action.

The nonresidential tenant now seeks to prevent the landlord from proceeding with the UD action claiming the landlord's acceptance of the partial rent payment invalidates the 3-day notice since the notice now states an amount of rent which is no longer due.

Can the nonresidential landlord accept a payment of partial rent after serving a 3-day notice and later file a UD action against the tenant without serving another 3-day notice?

Yes! A **nonresidential landlord** can accept a partial payment of rent after serving a 3-day notice before filing a UD action. Without further notice to the tenant, the nonresidential landlord can commence a UD action and evict the tenant. [Calif. Code of Civil Procedure §1161.1(b)]

Further, on accepting a partial payment of delinquent rent, a nonresidential landlord does not need to even agree to a due date for the remainder of rent. He also does not need to enter into any agreement regarding his acceptance of the partial payment if the tenant has previously been given a reservation of rights by the landlord, called a *nonwaiver provision* (which appears as a provision in nonresidential leases). [See **first tuesday** Form 552 §22]

However, the nonresidential landlord who memorializes his acceptance of the partial rent payment and the due date for payment of the remainder due eliminates conflicting claims by the tenant in a UD action about the tenant's expectations based on the landlord's acceptance of partial payment of rent.

Residential property distinguished

Now consider the same situation involving residential property instead of nonresidential property.

As for serving a 3-day notice and later accepting any amount of rent, a distinction exists between residential and nonresidential tenancies.

A **residential landlord** who accepts any amount of rent from a tenant after serving a 3-day notice waives his right to file a UD action based on the 3-day notice. A residential landlord must re-notice the tenant for the amount now remaining unpaid. [**EDC Associates, Ltd.** v. **Gutierrez** (1984) 153 CA3d 167]

Residential vs. nonresidential landlords

Acceptance of a partial payment on delinquent rent is within the discretion of the landlord.

A landlord may be willing to accept partial payments when:

- the partial payment is at least equal to the rent accrued at the time the tenant offers the payment;

- the tenant is creditworthy;

- the tenant has an adequate payment history; and

- the tenant is one the landlord wants to retain.

Both residential and nonresidential landlords may accept a partial payment of delinquent rent and at any time thereafter serve a 3-day notice demanding payment of the balance due or quit. However, a landlord could agree in a partial payment agreement not to serve a 3-day notice on receipt of the partial payment of rent conditioned on the payment of the balance at a later date. [See Form 558; see Form 559 accompanying this chapter]

The expiration of the 3-day notice to pay rent or quit without compliance establishes the tenant's unlawful detainer of the premises, which is the requisite for maintaining a UD action that will result in an eviction order. [CCP §1161; see Chapter 19]

Residential rent paid after notice

If a **residential landlord** files a UD action and later accepts a partial payment of rent, the UD action cannot be maintained. The reason lies in that a difference now exists between the rent demanded in the notice to pay to establish an unlawful detainer and the amount remaining delinquent at the UD hearing. In residential UD actions the amounts must be the same. The contrary rule applies to nonresidential tenancies.

Once the residential landlord accepts a partial payment of delinquent rent, the 3-day notice served on the tenant no longer states the correct amount which must be paid by the tenant to avoid losing his right to possession.

Any 3-day notice served on a residential tenant which overstates the amount of delinquent rent due at the **time of trial** on the UD action is invalid. The UD action in a residential eviction based on an overstated amount in the 3-day notice must fail. [**Jayasinghe** v. **Lee** (1993) 13 CA4th Supp. 33]

Thus, the residential landlord on accepting a partial payment of rent must serve another 3-day notice demanding payment of the remainder due on unpaid delinquent rent and file a new UD action if one has already been filed.

PARTIAL PAYMENT AGREEMENT
Nonresidential

DATE:_____, 20_____, at _____, California

Items left blank or unchecked are not applicable.

FACTS:

This partial payment agreement pertains to the collection of past due rent under a nonresidential lease or rental agreement dated _____, at _____, California, regarding leased premises referred to as: _____
_____

AGREEMENT:

1. Tenant has not paid the rent due for the month of _____, 20_____.
2. Landlord hereby accepts partial payment on past due rent in the amount of ....$_____
3. The balance of the unpaid rent owed is........................ $_____
   - 3.1 Plus late charge for delinquency of .... $_____
   - 3.2 Plus a deferred rent processing charge of................... $_____
   - 3.3 Total deferred rent due, including additional charges, is the sum of ....$_____
4. Tenant to pay the total deferred rent on or before _____, 20_____.
   - 4.1 Rent to be paid by ☐ cash, ☐ check, or ☐ cashier's check made payable to Landlord.
   - 4.2 Rent may be tendered by ☐ mail, or ☐ personal delivery to:
     - _____ (Name)
     - _____ (Address)
     - _____ (Phone)
     - a. Personal delivery of rent will be accepted during the hours of _____am to _____pm on the following days: _____
   - 4.3 Rent may also be paid by deposit into account number _____ at:
     - _____ (Financial Institution)
     - _____ (Address)
     - _____
   - 4.4 No grace period for payment of the deferred rent is granted to Tenant.
   - 4.5 Delinquent payment of the deferred rent incurs a late charge of $_____
5. If deferred rent is paid when due, any outstanding three-day notice to pay rent or quit is no longer valid.
6. If the deferred rent is not paid when due, Landlord reserves the right to:
   (Check one box only)
   - 6.1 ☐ Serve Tenant with a three-day notice to pay the remaining balance of the rent due or quit the premises.
     (Check if a three-day notice has not been served)
   - 6.2 ☐ Commence, without further notice, an unlawful detainer action to evict Tenant from the premises.
     (Check if a three-day notice has been served)
   - 6.3 ☐ Continue with the unlawful detainer action on file to evict Tenant from the premises.
     (Check if unlawful detainer action has been filed)
7. _____
   _____
   _____
   _____

I agree to the terms stated above.	I agree to the terms stated above.
Date:_____, 20_____	Date:_____, 20_____
Landlord: _____	Tenant: _____
Agent: _____	Tenant: _____
Signature: _____	Signature: _____
Address: _____	Signature: _____
_____	Address: _____
Phone: _____	Phone: _____
Fax: _____	Fax: _____

Nonresidential nonwaiver requirements

However, should a **nonresidential landlord** file a UD action and then accept a partial payment of rent, the landlord must then or previously have provided the tenant with notice that the acceptance of rent does not waive the landlord's rights, called a *nonwaiver of rights provision*. When the tenant receives a nonwaiver of rights notice on or before the landlord's acceptance of rent, the landlord can continue with the UD action and recover possession of the premises. [CCP §1161.1(c)]

Leases include a nonwaiver of rights provision which states the landlord's acceptance of partial rent does not constitute a waiver of the landlord's right to enforce any remaining breach of the lease. [See Form 552 §22]

Now consider a nonresidential tenant who defaults on a rent payment under a lease with a nonwaiver provision and fails to pay the rent before expiration of a 3-day notice to pay or quit. The notice to pay does not contain a notice of nonwaiver on acceptance of rent.

The nonresidential landlord files a UD action and then accepts a partial payment of rent without entering into any agreements, except to receipt the amount paid as being rent.

The tenant claims the landlord cannot now proceed with the UD action because he did not receive a notice of nonwaiver in the 3-day notice or on acceptance and receipt of the partial rent payment.

However, the nonresidential landlord may proceed with the UD action after receipt of partial rent. The nonwaiver provision in the lease agreement gives the tenant actual notice that the landlord's acceptance of any rent does not waive the landlord's rights. One such right is the right to proceed with a previously filed UD action. [**Woodman Partners** v. **Sofa U Love** (2001) 94 CA4th 766]

The 3-day notice or the partial payment agreement could include a nonwaiver provision to preserve the landlord's rights whether or not the lease contains the nonwaiver notice.

A nonwaiver provision in a 3-day notice or partial payment agreement provides the landlord with the same right to proceed with the UD action as though the provision existed in the lease.

On accepting a partial payment of rent after a UD action has been filed, the nonresidential landlord amends the UD complaint to reflect the partial payment received and the amount now remaining due from the tenant. [CCP §1161.1(c)]

Get it in writing

Without a written partial payment agreement, the tenant might well claim the landlord who accepted partial rent:

- treated acceptance as an accord and satisfaction of all the rent due in a dispute over the rent amount; or

- waived the right to continue eviction proceedings, sometimes called *estoppel*.

The tenant might also argue the deferred payment schedule for the month in question was a permanent modification of the lease establishing a semi-monthly rent payment schedule.

When a residential or nonresidential landlord accepts a partial payment of rent, the use of the partial payment agreement is evidence which bars the tenant from later claiming the landlord waived valuable rights by accepting rent.

Residential partial payment agreement

The partial payment agreement entered into by a residential landlord and tenant on acceptance of a portion of the rent due is evidence of:

- the landlord's receipt of partial rent;

- the tenant's promise to pay the remainder of the rent by the rescheduled due date; and

- notification of the landlord's right to serve a 3-day notice on failure to pay the remaining balance. [See Form 559]

PARTIAL PAYMENT AGREEMENT
Residential

DATE:_____, 20_____, at _____, California

Items left blank or unchecked are not applicable.

FACTS:

This partial payment agreement pertains to the collection of past due rent under a residential lease or rental agreement:

Dated _____, at _____, California,

regarding leased premises referred to as: _____

_____

AGREEMENT:

1. Tenant has not paid the full rent due for the month of _____, 20_____.
2. Landlord hereby accepts partial payment on the past due rent in the amount of....... $_____
3. The balance of the unpaid rent owed by Tenant is .... $_____
   - 3.1 Plus a late charge for delinquency of .... $_____
   - 3.2 Plus a deferred rent processing charge of.................... $_____
   - 3.3 Total deferred rent due, including additional charges, is the sum of .... $_____
4. Tenant to pay the total deferred rent on or before _____, 20_____.
   - 4.1 Rent to be paid by ☐ cash, ☐ check, or ☐ cashier's check made payable to Landlord.
   - 4.2 Rent may be tendered by ☐ mail, or ☐ personal delivery to:
     - _____ (Name)
     - _____ (Address)
     - _____ (Phone)
       - a. Personal delivery of rent will be accepted during the hours of _____ am to _____ pm on the following days: _____.
   - 4.3 Rent may also be paid by deposit into account number _____ at:
     - _____ (Financial Institution)
     - _____ (Address)
     - _____
   - 4.4 No grace period for payment of the deferred rent is granted to Tenant.
   - 4.5 Delinquent payment of the deferred rent incurs a late charge of............... $_____
5. If the deferred rent is not paid when due, a three-day notice to pay rent or quit may be served at any time.
6. No provision of the lease or rental agreement is affected by this agreement.
7. _____
   _____
   _____

I agree to the terms stated above.	I agree to the terms stated above.
Date:_____, 20_____	Date:_____, 20_____
Landlord: _____	Tenant: _____
Agent: _____	Tenant: _____
Signature: _____	Signature: _____
Address: _____	Signature: _____
	Address: _____
	_____
Phone: _____	Phone: _____
Fax: _____	Fax: _____

FORM 559   02-02   ©2003 **first tuesday**, P.O. BOX 20069 RIVERSIDE, CA 92516 (800) 794-0494

A partial payment agreement is not a notice to the tenant to pay the deferred portion of the delinquent rent or quit, which is required to establish an unlawful detainer and evict the tenant.

Consider a **residential tenant** who informs the landlord he is unable to pay the monthly rent due within the grace period, before the payment becomes delinquent.

The tenant offers to pay part of the rent prior to delinquency and the remainder ten days later.

Since the tenant is creditworthy, has not been delinquent in the past and the landlord wishes to retain the tenant, the residential landlord agrees to accept the partial payment.

However, to **avoid disputes** as to the amount of rent remaining due and when it will be paid, the residential landlord prepares and requires the tenant to sign a partial payment agreement formalizing their understanding.

Now consider a residential landlord who serves a 3-day notice and accepts a partial payment of rent before the notice expires. By accepting a partial payment, the residential landlord has rendered the 3-day notice invalid.

However, the residential landlord required the tenant to enter into a partial payment agreement when the rent was accepted.

The partial payment agreement will avoid any claims by the tenant about when the balance is due or that the landlord waived his right to serve another 3-day notice for the remainder of the delinquent rent.

Nonresidential partial payment agreement

The eviction rights reserved by a nonwaiver provision when a nonresidential landlord accepts partial rent are far less restrictive than for a residential landlord.

Before service of a 3-day notice to pay rent or quit on a **nonresidential tenant** who is delinquent in his rent payment, the nonresidential landlord can:

- accept partial payment of rent; and

- either concurrently or thereafter serve a 3-day notice, or agree not to serve a 3-day notice until the remainder of the rent is not paid as rescheduled. [See Form 558 §6.1]

When a 3-day notice has been served and the nonresidential landlord later accepts a partial payment of rent, the partial payment agreement acknowledging receipt of partial rent contains:

- the due date for payment of the delinquent rent remaining unpaid; and

- notice of the nonresidential landlord's right to file a UD action on nonpayment.

More importantly, a nonresidential landlord who accepts a partial payment of rent **after filing a UD action** and enters into a partial payment agreement with the tenant has notified the tenant he has not waived his right to continue the UD action and recover possession under the UD action previously filed.

Further, the nonresidential landlord could agree to reinstate the lease if the remainder of the delinquent rent is paid prior to the UD hearing date.

However, no agreement is necessary on acceptance of partial rent from a nonresidential tenant. The landlord can accept partial payment and immediately proceed with his next step in the eviction process — service of a 3-day notice or filing of the UD action or the UD hearing — if a nonwaiver provision is in a prior document, such as the lease.

Chapter 16

Changing terms on a month-to-month tenancy

This chapter reviews the requirements for the landlord's 30-day notice to alter the terms in a tenant's month-to-month rental agreement.

Landlord's 30-day notice

A landlord and tenant enter into a month-to-month tenancy which includes an option to purchase the property which expires on termination of the month-to-month tenancy.

Later, the landlord serves the tenant with a 30-Day Notice of Change in Rental Terms stating the option to purchase will expire in 30 days, unless exercised by the tenant. [See Form 570 accompanying this chapter]

After the 30-day notice expires, the tenant, who is still in possession, attempts to exercise the option.

The landlord refuses to sell the property under the option, claiming the tenant's right to exercise the option to purchase no longer exists.

The tenant claims the option to purchase is binding for the duration of the tenancy, and the month-to-month rental agreement has not been terminated.

Can the tenant enforce the option to purchase?

No! The option expired unexercised on the running of the 30-day notice of change in rental terms.

The option to purchase was part of the rental agreement. Thus, on expiration of the 30-day notice cancelling the option, the option — as a set of terms in the month-to-month rental agreement — was eliminated.

Like any other provision contained or referenced in a month-to-month rental agreement, the option to purchase is part of the month-to-month tenancy, subject to change on 30 days written notice from the landlord. [**Wilcox** v. **Anderson** (1978) 84 CA3d 593]

30-day notice to change rental terms

All covenants and conditions in a residential or nonresidential month-to-month rental agreement, also called *provisions, clauses, terms, conditions, addendums, etc.*, for any type of real estate may be changed on 30 days written notice by the landlord. [Calif. Civil Code §827]

For example, a residential or nonresidential landlord under a month-to-month rental agreement can increase the rent (not to exceed 10% within 12 months) or shift repair and maintenance obligations to the tenant by serving a 30-Day Notice of Change in Rental Terms. [See Form 570]

To be enforceable, the 30-day notice must be served in the same manner as a 3-day notice to pay rent or quit. [See Chapter 20]

However, only the landlord may unilaterally change the terms in a rental agreement. [CC §827]

A month-to-month tenant has no ability to alter the terms of his rental agreement, other than to terminate the tenancy and vacate. [CC §1946]

In rent control communities, a landlord or property manager must be fully apprised of how rent control ordinances affect their ability to alter provisions in leases and rental agreements.

30-day notice to increase rents

A landlord or property manager may serve a notice of change in rental terms under a periodic (month-to-month) rental agreement on **any day** during the rental period.

Once a notice of change in rental terms is served on a month-to-month tenant, the new terms stated in the notice immediately become part of the tenant's rental agreement. [CC §827]

However, the new rental terms stated in the notice do not take effect until expiration of the notice.

For example, a property manager prepares a 30-day notice of change in rental terms to be served on a month-to-month tenant to **increase the rent**.

The due date for the payment of rent is the first day of each month.

The tenant is properly served with the 30-day notice on the 10th of June. The tenant intends to remain in possession at the new rental rate.

Since June 11th is the first day of the 30-day **notice period**, the rent will not *begin to accrue* at the increased rate until July 11th — the day after the 30-day notice expires. However, rent for all of July is payable **in advance** on the first day of the month, including the number of days (21) affected by the rent increase.

The rent due and payable in advance for the calendar month of July will be prorated as follows:

- the old rate for the first ten days of the month; and

- the new rate for the remaining 21 days in the month of July.

Pro rata rent will be determined based on the number of days in the calendar month, unless the rental agreement contains a provision prorating rent on a 30-day month. [CC §14]

Note — Until January 1, 2006, unless extended, any residential landlord raising rent more than 10% within a 12-month period must furnish the tenant with a written 60-day notice of the rent increase. [CC §827; see **first tuesday** Form 574]

Tenant's response to a change

On being served with a 30-day notice of a change in rental terms, the month-to-month tenant has three options:

- remain in possession and comply with the new rental terms;

- serve the landlord with a 30-day notice of intent to vacate and pay pro rata rent on the next due date for days remaining unpaid through the end of the 30-day notice to vacate; or

- remain in possession, refuse to comply with the rental terms and raise defenses, such as retaliatory eviction, in the resulting unlawful detainer (UD) action. [See Chapter 34]

Note — To prevail on a defense of retaliatory eviction, circumstances showing retaliation for the exercise of rights must exist.

Consider the tenant who receives the landlord's notice but does not wish to comply with changes in the rental terms. Accordingly, the tenant serves the landlord with a 30-day Notice of Intent to Vacate. [See **first tuesday** Form 572]

If the change is a rent increase, the tenant is liable for pro rata rent at the new rate for the days after the rent increase becomes effective up to the expiration of the tenant's notice to vacate — payable in advance on the due date for the next scheduled payment of rent, usually the first.

30-DAY NOTICE OF CHANGE IN RENTAL TERMS

DATE:_____, 20_____, at _____, California

To Tenant: _____

Items left blank or unchecked are not applicable.

FACTS:

You are a Tenant under a rental agreement or expired lease
Dated _____, at

_____, California,

entered into by _____, Tenant,

and_____, Landlord,

regarding real estate referred to as: _____

_____

_____

<table>
<tr><td>NOTICE:
A landlord must furnish the tenant with a written 30-day notice of any change in the terms of a month-to-month tenancy. If rent is raised more than 10% within a 12-month period on a residential tenant, a 60-day notice of the increase is required. [Calif. Civil Code §827; See first tuesday Form 574]</td></tr>
</table>

NOTICE:

Thirty (30) days after service of this notice on you, the terms of your tenancy on the real estate are hereby changed as checked below:

1. ☐ Rent shall be $_____ ☐ monthly, or ☐ _____,
   payable in advance and due on the _____ day of the month.

   1.1 Rent to be paid by ☐ cash, ☐ check, or ☐ cashier's check made payable to Landlord.

   1.2 Rent may be tendered by ☐ mail, or ☐ personal delivery to:

   _____ (Name)

   _____ (Address)

   _____

   _____ (Phone)

   a. Personal delivery of rent will be accepted during the hours of _____ am to _____ pm on the
      following days: _____

   1.3 Rent may also be paid by deposit into account number _____ at:

   _____ (Financial Institution)

   _____ (Address)

   _____

2. ☐ The common area maintenance charge shall be $_____ per month, payable with each payment
   of rent.

3. ☐ Utilities now paid by Landlord to be paid by Tenant as checked:
   ☐ Gas   ☐ Electricity   ☐ Sewage and Rubbish   ☐ Water   ☐ Cable TV

4. ☐ Tenant to maintain and properly care for the lawns, gardens, tree, shrubs and watering system.

5. ☐ An additional security deposit of $_____ is payable with the next rent payment.

6. _____

   _____

This notice affects no other terms of your tenancy.

Date:_____, 20_____

Landlord/Agent:_____

Signature: _____

Address: _____

_____

Phone:_____

Fax: _____

E-mail: _____

FORM 570   02-02   ©2003 **first tuesday**, P.O. BOX 20069 RIVERSIDE, CA 92516 (800) 794-0494

Rent control restrictions

Most rent control ordinances allow a landlord or property manager to increase the rent to:

- obtain a fair return on his investment;

- recover the cost of capital improvements to the property; and

- pass through the cost of servicing the debt on the property.

Thus, without further authority from the rent control board, a landlord can make general adjustments to rents in one of three ways:

- increase rent by the maximum percentage set by ordinance;

- increase rent by the maximum percentage of the consumer price index (CPI) as set by ordinance; or

- increase rent by the maximum amount previously set by the rent control board.

Landlords of newly constructed units or individual units (SFRs/condos) held out for rent may establish their own rental rates, subject to limitations if they are controlled by rent control ordinances established prior to 1995. [See Chapter 39]

SECTION D

Enforcing Rents, Forfeiting Tenancies

Chapter 17

Forfeiture of the lease

This chapter discusses the effect a termination of the right to occupy has on the tenant's obligation to pay future rent agreed to in either a residential or nonresidential lease.

Tenant's monetary obligations survive

A tenant occupies real estate under a lease agreement which states that once the tenant's right to possession under the leasehold is terminated due to a default by the tenant, the landlord may collect rents for the period remaining until expiration of the lease agreement, called a *default remedies clause.* [See **first tuesday** Forms 551 and 552 §23]

The tenant fails to pay the rent, but does not vacate the premises. The landlord serves the tenant with a 3-day notice to pay rent or quit.

In the notice, the **landlord declares** the lease to be *forfeited* on expiration of the third day following service if the tenant does not pay the rent. If the tenant fails to pay during the three-day period, the right to possession is forfeited. [See **first tuesday** Form 575 §3]

The tenant does not pay the rent within the three-day period and remains in possession of the property, called a *holdover occupancy* or *unlawful detainer (UD)*, since the leasehold under which the tenant has the right to occupy the property has been **terminated** on the running of the third day due to the **forfeiture declaration** in the 3-day notice.

The landlord does not file a UD action to regain possession of the property, even though the tenant's possession is now unlawful and the tenant pays no further rent.

Note — The landlord may be benefiting by not evicting the tenant when no other tenant is available to immediately occupy the space. The rent earned during the holdover is the holdover rate set in the lease, which usually greatly exceeds the current rental rate for the space. Also, occupancy is often required by insurance carriers to retain hazard coverage.

The tenant later voluntarily vacates the property before the expiration of the lease.

The landlord then files a civil action to collect rent earned and unpaid for:

- the period prior to termination of the right to possession by forfeiture;

- the holdover (unlawful detainer) period prior to vacating; and

- the **future rent** scheduled for payment after the tenant vacated until *expiration* of the lease.

The tenant claims the landlord cannot collect rent called for in the lease agreement for any period after expiration of the 3-day notice since:

- the election to forfeit the lease contained in the 3-day notice to pay or quit terminated the entire lease agreement, not just the occupancy; and

- the landlord's failure to evict the tenant on termination of the lease agreement converted the tenant's continued occupancy into a periodic month-to-month tenancy — for which only reasonable rent is due, not the scheduled rent for a holdover as called for in the lease.

Can the landlord collect all rent unpaid during the occupancy and future rent due during the remaining term of the lease even though the lease was forfeited in the 3-day notice?

Yes! A 3-day notice to pay or quit which declares an election to forfeit the lease on failure to pay does not also cancel the lease agreement. The forfeiture election only terminates the **right to possession** held under the leasehold which was conveyed to the tenant by the landlord on entering into the lease agreement.

Here, a distinction must be made between the **lease** held by the tenant, called a *leasehold*, and the **lease agreement** which is a contract commonly referred to as the *lease*.

Independent of the termination of the tenant's right to possession on expiration of the 3-day notice due to a declaration of forfeiture, the tenant's **obligation to pay** future rent scheduled in the lease agreement until it expires remains unaffected and fully enforceable, either under the default remedies clause in the lease agreement or by statute. [Calif. Civil Code §1951.2(a)(3)]

Also, the holdover occupancy does not convert the unlawful possession after expiration of the 3-day notice into a month-to-month tenancy, unless monthly rent is tendered and accepted by the landlord.

Further, a landlord need not first evict the holdover tenant in a UD action before filing a separate money action to recover future rents called for in the lease agreement.

However, the tenant's leasehold **right to possession** must first be terminated, as it was by the forfeiture election and expiration of the 3-day notice (or by an eviction in a UD action or abandonment), before the landlord can recover holdover rents and **unearned future rents** due under the lease agreement. [**Walt** v. **Superior Court** (1992) 8 CA4th 1667]

First terminate the lease on default

"Termination of the lease" refers to the termination of the tenant's *right to possession* which was conveyed to the tenant on entering into the lease.

If a breach of the lease by the tenant is curable, the landlord terminates the tenant's right to possession on expiration of a 3-day notice period (without performance by the tenant) by serving the tenant with either a 3-day notice to pay rent or quit or a 3-day notice to perform or quit, which contains a *forfeiture-of-lease* clause. [**In re Windmill Farms Inc.** (9th Cir. 1988) 841 F2d 1467]

If the 3-day notice lacks a forfeiture declaration, the leasehold is not terminated until five days after a judgment on the UD action is entered awarding possession to the landlord.

The tenant's possession becomes unlawful when the tenant continues in possession without permission after the leasehold has been terminated, called an *unlawful detainer (UD)*, *holdover tenancy* or *tenancy at sufferance*.

With the leasehold right to possession terminated, the landlord may file a UD action and recover possession without concern about the tenant *reinstating* the lease and being *restored* to possession at trial. [Calif. Code of Civil Procedure §1161(2)]

One purpose of the UD action is for a court to determine whether the termination of the right to possession under the 3-day notice was proper. If proper, the landlord is awarded possession and the tenant evicted. If a forfeiture declaration did not exist in the notice, then the forfeiture cannot occur until a *five-day reinstatement period* has passed after entry of judgment.

Rent earned and unpaid up to the time of entry of the UD judgment may also be awarded in the UD action along with an eviction order. The UD award for money due from rent applies only to periods before the UD trial:

- before termination of the lease for rent at the rate due under the lease agreement; and

- during the holdover period up to trial for rent of a **reasonable amount** which is set by the court, not by prior agreement under a holdover rent provision.

A UD award may not include future, unearned rent. These are only collectible through a separate money action.

3-day notice without a forfeiture

A landlord who needs to evict a tenant by a court order in a UD action can recover possession and either:

- leave the leasehold interest unforfeited, its ownership remaining with the dispossessed (evicted) tenant; or

- terminate the leasehold by a declaration of forfeiture in the 3-day notice. [CCP §1174(a),(c)]

To terminate the tenant's leasehold interest under a lease or rental agreement on any material breach of provisions in the lease/rental agreement by the tenant, the 3-day notice served to establish the unlawful detainer must contain a declaration of the landlord's intent to forfeit the leasehold.

On termination of the leasehold and all tenant rights to the unexpired term of the tenancy, the landlord can reoccupy the property for his own account (if the tenant has vacated). The tenant has no continuing interest in the real estate after the 3-day notice expires due to the declaration of forfeiture. [CCP §1174(a)]

However, the landlord may not want to terminate the tenancy on evicting the tenant. The landlord may rather retake possession on behalf of the tenant, acting as the tenant's agent to relet the property for the account of the tenant, not himself.

Here, the landlord omits (by deletion) the declaration of forfeiture from the 3-day notice

since the landlord will take possession on behalf of the tenant. Although dispossessed, the tenant still owns the leasehold estate under the unexpired lease, now managed by the landlord on the tenant's behalf.

Also, the landlord faced with a tenant under an unexpired lease whose only breach is the **failure to pay rent** may want to give the tenant every opportunity to bring the rent up-to-date and remain the (otherwise) good tenant he has been.

Faced with delinquent rent (and failed promises to bring the rent current), the landlord can serve a 3-day notice to pay rent or quit and strike (delete) the declaration of forfeiture provision from the 3-day notice.

Thus, at the UD trial:

- the leasehold interest will not be terminated (or declared forfeited by the court) and will continue as retained by the tenant for the duration of the unexpired lease;

- the tenant will be given five days after the eviction judgment is entered to reinstate the lease agreement and remain in possession by paying the delinquent rent, interest, costs and other money losses due the landlord; and if rent is not paid to reinstate the lease agreement, the tenant will be ordered evicted after the fifth day, and the landlord will take possession and relet the premises on behalf of the tenant. [CCP §1174(c)]

Relief from forfeiture

When a forfeiture of the leasehold for an original period of **more than one year** is declared in the 3-day notice and the landlord is awarded possession in a UD action, the tenant who wishes to remain in possession must, within 30 days of the forfeiture, make an application on a petition to the court for *relief from forfeiture*. If granted, the tenant's right to possession under the lease is *restored*. [CCP §1179]

Thus, the relief from forfeiture is sought primarily by nonresidential tenants who have long-term leases and are prepared to cure any defaults.

Only a court order can **restore** possession to the tenant under the lease since the declaration of forfeiture in the 3-day notice **terminated** the tenant's lawful right to possession on expiration of the three days. The tenant has no ability to unilaterally restore the leasehold and his right to possession after the leasehold interest has been terminated by forfeiture.

A tenant's relief from forfeiture and a reinstatement of the lease by court order are based on the degree of *hardship* the tenant would suffer if evicted. The application for relief and reinstatement of the lease or rental agreement, and restoring the leasehold estate and tenancy to the tenant, can be filed anytime before the actual eviction and removal of the tenant by the sheriff and the return of the premises to the landlord.

The court's granting the tenant relief from forfeiture must be:

- conditioned on the payment of all amounts due the landlord, including **full payment** of the rent due; and

- **full performance** of all lease or rental agreement conditions, whether oral or written.

Also, whether the right to possession has already been terminated by a declaration of forfeiture in the 3-day notice is of no concern to the court. [CCP §1179]

If an attorney for the tenant seeking relief appears on behalf of the tenant, a copy of the application for relief and petition for the hearing must be served on the landlord or property manager filing the UD action at least five days prior to the hearing. [CCP §1179]

The landlord needs to be prepared at the UD trial to defend against a motion for relief of forfeiture (i.e., why relief from the forfeiture would be unfair to the landlord, and if fair, the amounts owed and lease/rental conditions to be cured, etc.) since the court on its own may initiate an inquiry into whether the tenant is entitled to relief from forfeiture.

If the tenant is *in proper*, the tenant can make an oral request of the court at the UD trial in the presence of the landlord (or other plaintiff) to be relieved of the forfeiture and allowed (on conditions) to remain in possession.

The obligation to pay future rent

On termination of the tenant's leasehold estate under any 3-day notice, by forfeiture or by statute, the landlord is entitled to:

- file a UD action to physically remove the defaulting tenant from actual possession, called *eviction*, and enforce collection of rent earned and unpaid through entry of the UD judgment; and

- file a separate action to recover money due during the remaining term of the lease, called *future rents*, and any prior unpaid rent earned, but not included in the UD judgment.

Consider the tenant whose leasehold estate and the accompanying right to possession created by a lease is terminated prior to expiration of the lease.

The landlord's right to collect future rent after the tenant has been evicted is **independent and separate** from the tenant's right to occupy the property. One is a *contract right* (to collect money) and the other is a *real property right* (the leasehold estate). Different rules of law apply to the enforcement of each. [Walt, *supra*]

In a money action separate from the UD action, the landlord is entitled to recover:

- all unpaid rent earned under the lease agreement up until abandonment or a notice to pay, perform, or quit terminates the right to possession [CC §1951.2(a)(1)];

- reasonable per diem rent from the termination of the right to possession, until entry of the judgment for rent [CC §1951.2(a)(2)];

- all unearned rent called for in the lease agreement for the remaining unexpired term of the lease, subject to *loss mitigation*, default remedies in the lease, the prior reletting of the premises, and the discounted *present worth* of the future rent [CC §1951.2(a)(3)];

- costs incurred by the landlord as a result of the tenant's breach [CC §1951.2(a)(4)]; and

- attorney fees incurred if the lease contains an attorney fees provision. [CC §1717]

The separate money action to recover future rents can be filed immediately after the tenant has vacated or been evicted and his right to possession terminated.

Of course, double recovery of rent is not allowed. If the landlord in his UD action is awarded (or denied) rents accrued prior to the UD award, the landlord cannot again seek to recover those amounts in the separate money action for rents.

For the landlord to recover future rents after an early termination of possession due to abandonment or any 3-day notice, the landlord must either:

- have **reserved his right** to collect future rent payments by a provision in the lease, called a *default remedies clause* [See Fig. 1]; or

- **relet the property** in good faith prior to being awarded the future rent if the lease does not contain a default remedies clause, called *statutory recovery*. [CC §1951.2(c)]

Collecting future rents after eviction

Now consider a tenant who breaches the lease by failing to pay the rent when due.

The lease agreement contains a *default remedies clause* allowing the landlord to collect all remaining unpaid rents due under the lease after an early termination of possession. [See Fig. 1]

The landlord serves the tenant with a 3-day notice to pay rent or quit which includes a forfeiture provision.

On expiration of the three days and failure of the tenant to either pay or quit, the landlord brings a UD action to evict the tenant.

The landlord is awarded possession.

The UD judgment includes an award for rent earned and unpaid for the periods prior to entry of the UD judgment, and attorney fees.

Later, the landlord brings a separate money action to recover the unpaid rent due over the remaining term of the lease to expiration.

The tenant claims the landlord is barred from recovering the unpaid rent since a forfeiture of the lease was declared.

However, the declaration of a forfeiture in the 3-day notice does not bar the landlord from collecting future rents called for in the lease. [**Danner** v. **Jarrett** (1983) 144 CA3d 164]

The declaration of the forfeiture terminates the tenant's right to cure the breach after the 3-day notice expires, unless the tenant can show *hardship* and fully perform on the lease. [CCP §§1174.5; 1179]

Even if the lease agreement does not contain a default remedies clause, statutory provisions permit the landlord to recover future rents after termination of possession. However, without a default remedies clause, the landlord must first relet the premises before seeking recovery of the future rent. [CC §1951.2(a)(3),(c)]

Loss mitigation affects future rents

With or without a default remedies clause in a lease, the landlord who seeks to recover future rents is compelled to *mitigate his loss* of rent after the tenant vacates or is evicted.

If the landlord does not act to reduce his loss of future rental income, a tenant has the right to offset any future rent due under his lease by the amount of rent the landlord could have reasonably collected by reletting the space. [CC §1951.2(c)]

Consider the tenant who fails to pay rent called for in the lease.

Ultimately, a UD judgment is entered in the landlord's favor, and the tenant is evicted under a *writ of possession* issued by the court.

Having repossessed the property, the landlord, in an effort to mitigate his losses, takes steps to relet the property. The property is listed with a real estate broker to locate a tenant for the property.

During the effort to relet, the evicted tenant offers to lease the property at the old rental rate.

The owner refuses the evicted tenant's offer. Later, he relets the property at a lower rental rate to a more creditworthy tenant.

The landlord then seeks to recover his money losses from the evicted tenant for the difference between the lesser amount of rent the new tenant has agreed to pay — the offset — and the greater amount of rent due and unpaid through the expiration of the evicted tenant's lease.

The evicted tenant claims the landlord is barred from collecting any unpaid future rent since the landlord could have recovered the full amount of rental payments had the landlord not rejected his offer to lease.

Is the evicted tenant liable for the deficiency created by the difference between all rent remaining unpaid on his lease and the amount of rent the new tenant has agreed to pay?

Yes! The tenant owes the deficiency remaining in future rents on the terminated lease after reletting the premises. The landlord's effort to mitigate the loss of rents by reletting the property was in good faith and reasonable.

The reasonableness of the landlord's conduct undertaken to relet the space is determined based on the **actions actually taken** by the landlord, not by evaluating courses of action which were available or that the landlord could have taken to mitigate damages (such as re-renting to the evicted tenant).

Here, the landlord actively sought a new tenant and was unable to get the full amount of the rent the evicted tenant had agreed to pay through the expiration of his lease. [**Zanker Development Co.** v. **Cogito Systems Inc.** (1989) 215 CA3d 1377]

Thus, a landlord must pursue a course of action which is likely to reduce the amount of future rent the tenant owes under the lease agreement after the tenancy (leasehold) is terminated.

If not, the tenant is permitted to offset future rents by showing the landlord's efforts (or lack thereof) to relet the property were unreasonable efforts to *mitigate* the loss of rent.

Future rent discounted

From the time the tenant defaults in the payment of rent to the time of the award of rent, the landlord is entitled to **recover interest** on the earned and unpaid amounts of rent from the date each payment of rent became due until trial.

Fig. 1 *Excerpt from* **first tuesday** *Form 552 — Nonresidential Lease Agreement*

23. Default Remedies:

    23.1 If the Tenant breaches any provision of this lease, the Landlord may exercise its rights, including the right to collect future rental losses after forfeiture of possession.

The interest accrued prior to judgment is calculated at the rate agreed to in the lease. If the interest rate is not stated in the lease, the interest will accrue at 10% per annum from the date of default to entry of the money judgment. Thereafter, interest accrues (at 10%) on the money judgment until paid. [CC §§1951.2(b); 3289]

However, the landlord who recovers **future rent** which became due under the lease after entry of judgment will only be awarded the *present value* of the unearned future rents.

To determine the **present value** of unearned rent at the time of the court's money award, the future rents will be discounted (to their present value) at the annual rate of 1% over the Federal Reserve Bank of San Francisco's discount rate. The bank's discount rate during most of 2002 was 1.75%. Thus, the discount rate for 2002 was 2.75%. [CC §1951.2(b)]

Costs to relet

Since the landlord has a duty to mitigate rental losses over the remaining term of a lease after abandonment or eviction, the landlord is also entitled to recover all **reasonable costs** he incurs to relet the property to mitigate the loss of rental income after the tenant is no longer in possession. [CC §1951.2(a)(4)]

Costs are expenses incurred to relet the property, including:

- costs to clean up the property;

- brokerage and legal fees to find a new tenant;

- permit fees to construct necessary improvements or renovations; and

- any other money losses incurred as a result of the tenant's breach. [**Sanders Construction Company, Inc.** v. **San Joaquin First Federal Savings and Loan Association** (1982) 136 CA3d 387]

Cancellation of the lease agreement

Future rents will become uncollectible if the landlord and tenant agree the right to possession (under real estate law) and the tenant's obligation to pay rent (under contract law) are both terminated, called a *surrender* or *cancellation* of the lease agreement.

Termination of the lease only refers to the landlord's forfeiture of the tenant's right to possession under the leasehold conveyed by the landlord under the lease agreement.

To avoid a surrender, the landlord must ensure all 3-day notices and other communication, including those of his agents, state the landlord's only intent is to declare a *forfeiture* of the lease (leasehold), not a *cancellation* of the lease (agreement).

A cancellation of the lease agreement results in a termination of the tenant's contract obligation to pay future rent. The cancellation is comparable to an owner's deed-in-lieu of foreclosure, given to a lender, in exchange for the lender's cancellation of the debt owed on a trust deed note.

Chapter 18

Delinquent rent and notice to pay

This chapter discusses the requirements and results of the 3-day notice to pay rent or quit in residential and nonresidential income properties.

Forfeit possession in three days

A tenant, residential or nonresidential, fails to pay the agreed rents on the *due date* or prior to expiration of the *grace period*. The rent is now *delinquent*.

The landlord's property manager *serves* the tenant with a 3-day notice to pay rent or quit the premises. [See Form 575 accompanying this chapter]

The 3-day notice states the **exact amount** of delinquent rent and any other amounts owed the landlord which are delinquent, the monetary aspect of the lease or rental agreement entered into by the tenant.

Further, the notice contains a *lease forfeiture clause* which states the landlord's *election to forfeit* the tenant's possessory interest in the property — the leasehold interest conveyed under the lease or rental agreement — and recover possession of the property in the event the tenant fails to pay the delinquent rent before the notice expires.

After the 3-day notice expires, the tenant still in possession tenders payment of the delinquent rent to the landlord.

The landlord refuses to accept the payment. The tenant refuses to voluntarily vacate.

The landlord files an unlawful detainer (UD) action seeking to evict the tenant and regain possession of the premises. The landlord claims the tenant's possessory rights to the property have been terminated by the expiration of the 3-day notice and election to forfeit, and cannot now be *reinstated*.

Can the landlord evict the tenant even though the tenant tendered the delinquent rent in full after expiration of the 3-day notice and before the UD trial?

Yes! The tenant's right to possession was terminated by the election to forfeit the lease and expiration of the 3-day notice. Thus, his occupancy became unlawful on expiration of the 3-day notice since the landlord or the landlord's property manager did not receive the delinquent rent before expiration of the notice containing a forfeiture declaration. [Calif. Code of Civil Procedure §§1161(2); 1174(a)]

On expiration, the landlord is no longer obligated to accept delinquent rent payments and allow the lease or rental agreement to be *reinstated* when:

- the landlord **does not actually receive payment before** the notice expires; and

- the landlord declares in the 3-day notice his **election to forfeit** the tenant's right to possession on expiration of the notice. [CCP §1174(a)]

Default, notice and cure/vacate

A tenant *defaults* on his rental or lease agreement by failing to:

- pay rent and any other **amounts due** called for in the lease or rental agreement; or

- perform nonmonetary obligations called for in the lease or rental agreement.

On a tenant's default, the landlord may make a demand on the tenant to cure the default or quit the premises.

However, only a default by the tenant which is a *material breach* allows for the forfeiture of the tenancy.

Failure to pay rent or perform other obligations called for in the lease or rental agreement is a material breach. Conversely, the tenant's failure to pay late charges, interest penalties, bad check charges or security deposits are minor breaches, which alone does not justify a demand to cure or quit under a 3-day notice. [**Keating** v. **Preston** (1940) 42 CA2d 110]

A failure to pay additional sums agreed on to increase the security deposit is not a failure to pay *rent*. Rent must be delinquent before a 3-day notice can be served to collect all amounts due and unpaid. A security deposit is *security* for the payment of rent. A security deposit is not rent. Thus, failure to make a security deposit payment is not a basis for a 3-day notice since it is not rent.

Some nonmonetary defaults by a tenant cannot be cured, such as waste to the premises, alienation of the leasehold or significant criminal activity which has occurred on the property, called *incurable breaches*. The landlord's remedy for an incurable breach is to serve notice on the tenant to quit the premises within three days after service, leaving no alternative but to vacate. Here, a lease forfeiture clause is not required, as nothing remains to be cured or reinstated. [CCP §1161(4)]

Three days between notice and UD

When a tenant does not *timely pay* the agreed rent, the landlord is entitled to serve the tenant with a written notice demanding the tenant pay all amounts due or vacate the premises within three days, called a *3-day notice to pay rent or quit*.

A tenant has three calendar days, day one being the **day after service** of the notice, to pay the delinquent rental amounts and avoid forfeiture of the lease and eviction. [Calif. Civil Code §10]

The tenant cures the default and retains his right to possession by paying the amount stated before the 3-day notice to pay or quit expires. [CCP §1161.5]

To cure the default in rent payments, the tenant may deliver the payment by an electronic funds transfer if the **electronic transfer** has been previously established between the landlord and the tenant.

If such a procedure has not been established, the tenant must deliver the total amount due as directed in the 3-day notice:

- to the person named on the 3-day notice at the address listed (and if personal delivery is requested, during the hours and days noted); or
- into the bank account number of the financial institution given on the 3-day notice.

During the three-day notice period, the tenant may **tender payment** of the rent in the same manner the tenant made past rental payments — by personal or company check, money order, cashier's check, cash or electronic transfer. [**Strom** v. **Union Oil Co.** (1948) 88 CA2d 78]

A tenant's rent which is paid by check and received on time by the landlord sometimes becomes delinquent due to the tenant's lack of sufficient funds on deposit with his bank. The landlord can now serve a 3-day notice to pay or quit since the rent is delinquent. However, he cannot demand payment by cash or money order in the 3-day notice since the tenant has been paying rent by check.

Further, the rent check received by the landlord during the 3-day notice period must be paid by the tenant's bank. If it is returned for lack of sufficient funds, the delinquent rent has not been paid, the notice has expired and the landlord may file a UD action.

THREE-DAY NOTICE TO PAY RENT OR QUIT

DATE:_____, 20_____, at _____ , California

To Tenant: _____

Items left blank or unchecked are not applicable.

FACTS:

You are a Tenant under a lease or rental agreement

Dated _____, entered into by

_____ , Tenant,

and _____ , Landlord,

recorded _____, as Instrument No. _____,

in _____County Records, California,

regarding real estate referred to as: _____

NOTICE:

1. You are in breach of the payment of amounts due under the lease or rental agreement

2. Within three (3) days after service of this notice you are required to either:

2.1 Pay rent and other amounts now due and unpaid in the **Total Amount** of . . . . $_____,
representing rent for the periods of:

_____, 20_____ to _____, 20_____ Amount $_____
_____, 20_____ to _____, 20_____ Amount $_____
_____, 20_____ to _____, 20_____ Amount $_____

and amounts due for:

☐ returned check fees of .... $_____
☐ late charge fees of .... $_____
☐ common area maintenance of .... $_____
☐ association assessments of .... $_____
☐ property taxes of .... $_____
☐ interest on delinquent rent of .... $_____

The Total Amount due to be paid in one of the following manners:

a. to: _____ (Name)
_____ (Address)
_____
_____ (Phone)

Personal delivery of the Total Amount due will be accepted at the above address during the hours of
_____am to _____pm on the following days:_____

b. By deposit into account number _____
at: _____ (Financial Institution)
_____ (Address)
_____

c. By the electronic funds transfer previously established between Landlord and Tenant.

OR

2.2 Deliver possession of the premises to the Landlord or: _____
_____

3. If you fail to pay the Total Amount due, or to deliver possession of the premises within three (3) days, legal proceedings will be initiated against you to regain possession of the premises and to recover the amounts owed, treble damages, costs and attorney fees.

4. The Landlord hereby elects to declare a forfeiture of the lease or rental agreement if you fail to pay the Total Amount demanded above.

4.1 Landlord reserves the right to pursue collection of any future loss of rent allowed by Civil Code §1951.2.

Date:_____, 20_____

Landlord/Agent: _____

Signature: _____

Address:_____

Phone:_____ Fax: _____

FORM 575   07-02   ©2003 **first tuesday**, P.O. BOX 20069 RIVERSIDE, CA 92516 (800) 794-0494

Note — Consider a tenant under a month-to-month rental agreement whose rent checks are returned due to insufficient funds. To modify the method of payment, the landlord must serve the tenant with a written 30-day notice advising the tenant he now is to pay rent by cash or cashier's check. [CC §827]

One year rent limitation

Unpaid rents which **became due** more than one year before service of a 3-day notice may not be included in a 3-day notice.

If rents due for more than one year are included, the 3-day notice is defective and will not terminate the right to possession. More rent has been demanded than will be awarded by a court in a UD action. Thus, any UD action based on the defective notice will fail due to the excessive rent demanded in the UD action. [**Bevill** v. **Zoura** (1994) 27 CA4th 694]

However, the landlord may recover rents and other amounts delinquent for more than one year by pursuing collection in a separate civil action and not in an eviction (UD) action.

The time period for a landlord's recovery of due and unpaid amounts in a separate money action from a UD action is four years, called a *statute of limitations*. [CCP §337]

Before a landlord or his property manager serves a tenant with a 3-day notice to pay rent or quit, the following questions must be answered:

- Is the rent delinquent?

- What amounts are due and unpaid?

- When can rent earned be estimated in the 3-day notice?

- What is a reasonable estimate of delinquent rent?

- When does the 3-day notice expire?

- When does the tenant's right to possession terminate? and

- How are subtenants evicted?

The holdover tenant

When a lease contains a holdover provision, the landlord's failure to evict the tenant after serving a 3-day notice does not create a month-to-month tenancy with rent due as stated in the holdover provision. [**Walt** v. **Superior Court** (1992) 8 CA4th 1667]

Similarly, a 3-day notice is not required once a 30-day notice to vacate served on a tenant has expired since a 30-day notice also establishes an unlawful detainer. [CC §1946]

A holdover occurs when a tenant remains in possession after the agreed-to lease term expires, not when the 3-day notice expires. When a tenant holds over, the landlord may immediately file a UD action without serving any notice. [CCP §1161(1)]

However, a landlord under an expired lease should only seek to recover possession, not rent, in a UD action filed against the holdover tenant.

Then in a separate action, the landlord can recover money losses under the holdover provision for the period of the tenant's unlawful detainer.

Typically, holdover rent exceeds fair rental value and will not be the basis for rent awards in a UD action.

When is the rent delinquent?

Rent must be delinquent before a 3-day notice to pay or quit may be served.

Rent becomes **delinquent**:

- the day following the last calendar day of the *grace period* established in the lease or rental agreement; or

- the day following the due date, when the lease or rental agreement does not provide for a grace period.

However, when the last day scheduled for payment of rent falls on a legal holiday, the payment may be *tendered* on the **next business day**.

A *legal holiday* is every Saturday, Sunday and any other day designated by the state as a holiday, which includes federal holidays. [CCP §§10; 12a]

Thus, if the last day of a *grace period* for payment of past due rent (which could be the due date) falls on a legal holiday, the tenant's rent payment is not delinquent if it is received by the landlord on the first business day following the legal holiday. [CCP §13; Calif. Government Code §6706]

To initiate the **rent collection process**, a landlord serves a tenant with a 3-day notice to pay rent or quit. The notice may be served on any day after the grace period has expired without the payment of the rent, called a *delinquency*.

A *grace period* is stated in a lease or rental agreement as a set time period following the due date during which rent may be paid without incurring a late charge.

While rent may be unpaid and past due, it is not *delinquent* until the grace period expires and a late charge may be demanded.

Consider a landlord and tenant who enter into a lease which states rent is due on the first day of each month, the *due date*.

The lease also contains a **late charge provision** which imposes an additional charge if rent payments are not *received* on or before the tenth of the month. A grace period is not mentioned in the lease.

Each month, the tenant pays his rent after the late charge would be incurred. The landlord accepts the tenant's late rental payments every month, but makes no demand for payment of the late charge. [See **first tuesday** Form 569]

Finally, on receipt of yet another late payment, the landlord informs the tenant all future rent payments, including the next month's rent which is due in a few days, must be received by the landlord prior to incurring a late charge.

The next month, the late charge period runs and rent has not been paid.

The day the late charge is incurred, the landlord serves the tenant with a 3-day notice to pay rent or quit. The tenant does not pay rent before the 3-day notice expires. The landlord files a UD action.

As in the prior months, the tenant tenders the rent payment to the landlord after the late charge is incurred. However, the landlord refuses to accept the payment.

Has the landlord established an unlawful detainer on expiration of the 3-day notice?

No! The 3-day notice is premature and useless. The tenant's rent had not yet become **delinquent** since rent is not delinquent until the grace period — including *extensions* authorized by the landlord's acceptance of late payments — has run.

The lease established a **grace period** by calling for an additional charge after the tenth. Thus, payments received after the tenth are delinquent. However, the landlord's consistent acceptance of rent payments after the grace period *without imposing the late charge* was conduct which extended the grace period. [**Baypoint Mortgage** v. **Crest Premium Real Estate Investments Retirement Trust** (1985) 168 CA3d 818]

Thus, the tenant's tender of rent after the written grace period ran, but on or before the extended date set by conduct, was timely.

For the landlord to **re-establish his ability** to enforce payment within the written grace period, the landlord must give reasonable advance notice of the change in terms of payment — 30 days — to the tenant of his intent to enforce the written grace period.

The 30-day notice to reinstate the grace period agreed to in the lease or rental agreement should state all rent payments due following the expiration of the 30 days must be received within the written grace period, prior to delinquency. If not received, a 3-day notice will be served and the late charge imposed in the agreed-to amount.

Note — For payments made on loans secured by single-family, owner-occupied residential dwellings:

- *the borrower is given a statutory 10-day grace period; and*

- *the amount of the late charge is limited to the greater of 6% of the installment due or $5. [CC §2954.4(a)]*

No statutory grace period or late charge limitations exist for rent payments made by tenants. The legislature should provide residential tenants with similar statutory protection (and landlord guidance) to establish consistent expectations among residential tenants and residential landlords.

Accurate residential rent demands

To be valid, the 3-day notice to pay rent or quit served on a **residential tenant** must state the *exact amount* of money due which has not been paid. This is not the case for nonresidential rent when the exact amount cannot be accurately ascertained when the notice is served.

A residential tenant is not required to pay more than the amount due and unpaid to retain his possessory right under his lease or rental agreement. Likewise for nonresidential tenants, even if their rent paid is estimated.

Collecting late charges

Late charges demanded and unpaid are properly included in a 3-day notice to pay rent or quit since delinquent late charges are sums due under the lease. [**Canal-Randolph Anaheim, Inc.** v. **Moore** (1978) 78 CA3d 477]

However, in a UD action, many municipal court judges, as a matter of discretion, will declare invalid a 3-day notice which includes any late charges. [See Chapter 20]

Conversely, a UD action based solely on the failure to pay late charges, bad checks fees, accrued interest or the deposit of additional security will not stand. [See Chapter 20]

To collect unpaid late charges other than by a deduction from the security deposit, the landlord may file a small claims or municipal court action.

A property manager retained by a landlord to manage his residential or nonresidential rental property may represent the landlord in small claims court to recover money due under a lease or rental agreement related to the property managed. [CCP §116.540(h)]

If the amount stated in a 3-day notice served on a **residential tenant** exceeds the amounts due and unpaid at the time of the UD trial, the notice is invalid. [**Jayasinghe** v. **Lee** (1993) 13 CA4th Supp. 33]

For both residential and nonresidential tenants, if the amount stated in the 3-day notice is less than the actual amount due and unpaid, the tenant may pay the amount stated and avoid eviction.

To collect any omitted amounts, the landlord must serve another 3-day notice to pay the balance or quit.

Estimated nonresidential rent

When the property leased is nonresidential, the 3-day notice may include an *estimate* of the amounts due if:

- the notice states the amount due is an estimate; and

- the amount estimated is reasonable. [CCP §1161.1(a)]

Failure to indicate in the 3-day notice that an estimate of the amount due is **an estimate** renders the 3-day notice invalid.

Further, if the landlord knows the **exact amount** of the delinquent rent and other monies owed, and then states a different amount as the amount due in the 3-day notice and declares it an estimate, the landlord will be unable to evict the tenant. The notice is defective for terminating the right to possession since the exact amount of the delinquency is known.

Also, including amounts in the 3-day notice which are not yet due, such as unbilled common area maintenance expenses (CAMs), is not a reasonable estimate of *delinquent amounts*. [**WDT-Winchester** v. **Nilsson** (1994) 27 CA4th 516]

An estimate of rent owed in a 3-day notice is **considered reasonable** if the actual amount owed is in question and the delinquent amount demanded is neither 20% **more or less** than the amount determined due at the UD hearing. [CCP §1161.1(e)]

Estimating known amounts

Consider a tenant who leases nonresidential property. The lease agreement states the tenant will pay his proportionate share of the property taxes and assessments.

It is agreed the landlord will first pay all property taxes and assessments on the premises before making a written demand on the tenant for payment of the tenant's proportionate share.

Before the landlord pays the property taxes, the landlord makes a written demand on the tenant for payment of his portion of the unpaid property taxes.

The tenant does not pay his share of the taxes demanded by the landlord. The tenant also fails to make his regular monthly rental payment.

The landlord serves the tenant with a 3-day notice to pay rent or quit. The 3-day notice states the amount due includes unpaid rent and the tenant's proportionate share of the property taxes.

The total amount does not exceed 20% of the periodic rent, and the notice indicates the amount is an estimate.

The tenant neither pays the amount stated in the notice nor vacates the premises.

The landlord files a UD action.

The tenant claims the 3-day notice is invalid and does not terminate his possessory interest and establish an unlawful detainer since he did not yet owe property taxes on the date the notice was served.

The landlord claims the 3-day notice is valid since the estimated amount was within 20% of the actual amount due.

Is the 3-day notice valid?

No! The 3-day notice is invalid. It is not reasonable for the landlord to estimate rents when he knows the exact amount owed by the tenant. [WDT-Winchester, *supra*]

Further, the portion of taxes demanded from the tenant as additional rent was not yet due or delinquent. The landlord had not yet paid the property taxes, an agreed-to requisite to a demand for reimbursement.

Under the lease, the tenant's obligation to pay the tenant's share of the property taxes only arises after the landlord actually pays the property taxes, demands reimbursement and payment of the reimbursement becomes delinquent.

(Guess)timating unknown amounts

Now consider a tenant who takes possession of property under a "percentage" lease agreement.

The rent provisions in the lease state:

- the rent is payable annually on each anniversary of the lease in an amount equal to 20% of the gross sales proceeds; and

- the tenant is to provide the landlord with the amount of his gross sales proceeds.

The tenant fails to either furnish the landlord with the sales proceeds figure or make the annual rental payment.

The landlord serves the tenant with a 3-day notice to pay rent or quit. The notice states:

- the amount of rent which is due and unpaid in an amount equal to 20% of the tenant's gross sales proceeds; and

- only the tenant knows the amount of the sales proceeds.

The tenant does not pay the rent before the 3-day notice expires.

The landlord files a UD action.

The tenant claims the 3-day notice is invalid since the notice did not state the amount of rent due.

Can the landlord evict the tenant even though the 3-day notice did not state the dollar amount of the unpaid and delinquent rent?

Yes! The tenant cannot prevent the landlord from enforcing his right to receive rent or recover possession by failing to provide the landlord with the means needed — the amount of his sales proceeds — to determine the rental amount and then claim the 3-day notice is defective.

The purpose of a 3-day notice is to give a tenant the opportunity to avoid forfeiture of his leasehold estate by paying the delinquent rent. [**Valov** v. **Tank** (1985) 168 CA3d 867]

Rent estimates by nonresidential tenants

On receiving a 3-day notice which states the rental amount due is an estimate, the nonresidential tenant in response may tender the amount of rent the tenant estimates is due. [CCP §1161.1(a)]

If the amount estimated and tendered by the tenant is determined in the UD action to be equal or greater than the rent due, the tenant will retain his right to possession. Likewise, if the amount tendered as the tenant's estimate of the rent due was reasonable, but less than the amount actually due, the tenant can retain possession by paying within five days after entry of the UD judgment:

- the amount of back rent determined due if the landlord refused tender, or the difference between the tenant's payment and the amount due if the landlord accepted the tenant's payment; and

- other sums awarded the landlord. [CCP §1161.1(a)]

Three days to pay after notice

The time period for expiration of the 3-day notice and when a UD action may be filed is controlled by statute. [See Chapter 19]

For example, a landlord serves a tenant with a 3-day notice on a Wednesday.

The first calendar day of the 3-day notice period is the next day, Thursday. The second day is Friday. Saturday is the third calendar day, but Saturday, the third and final day to cure the default, is not a business day on which the notice can expire; nor is Sunday, since the weekend days are legal holidays in California.

Further, Monday is Memorial Day, a legal holiday, not a business day. Thus, the final day on which the tenant may pay delinquent rent and avoid eviction is Tuesday — the first business day on which the notice can expire.

Thus, the landlord can file a UD action no sooner than the next court day after the notice actually expires, which is Wednesday, if the tenant does not pay the rent on or before Tuesday. In this "expiration on a business day" situation, the landlord could have waited until Friday to serve the 3-day notice and obtained the same end result.

Therefore, when the final day of the 3-day notice falls on a holiday such as a Saturday, Sunday or legal holiday, the 3-day notice expires on the next business day. [**Lamanna** v. **Vognar** (1993) 17 CA4th Supp. 4; CCP §12a]

However, unlike the service of documents in civil actions, mailing of the 3-day notice for failure of personal service does not extend the three-day notice period an additional five days. [**Losornio** v. **Motta** (1998) 67 CA4th 110]

Subtenant evictions by the landlord

For a landlord to regain possession when the (master) tenant defaults and a subtenant occupies the premises, the 3-day notice must also **name** the subtenant as a tenant in default and be served on the subtenant. [CCP §1161]

Thus, serving a subtenant with a copy of the 3-day notice which only names the master tenant will result in the subtenant retaining his right to possession. [**Briggs** v. **Electronic Memories & Magnetic Corporation** (1975) 53 CA3d 900]

Conversely, a landlord who wishes to evict a defaulting master tenant but retain the subtenant may do so. The landlord is not required to serve the subtenant with a 3-day notice when only the master tenant is being evicted. [**Chinese Hospital Foundation Fund** v. **Patterson** (1969) 1 CA3d 627]

For example, a landlord consents to a sublease which contains an *attornment provision*. Should the master tenant default and forfeit his right to possession, the landlord can take over the sublease under the attornment clause and be assured the subtenant will remain obligated to perform on the sublease. [See Chapter 40]

Under the sublease's **attornment provision**, the subtenant has agreed to recognize the landlord as his landlord in lieu of the master tenant should the landlord elect to forfeit the master tenant's leasehold and recognize the subtenant as the landlord's tenant.

However, a subtenant who takes possession of the premises after the master tenant has been served with a 3-day notice will be evicted on the landlord's successful completion of a UD action. [CCP §1164]

Chapter 19

Three-day notices to quit

This chapter discusses the proper 3-day notice to serve on a tenant for a material breach of a lease, other than for past due amounts of money.

Curable and incurable nonmonetary breaches

On a routine inspection of an apartment complex, the property manager observes a pet in one of the units. All the leases and rental agreements with tenants of the complex prohibit the keeping of a pet on the premises.

As a courtesy, the tenant of the unit is asked, both orally and by a personal note left with the tenant, to remove the pet. However, the tenant retains the pet. [See Chapter 37]

To enforce the pet provision in the tenant's lease, the property manager prepares a 3-day notice to **perform or quit**. The notice is served on the tenant.

The notice gives the tenant an ultimatum — either remove the pet (the performance required) or vacate the unit within three days. [See Form 576 accompanying this chapter]

The tenant fails to remove the pet from the premises and remains in the unit after the 3-day notice expires.

Can an unlawful detainer (UD) action be maintained to evict the tenant for failure to either remove the pet or vacate under the 3-day notice?

Yes! On expiration of the 3-day notice to perform by removing the pet or vacating, the tenant may be evicted if the conditions have not been met. The tenant has breached the provision in his lease which prohibits him from keeping a pet on the premises. [Calif. Code of Civil Procedure §1161(3)]

However, had the tenant breached a provision in his lease or rental agreement which the tenant could not perform within three days, the landlord or property manager would serve a 3-day **notice to quit** the premises giving no alternative to perform and remain on the premises. [CCP §1161(3)]

Types of 3-day notices

The 3-day notice served on a tenant must be the correct type before the tenant's unlawful detainer (holdover) of a premises can be established and the tenant evicted.

Depending on the nature and extent of the tenant's breach, one of the following types of 3-day notices may be served:

- a 3-Day Notice to Pay Rent or Quit [See **first tuesday** Form 575];

- a 3-Day Notice to Perform or Quit [See Form 576]; or

- a 3-Day Notice to Quit. [See Form 577 accompanying this chapter]

When a tenant's breach is the failure to pay rent or other money obligation which is due, the tenant is served with a 3-day notice *to pay rent or quit*. [See Chapter 18]

When the lease provision breached is not for rent or other money obligation, called a *nonmonetary breach*, and the breach can still be quickly corrected by the tenant, the tenant is served with a 3-day notice *to perform or quit*. [See Form 576]

Should the tenant be in default on both the payment of money and a curable nonmonetary provision in the lease, such as the obligation to maintain the landscaping, a 3-day notice to perform or quit is used.

The demand to pay rent is listed as an additional (monetary) breach to be cured under the notice to perform or quit.

A 3-day notice *to quit* which contains no alternative to vacating is served on a tenant if the tenant's breach is:

- impossible to cure in three days [**Matthew** v. **Digges** (1920) 45 CA 561]; or

- a statutory breach, such as an unauthorized subletting of the premises, nuisance or unlawful conduct on the premises. [CCP §1161(4); see Form 577]

The 3-day notice to quit requires the tenant to vacate the premises.

Notice to perform or quit

The 3-day notice to perform or quit requires the tenant to either:

- perform under the breached lease provision; or

- vacate the premises. [CCP §1161(3)]

The tenant's breach of the lease or rental agreement must be a *significant breach*, called a *material breach*, to justify serving a 3-day notice to perform or quit. A minor or trivial breach of the lease, such as a failure to pay late charges or bad check fees, will not support a 3-day notice. [**Baypoint Mortgage** v. **Crest Premium Real Estate Investments Retirement Trust** (1985) 168 CA3d 818]

In order for the tenant to avoid a forfeiture of his right to occupy the property, he must be given an opportunity to *reinstate* the lease or rental agreement — if the breach can be cured in three days.

The 3-day notice to perform or quit will specify the provision breached and the action required to cure the breach.

When the tenant cures the breach before the 3-day notice expires, the lease or rental agreement is *reinstated* and possession continues as though no breach occurred.

To eliminate the tenant's right to also **reinstate** the lease or rental agreement after the 3-day notice expires (for a period ending five days after the UD trial), the notice must clearly state the landlord's **election to terminate** the tenant's right to possession should the tenant fail to perform, called a *lease forfeiture clause*. [CCP §1174(a); see Chapter 17]

The tenant who vacates instead of performing forfeits his **possessory right** to occupy the lease premises. Further, the tenant cannot reinstate the lease after expiration of the 3-day notice to perform or quit if the landlord declares his election to terminate possession by a forfeiture in the notice.

In spite of the forfeiture of the right to possession, the lease agreement, including provisions imposing obligations on the tenant to pay money, remains fully enforceable by the landlord after the tenant's leasehold interest is terminated.

The tenant's failure to either cure the breach by performance or vacating within the three days following service of a notice which contains an election to forfeit allows the landlord to initiate a UD action and have the tenant removed. [CCP §1161(3)]

Curable nonmonetary breaches

A tenant operates a retail business on leased premises. The lease agreement calls for the tenant to periodically provide the landlord with a list of his inventory of sales merchandise. Also, the landlord is permitted to examine the tenant's business records.

Upon the landlord's request, the tenant does not provide the inventories or permit the landlord to examine his business records.

30-DAY NOTICE TO PERFORM OR QUIT

DATE:_____, 20_____, at _____, California

To Tenant: _____

Items left blank or unchecked are not applicable.

FACTS:

You are a Tenant under a rental agreement or expired lease

Dated _____, at

_____, California,

entered into by _____, Tenant,

and _____, Landlord,

recorded _____, as Instrument No. _____,

in _____ County Records, California.

<table>
<tr><td>

NOTICE:

A tenant who fails to perform any terms of the lease/rental agreement which can be performed or rectified must within three (3) days after service of written notice of the breach either cure the breach or vacate and deliver possession of the premises to the landlord. [California Code of Civil Procedure §1161(3)]

</td></tr>
</table>

NOTICE:

1. You are in breach of the terms of your lease/rental agreement as follows: _____

    _____

    _____

2. Within three (3) days after service of this notice, you are required to either:

    2.1 Perform or rectify the breach by: _____

    _____

    OR

    2.2 Deliver possession of the premises to Landlord or: _____

    _____

3. If you fail to cure the breach or to deliver possession within three (3) days, legal proceedings may be initiated to regain possession of the premises and to recover the rent owed, treble damages, costs and attorney fees.

4. Landlord hereby elects to declare a forfeiture of your lease/rental agreement if you fail to cure the breach noted above.

    4.1 Landlord reserves the right to pursue collection of any future rental losses allowed by Civil Code §1951.2.

Date:_____, 20_____

Landlord/Agent: _____

Signature: _____

Address:_____

_____

Phone: _____

Fax: _____

E-mail: _____

The landlord serves the tenant with a 3-day notice to quit the premises — no alternative performance to vacate is given to allow the tenant to rectify the failures and stay.

The tenant does not vacate the premises.

The landlord files a UD action, seeking to evict the tenant since he breached a material lease obligation.

The tenant claims he cannot be evicted since the 3-day notice did not give the tenant the alternative to perform his lease obligations by delivering inventory lists and records to avoid a forfeiture of possession.

Can the landlord maintain a UD action against the tenant based on the 3-day notice to quit?

No! The 3-day notice served on the tenant must be in the alternative — perform or quit — since the tenant could have handed over an inventory to the landlord and given the landlord access to the business records, all within three days. [**Hinman** v. **Wagnon** (1959) 172 CA2d 24]

A landlord must allow a tenant to cure a breach, monetary or nonmonetary, within three days after notice when the lease provision breached calls for the tenant's performance of an act which the tenant is capable of performing within three days. [CCP §1161(3)]

Notice to quit with no alternative

If the provision breached by the tenant calls for or prohibits an activity which cannot be performed or rectified within three days, the tenant may be served with a 3-day notice to quit. No alternative need be included, as nothing can be done or remains to be done which the tenant can do (or stop doing) within three days. [CCP §1161(3); see Form 577]

For example, possession can be recovered by service and expiration of a 3-day notice to quit based on *statutory forfeitures* when a tenant:

- maintains a *nuisance* on the premises;

- uses the premises for an *unlawful purpose*; or

- *assigns, sublets* or *commits waste* to the premises in breach of a lease provision. [CCP §1161(4)]

The 3-day notice to quit does not need to indicate the provision breached or the activity of the tenant that constitutes the breach, such as an unlawful use, nor does it need to include a lease forfeiture declaration by the landlord.

The right to possession is *automatically forfeited* by the breach, not by the 3-day notice, and possession may not be reinstated unless the landlord chooses to waive the forfeiture.

The landlord serves a 3-day notice to quit only because the notice is a requisite to the recovery of possession in a UD action, as a forfeiture of the lease has already occurred by statute. [CCP §1161(4)]

Quit! The breach cannot be undone

Consider a tenant who leases agricultural property. The lease states the tenant's use of the property is limited to grazing sheep. However, the tenant plants a crop on the property, a breach of the use provision in the lease.

Based on the tenant's **unauthorized use** of the premises, the landlord initiates the eviction process by serving a 3-day notice to quit on the tenant.

Here, the tenant's use of the property to raise a crop, instead of the single agreed-to use as a pasture, is an *incurable nonmonetary breach* of the tenant's lease. The tenant cannot reverse the effects of raising the crop on the soil as it has occurred and cannot now be undone. [**Harris** v. **Bissell** (1921) 54 CA 307]

Consider also a tenant of agricultural property which contains an orchard. The lease obligates the tenant to poison squirrels on the property to control the agricultural pest.

The tenant does not take the required action to poison the squirrels, and the premises becomes infested with squirrels.

30-DAY NOTICE TO QUIT

DATE:_____, 20_____, at _____, California

To Tenant: _____

Items left blank or unchecked are not applicable.

FACTS:

You are a Tenant under a lease or rental agreement

Dated _____, at

_____ , California,

entered into by _____ ,Tenant,

and _____ , Landlord,

recorded _____, as Instrument No. _____,

in _____ County Records, California,

regarding real estate referred to as: _____

_____

_____

> **NOTICE:**
> A tenant must vacate and deliver possession to the landlord within three (3) days after service of written notice for breach of any terms of the lease/rental agreement which cannot be performed or rectified. [California Code of Civil Procedure §1161(4)]

NOTICE:

1. You are in breach of the terms of your lease/rental agreement as follows:

    _____

    _____

    _____

    _____

    _____

2. Within three (3) days after service of this notice you are required to vacate and deliver possession of the premises to Landlord or:_____

3. If you fail to vacate and deliver possession of the premises within three (3) days, legal proceedings may be initiated to regain possession of the premises and to recover the rent owed, treble damages, costs, and attorney fees.

4. Landlord hereby elects to declare a forfeiture of your lease or rental agreement.

    4.1 Landlord reserves the right to pursue collection of any future rental losses allowed by Civil Code §1951.2

    Date:_____, 20_____

    Landlord/Agent: _____

    Signature:_____

    Address: _____

    _____

    Phone: _____

    Fax: _____

    E-mail: _____

The landlord serves the tenant with a 3-day notice to quit the premises for the tenant's failure to poison the squirrels.

The tenant does not vacate the premises. The landlord files a UD action to evict the tenant. The tenant claims he cannot be evicted since the proper notice to serve for the failure to poison the squirrels is a 3-day notice to perform or quit, allowing the tenant to cure his breach.

However, the 3-day notice to quit is the proper notice. The elimination of squirrels by poisoning cannot be performed within three days — before the 3-day notice to quit would expire. [Matthews, *supra*]

Breach of statutory prohibitions

A tenant may be evicted for maintaining a *nuisance or unlawful use* of the premises, even if these activities are not prohibited by the lease. [CCP §1161(4)]

A **nuisance** includes anything which:

- is *injurious to health*, such as contamination of the property's soil;

- is *offensive to the senses*, such as excessive noise levels or obnoxious fumes; or

- *obstructs the use and enjoyment* of surrounding property. [Calif. Civil Code §3479]

For example, a tenant in a multi-unit property maintains a nuisance on the premises, such as excessive late-night noise, which interferes with another tenant's **use or enjoyment** of his premises. As a result, the landlord may serve the tenant with a 3-day notice to quit.

Also, a tenant who illegally sells, grows or manufactures controlled substances on the premises, has by his actions, triggered an automatic forfeiture of the leasehold. The tenant may be served with a notice to quit for maintaining a nuisance, and if he does not vacate, be evicted by a UD action. [CCP §1161(4)]

A tenant's **unlawful use** of the premises includes violations of local laws or ordinances, such as noncompliance with zoning ordinances that restrict the use of the premises. Again, the leasehold is forfeited automatically due to the violation. The 3-day notice is required only as a requisite to a UD action should the tenant remain in possession. [**Haig** v. **Hogan** (1947) 82 CA2d 876]

However, before the unlawful use *justifies* a notice to quit, the use must:

- threaten the physical safety of the property;

- stigmatize the premises; or

- impair the landlord's continued receipt of rent.

For example, a tenant's lease contains a provision stating the tenant agrees not to use the premises for any unlawful purpose or to violate any laws, a provision which restates codified law.

The tenant's business, which is authorized to operate on the premises, is penalized for violation of federal anti-trust laws. The landlord seeks to evict the tenant for unlawful use of the premises in violation of the lease.

Here, the landlord may not evict the tenant. The tenant's violation of anti-trust laws in the conduct of his **lawful business** is not an unlawful use of the premises. [**Deutsch** v. **Phillips Petroleum Co.** (1976) 56 CA3d 586]

When a tenant's activity is considered a nuisance or an unlawful use, a 3-day notice to quit may be served on the tenant even if the tenant is able to cure the breach by terminating or eliminating the activity within three days. The mere occurrence of the unlawful and endangering activity automatically forfeits the lease, leaving nothing for the tenant to do except vacate or be evicted based on the 3-day notice to quit.

Forfeiture on assigning or subletting

Consider a lease prohibiting the tenant from *assigning* the lease or *subleasing* the premises without first obtaining the landlord's written consent.

Unknown to the landlord or his property manager, the tenant subleases the premises. The property manager discovers the premises is occupied by a subtenant.

The property manager names and serves both the tenant and the subtenant with a 3-day notice to quit.

The subtenant does not vacate the premises, and a UD action is filed to regain possession from both the tenant and the subtenant.

The tenant claims his leasehold interest cannot be terminated by the 3-day notice to quit since the landlord cannot unreasonably withhold his consent to a sublease of the premises.

Can the landlord serve a 3-day notice to quit on a tenant who subleased without his consent and evict the tenant?

Yes! The landlord can proceed to have the subtenant evicted by serving a 3-day notice to quit. The tenant failed to request the landlord's consent prior to subletting the premises, thus breaching the lease and at the same time forfeiting the right to possession.

The tenant cannot avoid the forfeiture of his leasehold due to the subletting by claiming the landlord cannot unreasonably withhold consent when the landlord was not given the opportunity to grant or withhold his consent. [**Thrifty Oil Co.** v. **Batarse** (1985) 174 CA3d 770]

When provisions in a lease prohibit subleasing or assignment of the lease by the tenant without the landlord's consent, and the tenant subleases or assigns without obtaining consent, a 3-day notice to quit may be served on the tenant to recover possession. By statute, the act is an incurable activity which terminates the lease, leaving no alternative to vacating. [CCP §1161(4)]

However, the landlord need not consider the lease terminated when the tenant subleases the premises or assigns the lease without the landlord's consent. The landlord can waive the statutory forfeiture.

Thus, a 3-day notice to **perform or quit** may be served on the tenant requiring the tenant to remove the subtenant from the premises — within three days — and retain his right to possession. [CCP §1161(3)]

Waste forfeits the lease

Waste to the leased premises by a tenant is a breach which cannot be cured. Thus, the right to possession has been terminated. The tenant must vacate if the landlord serves a 3-day notice to quit.

However, *waste* is only grounds for eviction when the **value** of the leased premises is substantially or permanently diminished — *impaired* — due to the tenant's conduct.

Waste occurs when a tenant:

- *intentionally damages* or destroys the leased premises; or

- neglects the premises and *impairs its value* by failing to care for and maintain it as agreed.

Consider a tenant in an office building. The tenant's lease obligates the tenant to follow all building rules.

The building rules prohibit tenants from adjusting the temperature controls. The tenant's employees adjust the temperature controls, resulting in damage to the thermostat.

The landlord serves the tenant with a 3-day notice to quit the premises. The tenant does not vacate.

The landlord files a UD action, claiming the tenant committed waste to the premises since the adjusting of the temperature controls by the tenant's employees damaged the building's thermostat.

However, the tenant cannot be evicted for waste since the damage to the thermostat was minor. Further, the damage was reparable within three days. Also, the landlord was unable to demonstrate the tenant's conduct *substantially diminished* the property's market value. [**Rowe** v. **Wells Fargo Realty, Inc.** (1985) 166 CA3d 310]

Now consider a landlord who discovers a tenant's pets have damaged the wooden floors, doors and plastered walls of the tenant's apartment unit. Unsanitary conditions also exist in the unit.

A 3-day notice to quit is served based on the tenant's waste to the unit.

Again, the landlord is unable to evict the tenant for waste. The tenant's failure to maintain the unit has not significantly or permanently lowered the market value of the unit. [**Freeze** v. **Brinson** (1991) 4 CA4th 99]

The damage created by the tenant's pets could be repaired, and the unit quickly returned to a marketable condition. Thus, a 3-day notice to perform or quit was the appropriate notice.

Waiver of breach by conduct

Consider a tenant of nonresidential property who wants to add further improvements to the leased premises.

The lease requires the landlord's written consent before the tenant makes improvements to the premises.

The tenant submits a request to the landlord for approval of additional improvements he wants to make. The landlord does not respond to the tenant's request.

Without the landlord's consent, the tenant begins construction of the improvements.

The landlord becomes aware of the construction. The landlord also discovers the construction encroaches beyond the area of the leased premises onto other property owned by the landlord.

The landlord demands the tenant remove the improvements he has constructed.

As a result, the landlord and tenant commence lease negotiations to expand the leased premises to include the property on which the improvements now encroach.

During negotiations, the landlord accepts all rent payments made by the tenant.

Ultimately, the landlord and tenant are unable to reach an agreement and resolve the unauthorized construction.

The landlord then serves a 3-day notice to quit followed by a UD action to evict the tenant.

The tenant claims the landlord's acceptance of rent payments waived the landlord's right to terminate the tenant's possession based on the tenant's failure to obtain the landlord's consent before improving the property.

Can the landlord evict the tenant?

Yes! The landlord did not waive his right to terminate the tenant's possession by accepting rent called for in the lease since the landlord **continuously objected** to the construction of the improvements.

While the landlord accepted rent payments, the landlord did not intend for the tenant to construct the improvements and continue to occupy the premises on the terms of the existing lease. [**Thriftimart, Inc.** v. **Me & Tex** (1981) 123 CA3d 751]

Many lease agreements contain a provision stating a waiver by the landlord of a tenant's breach of the lease is not a waiver of similar, subsequent breaches or other breaches by the tenant, called a *nonwaiver provision*. [See Chapter 33]

When a nonwaiver clause is in the lease, the landlord's acceptance of rent does not constitute a waiver of his right to evict the tenant for a separate breach, such as an assignment of the lease. [**Karbelnig** v. **Brothwell** (1966) 244 CA2d 333]

Covering your bases with alternatives

A tenant's failure to comply with building rules or to maintain the premises in a clean and sanitary manner are breaches of a lease agreement which generally can be performed within three days.

The landlord who serves a 3-day notice to **perform or quit** provides the tenant with the opportunity to comply with building rules or clean the premises and stay. Should the tenant's breach remain uncured after three days and the tenant remain in possession, the landlord may file a UD action to evict the tenant if he so chooses.

For example, the tenant whose authorized pets damage his unit may be unable to replace wood floors and replaster walls within three days. If the tenant fails to perform, the landlord can evict him.

Consider again the tenant who could not be evicted for waste since his failure to follow building rules did not permanently lower the market value of the premises.

A tenant whose breach results from the failure to follow building rules may stop the activity constituting a violation on receiving a 3-day notice to perform or quit. Should the tenant perform the notice to comply with building rules within the three-day period, the tenant cannot be evicted.

However, the tenant might later resume the breaching activity. The tenant's repeat conduct may then constitute a *nuisance*, perhaps obstructing the ability of the landlord or other tenants to enjoy the use of the building due to the constant interference.

The tenant will likely contest a 3-day notice to quit for nuisance. The landlord will then be forced to show how the tenant's conduct constitutes a *continuing nuisance*.

A 3-day notice to quit results in a forfeiture of the tenant's right to possession, as no alternative exists — a harsh result courts do not favor.

Thus, if the tenant's breach is non-statutory and can be cured within three days, a 3-day notice to perform or quit is the proper notice to serve.

When uncertainty exists whether or not the breach can be cured within three days or a tenant's conduct meets the requirements for serving a 3-day notice to quit, a 3-day notice to perform or quit will either:

- cause the tenant to cure the breach within three days; or

- support the landlord's UD action to evict the tenant.

Consider a tenant who operates a concession stand on the leased property. The lease prohibits camping on the premises and contains a nonwaiver provision.

The tenant is unable to stop campers from using the premises. The tenant installs a sign stating camping is not allowed and erects fences to keep overnight campers off the premises. On a demand from the landlord, the tenant takes down the sign and fences.

On removal of the fence, the tenant advises the landlord of his inability to restrict campers from using the premises. The landlord does not respond, but continues to accept rent.

After an extended time, the landlord serves a 3-day notice to quit for breach of the lease provision prohibiting camping on the premises. The landlord files a UD action to evict the tenant.

Can the landlord evict the tenant?

No! When a landlord's conduct misleads a tenant into believing the breaching conduct is no longer a concern of the landlord, the landlord will be prevented or estopped from completing the eviction on what has become tenant activity authorized by the landlord, even if the lease contains a nonwaiver provision. [**Salton Community Services District** v. **Southard** (1967) 256 CA2d 526]

Once the tenant's actions which were the breach of a lease provision have been condoned by the landlord, the landlord has waived the nonwaiver provision and must take reasonable steps if he intends to *reinstate* the provision so he can enforce it.

A reasonable step to reinstate enforceability would be a written 30-day notice to the tenant stating the landlord intends to enforce the lease provision on expiration of the 30-day notice, if 30 days is sufficient time for the tenant to cure the breach. [See **first tuesday** Form 570]

If the tenant continues to breach after expiration of the notice reinstating the provision, the landlord may serve a 3-day notice to perform or quit.

For example, the due date and grace period for rent payments are waived by the landlord's conduct if he consistently accepts late payments without demanding a late charge or serving a 3-day notice to pay or quit. The waiver of the late charge provision occurs in spite of the existence of a nonwaiver provision in the lease and must be reinstated by a 30-day notice of change in terms.

Service of notice

Statutory requirements must be strictly followed when preparing and serving a 3-day notice.

If the 3-day notice is incorrectly or inaccurately prepared, or improperly served on the tenant, the notice is invalid. To evict the tenant, a new 3-day notice must be correctly prepared and properly served. [**Lamey** v. **Masciotra** (1969) 273 CA2d 709]

A proof of service form must be filled out and signed by the person who serves the 3-day notice. Without a proof of service, a UD action cannot be maintained. [See **first tuesday** Form 580]

Concurrent service of two notices

When concurrently serving a 3-day notice to pay, perform or vacate and a 30-day notice to vacate or change terms, the notices must not be attached to one another and must be separated when served. If attached to one another or combined in any way, they may be reasonably confused as one and defeat any UD action based on the 3-day notice.

Also, each notice should be accompanied by its own separate *proof of service*. [See **first tuesday** Form 580]

For example, a tenant is again breaching his obligation to maintain the premises. The landlord concurrently serves the tenant with both a 3-day notice to perform or quit and a 30-day notice to vacate. Both notices are served concurrently. Each notice stands alone, unattached to one another, and is separately, but concurrently, handed to the tenant. Each service is returned by the server accompanied by a separate proof of service.

The tenant fails to maintain the premises under the 3-day notice and remains in possession.

The landlord files a UD action based on the service of the 3-day notice.

At the UD hearing, the tenant claims he thought he did not have to vacate within three days since the 30-day notice did not mention a breach and gave him 30 days to vacate.

The court, under the "reasonable man" analysis, on examining the content of the separate notices, grants the tenant **relief from forfeiture** of possession under the 3-day notice; confusion may have caused the tenant not to protect his interest in the property. The tenant could be allowed to stay, **on the condition** he immediately perform the maintenance called for in the 3-day notice. [CCP §1179]

Thus, regardless of any confusion he may have, the tenant will either:

- retain the right to possession after the UD proceedings on the 3-day notice (subject to the outstanding 30-day notice to vacate) on the condition he immediately perform the maintenance called for in the notice; or

- be evicted from the property if he fails to perform the maintenance called for in the notice.

Now consider a tenant who is concurrently served with a 3-day notice and a separate 30-day notice, each with its own proof of service statement.

The **3-day notice** to pay or quit states a tenant who fails to pay amounts due under a lease or rental agreement must, within three days after service of written notice of the breach, either pay or vacate and deliver possession to the landlord.

The **30-day notice** to vacate states the tenant is required to vacate and deliver possession of the premises to the landlord within 30 days after service of the notice. [See Chapter 21]

The 30-day notice does not request that the tenant pay any delinquent rent which is due, only the amount which will become due within 30 days.

The tenant pays the rent before the three-day period expires.

Later, at the end of the 30-day period, the tenant refuses to leave.

The landlord initiates a UD action on the 30-day notice to vacate. At the UD hearing, the tenant claims he believed if he paid the delinquent rent, the 30-day notice would no longer be applicable, since the notices all related to his difficulty in paying rent on time.

Again, the court will apply the *reasonable man test* — examining the contents of both notices and determining if confusion could occur in the mind of the tenant.

The court also must enforce the **legislative scheme** to make sure the landlord followed all statutory requirements regarding the contents and service of the notice. If the landlord is in compliance, the court must award the landlord the relief available under the legislative scheme.

Here, the contents of the notices show they are mutually exclusive of one another.

The 30-day notice makes no mention of the delinquent rent owed or, if rent is paid, that the tenancy will continue beyond 30 days.

Also, while served concurrently, the landlord did serve the notices separate from one another. Both notices followed their respective statutory schemes:

- one for collecting delinquent rent; and

- the other for terminating the month-to-month tenancy.

Thus, a court should find that the tenant's purported confusion is not a legal excuse for failing to vacate.

Retaliatory eviction

A tenant might claim the service of the 30-day notice is a *retaliatory eviction* triggered by his nonpayment of rent when due. [See Chapter 34]

For example, a landlord concurrently serves a tenant with a 3-day notice to pay or quit and a 30-day notice to vacate — merely because the tenant continuously fails to timely pay rent and is again delinquent. The tenant claims the 30-day notice was served to terminate his tenancy **in retaliation** for being late with the rent, which is probably true although it was not and need not be stated in the 30-day notice.

However, *retaliatory eviction* only occurs when the tenant:

- exercises his right to file a complaint with an appropriate agency regarding the *habitability* of the premises;

- orally complains to the landlord about the *habitability* of the premises;

- files documents to initiate a judicial or arbitration proceeding regarding the *habitability* of the premises;

- *organizes or participates* in a tenant association or an association for tenant's rights; or

- lawfully exercises any rights, such as the refusal to authorize credit reports or personal investigation after vacating the premises. [CC §1942.5]

Thus, the tenancy was not terminated in retaliation for complaints about the habitability of the premises or for a legal right exercised by the tenant. Instead, the tenant was being evicted for his delinquency in rent payments — a breach by the tenant of the month-to-month rental agreement.

Chapter 20

Other amounts due under 3-day notices

This chapter discusses the inclusion of amounts due the landlord other than "rent" in a 3-day notice to pay rent or quit.

Know what the judge will allow

A lease between a landlord and his tenant contains a rent provision with a clause calling for the **accrual of interest** from the due date on any amount of rent which becomes delinquent, called a *late payment clause*.

The tenant fails to pay rent when due or before it becomes delinquent. The landlord then prepares a 3-day notice to pay rent or quit and serves the notice on the tenant. [See **first tuesday** Form 575]

The 3-day notice itemizes the amounts of delinquent rent and daily interest accrued which are due and unpaid on the date the notice is prepared.

The tenant fails to pay or quit during the 3-day period. The landlord files an unlawful detainer (UD) action asking the court to order the removal of the tenant from possession.

At the UD hearing, the tenant claims the landlord cannot terminate his possession of the premises under the 3-day notice since the notice demands payment of an amount which is greater than the **rent due** under the lease, and thus is defective as the demand includes *other amounts due* the landlord.

May the 3-day notice include amounts due under monetary provisions in the lease in addition to "technical rent"?

Yes! **Amounts due** under rent provisions in the lease or rental agreement which may be demanded in the 3-day notice to pay or quit are not limited to the scheduled amount of periodic rent which is delinquent.

While the notice to pay may not be served until rent is delinquent, the notice itself is limited to stating the *total amount which is due*, not only the amount of rent due. Thus, the notice may include all sums of money which are **due and unpaid** under the lease or rental agreement at the time the notice is served, including the delinquent rent. [**Canal-Randolph Anaheim, Inc.** v. **Moore** (1978) 78 CA3d 477]

Examples of amounts due periodically under a lease or rental agreement, in addition to scheduled rent, include:

- common area maintenance charges (CAMs);

- association charges;

- pro rata insurance premiums, property taxes and assessments;

- late payment and bad check charges;

- expenses incurred by the landlord to cure waste or failure to maintain the property, called *future advances*; and

- other amounts of money properly due as compensation or reimbursement of expenses arising out of the occupancy.

A 3-day notice to pay rent or quit form should provide for the itemization of rent and other amounts due which are unpaid and delinquent. [See **first tuesday** Form 575]

Lump sum late charges

Under a nonresidential lease agreement entered into by a tenant, rent is typically due and payable on the first day of each month, called the *due date*. The lease contains a late charge provision stating the tenant agrees to pay a charge in the amount of $150 in the event the rent is not **received by** the landlord on or before the fifth day of each month, called a *grace period*. [See **first tuesday** Form 552 §3.9]

Under the lease, rent is *delinquent* the day after the grace period runs, the sixth day of the month. The delinquency triggers the landlord's right to demand the late charge or do nothing and waive it.

The lease also provides for the tenant to pay $25 for each rent check returned for insufficient funds (NSF). [See **first tuesday** Form 552 §3.10]

One month, the landlord receives the rent after the grace period has run. As he must, the landlord accepts the rent since the right to possession has not been terminated. The landlord then notifies the tenant in writing that he is imposing the agreed-to late charge, payable as agreed with the following month's rent.

The following month the landlord receives the regularly scheduled rent within the grace period. However, the tenant does not also tender the late charge the landlord demanded on the prior month's delinquent payment.

Landlord's options for collection

On the tenant's failure to pay additional charges, the landlord's options to enforce payment, viable or not, include:

- returning the rent check to the tenant as insufficient payment for the amount due;

- serving the tenant with a 3-day notice to pay or quit;

- deducting the additional charge from the security deposit on written notice to the tenant; or

- filing an action against the tenant in small claims court to collect the late charge.

Returning the rent check to the tenant will result in one of two scenarios:

1. The tenant will submit another check which includes payment of the late charge (which payment will be delinquent and presumably incur another late charge); or

2. The tenant will retain the rent check as having been properly tendered and therefore paid, and do nothing more until he sends a check for the following month's rent.

A tenant who fails to pay rent or otherwise *materially breaches* the lease, may be served with the appropriate 3-day notice. The 3-day notice based on a material breach properly includes a demand for late charges and any other *amounts past due*. [Canal-Randolph Anaheim, Inc., *supra*]

If the tenant fails to cure the breach within three days following service of the notice and remains in possession, the landlord may file an unlawful detainer (UD) action to regain possession. [Calif. Code of Civil Procedure §1161]

However, a landlord will not succeed in a UD action when the landlord's refusal to accept the tenant's timely tender of a rent check is based solely on the tenant's refusal to pay late charges, which is a minor breach. [Canal-Randolph Anaheim, Inc., *supra*]

Thus, the landlord has two **viable options** for the collection of unpaid late charges from the tenant:

- accept the rent check and deduct the amount of the unpaid late charge from the security deposit and advise the tenant of the deduction; or

- accept the rent check and file an action in small claims court or municipal court for the unpaid late charge amounts.

The only financially practical action the landlord can take when the tenant refuses to pay a late charge is to accept the rent and deduct the late charge from the security deposit.

A UD action cannot be maintained if the sole existing breach of the lease is the failure to pay the late charges. A *material breach* is required to support a UD action, such as a delinquency in the scheduled rent and other scheduled periodic compensation for occupancy and use of the property. A late charge is properly sought when pursuing delinquent rent, but a late charge (or bounced check charge) is a *minor breach* and will not independently support a UD action. [**Baypoint Mortgage** v. **Crest Premium Real Estate Investments Retirement Trust** (1985) 168 CA3d 818]

Late charges

To be enforceable, late charges must be *reasonably related* to the actual costs of collecting the delinquent rent (the time and effort involved) and the delay in its receipt (loss of use, such as interest).

A lump sum (or interest rate) late charge becomes an unenforceable liquidated damage if the amount of the charge imposed is significantly greater than the actual out-of-pocket losses suffered by the landlord due to the tenant's late payment of rent, in which case the charge is called a penalty. [**Garrett** v. **Coast and Southern Federal Savings and Loan Association** (1973) 9 CA3d 731]

Note — Some may argue any lump sum late charge on residential property is void as a liquidated damage since losses due to a late payment in any real estate transaction, especially residential, are readily ascertainable.

A liquidated damages provision in a residential lease is void, unless the loss covered is impracticable or impossible to calculate (which it is not), or the amount agreed to is a reasonable estimate of the landlord's out-of-pocket expenses for the collection effort. [Calif. Civil Code §1671(c)(2)]

When setting the amount of a late charge for a residential tenant's failure to timely pay rent under a lease or rental agreement, consider charging an amount equivalent to the late charge allowed on a residential loan since it is a good indicator of *reasonableness.*

The late charge which can be charged for receipt of a delinquent payment on a loan secured by residential property is controlled by statute. Not so for rent.

For example, the lump sum late charge allowed on a loan secured by an owner-occupied, single-family residence cannot exceed 6% of the delinquent payment (principal and interest only). [CC §2954.4(a)]

Rent is the economic equivalent of interest. For purposes of late charges, rent payments should be treated no differently than interest payments.

Late charges as liquidated damages

A lump sum late charge set forth in a real estate lease is a *liquidated damages* provision. The charge is a one-time, predetermined fixed amount intended to reimburse the landlord for the delay in receipt of the rent money and his costs and effort spent to collect the delinquent rent. [CC §1951.5]

A late charge provision which calls for *interest to accrue* at a predetermined annual percentage rate on amounts earned and unpaid (delinquent rent) is not a liquidated damages provision and is fully enforceable. [Canal-Randolph Anaheim, Inc., *supra]*

However, some landlords wrongfully view late charges as a means for **coercing tenants to pay** the rent on time. Thus, they set the late charge at an amount which more than reimburses the landlord for his actual losses, a penalty assessment that is unenforceable.

A lump sum late charge provision in a **nonresidential lease** is valid unless the tenant can show the amount of the late charge is an unreasonable reimbursement for the delay in receipt of the rent. [CC §1671(b)]

A late charge is unenforceable if the charge is so great in comparison to actual losses that it *imposes a penalty* on the tenant for his late rental payment. [Garrett, *supra]*

An appropriate late charge in a lease for single-user residential or nonresidential property encumbered by a loan is the amount of the late charge imposed when a monthly payment on the loan is delinquent. The landlord is simply "passing through" the loss incurred by his late receipt of the tenant's rent payment.

However, in a residential lease agreement, a late charge provision setting a fixed amount is void unless the losses suffered by the landlord due to late payment are impracticable to calculate. [CC §1671(c)(2)]

Note — Determining money losses suffered due to late payments in any real estate transaction, especially in a residential lease, is not impracticable to calculate since it is merely an accounting of known amounts incurred as expenses in the collection and lost use of the funds until received.

Imposing the late charge

A late charge is not automatically due and payable by the tenant when the landlord fails to receive the rent payment within the grace period.

The landlord must first make a written demand on the tenant for payment of the late charge and include the date when the charge is payable before the amount is delinquent and collection can be enforced.

Thus, a written billing demanding payment of the late charge with the next month's rent is delivered to the tenant to ensure the late charge is imposed. [See **first tuesday** Form 568]

The **late charge notice** advises the tenant the landlord is entitled to enforce collection of unpaid late charges by:

- deducting the unpaid delinquent amount from the tenant's security deposit; or

- filing a small claims or municipal court action for unpaid delinquent amounts.

Too late to collect

Within one year from the date rent became delinquent or some other *material breach* of a monetary provision in the lease or rental agreement occurred, the landlord must serve a 3-day notice on the tenant to be able to enforce collection of the amounts due in a UD action. [CCP §1161(2)]

As an alternative to seeking a recovery of money in a UD action, the landlord can file a separate action for money within four years of the breach, to collect unpaid late charges, returned check handling charges and any other amounts due under the lease. [CCP §337]

Ultimately, the landlord can deduct the late charges from the tenant's security deposit as payment of unpaid amounts due the landlord under the lease. [CC §§1950.5(b)(1); 1950.7(c)]

*Note — Within three weeks after vacating **residential property**, a residential tenant is entitled to an accounting statement itemizing the prior deduction from the security deposit for the unpaid late charges, as well as any other deductible expenses incurred by the landlord. [CC §1950.5(f)]*

*Within two weeks after the landlord of **nonresidential property** receives possession from the tenant, the landlord must return the portion of the security deposit remaining after deductions for necessary cleaning, repair and other amounts due. [CC §1950.7(c)]*

However, a nonresidential landlord is not required to set forth an itemized accounting of amounts deducted from a security deposit unless agreed to in the lease.

The UD court problem

While the enforcement of lump sum late charges for the recovery of collection efforts has not been the subject of reported cases, the court in *Canal-Randolph Anaheim, Inc.* ruled an interest-rate late charge on delinquent rent to cover the loss of use of the payment can be included as *amounts due* under a lease or rental agreement.

Canal-Randolph Anaheim, Inc. clarified that a landlord may include any sums due under the lease as amounts due in the 3-day notice.

Also, no statutes exist which forbid (or limit) the collection of a late charge in a lease or rental agreement. Cases do limit the charge to an amount reasonably calculated to cover the losses inflicted by late payment.

However, not all trial judges agree late charges are part of the *amount due* under a 3-day notice. Despite the holding of *Canal-Randolph Anaheim, Inc.*, some judges declare late charges are not *rent*, the delinquency of which triggers use of a 3-day notice to pay or quit. [CCP §1161(2)]

Thus, these judges hold a late charge or bad check charge cannot be included in the 3-day notice as part of the *amount due*. If included, the demand would bar an eviction before those judges.

Before a landlord or a property manager includes any late charge (or other amounts due besides technical rent) in a 3-day notice as part of the total amount due, it should first be determined if the judge presiding over UD actions in their jurisdiction will allow a demand for late charges.

Judges vary in their approach to late charges:

- some judges allow *masked late charges* cloaked as a forgiveness of 6% to 10% of the scheduled rent, if paid before the rent (including the masked late charge) is considered delinquent — within five to 10 days after it is due;

- some judges allow a late charge of up to 6% of the delinquent rent as a reasonable amount;

- some judges disallow late charges as an unenforceable penalty for being delinquent;

- some judges disallow late charges as a forfeiture of money (since the amount exceeds the costs of collection); and

- some judges just disallow late charges altogether as an exercise of their discretion.

Information on the treatment given by the local trial court judge can be obtained from an attorney or other landlords who have experience in front of the judge.

If the judge will not allow the late charge as part of the amount due from the tenant, the landlord should leave it out of the 3-day notice. Instead, either deduct the late charge from the security deposit (if any remains when refunded), or pursue collection in a separate action for money, both of which avoid the issue of demands placed in the 3-day notice. Do not risk getting an erroneous judicial determination that late charges or other amounts due were improperly included in the 3-day notice and therefore a denial of the eviction.

Note — An obvious solution to the inconsistent rules applied to late charges is legislation to establish public policy by defining the nature of late charges and acceptable limits for recovery of the cost of collecting delinquent rent — guidance for all involved in the UD process.

Late charges for rent should be treated like late charges on mortgages. Both serve the same economic function — recovery of costs incurred due to the delay of receipt of funds and collection efforts. Also, the number of homeowners with mortgage payments is almost equal to the number of renters with rental payments in California. Both mortgage payments and rental payments are part of the cost of occupancy and entitled to equivalent legislative controls.

Chapter 21

Notices to vacate

This chapter presents the 30/60-day notices to vacate used by landlords and tenants to terminate month-to-month tenancies.

Termination of periodic tenancies

A tenant occupies a single-family residential property under a lease. The lease obligates the tenant to maintain the property's landscaping.

Soon the landlord receives complaints from surrounding property owners about excessive noise and a high number of visitors at the rental late at night. On more than one occasion, the police have responded to calls from neighbors regarding the noise.

Also, the city ordinance compliance department has given notice for the removal of disabled vehicles from the property.

On a drive-by inspection, the landlord also discovers the landscaping and lawn have deteriorated since the tenant has not watered.

While the tenant consistently pays the rent on time, the landlord feels the tenant must be evicted even though several months remain on the term of the lease. The tenant is creating a *nuisance* by interfering with his neighbors' use and enjoyment of their property and has failed to maintain the leased premises.

The landlord prepares and serves the tenant with a 30-day notice to vacate. The landlord avoids stating his reason for terminating the tenancy. [See Form 569 accompanying this chapter]

The tenant remains in occupancy of the premises after the 30-day notice expires and tenders the next rent payment on time.

The landlord refuses to accept the rent payment and files an unlawful detainer (UD) action to evict the tenant.

Can the landlord, subject to an unexpired lease which the tenant has breached, evict the tenant from the premises with a 30-day notice?

No! The tenant occupies the property under an unexpired lease. The landlord cannot terminate the lease by using a notice to vacate, much less use the notice to vacate to establish an unlawful detainer.

A **residential or nonresidential** 30-day notice to vacate the premises is only effective when used by a landlord or tenant to terminate a periodic tenancy. The term of the periodic tenancy does not matter, unless:

- the property is **residential** and the tenant has occupied the premises for **one year or more**, in which case the landlord, not the tenant, must use a 60-day notice to vacate [Calif. Civil Code §1946.1; see **first tuesday** Form 579]; or

- the property is **nonresidential** and the rental agreement calls for a greater or lesser period for notice, but not less than seven days. [CC §1946]

If agreed, a residential or nonresidential **lease** can provide for the tenant to terminate his occupancy prior to expiration of the lease on 30 days notice or any other period for notice, conditioned on the payment of a penalty for vacating prematurely. A lease is not controlled by the periodic tenancy rules prohibiting a forfeiture on the tenant's voluntary termination of a rental agreement.

Periodic tenancies extended/terminated

Unlike the extension of a lease, the 30-day rental period under a **month-to-month rental agreement** is *automatically extended* on the same terms.

Any landlord under a month-to-month rental agreement (or any other periodic rental agreement) may **interfere at any time** with the automatic renewal of the rental agreement and terminate the tenancy. Thus, the tenant's right to occupy under the periodic rental agreement is terminated by serving a 30-day notice to vacate.

However, if the property is residential and the tenant has resided on it for **one year or more**, then the landlord (not the tenant) is required to give the residential tenant a 60-day notice to vacate. [CC §1946]

Likewise, any tenant under a month-to-month rental agreement may at any time stop the automatic renewal process and terminate the tenancy by giving the landlord a 30-day notice of his intent to vacate the premises. [CC §§1946; 1946.1; see Form 572 accompanying this chapter]

An expired notice to vacate on a month-to-month tenancy, whether given by the tenant or the landlord, establishes a tenant's unlawful detainer (UD) should the tenant remain in possession. [**Palmer** v. **Zeis** (1944) 65 CA2d Supp. 859]

Thus, once the notice to vacate expires, the landlord may file a UD action to evict the month-to-month tenant without further notice.

Lease becomes a periodic tenancy

Consider a tenant who enters into a one-year lease of a unit in an apartment building. The lease term expires, and the tenant remains in possession of the unit. The tenant continues to pay rent monthly, which the landlord accepts.

Later, the landlord serves the tenant with a 60-day notice to vacate the property since the tenant has resided on the property for over one year. The tenant remains in possession of the property after the 60-day notice expires.

The landlord files a UD action to evict the tenant, claiming the tenant is now unlawfully detaining the unit.

The tenant claims he cannot be evicted based on a 60-day notice to vacate since he holds possession of the unit under a lease agreement, which was automatically extended for the same terms as the original lease when the landlord continued to accept rent after the initial lease expired.

Here, the notice to vacate is proper and the tenant can be evicted. The landlord's acceptance of monthly rent after the lease expired, without an extension or renewal agreement, establishes a month-to-month tenancy on the same terms as the lease. [CC §1945]

The lease term expired and the tenant now occupies the premises under a month-to-month tenancy based on all the provisions in the lease, except the term of the tenancy.

For nonresidential landlords, a 30-day notice to vacate is sufficient to terminate the tenancy created by accepting rent under an expired nonresidential lease of any term.

Landlord's intent to evict

A landlord terminates a month-to-month tenancy by preparing and serving the tenant with the appropriate 30/60-day notice to vacate. If a breach exists, a 3-day notice to quit is used. [See **first tuesday** Forms 571 and 579; see Chapter 19]

A notice to vacate form used by a landlord contains:

- the name of the tenant;

- the address of the premises;

- a reference to the rental agreement or expired lease;

30-DAY NOTICE TO VACATE
(For Use by Residential Landlord)

DATE:_____, 20_____, at _____, California

To Tenant: _____

Items left blank or unchecked are not applicable.

FACTS:

You are a Tenant under a rental agreement or expired lease

Dated _____, at

_____, California,

NOTICE:
A residential landlord may terminate a month-to-month tenancy by giving at least thirty (30) days written notice to the tenant, unless the tenant has occupied the unit one year or more, in which case at least a 60-day notice period is required. [Calif. Civil Code §1946]

entered into by _____ , Tenant,

and _____ , Landlord,

regarding real estate referred to as:_____
_____

NOTICE:

1. This notice is intended as at least a thirty (30) day notice prior to termination of your month-to-month tenancy.

2. On or before _____, 20_____, a date at least thirty (30) days after service of this notice, you will vacate and deliver possession of the premises to Landlord or:
_____

3. Rent due and payable by you prior to the date to vacate includes prorated rent of $_____, due _____, 20_____.

4. Landlord acknowledges the prior receipt of $_____ as your security deposit.

    4.1 Within 21 days after you vacate, Landlord will furnish you a written statement and explanation of any deductions from the deposit, and a refund of the remaining amount. [Calif. Civil Code §1950.5(f)]

    4.2 Landlord may deduct only those amounts necessary to:

        a. Reimburse for Tenant defaults in rental payments;

        b. Repair damages to the premises caused by Tenant (ordinary wear and tear excluded);

        c. Clean the premises, if necessary;

        d. Reimburse for Tenant loss, damage or excessive wear and tear on furnishings provided to Tenant.

5. Landlord may show the leased premises to prospective tenants during normal business hours by first giving you written notice at least 24 hours in advance of the entry. The notice will be given to you in person, by leaving a copy with an occupant of suitable age and discretion, or by leaving the notice on or under your entry door.

6. Please contact the undersigned to arrange a time to review the condition of the premises before you vacate.

7. If you fail to vacate and deliver possession of the premises by the date set for you to vacate, legal proceedings may be initiated to regain possession of the premises and to recover rent owed, treble damages, costs and attorney fees.

8. The reason for termination is _____
(complete if required by rent control ordinance or Section 8 housing)

Date: _____
Landlord/Agent: _____
Signature: _____
Address:_____
_____
Phone: _____
Fax: _____
E-mail: _____

- a statement that the unit must be vacant within the applicable number of days (30 or 60) after service of the notice;

- the amount of pro rata rent to be paid when rent is next due; and

- a statement regarding the security deposit and its disposition.

A *forfeiture provision* is not properly included in any notice to vacate since no forfeiture can exist on its expiration — the tenancy merely expires when the notice expires, with no tenancy remaining to be forfeited.

Due to its contents, the landlord's notice to vacate form eliminates any confusion as to the amount of pro rata rent to be paid and when the rent is due. [See Form **first tuesday** 571 §3]

Tenant's intent to vacate

A tenant, residential or nonresidential, who intends to vacate and avoid further liability under a month-to-month rental agreement must give notice to the landlord of his termination of the tenancy. The tenant must give 30 days notice of his intent to vacate which may be done by letter personally delivered to the landlord or his agent, or sent by certified or registered mail. [CC §§1946; 1946.1]

Some landlords accept oral notice of the tenant's intent to vacate without reducing the notice to a writing signed by the tenant.

However, both the tenant and the landlord are better served when the landlord provides the tenant with a 30-Day Notice to Vacate form when entering into a rental agreement or when oral notice is given. The tenant will then have the correct paperwork to complete and deliver to the landlord or property manager. Use of a form lends certainty to the tenant's understanding of a critical event. [See Form 572]

A tenant's notice to vacate form documents and acknowledges:

- the tenancy is terminated on expiration of 30 days after service of the notice on the landlord or his manager;

- the tenant's intent to pay pro rata rent;

- the amount of the security deposit and an entitlement to an itemized statement for any deductions from the security deposit; and

- a statement relating to final review of the premises with the landlord or property manager for any cleaning and repairs.

If the tenant serves the landlord with a written 30-day notice to vacate and the **tenant fails** to vacate within 30 days after service, the landlord may immediately file a UD action. [CCP §1161(5)]

Service of the notice to vacate

A notice to vacate may be served at any time during the month.

However, a **nonresidential landlord** and tenant may limit the right to serve the notice at any time by agreeing in the rental agreement that the 30-day notice to vacate cannot be served during the last six days of the month. This is not true for residential tenancies since service can be at any time. [CC §§1946; 1946.1(a)]

To be effective, the notice to vacate from a tenant or landlord must be served:

- in the same manner as a 3-day notice (in person, by substitution or post and mail); or

- by certified or registered mail, a method of service not available for 3-day notices to quit. [CC §§1946; 1946.1(e); see Chapter 19]

Thus, the date of service is the date the notice is:

- personally served;

30-DAY NOTICE TO VACATE
From Tenant

DATE:_____, 20_____, at _____, California

To Landlord: _____

Items left blank or unchecked are not applicable.

FACTS:

I am a Tenant under a lease or rental agreement

Dated _____, at

_____, California,

entered into by _____, Tenant,

and_____, Landlord,

regarding real estate referred to as: _____

_____

<table>
<tr><td>

NOTICE:

Unless otherwise agreed, a Tenant may terminate a month-to-month tenancy by giving thirty (30) days written notice to the landlord. [California Civil Code §1946]

</td></tr>
</table>

NOTICE:

1. Within thirty (30) days after service of this notice, I will vacate and deliver possession of the premises to Landlord or _____.

2. This notice is intended as a Thirty-Day Notice to terminate my month-to-month tenancy.

3. I understand:

   3.1 I will owe prorated daily rent for any days in the 30-day period I have not prepaid rent.

   3.2 I have previously given Landlord a security deposit of $_____.

   3.3 Within 21 days after I vacate, Landlord will furnish me a written statement and explanation of any deductions from the deposit, and a refund of the remaining amount. [California Civil Code §1950.5(f)]

   3.4 Landlord may deduct only those amounts necessary to:

      a. Reimburse for Tenant defaults in rental payments;

      b. Repair damages to the premises caused by Tenant (ordinary wear and tear excluded);

      c. Clean the premises, if necessary;

      d. Reimburse for Tenant loss, damage or excessive wear and tear on furnishings provided to Tenant.

   3.5 Landlord may show the premises to prospective tenants by giving reasonable notice as called for in the lease or rental agreement. Otherwise, twenty-four (24) hours will be presumed to be reasonable notice. Showings will only occur during normal business hours.

4. I will contact Landlord or Manager to review the condition of the premises before I vacate.

5. The reason for termination is_____.
   _(optional)

6. I have served this notice on Landlord or Manager by ☐ certified or registered mail, or ☐ personally.

This statement is true and correct.	For Landlord/Agent's use:
Date:_____, 20_____	Date Received: _____
Tenant:_____	
Signature: _____	
Forwarding Address: _____	
_____	
Phone: _____	
Fax: _____	
E-mail: _____	

FORM 572   10-00   ©2003 **first tuesday**, P.O. BOX 20069 RIVERSIDE, CA 92516 (800) 794-0494

- handed to a person of suitable age and discretion and mailed;

- posted on the leased premises and mailed; or

- mailed by certified or registered mail.

The 30- or 60-day minimum period within which the tenant must vacate begins to run the day after the date of service, which is day one of the 30- or 60-day period. [CC §10]

If the day for expiration of the notice is a Saturday, Sunday or legal holiday, the tenant is not required to vacate until the next business day. [CCP §12a]

However, most notice to vacate forms give a **specific date** by which the tenant must vacate, which is at least 30 or 60 days after service of the notice. Thus, the day is not left to chance and not set as a weekend day or holiday.

Rent control limitations on eviction

If residential rental property is located in a rent control community, the landlord is limited in his ability to terminate the tenancy and evict the tenant.

Typically, evictions are allowed in rent control communities when:

- the tenant fails to pay rent or otherwise materially breaches the lease agreement;

- the tenant creates a nuisance;

- the tenant refuses to renew a lease;

- the tenant uses the residence for an illegal purpose; or

- the landlord or a relative will occupy the unit.

A landlord who owns properties subject to rent control and his property manager must make themselves aware of the local restrictions imposed on the eviction of tenants.

Good reason to evict

A landlord is not required to state his reasons, or even have good cause, for evicting a month-to-month tenant in a notice to vacate — with the exceptions of rent control and Section 8 housing.

When a tenant's rent is subsidized by the Department of Housing and Urban Development's (HUD) Section 8 housing program, the landlord must set forth the reasons for the termination in the notice to vacate, and the reasons must be for a good cause. [**Mitchell** v. **Poole** (1988) 203 CA3d Supp. 1]

However, under no condition may a landlord evict a tenant for the wrong reason.

The landlord may find himself not only unable to evict the tenant, but defending against the tenant's claim the eviction is:

- in retaliation for the tenant making official complaints about the property or against the landlord;

- based on discriminatory reasons, such as the tenant's ethnicity or marital status; or

- improper because of the failure to maintain the property in a habitable condition.

Chapter 22

Personal property recovery by tenant

This chapter explains the steps residential and nonresidential landlords must take when confronted with personal property left by a tenant who has vacated.

Reclaim it or lose it on notice

A tenant vacates a rental property, residential or nonresidential, leaving behind personal belongings.

The tenant's right to possession of the space has been **terminated** by notice from the landlord due to the tenant's breach of the lease. The space is immediately re-rented and needs to be made ready for the new tenant.

The landlord removes the tenant's belongings from the leased space and stores them in a place of safekeeping. The value of the personal property is determined by the landlord to be less than $300.

Immediately, the landlord mails the tenant a notice, called a *Notice of Right to Reclaim Personal Property*, which:

- describes each item or lot of personal property left on the premises; and

- advises the tenant that the personal property will be discarded if not reclaimed by the tenant within 18 days of mailing the notice. [Calif. Civil Code §1983; see Form 584 accompanying this chapter]

The tenant does not respond to the notice and it expires. The landlord and his property manager dispose of the tenant's belongings.

Later, the tenant sends the landlord a letter requesting the landlord arrange for him to pick up the property. The landlord does not respond, believing he can ignore the tenant's late response.

The tenant then demands payment for the value of the items left behind.

Here, the landlord is not liable for the value of the personal property left in the unit and unclaimed by the tenant. The landlord followed the statutory procedure for notice and disposal of property worth less than $300. [CC §§1982; 1984]

The statutory notice procedure:

- provides the tenant with time in which to reclaim his personal property; and

- protects the landlord from liability on disposition of the personal property should the tenant fail to respond prior to expiration of the notice to reclaim.

Removal of personal property

Before removing a tenant's personal property from a vacant unit, a landlord must first be legally entitled to enter and take possession of the unit.

The landlord can enter, take possession and dispose of a tenant's personal property when the tenant has vacated and the tenant's right to possession of the premises has been *terminated*.

A tenant's right to possession is **terminated** when:

- the tenant's lease expires;

- a notice to vacate containing a declaration of forfeiture is served on the tenant and expires [See Chapter 21];

- the tenant's abandonment of the premises has been established by the statutory abandonment procedure; or

- the tenant has been evicted by an unlawful detainer (UD) action.

Returning personal property

Two separate statutory procedures exist for the return of personal property left on the premises by a tenant. One is initiated by the landlord, the other by the tenant.

One procedure allows residential and nonresidential landlords to initiate (and control) the process of returning or disposing of the tenant's personal property. A notice is personally served or mailed to the tenant who vacated and left the personal property advising him of his right to **reclaim or abandon** the personal property, called the *landlord-initiated disposition procedure*. [See **first tuesday** Form 581 and Form 584]

The other procedure allows a residential tenant who acts within 18 days of vacating the premises to initiate a return of his personal property he left behind by handing or mailing to the landlord or the property manager a *request to surrender* personal items he left behind, called the *tenant-initiated recovery procedure*. [CC §1965; see Form 582 accompanying this chapter]

The landlord is not required to employ the landlord-initiated procedure when confronted with the disposition of the tenant's personal property. [CC §1981]

However, a landlord who sells or disposes of a tenant's personal property by any procedure other than established by these two procedures can be challenged for his handling of the belongings by the tenant. The statutory procedures are sometimes called *safe harbor rules*.

For example, a tenant claims his personal property was inadvertently left behind, not abandoned. Thus, the landlord would not be entitled to sell or dispose of the property unless the landlord first establishes the tenant's actual intent is not to reclaim the property and thus to have abandoned it.

For abandonment and landlord disposal, the preferred method for establishing the tenant's intent not to reclaim the property left behind is the landlord-initiated disposition procedure. The tenant is notified of his right to reclaim the property he left behind and his need to respond to avoid its disposal. [See **first tuesday** Form 581 or Form 584]

Residential tenant-initiated recovery

Only a residential tenant may deliver to the landlord or the landlord's agent a written request for the return of personal property left in the vacated unit, called a *Notice to Landlord to Surrender Personal Property*. [See Form 582]

The tenant's request for the release of his belongings by the landlord, called *surrender*, must:

- be written;

- be mailed or handed to the landlord within 18 days after he vacates the unit;

- include his current mailing address;

- contain an identifiable description of the personal property left behind;

- be received by the landlord while the landlord or his agent is in control or possession of the personal property; and

- be received by the landlord or his agent before they have mailed to him a notice to reclaim the personal property, commencing the landlord-initiated disposition. [CC §1965(a)]

In response to receipt of the tenant's notice of surrender, the landlord must respond with a written demand on the tenant for reasonable removal and storage costs which:

NOTICE OF RIGHT TO RECLAIM PERSONAL PROPERTY
(To Tenant after Termination of Tenancy)

DATE:_____, 20_____, at _____, California

To Former Tenant:

  Name:_____

  Address:_____

  _____

Items left blank or unchecked are not applicable.

FACTS:

You were a Tenant under a lease or rental agreement dated

_____, at _____, California,

entered into by _____, Tenant,

and _____, Landlord,

regarding real estate referred to as:_____

_____

> **NOTICE:**
> This notice may be given to a residential and nonresidential tenant who left personal property on the premises which remains after he vacated the premises and his tenancy terminated. On expiration of this notice, the landlord may dispose of the unclaimed property. [CC §1983]

NOTICE:

1. This notice expires unless you respond by _____, 20_____, which date is at least:

   ☐ 15 days after this notice was personally served, or

   ☐ 18 days after this notice was deposited in the mail.

2. When you vacated the premises referenced above, the following personal property remained:

   _____

   _____

   _____

   _____

3. You may claim the personal property at: _____

   _____

4. **YOU MAY AVOID DISPOSAL OF PERSONAL PROPERTY** by doing the following before expiration of this notice:

   4.1 Pay the reasonable cost of removal and storage of all the personal property; **AND**

   4.2 Take possession of the personal property.

5. **The personal property to be claimed or disposed of is valued as:**

   5.1 ☐ Worth more than $300. If you fail to reclaim the property, it will be sold at a public sale after published notice of the sale. You have the right to bid on the property at this sale. After the property is sold and the cost of storage, advertising and sale are deducted, the remaining money will be handed to the county. You may claim the remaining money within one year after the county receives the money.

   5.2 ☐ Worth less than $300. This property is believed to be worth less than $300. Therefore, it may be kept, sold or destroyed without further notice if you fail to reclaim it prior to expiration of this notice.

This statement is true and correct.

Date:_____, 20_____

Landlord/Agent: _____

Signature: _____

Address: _____

_____

Phone: _____

Fax: _____

E-mail: _____

FORM 584   09-02   ©2003 **first tuesday**, P.O. BOX 20069 RIVERSIDE, CA 92516 (800) 794-0494

- the landlord will mail or hand to the tenant within five days after the landlord receives the tenant's request to surrender the property; and

- itemizes any costs for removal and storage to be paid before the tenant can remove the property. [CC §1965(a)(3); see **first tuesday** Form 588]

It is then incumbent upon the tenant to contact the landlord and arrange a mutually agreed-to date, time and location for the tenant to claim and remove the personal property.

However, the tenant or the tenant's agent must remove the personal belongings within 72 hours **after the tenant pays** storage charges demanded by the landlord. [CC §1965(a)(4)]

After a tenant mails the landlord a request to surrender personal property, the landlord might receive **another request** for the same items from the tenant's roommate, a secured creditor or other person with an interest in the property.

The first request received by the landlord controls the return of the property left behind. [CC §1965(d)]

The landlord is not obligated to the roommate or anyone else who makes a later request for the same personal belongings.

Which process controls

The tenant-initiated process for residential rentals does not apply if the landlord first mails or personally delivers the notice to reclaim personal property to the tenant before he receives the tenant's notice to surrender. [CC §1965(c)]

But what if the landlord's notice to reclaim property and the tenant's request to surrender the property pass in the mail?

Here, the landlord-initiated process begins the moment the landlord deposits the notice of the tenant's right to reclaim property in the mail (first-class, postage prepaid). The tenant-initi-ated process does not begin until the landlord or his agent personally receives the tenant's request.

Thus, the landlord who neglects to mail the notice before actually receiving a tenant's request must respond to the tenant's request since the landlord no longer controls disposition under abandonment rules.

Conversely, if the landlord can show he or his agent deposited either the Notice of Belief of Abandonment or the notice to reclaim personal property in the mail before they actually received the tenant's notice to surrender, the tenant must abide by the landlord-initiated disposition procedure.

Residential landlord violations

Consider a residential tenant who has vacated and timely hands the landlord a notice to surrender personal items he left behind.

The landlord makes a demand on the tenant to pay removal and storage costs. The tenant promptly pays the removal and storage costs.

Should the landlord fail to hand over the items within 72 hours after the tenant (or tenant's agent) pays storage and removal fees, the landlord is liable for:

- damages for the value of the personal items;

- $250 for each violation; and

- attorney fees. [CC §1965(e)]

This tenant-initiated procedure is entirely avoided if the landlord merely sends by first-class mail either the notice of abandonment (both real estate and personal property) or a notice to reclaim personal property before he receives the tenant's notice to surrender the property. [See **first tuesday** Form 581 and Form 584]

NOTICE TO LANDLORD TO SURRENDER PERSONAL PROPERTY
(For Use by Residential Tenants Only)

DATE:_____, 20_____, at _____, California

To Landlord: _____

Items left blank or unchecked are not applicable.

FACTS:

I am a former Tenant under a residential lease or rental agreement

Dated _____, at

_____, California,

entered into by _____, Tenant,

and _____, Landlord,

regarding real estate referred to as: _____

> **NOTICE:**
> If the landlord has not initiated the abandonment remedy, the tenant by this request may reclaim personal property from vacated residential rental premises within 72 hours after payment of removal and storage fees. [Calif. Civil Code §1965]

NOTICE:

1. Within eighteen (18) days prior to mailing or handing this notice to the Landlord, I vacated and delivered possession of the premises to Landlord or
_____

2. This notice is a request for Landlord to surrender to me or
_____

   personal property not owned by Landlord and described below which was left on the vacated premises.

3. I understand:

   3.1 This notice must be mailed within eighteen (18) days after I vacated the premises.

   3.2 Landlord or the landlord's manager must have control or possession of the personal property at the time the Landlord actually receives this notice.

   3.3 I will pay all reasonable costs actually incurred by Landlord for the removal and storage of the personal property as a condition for the release and return of the personal property.

   3.4 Landlord will provide a written itemized demand for payment of reasonable removal and storage fees within five (5) days of actual receipt of this notice unless the property is first returned. The demand for payment of removal and storage fees will be mailed to the address given below or handed to me personally.

   3.5 I will claim and remove the personal property at a reasonable time mutually agreed upon by Landlord and myself to occur within 72 hours after my payment of reasonable removal and storage fees demanded by landlord.

4. Description of personal property to be reclaimed: _____
_____
_____
_____

This statement is true and correct.	**For Landlord/Manager's use:**
Date:_____, 20_____	Date Received: _____
Tenant:_____	By: _____
Signature: _____	
Current mailing address: _____	
_____	
Phone: _____	
Fax: _____	
E-mail: _____	

FORM 582   09-02   ©2003 **first tuesday**, P.O. BOX 20069 RIVERSIDE, CA 92516 (800) 794-0494

Landlord-initiated abandonment

On mailing or personally delivering the notice of abandonment to the tenant, and any other possible **owner or creditor known** to have an interest in the belongings, a residential or nonresidential landlord commences the landlord-initiated disposition process. [See **first tuesday** Form 581]

The notice to dispose of the tenant's property must be delivered to the tenant by either:

- personal service; or

- first-class mail to the tenant's last known address with a duplicate notice mailed to the address of the vacated premises. [CC §1983(c)]

Notice should be given promptly on termination of the tenancy, but may be given at any time after the tenant has vacated the premises. [CC §1983]

As a matter of practice, the tenancy should first be terminated before entering the premises and determining whether the tenant left personal property, unless the abandonment procedure is used.

Abandonment notices

A landlord may combine the abandoned personal property notice with the notice of abandonment of the premises.

The landlord combines the two notices when he believes the tenant has abandoned both the personal property and the premises, and the landlord **chooses to terminate** the tenant's right to possession by establishing an abandonment of the premises. [CC §1991; see Form 581]

Both notices from the landlord to the tenant must include:

- a description of each item;

- notice that reasonable storage costs will be charged;

- the location where the property may be reclaimed;

- expiration of the notice — the date by which the tenant must reclaim his property;

- notice the property will be kept, sold or destroyed if the value is estimated at less than $300; and

- notice the property will be sold by public sale if it is worth $300 or more and is not reclaimed. [CC §§1983(b); §1984(b)]

If the notice is personally served on the tenant, the notice may expire no less than 15 days after service.

If the notice is mailed, the notice may expire no less than 18 days after posting in the mail. [CC §1983(b)]

If personal property worth less than $300 is not reclaimed by a tenant before the notice expires, the landlord may keep, sell or destroy the property without further notice to the tenant. [CC §1984]

Notice to third-party owners

Under the landlord-initiated procedure, the landlord must also notify any other persons he **reasonably believes** may have any ownership interest in the personal property left on the premises. [CC §1983(a); see Form 587 accompanying this chapter]

For example, if a landlord is aware a co-tenant or guest left behind some personal property, he must notify the co-tenant or guest as well as the tenant.

NOTICE OF RIGHT TO RECLAIM PERSONAL PROPERTY
(To Others with an Interest in Property Left by Tenant)

DATE:_____, 20_____, at _____, California

To: Name:_____

    Address:_____

    _____

Items left blank or unchecked are not applicable.

NOTICE:

1. This notice to claim personal property you may have an interest in expires on _____, 20_____, which date is at least:

   ☐ 15 days after this notice was personally served on you; or

   ☐ 18 days after this notice was sent by first class mail, postage prepaid, to your last known address.

2. When our former tenant named_____,

   vacated premises known as _____

   _____,

   the following personal property remained:_____

   _____

   _____

   _____

   _____

   _____.

3. If you have an interest in any of this personal property, you may claim it at:

   _____

   _____

4. You must pay the cost of storage on or before taking possession of the personal property you claim. [**first tuesday** Form 588]

5. Unless you take possession of the personal property you have an interest in prior to the expiration of this notice, the personal property not claimed will be sold at a public sale by competitive bidding. [CC §1988]

> **NOTICE:**
> This notice may be given to persons who are believed to own or hold a security interest in personal property left on residential or nonresidential premises by a tenant who has vacated and whose tenancy has been terminated. On expiration of this notice, the landlord may dispose of itemized unclaimed property [CC §1983]

This statement is true and correct.

Date:_____, 20_____

Landlord/Agent: _____

Signature: _____

Address: _____

_____

Phone: _____

Fax: _____

E-mail: _____

FORM 587   09-02   ©2003 **first tuesday**, P.O. BOX 20069 RIVERSIDE, CA 92516 (800) 794-0494

The *reasonable belief* of ownership of the abandoned personal property imposed on a landlord means the **actual knowledge** a prudent person in the landlord's (or property manager's) position would have without making an investigation, unless such an investigation is of probable value and reasonable cost. [CC §1980(d)]

For example, the landlord is not required to investigate public records unless it is likely he will find information pertinent to locating the owner of the personal property.

Also, if a landlord notices a name or phone number inscribed on the personal items, such as a furniture rental company, the landlord will not be protected from liability for failure to investigate the name or phone number.

Identification of personal property

First, the identification of the personal property in notices to reclaim initiated by the landlord should list every significant item or "lot of items" left behind.

Although the landlord may choose to describe only a portion of the personal property left behind, he is protected from liability only for those items he identifies.

A landlord may identify items as simply as a "bundle," a "lot" or a "box" of items, or the landlord may look inside the bundle or boxes to determine the contents and their worth. The **total value** of the bundled, boxed or similar items in a lot will determine the method the landlord must employ to dispose of them.

Proof of value statement

The landlord may use his reasonable belief to estimate the value of the items. Should the tenant leave behind items with a total worth exceeding $300, the landlord must put them up for sale at a **public auction**. [CC §1988(a)]

The landlord, property manager or resident manager should use a witness to inventory the items and confirm their estimated worth. The witness will assist the landlord should the tenant claim the landlord confiscated or damaged items.

Storage and release of property

As in the tenant-initiated procedure for reclaiming items, the landlord may charge the tenant for the cost of removal and storage of the property.

The landlord may store the personal property in the unit, or remove it to another place of safekeeping, for which he may charge a fee.

While the landlord must exercise care in storing the property, he may be held liable only for damages caused by his intentional or negligent treatment of the items when removing and storing them. [CC §1986]

The landlord **must release** the personal property to the tenant, or the person who first notifies the landlord of his right to reclaim, within 72 hours of payment of the storage costs.

The tenant or owner reclaiming the personal items is responsible for the storage costs. Any owner other than the tenant is responsible only for the storage costs of property he claims.

The landlord may not, however, charge more than one party for storage of any one item. [CC §1990]

Sale of the abandoned property

If the total worth of the abandoned personal items is $300 or more, they must be sold at a public sale by the landlord.

If the abandoned personal property notice states the property (because of its value) is **subject to public sale**, the landlord must surrender the personal property to the tenant any time prior to the sale, even after the date specified for expiration in the notice of abandonment. [CC §1987]

However, the tenant or the owner must then pay advertising and sale costs in addition to storage costs. [CC§ 1987]

The landlord must advertise the public sale prior to its scheduled date in a local county newspaper of general circulation. [CC §1988(b)]

The **notice of sale** must appear twice — once each week for two consecutive weeks. The last advertisement may not be later than five calendar days before the date of the sale.

The notice of sale must specify the date, time and location of the sale. Also, the notice of sale must sufficiently describe the personal property to allow the owner to identify the property as his.

The timetable before sale becomes the combination of the 15-or 18-day period for the notice of abandonment and the 12 days of advertising.

The highest bidder (including the tenant or landlord) may buy the property.

Any proceeds from the sale, minus the costs of sale, advertising and storage, are given to the county treasurer within 30 days of the sale. Once the remaining proceeds have been given over to the county treasurer, the tenant or owner of the personal property has one year to claim the proceeds. [CC §1988]

Chapter 23

Constructive eviction cancels the lease

This chapter reviews the tenant's remedies when a landlord breaches a nonresidential lease.

Interference forces tenant to vacate

A nonresidential tenant occupies a building in which he operates his restaurant business.

The tenant's lease agreement obligates the landlord to make all necessary repairs to the exterior walls and roof during the term of the lease.

During the tenancy, the roof begins to leak. The tenant notifies the landlord about the leak and the need for repairs. The landlord makes several personal attempts to repair the roof. However, the roof is never properly repaired and the leak persists.

The leaking water causes damage to the interior walls. During rain storms, puddles form on the floors creating hazardous conditions for employees and patrons.

Fed up, the tenant **vacates the premises**.

The tenant then makes a demand on the landlord to recover his security deposit and business losses.

The tenant's losses include lost income from business operations, loss of goodwill, relocation expenses, employee medical expenses and water damage to furnishings and equipment.

Also, the tenant claims the lease agreement has been cancelled due to the landlord's interference with the tenant's occupancy since the landlord's failure to meet his lease obligation to repair the roof caused him to vacate the leased premises, called a *constructive eviction*.

The landlord claims his failure to repair the roof was not conduct so intrusive as to result in a constructive eviction, but was merely an inconvenience to the tenant for which the tenant is only entitled to money for his losses, not a cancellation of the lease agreement.

Here, the landlord's failure to meet his obligation to repair the roof was conduct which *terminated* the tenant's right to possession and *cancelled* the lease agreement. The leaking roof significantly interfered with the tenant's ability to use the premises to operate a restaurant as intended in the lease.

Thus, both the landlord's **failure to maintain** the property and the tenant **vacating the premises** constituted a *constructive eviction* allowing the tenant to recover the security deposit and any money losses caused by the landlord's interference. [**Groh** v. **Kover's Bull Pen, Inc.** (1963) 221 CA2d 611]

A tenant is not obligated to continue to occupy the premises and pay rent if the premises can no longer be used as intended due to the landlord's conduct.

If the landlord's failure to repair does not deprive the tenant of his use of the premises, the tenant's right to possession and obligations under the lease agreement remain intact.

Recovery of any money losses a tenant incurs due to the landlord's failure to repair, which does not significantly interfere with the tenant's use of the premises and justify his vacating as a constructive eviction, must be pursued in a separate action, not as an offset to rent.

Note — The constructive eviction could easily have been avoided in Groh *had the landlord hired competent help to promptly and properly repair the roof.*

Landlord's breach terminates possession

Both the landlord and the tenant must perform their obligations under the provisions contained or implied in the lease agreement. If either the landlord or tenant do not fully perform, they breach the lease.

A breach, due to the landlord or tenant's failure to perform their respective obligations under the lease agreement, is either a *minor breach* or a *material breach*.

A **minor breach** of the lease agreement provisions by either the landlord or the tenant is not a justifiable basis for terminating the leasehold. Examples of minor breaches include the landlord's failure to maintain landscaping or the tenant's failure to pay late charges.

However, a **material breach** of the lease by either the tenant or landlord justifies a termination of the tenant's right or ability to possess the premises — his leasehold estate in the property.

As a material breach, a landlord's failure to meet significant obligations imposed on him by the lease agreement **allows the tenant** to:

- terminate his possession of the leased premises, causing the leasehold estate to revert to the landlord; and

- cancel the lease agreement, including all future rent obligations.

Constructive eviction

A **constructive eviction** occurs when:

- the landlord or his agent *substantially interferes* with the tenant's use and enjoyment of the premises during the term of the lease or rental agreement; and

- the *tenant vacates* the premises due to the interference.

A constructive eviction due to the landlord's interference does not occur until the tenant vacates. Eviction does not exist as long as the tenant remains in possession.

Examples of **substantial interference** by the landlord which justify the tenant's vacating the premises include:

- a material breach of the lease, such as failing to repair and maintain the leased premises to accommodate the use intended by the lease [Groh, *supra*];

- extensive alteration of the leased premises which is not authorized in the lease or by the tenant and interferes with the intended use [**Reichhold** v. **Sommarstrom Inv. Co.** (1927) 83 CA 173];

- the sale of adjacent property owned by the landlord without reserving the tenant's parking and water rights given to the tenant under the lease [**Sierad** v. **Lilly** (1962) 204 CA2d 770]; or

- the failure to abate a sanitation, noise or safety nuisance over which the landlord, but not the tenant, has control. [**Johnson** v. **Snyder** (1950) 99 CA2d 86]

In a constructive eviction, neither a 3-day notice nor an unlawful detainer (UD) action is used to force the tenant to vacate. [Reichhold, *supra*]

Tenant's losses and remedies

Every lease and month-to-month rental agreement contains an **implied covenant**, an unwritten lease provision, which prohibits the landlord from interfering with the tenant's agreed use and possession of the property, called the *covenant of quiet enjoyment*. [Calif. Civil Code §1927]

When a landlord breaches the *covenant of quiet enjoyment*, or other significant lease provision, the tenant can:

- **vacate** the leased premises, recover his money losses incurred and cancel his obligation to pay future rents based on his constructive eviction; or

- **retain possession**, continue to pay rent and sue for any income lost or expenses incurred due to the landlord's interference.

The **losses** a tenant can recover when the tenant vacates upon his constructive eviction include:

- advance payments of rent and security deposits;

- the cost of removing trade fixtures [Reichhold, *supra*];

- relocation expenses; and

- loss of business goodwill. [Johnson, *supra*]

The breaching landlord's remedies

A tenant who fails to pay rent and later vacates the premises due to a constructive eviction owes the landlord rent for the period of occupancy prior to vacating.

However, any unpaid back rent the landlord is entitled to collect is offset by money losses the tenant incurs due to the constructive eviction. **[Petroleum Collections Incorporated** v. **Swords** (1975) 48 CA3d 841]

Breach of anti-competition clause

The landlord's breach of an anti-competition provision is a material breach of the lease agreement. The tenant may respond by vacating the premises as a constructive eviction.

Consider a nonresidential lease containing an *anti-competition clause* stating the landlord will not lease other space in the commercial complex to competitors of the tenant.

The lease also contains a *remedies provision* stating the landlord may relet the premises **without notifying** the tenant should the tenant vacate prior to the lease expiration date.

Later, the tenant holds a sale to liquidate his stock. The tenant then closes down his business operations, vacates the premises and returns the keys to the landlord with instructions to find another tenant. The tenant's lease does not expire for a few years.

The landlord does not respond by entering into an agreement to cancel (surrender) the lease, nor does he take possession of the premises. Further, the landlord does not take **steps to forfeit** the tenant's right to possession (by abandonment or 3-day notice).

The tenant pays no further rent and the landlord makes no demand on the tenant for delinquent rent.

The landlord tries to locate a new tenant, but is unable to find one.

Several months after closing the business, the tenant re-enters the premises and prepares to reopen for business.

Meanwhile, the landlord leases another space in the building to a competitor of the tenant.

On discovering a competitor will now occupy the same commercial complex, the tenant vacates the premises and notifies the landlord he has elected to cancel the lease since the landlord breached the anti-competition clause in the lease by renting another space in the building to his competitor.

The landlord makes a demand for all rents due until the expiration of the lease agreement, claiming the obligation to pay rent under the lease has not been terminated.

The tenant claims he is liable only for the rents due prior to his vacating the premises (the second time) since the landlord's breach of the anti-competition provision in the lease constituted a constructive eviction.

Can the tenant cancel the lease, thus terminating his obligation to pay rent for the remaining term of the lease?

Yes! The tenant's right to possession under the lease has been terminated and the tenant's lease obligation to pay rent is cancelled due to the landlord's interference and the tenant vacating the premises. The landlord's breach of the anti-competition clause constitutes a constructive eviction of the tenant which justifies his vacating the premises and cancelling the lease agreement. [**Kulawitz** v. **Pacific Woodenware & Paper Co.** (1944) 25 CA2d 664]

Failure to forfeit leads to breach

The landlord in the prior scenario failed to terminate the tenant's right to occupy the premises by declaring a forfeiture of the leasehold estate when the tenant first vacated the premises and became delinquent on rent. Due to the landlord's administrative error, the tenant retained all his property and contract rights under the lease.

The landlord could have terminated the leasehold when the tenant closed his business and delivered the keys to the landlord by:

- a surrender (accepting the possession of the premises in exchange for cancellation of the lease agreement and loss of future rents); or

- a 3-day notice to pay rent or quit with a declaration of forfeiture of the leasehold (or a notice of abandonment).

Without a termination of the tenant's leasehold rights, the tenant's right to possession as agreed to in the lease remained in effect throughout the delinquency.

Since the tenant's right to possession had not been terminated, the landlord's lease obligation to the tenant to abide by the anti-competition clause remained in effect.

A landlord cannot reasonably expect to recover rents remaining due for the unexpired duration of a lease agreement which he has breached, causing the tenant to vacate as a constructive eviction.

Independent obligations to perform

Now consider a tenant who leases a gas station.

A modular sign on the premises advertising the service station can be seen from a nearby freeway.

However, the sign was installed without a permit. The city orders the removal of the sign since its proximity to the gas tanks constitutes a fire hazard.

The landlord removes the sign and replaces it with a billboard which cannot be seen from the freeway.

The tenant demands the landlord provide a sign which can be seen from the freeway, and is of comparable likeness to the one removed.

When the landlord fails to provide a similar sign, the tenant stops paying rent but remains in possession of the premises.

Months later, the lease agreement is cancelled by the mutual agreement of the landlord and tenant. The tenant then vacates the premises.

The landlord now makes a demand on the tenant to pay rent for the period of time the tenant did not pay rent prior to vacating the premises.

The tenant claims he is not liable for the rent during his period of occupancy after removal of the sign since the landlord constructively evicted the tenant from the premises by removing the sign, a breach of the covenant of quiet enjoyment and use of the property.

Is the tenant liable for the unpaid back rent during his entire period of occupancy?

Yes! The tenant is liable for the agreed-to rent for the period of his occupancy since a constructive eviction — which relieves the tenant of his rent obligation — cannot occur until the tenant **actually vacates** the premises (and thus owes no more rent). [Petroleum Collections Incorporated, *supra*]

While the landlord's failure to replace the sign that could be seen from the freeway with a similar sign significantly interfered with the tenant's use of the property as intended by the lease, the fact is the tenant remained in possession after the breach without negotiating a modification of the lease agreement.

A tenant owes rent under the lease in exchange for his use and possession of the leased premises. Rent at the agreed price is due even though the use may be diminished by the landlord's interference.

Thus, when the tenant remains in possession and **fails to pay rent**, the interfering landlord may forfeit the tenant's right to occupy the property by a 3-day notice and declaration of forfeiture.

Conversely, a landlord whose conduct interferes with the tenant's use and possession allows the tenant to vacate without paying future rents — a constructive eviction due to a breach of the implied covenant of quiet enjoyment.

Quiet enjoyment waiver

A tenant leases space in a retail center.

The nonresidential lease agreement contains a **remedies clause** stating:

- the tenant may not terminate the lease agreement on any failure of the landlord to fully perform on the lease; and

- the tenant may only recover money losses should the landlord breach the lease.

The landlord leases the adjoining space to a dry cleaning business. The dry cleaning business emits fumes that enter the ventilation system and permeate the tenant's premises, negatively impacting his employees and business operations.

The landlord is notified of the interference but fails to remedy the ventilation problems over which he has control.

The tenant stops paying rent and vacates the premises, claiming the dry cleaning fumes were noxious and endangered his employees' health.

The landlord makes a demand on the tenant to pay rent for the remainder of the lease term.

The tenant rejects the demand and then seeks to recover his lost profits, relocation expenses and employee medical expenses from the landlord.

The tenant claims the landlord's failure to prevent the fumes from invading his leased premises is a breach of the implied covenant of quiet enjoyment and constitutes a constructive eviction which cancelled the lease when he vacated.

The landlord claims the tenant is liable for the remaining rent whether or not the tenant vacated since the lease contains a remedies clause which waives the tenant's right to terminate the lease.

Is the tenant liable for the rent due for the remaining term of the lease?

Yes! The nonresidential tenant is liable for the rent remaining unpaid on the lease. While the tenant was constructively evicted, he remains liable for all future unpaid rent under the lease. The tenant contracted to limit his remedies on the landlord's material breach of the lease to a demand for money. The tenant's claim for money losses is separate from the rent due under the lease. [**Lee** v. **Placer Title Company** (1994) 28 CA4th 503]

Thus, the tenant is obligated to:

- remain in possession (and care) of the premises even though he has been constructively evicted;

- continue paying the agreed rent for the entire duration of the lease; and

- sue the landlord to recover any money losses caused by the landlord's breach of the lease agreement.

Note — For residential tenants, any waiver or limitation on the remedies for breach of the covenant of quiet enjoyment is void as against public policy; not so for nonresidential tenants. [CC §1953]

However, if the landlord's conduct prevents, not just interferes with, the tenant from operating his business on the property and forces him to vacate, then the value of the tenant's leasehold interest has been completely diminished.

While the nonresidential tenant waived his right to terminate the lease on the landlord's breach of the covenant of quiet enjoyment, he may vacate the property and sue for money, including:

- a 100% offset against future rents due on the lease for his money losses occurring after the breach and until the landlord performs or the lease term expires; and

- lost profits, relocation expenses, rent for the replacement space and loss of goodwill.

Landlord interference with subtenants

A tenant may convey part of his leasehold right to possess part or all of the real estate to a subtenant by entering into a *sublease.*

Most leases (and subleases) held by single-user tenants prevent the tenant from subleasing (or assigning) without the landlord's permission.

On entering into a sublease, the subtenant becomes a third-party beneficiary to the master lease entered into by the landlord, which includes the benefit of the implied covenant of quiet enjoyment, when:

- the master lease permits subleasing; or

- the landlord consents to a sublease under a restraint on alienation provision in the master lease.

The master lease should be attached to the sublease as an exhibit, as the rights of the subtenant are limited by the terms of the master lease.

Thus, if a landlord's conduct interferes with the subtenant's use of the premises as agreed in the sublease (and limited by the master lease), the subtenant may vacate and recover losses from the landlord for a constructive eviction. [**Marchese** v. **Standard Realty and Development Company** (1977) 74 CA3d 142]

When a **subtenant** has been constructively evicted by the landlord, the master tenant may:

- vacate the entire premises, cancel the lease and recover losses from the landlord for a constructive eviction of the master tenant; or

- remain in possession and recover money losses for breach of the implied covenant of quiet enjoyment.

Constructive eviction vs. the warranty of habitability

Constructive eviction of either a residential or nonresidential tenant is distinct from the implied warranty of habitability enforced against landlords only in residential rental and lease agreements. Constructive eviction requires the tenant to vacate; the warranty of habitability does not.

Both residential and nonresidential leases contain written conditions which, if breached by the landlord, result in termination of the tenant's possession — constructive eviction.

However, the warranty of habitability is not a written provision but is implied; it is judicially and legislatively considered to exist in all residential lease and rental agreements.

The implied warranty of habitability requires a landlord to maintain safe and sanitary conditions in his residential units. On the landlord's failure to maintain habitable conditions, the residential tenant may remain in possession and pay a reduced rent that will be set by the court. Thus, a constructive eviction has not taken place since the residential tenant remains in possession. [**Green** v. **Superior Court of the City and County of San Francisco** (1974) 10 C3d 616; Calif. Code of Civil Procedure §1174.2; see Chapter 37]

However, both residential and nonresidential tenants can vacate the premises based on the landlord's significant interference with possessory rights and recover any losses from their landlords which flow from the constructive eviction.

Consider a nonresidential landlord who fails to meet his obligations under a lease to maintain the property for the intended use. The nonresidential tenant retaliates by failing to pay rent. However, the tenant does not vacate the premises.

The landlord files a UD action to evict the tenant for his failure to pay rent. At trial, the tenant is unable to raise the defense of a breach of the implied warranty of habitability since his lease is nonresidential. The nonresidential tenant is without an excuse for his failure to pay rent and will be evicted. [**Schulman** v. **Vera** (1980) 108 CA3d 552]

SECTION E

Maintenance and Security

Chapter 24

Defective building components

This chapter discusses a landlord's lack of liability for injuries caused by defects in components installed on the property which were supplied by manufacturers, distributors and retailers.

Liability for neglect, not strict liability

An occupant of a residential rental unit slips and falls in the bathtub. The occupant sustains injuries from the fall. The bathtub does not have an anti-skid surface and is very slippery when it is wet.

The occupant claims the landlord is strictly liable for the injuries since the bathtub without an anti-skid surface is defective.

Is the landlord liable to the occupant for the injuries caused by the defective bathtub surface?

No! Landlords are not strictly liable for injuries to the occupant caused by a defective bathtub surface. To be liable for another's injuries without concern for fault, called *strict liability*, the landlord must be part of the **chain of distribution** for the equipment or fixtures installed in the unit.

It is unreasonable to extend strict liability to hotel operators and residential landlords for defects in products manufactured and marketed by others which are used in the construction of the property. [**Peterson** v. **Superior Court** (1995) 10 C4th 1185]

Strict liability

Strict liability for an injury caused by a product applies primarily to the manufacturer of the product, since it is the manufacturer who places the product on the market and knows it will not be inspected for defects before it is used. Thus, the manufacturer is liable for defects.

The primary **social purpose** of strict liability is to insure the manufacturer, not the user who is injured, bears the costs of injuries caused by its products when used for the purpose intended.

Secondarily, strict liability for defect-related injuries also extends to distributors and retailers who are part of the "stream of commerce" in marketing products for use by the end user, the customer. Distributors and retailers are considered to be in the best position to **assert influence** over the manufacturer to create a product that is free of defects.

Strict liability is imposed on retailers and distributors since the added liability exposure is considered an incentive for their attention to the safety of the products they purchase from manufacturers for resale to the public.

However, the social goal of imposing strict liability on all involved in the manufacturing, distribution and resale of a product to the consumer is not to **ensure the safety** of the product. The goal is to spread the risks and costs of injury due to **lack of safety** in the use expected to be made of the product among those most able to bear the burden of the costs.

Previous strict liability rulings

The *Peterson* case barring tenants from pursuing landlords and hotel operators for strict liability for injuries resulting from dangerous and defective construction materials and fixtures overruled a previous California Supreme Court decision. The court previously held a residential landlord was strictly liable for injuries caused by hidden defects in components which were part of the construction of the property. [**Becker** v. **IRM Corporation** (1985) 38 C3d 454]

In *Becker*, a tenant slips in the shower and is injured when the shower door shatters — the door was defective since it was made from untempered glass.

The tenant claims the landlord's use of the product caused his injuries and the landlord is responsible under the strict liability doctrine.

The landlord claims he is not liable for the injuries since the defect in the shower door was hidden, and the accident was not foreseeable as no similar accidents had occurred to put the landlord on notice of the defect so he could prevent future occurrences.

In *Becker*, which is no longer law, the landlord was held strictly liable for the tenant's injuries caused by the latent defects in materials and fixtures installed in the unit, regardless of whether the landlord was aware of the defect, since the landlord was in the business of renting property.

Becker held the landlord is part of the enterprise of producing and marketing components built into the rental units when constructed.

However, *Peterson* overruled *Becker*. The *Peterson* court held the theory of strict liability could not be extended to residential landlords. Landlords are not distributors or retailers. Landlords and hotel operators, unlike distributors and retailers, cannot exert influence over the manufacturer to make a product safe. For the most part, landlords and hotel operators are not builders and do not have a business relationship with the manufacturer or the suppliers of the defective product.

Landlords and hotel operators are not retailers of products simply because the products are components of the structure and are used by the tenant. Once the product is purchased and installed by the builder, the product leaves the stream of commerce — distribution and resale has come to an end. The later use of the product by occupants, be they tenants or guests, does not transform the landlord and hotel operator into a retailer of the product.

Note — Peterson refused to decide whether strict liability can be imposed on a landlord or a hotel operator who participates in the construction of the building. Specifications established by planners, designers and construction contractors will play a role in deciding whether strict liability will be imposed on owner-builders of rental and hotel units.

Duty to correct known defects

It is the residential landlord's inaction when confronted with a **known dangerous** condition, called *negligence*, which gives rise to liability for injury to others.

Thus, a residential landlord who fails to cure known dangerous defects will be liable under general *tort principles of negligence* for injuries caused by the breach of his duty to correct known defects.

Tenants should be able to rely on the landlord's inspection of the rented space and the correction of all visible and known defects.

Residential landlords are in the business of leasing property for human habitation.

The residential landlord must provide a clean, safe and habitable premises during the term of the lease. Further, the landlord is obligated to repair all known patent or latent defects, unless the tenant agrees to undertake repairs and maintenance. [Calif. Civil Code §1942]

Thus, the residential landlord is personally liable to the tenant for injuries occurring on the rental property as a result of the landlord's failure to inspect, locate and repair defective and dangerous property conditions which are known or should be known to the landlord. [CC §1941]

The residential landlord is obligated to repair uninhabitable conditions which could affect the tenant's health and safety, and to make these repairs immediately. [See Chapter 26]

Further, if the cause of the tenant's injuries are from latent (hidden) defects in products, and the defects are unknown to the landlord, the tenant can still recover under the strict liability doctrine from the manufacturer, distributor and retailer of the product causing the injury. [Peterson, *supra*]

Note — The tenant will be able to recover from the landlord if the tenant can show the landlord could have reasonably foreseen the accident.

*A landlord or hotel operator who is aware of injuries caused by latent defects in products will be liable if other similar latent defects are not cured, since it is reasonably foreseeable injuries caused by similar defects throughout the project will occur. [***Sturgeon*** v. **Curnutt** (1994) 29 CA4th 301]*

Chapter 25

Care and maintenance of property

This chapter outlines the respective duties of the landlord and tenant to care for and maintain leased property, and the tenant's remedies should the landlord fail to perform.

Tenant's obligations and remedies

A landlord and a tenant enter into a lease for a furnished unit in an apartment complex.

The lease agreement contains a provision stating the landlord will maintain the premises and common areas in a safe and sanitary condition, and comply with all applicable ordinances and regulations. [See **first tuesday** Form 550 §6.2]

The lease further provides for the tenant to keep the unit clean and sanitary, and properly operate all electrical, gas and plumbing fixtures. [See **first tuesday** Form 550 §§5.3, 5.4]

Before the tenant takes possession, the resident manager and the tenant do a "walk-through" of the unit and agree on the condition of the premises.

The tenant and the resident manager complete a condition of premises form which is attached as an addendum to the lease agreement. [See Form 560 accompanying this chapter]

On the condition of premises form, the tenant notes any defects existing on the premises.

For example, the tenant marks if appliances are dented, screens have holes or are missing from windows, plumbing fixtures are broken or leaking, linoleum is peeling or damaged, carpeting has stains, etc.

Since the unit is furnished, the tenant and the resident manager also complete a condition of furnishings addendum during the "walk-through." [See Form 561 accompanying this chapter]

The tenant records any defects in the furniture on the condition of furnishings form, such as tears or burns in upholstery or scratches in wood furniture.

No minor or major defective conditions are observed by the tenant or the landlord during the "walk-through."

Later, when the tenant vacates the unit, the tenant and the resident manager will conduct a "walk-through" to determine if the unit and the furnishings have suffered any damage other than normal wear and tear during the occupancy.

The purpose of the condition of premises and condition of furnishings forms is to determine if any defective conditions exist in the rental unit and to repair them before the tenant takes possession.

When the tenant vacates, the landlord wants to be able to recover the cost of any damage to the unit or the furnishings caused by the tenant. The completed forms document the condition of the unit and its furnishings at the time of occupancy.

On the other hand, the tenant wants to avoid liability for damage he did not cause.

Tenant's duty to maintain

A tenant must repair all deterioration and damage to the premises caused by his failure to use ordinary care in his use of the premises. [Calif. Civil Code §1929]

Further, a residential tenant has a duty of care and maintenance in the use of the leased premises which includes:

CONDITION OF PREMISES ADDENDUM

DATE:_____, 20_____, at _____, California

Items left blank or unchecked are not applicable

FACTS:

This is an addendum to the following:

☐ Lease agreement

☐ Occupancy agreement

☐ Rental Agreement

Dated:_____, 20_____

Entered into by: _____

Landlord: _____

Tenant: _____

Regarding real estate premises referred to as:

_____

_____

_____

AGREEMENT:

1. Landlord and Tenant have jointly inspected the premises and common areas and agree the premises and unchecked items such as fixtures, appliances, and furnishings are in a satisfactory and sanitary condition.

2. Check only those items which are unsatisfactory and state why in "REMARKS."

EXTERIOR/COMMON AREAS:

☐ Garage/parking lot	☐ Garbage facilities	☐ Storage area	☐ TV antenna
☐ Pool/spa	☐ Satellite dish	☐ Patio/decks	☐ CATV hookup
☐ Stairs/railings	☐ Garage door openers	☐ Hallway/lobby	☐ Laundry area
☐ Fencing	☐ Roof	☐ Exterior lighting	☐ Eaves/gutters
☐ Sprinklers/hose	☐ Mailbox	☐ Walkways	☐ _____

ENTRY:

☐ Door	☐ # of keys _____	☐ Doorbell/knocker	☐ Closet
☐ Intercom/security	☐ Shelves	☐ Locks	☐ _____

KITCHEN:

☐ Range	☐ Trash compactor	☐ Oven	☐ Water purifier
☐ Refrigerator	☐ Counters/laminate	☐ Garbage disposal	☐ Cabinets/drawers
☐ Exhaust fan(s)	☐ Pantry/shelves	☐ Dishwasher	☐ Tile/linoleum
☐ Microwave	☐ Sink/faucets		

BATHROOM:

☐ Sink	☐ Tile/linoleum	☐ Faucets/hardware	☐ Closet/shelves
☐ Toilet	☐ Exhaust fan(s)	☐ Shower	☐ Shower enclosure
☐ Tub	☐ Medicine cabinet		

ELECTRICAL:

☐ Outlets	☐ Lighting	☐ Switchplates	☐ Thermostat
☐ Fixtures	☐ Furnace	☐ Smoke detectors	☐ Ventilation
☐ Air conditioning	☐ _____		

PLUMBING:
- ☐ Water heater
- ☐ Gas hookups
- ☐ Washer
- ☐ _____
- ☐ Hot/cold water
- ☐ Dryer

INTERIOR:
- ☐ Wall coverings
- ☐ Draperies
- ☐ Doorknobs
- ☐ Floors
- ☐ Closets
- ☐ Chimney/flue
- ☐ Floor coverings
- ☐ Rods/tracks
- ☐ Fireplace
- ☐ Baseboards/trim
- ☐ Screens
- ☐ _____
- ☐ Ceilings
- ☐ Glass doors
- ☐ Hardware/fittings
- ☐ Doors
- ☐ Sills/jambs
- ☐ Walls
- ☐ Windows
- ☐ Paint
- ☐ Shades
- ☐ Kickplates/stops

REMARKS:
_____
_____
_____
_____
_____

REPAIRS PROMISED:

1. _____
_____
by: _____
2. _____
_____
by: _____

I agree to the terms stated above.	I accept the premise as stated above.
Date:_____, 20_____	Date:_____, 20_____
Landlord/Manager: _____	Tenant: _____
Signature: _____	Signature: _____
Address: _____	Signature: _____
_____	Address: _____
Phone: _____	_____
Fax: _____	Phone: _____
E-mail: _____	Fax: _____
	E-mail: _____

FORM 560   10-00   ©2003 **first tuesday**, P.O. BOX 20069 RIVERSIDE, CA 92516 (800) 794-0494

- keeping the premises occupied by the tenant clean and sanitary;

- disposing of all rubbish, garbage and waste in a sanitary manner;

- properly operating all electrical, gas and plumbing fixtures, and keeping them clean and sanitary;

- allowing no person who is on the premises with the tenant's permission to intentionally destroy, damage, waste or remove any part of the premises or the facilities, equipment or appurtenances; and

- occupying and using the premises for the purpose it is intended to be used. [CC §1941.2]

The landlord can agree in the lease to be responsible for the cleanliness of the common areas, and the disposal of garbage and rubbish, i.e. the hiring of a sanitation service. [CC §1941.2(b)]

The tenant breaches his duty to care for and maintain the premises when the tenant:

- contributes substantially to the dilapidation of the premises; or

- substantially interferes with the landlord's duty to maintain the premises. [CC §1941.2(a)]

For example, a tenant does not notify his landlord of a leak in the roof which is causing damage to the ceiling of the rental unit.

Finally, the ceiling falls down, causing damage to the tenant's personal property, the walls and the floor coverings.

Here, the tenant interfered with the landlord's duty to maintain the property since the tenant failed to:

- notify the landlord of the leak in the roof; or

- repair the leak himself.

Also, the landlord is not liable for any damage to the tenant's personal property resulting from the falling ceiling.

Further, the tenant is liable for the cost of the damage to the rental unit for failure to report the need for repairs on the first sign of leakage.

A landlord can recover the cost of repairs made to correct excessive wear and tear by deducting the cost of repairs from the security deposit and demanding payment for any deficiency in the deposit to cover the expenses of any excess charges. [CC §1950.5(b)]

If the tenant fails to pay any charges remaining unpaid after deductions from the security deposit, the landlord can file an action against the tenant to recover amounts not covered by the security deposit. [CC §1950.5(m)]

Landlord's duty to maintain

A residential landlord has a general obligation to:

- put a residential unit in a condition fit for occupancy **prior to leasing**; and

- repair all unsafe and unsanitary conditions which occur **during occupancy** and render the unit uninhabitable. [CC §1941]

Further, all residential leases and rental agreements automatically contain an implied *warranty of habitability*. The unwritten warranty imposes a contractual duty on a landlord to repair and maintain his residential units so the units are fit for human occupancy at all times. [**Green** v. **Superior Court of the City and County of San Francisco** (1974) 10 C3d 616; see Chapter 26]

Both the landlord's statutory obligation to maintain his residential units and the implied warranty of habitability require the landlord to correct **major defects** that interfere with the tenant's ability to live on the property, such as a lack of hot water or heating, or a leaky roof.

CONDITION OF FURNISHINGS ADDEDUM
and Inventory

DATE:_____, 20_____, at _____, California

FACTS:

This is an addendum to the following:

☐ Lease agreement
☐ Rental agreement
☐ Occupancy agreement
☐ Other

Dated: _____, 20_____

Entered into by:

Landlord: _____

Tenant: _____

Regarding real estate referred to as: _____

_____

AGREEMENT:

1. Landlord and Tenant have jointly inspected the furniture and furnishings, and agree they are in satisfactory and sanitary condition.

2. Only those items checked are unsatisfactory and explained under "REMARKS."

3. The quantity of furnishings entered on this form are accepted by the Tenant.

4. Reimbursement for any loss damage or excess wear and tear on furnishings provided to the Tenant will be deducted from Tenant's security deposit.

LIVING ROOM:

☐ Carpet   ☐ Chairs   #_____
☐ Draperies   ☐ End tables   #_____
☐ Window coverings   ☐ Coffee tables   #_____
☐ Wall coverings   ☐ Lamps   #_____
☐ Couch   #_____   ☐ Shelves
☐ Pictures   #_____   ☐ _____

KITCHEN:

☐ Tile/linoleum   ☐ Chairs   #_____
☐ Window coverings   ☐ Range
☐ Refrigerator   ☐ Cabinets
☐ Table   #_____   ☐ _____

BEDROOM:

☐ Double bed   #_____   ☐ Night stands #_____
☐ Single bed   #_____   ☐ Lamps   #_____
☐ Headboards   #_____   ☐ Bureau   #_____
☐ Mattress   #_____   ☐ Pictures   #_____
☐ Box springs   #_____   ☐ Mirror   #_____
☐ Bed frame   #_____   ☐ _____

SECOND BEDROOM:

☐ Double bed   #_____   ☐ Night stands #_____
☐ Single bed   #_____   ☐ Lamps   #_____
☐ Headboards   #_____   ☐ Bureau   #_____
☐ Mattress   #_____   ☐ Pictures   #_____
☐ Box springs   #_____   ☐ Mirror   #_____
☐ Bed frame   #_____   ☐ _____

BATHROOM:

☐ Medicine cabinet   ☐ Shower/tub
☐ Shelves/fittings   ☐ Shower enclosure
☐ Toilet   ☐ _____

REMARKS:

_____
_____
_____
_____
_____
_____
_____
_____
_____
_____
_____
_____
_____
_____
_____
_____

I agree to the terms stated above.

Date:_____, 20_____

Landlord/Agent: _____

Address: _____

_____

Phone: _____

Fax: _____

Signature: _____

I agree to the terms stated above.

Date:_____, 20_____

Tenant: _____

Address: _____

Phone: _____

Fax: _____

Signature: _____

Signature: _____

FORM 561   10-00   ©2003 **first tuesday**, P.O. BOX 20069 RIVERSIDE, CA 92516 (800) 794-0494

While the residential landlord has an obligation to care for and maintain all major and structural components of residential rental units, the landlord is further obligated to repair **minor defects**.

Minor defects include such conditions as leaky faucets, faulty electrical switches and failed locks or latches.

Typically, a residential landlord agrees in the lease or rental agreement to care for and maintain the property, which includes the repair of minor defects. [See **first tuesday** Form 550 §6.2]

Thus, the landlord's failure to repair or replace minor defects constitutes a breach of provisions in the lease or rental agreement.

The landlord who breaches the lease by failing to make minor repairs must reimburse the tenant for reasonable costs incurred by the tenant to cure the defects.

Minor repairs and habitability

During his occupancy, a residential tenant discovers the electrical wiring for the garbage disposal under the kitchen sink is exposed.

The tenant asks the landlord to correct the faulty wiring. The landlord does nothing.

Later, other minor repairs become necessary. A roof leak develops, causing a stain in a bedroom ceiling, and the water closet on the toilet bowl leaks, requiring repair or replacement.

The tenant notifies the landlord of the need for repairs. Neither the landlord nor the tenant correct any of the minor defects.

Frustrated with the landlord's lack of cooperation, the tenant stops paying rent.

The landlord serves the tenant with a 3-day notice to pay rent or quit. [See **first tuesday** Form 575]

The tenant still refuses to pay rent, and the landlord files an unlawful detainer (UD) action.

The tenant defends his nonpayment of rent by claiming the landlord breached the warranty of habitability since he failed to repair the numerous defective conditions on the premises.

However, the landlord did not breach the warranty of habitability. The defective conditions did not interfere with the tenant's ability to live on the premises for the purposes intended, despite the inconveniences.

The landlord breaches the warranty of habitability only when he fails to provide and maintain residential rental units in a habitable — safe and sanitary — condition. [Green, *supra*]

Tenant's options to repair

When the residential landlord fails to repair minor defective conditions on the property, the tenant may exercise one of three remedies:

- repair the defect and deduct the costs of contracting for the repair from the rent [CC §1942(a)];

- make the repairs, continue to pay rent and sue the landlord to recover the cost of repairs; or

- vacate the premises. [CC §1942(a)]

However, if the premises are so unsafe and unsanitary they qualify as *uninhabitable*, the tenant can remain in occupancy and withhold payment of the rent.

In an ensuing UD action, the tenant would raise the defense of the landlord's breach of the implied warranty of habitability to force the landlord to make the necessary repairs to eliminate the unsafe and unsanitary condition.

The court would then set the amount of rent due during the period of nonpayment of rent based on the percentage of uninhabitability.

The repair-and-deduct remedy

If the leased premises is in need of repair, whether minor or major, the tenant must notify the landlord orally or in writing of the condition.

After advising the landlord of the need for repairs, the tenant can make the repairs himself and deduct the cost of the repairs from the next month's rent if:

- the landlord fails to make the necessary repairs within a *reasonable time*; and

- the cost of repairs does not exceed the amount of one month's rent, called *the repair-and-deduct remedy*.

The tenant cannot exercise the repair-and-deduct remedy more than twice in any 12-month period. [CC §1942(a)]

Also, any agreement by the tenant to waive or modify his right to repair and deduct the costs from the rent is unenforceable. [CC §1942.1]

A **reasonable time** for the landlord to repair after notice is 30 days, unless the need to repair is urgent and requires more immediate attention. [CC §1942(b)]

Obviously, the repair-and-deduct remedy is not available to the tenant when the need for repair is created by the tenant's conduct. [CC §1942(c)]

Repairs exceeding one month's rent

If the cost of repairs would exceed one month's rent, the tenant, while continuing to occupy and pay rent, may make the necessary repairs and file an action against the landlord to recover the cost of the repairs.

However, it may be impossible for the tenant to make the necessary repairs when:

- the tenant rents a unit in a large complex; or

- is unable to cover the cost of repairs.

If the nonresidential tenant is unable or does not want to cover the cost of repairs which the landlord has failed to make, the tenant can **vacate the premises** and is relieved of any further obligation under the lease. [CC §1942(a)]

Maintaining property with care

Just as a residential landlord has a duty to repair and maintain the leased premises, a **nonresidential landlord** who retains responsibility for maintenance and repair under the lease also has a duty to use care in doing so.

Consider a tenant, residential or nonresidential, who notifies his landlord a window is broken and will not stay open.

The landlord begins work to repair the window, but does not complete the work. The tenant gives the landlord permission to enter the premises when the tenant is out to finish the repairs, which the landlord does not do.

Finally, the window falls, injuring the tenant.

Here, the landlord is responsible for the injuries.

Once a landlord of residential or nonresidential premises undertakes to make repairs on the premises to correct a dangerous condition, the landlord must complete the repairs in a timely and proper manner. [**Minoletti** v. **Sabini** (1972) 27 CA3d 321]

Landlords of both residential and nonresidential property are also responsible to tenants, guests of tenants and members of the public for injuries caused to them by the landlord's lack of ordinary care or skill in the maintenance of his property. [CC §1714]

Nondelegable duty to repair

Now consider a nonresidential landlord who hires a contractor to repair the roof on leased property.

A tenant is injured as a result of the contractor's negligence while performing the repair.

The tenant claims the landlord is liable for his injuries since the landlord is responsible for maintaining the property, and the maintenance undertaken created a dangerous condition which injured the tenant.

The landlord claims he is not liable since it was the roofing contractor's negligence while on the job which caused the tenant's injury, not the landlord.

Is the landlord liable for injuries to a tenant caused by a contractor hired to perform repairs?

Yes! A landlord's duty to exercise care (not to be negligent) in the repair and maintenance of a leased premises is a *nondelegable duty* — it cannot be transferred or assumed by another person, such as a property manager or contractor. [**Srithong** v. **Total Investment Company** (1994) 23 CA4th 721]

Thus, the landlord is liable for injuries caused to persons (excluding the contractor's employees) during the fulfillment of the landlord's duty to maintain the property, whether the maintenance is accomplished by the landlord or by contractors he or his property manager employs.

Punitives for failure to maintain

A landlord is aware various felonious crimes have recently been committed in the common areas of his apartment complex.

The tenants of the complex complain to the landlord about the crimes. The tenants request the broken doors, gates and locks be repaired and adequate lighting be provided as security to prevent the crimes from reoccurring.

The landlord fails to make the repairs or provide the security measures requested.

Later, while in a common area, a tenant is assaulted and suffers injuries.

The tenant seeks to recover losses from the landlord for his injuries, as well as *punitive damages*. The tenant claims the landlord breached his duty to protect him from known criminal activity in the complex by **failing to maintain** and provide adequate security measures in the common areas.

Further, the tenant claims the landlord is liable for breaching the warranty of habitability.

First, can the tenant recover punitive damages from the landlord?

Yes! The landlord was aware of the dangerous condition created by the lack of maintenance. By failing to correct the deferred maintenance, the landlord conducted himself with a conscious disregard for the rights or safety of others.

The landlord's deliberate **failure to maintain** the premises, and thus eliminate the dangerous conditions which were known to him and over which he alone had the power to correct, exposes him to liability for punitive damages. [**Penner** v. **Falk** (1984) 153 CA3d 858]

Also, a landlord is liable for punitive damages **for failure to disclose** a dangerous condition about which he has actual knowledge. [**O'Hara** v. **Western Seven Trees Corporation Intercoast Management** (1977) 75 CA3d 798]

However, the landlord is not liable for breaching the warranty of habitability. The living quarters were habitable, and the housing complied with local codes.

Thus, the defense of uninhabitable premises for failure to pay rent based on a lack of security will fail and the nonpaying tenant will be evicted. [Penner, *supra*]

Chapter 26

Implied warranty of habitability

This chapter examines the purpose of the implied warranty of habitability and its effect on residential landlords.

Minimum quality low-income housing

A landlord, aware an apartment complex he owns is in a state of disrepair, does nothing to correct the defective conditions on the property.

Due to the location of the property and its below market rents, the landlord is able to rent out units in the complex without repairing any of the defective conditions.

A tenant, fully aware of the unsafe and unsanitary slum-like conditions, enters into a lease with the landlord.

Soon after occupying, the tenant asks the landlord to exterminate the rodents and cockroaches in his unit. The tenant also requests that plumbing blockages, exposed electrical wiring and the collapsing bathroom ceiling in the unit be repaired.

The landlord does not correct or repair any of the defective conditions.

In retaliation, the tenant stops paying rent and continues to occupy the unit.

The landlord serves a 3-day notice for nonpayment of rent and declares a forfeiture of the tenant's right to possession. The notice expires without payment and the landlord files an unlawful detainer (UD) action to evict the tenant.

The tenant defends his right to occupy by claiming the landlord failed to maintain the premises in a habitable condition, which permits the tenant to:

- retain possession; and

- pay a reduced rent set by the court.

The landlord claims the tenant must pay the agreed amount of rent even though he failed to make repairs since the tenant must either:

- quit the premises; or

- make the repairs himself and deduct the cost of the repairs from his rent as authorized by law.

Can the tenant continue to occupy the premises and pay a reduced court-ordered rent to the landlord?

Yes! The landlord's failure to maintain the premises in a habitable condition constitutes a breach of the *implied warranty of habitability* which all residential leases and rental agreements are subject to. Not so for nonresidential properties.

Also, the **court-ordered reduced rent** will remain for as long as the landlord fails to make the necessary corrections or repairs. [**Green** v. **Superior Court of the City and County of San Francisco** (1974) 10 C3d 616]

Note — Nonresidential leases do not contain an implied warranty of habitability. [See Chapter 23]

However, if the nonresidential landlord fails to make the significant repairs he is obligated to make under the lease, the tenant has two options:

- *pay for the repairs himself, demand reimbursement from the landlord, and if unpaid, file an action against the landlord to recover the cost of the repairs; or*

- *vacate the premises and file an action against the landlord for losses resulting from a constructive eviction.*

Implied warranty of habitability

The typical residential tenant under a lease agreement acquires a leasehold interest in the leased property for a specific period of time. The tenant expects the premises and appurtenances (common areas, parking and storage) available to him to be fit for the purpose leased — to be a sanitary place in which he may safely reside.

However, a residential tenant, especially an apartment dweller, is not just acquiring an interest in real estate, he is *contracting* for, and is entitled to, a **safe and sanitary** place to live, called a *habitable dwelling*. [See **first tuesday** Form 550 §6.2]

The implied warranty of habitability is judicially and legislatively included in all residential lease and rental agreements, whether or not it is included as a written provision.

The implied warranty requires the residential landlord to care for the premises by maintaining habitable conditions — the minimum level of living conditions for a safe and sanitary dwelling unit permitted by law. [**Hinson** v. **Delis** (1972) 26 CA3d 62; Calif. Code of Civil Procedure §1174.2]

Thus, residential property which is not in a habitable condition cannot be rented or leased "as-is," even though defective property conditions have been fully disclosed and the substandard conditions consented to by the tenant.

The implied warranty applies not only to the space rented by the tenant as housing, but also to common areas the tenant may use, such as laundry facilities, parking, recreational areas and storage spaces, called *appurtenances*. [Hinson, *supra*]

The public policy establishing the warranty of habitability arose due to the scarcity of available low-cost housing. This economic situation left residential tenants in some areas without the bargaining power possessed by more affluent and mobile tenants when negotiating with landlords for better property conditions.

Thus, market forces are not allowed to control over the higher public policy requiring safe and sanitary housing.

The warranty of habitability serves to punish slumlords and discourage slum-like conditions in low-income housing.

A landlord who invests money in real estate must maintain his property. Otherwise, the value of his investment will eventually disintegrate due to pressures in the rental market and court orders.

Landlord's warranty

The landlord breaches the implied warranty of habitability when the landlord fails to comply with building and housing code standards which *materially affect* health and safety. [CCP §1174.2(c)]

A habitable place to live is a dwelling free of **major defects**, not mere inconveniences, which would interfere with the tenant's ability to use the premises as a residence.

A residential dwelling is uninhabitable if any features of the dwelling are not properly maintained or do not substantially comply with building and housing codes, including:

- effective waterproofing and weather protection of roof and exterior walls, including unbroken windows and doors;

- plumbing and gas facilities;

- a hot and cold running water system with appropriate fixtures which are connected to a sewage disposal system;

- heating facilities;

- electrical lighting; and

- floors, stairways and railings. [Calif. Civil Code §1941.1]

In applying the guidelines, a leaky faucet would not render a residential unit uninhabitable, despite the inconvenience.

However, a lack of running water, or no hot water, is a significant defect which materially interferes with the tenant's ability to live on the property.

At the time the lease or rental agreement is entered into, the building grounds and appurtenances, such as a pool, laundry facilities, storage areas and parking structures, must be clean, sanitary and free from all accumulations of debris, filth, rodents and vermin to meet habitability guidelines. [CC §1941.1(f)]

Further, the landlord must provide an adequate number of garbage and rubbish receptacles in clean condition and good repair. [CC §1941.1(g)]

Typically, a residential tenant in an apartment complex is not expected to make repairs to major components of the complex, such as a central heating system, an electrical or plumbing system or the roof.

If a residential landlord fails to make necessary repairs, and the cost of the repair is less than one month's rent, the tenant may order out and pay for the needed repairs and deduct the cost from the rent, called the *repair and deduct remedy*. [CC §1942; see Chapter 25]

However, the repair-and-deduct remedy is not often feasible in apartment dwellings since areas where repairs must be made are in the possession and control of the landlord.

Thus, the residential tenant must resort to other remedies, such as:

- vacating the premises, called a *constructive eviction* [See Chapter 23];

- stop paying rent and, in any ensuing UD action, prove the landlord breached the implied warranty of habitability; or

- raise and prove the defense of retaliatory eviction.

Pre-leasing maintenance program

Before renting a residential unit in a building intended for human habitation, the landlord, in addition to maintenance for habitability, must:

- install and maintain an operable dead bolt lock on each main swinging entry door of a unit, unless the door is a horizontal sliding door;

- install and maintain operable window security or locking devices for windows which are designed to be opened, unless the window is a louvered window, casement window, or more than 12 feet vertically or six feet horizontally from the ground, roof or other platform; and

- install locking mechanisms in compliance with fire and safety codes on the exterior doors of the building leading to common areas that provide access to dwelling units in an apartment complex — installation of a door or gate is not required if none existed on January 1, 1998. [CC §1941.3(a)]

A tenant is responsible for promptly notifying the landlord of an inoperable dead bolt lock, window security or locking device in the unit.

The landlord will only be liable for injuries caused by his failure to correct the defect within a reasonable period of time after being notified or becoming aware of the defect. [CC §1941.3(b)]

A residential landlord who fails to comply with the required security measures entitles the tenant to do any of the following:

- repair and deduct the cost from rent;

- vacate the premises;

- recover money losses incurred due to the condition of an uninhabitable building;

- recover losses caused by any landlord retaliation;

- file an action for breach of contract; or

- seek injunctive relief to stop the landlord from keeping an uninhabitable building. [CC §1941.3(c)]

Warranty of habitability defense

In a UD action, a tenant who successfully raises the *defense* of the landlord's breach of the implied warranty of habitability will be allowed:

- to **retain possession** of the premises; and

- to **pay a reduced amount** of rent based on the uninhabitable condition of the property. [CCP §1174.2(a)(1)]

To retain possession, the tenant must pay the rent awarded to the landlord, offset by the tenant's attorney fees, within:

- five days of the entry of judgment; or

- ten days, if the UD judgment is served on the tenant by mail. [CCP §1174.2(a)]

If the tenant fails to timely pay the rental amounts set by the court, the landlord is awarded possession of the premises. [CCP §1174.2(b)]

The landlord may or may not be ordered to make all repairs necessary to return the premises to a safe and sanitary condition.

When a landlord is ordered to correct the uninhabitable conditions by returning the premises to a safe and sanitary condition:

- the tenant who remains in possession must pay the reasonable monthly rental value of the premises in its uninhabitable condition until the repairs are completed; and

- the court retains control to oversee compliance by the landlord. [CCP §1174.2(a)]

The tenant who raises the habitability defense instead of paying the rent **takes the risk** of being evicted. The landlord's failure to make repairs may not rise to the level of a *substantial breach* of the warranty of habitability if the repairs are minor in nature and are judged to create only an inconvenience or annoyance to the tenant.

If the landlord has not substantially breached the warranty of habitability:

- the landlord is awarded the right to possession; and

- the tenant is liable for rent accrued through the date of judgment. [CCP §1174.2(b)]

Further, the prevailing party in a UD action is entitled to his **attorney fees** even if the lease or rental agreement does not contain an attorney fees provision. Whoever is awarded possession of the premises is the prevailing party. [CCP §1174.2(a), (b)]

Determining reasonable rental value

To calculate the reasonable rental value of the premises when a breach of the implied warranty of habitability exists, the court will:

- establish the percentage attributable to the tenant's diminished habitability or use of the premises due to the substandard living conditions; and

- reduce the agreed-to monthly rental payment by that percentage. [**Cazares** v. **Ortiz** (1980) 109 CA3d Supp. 23]

If the agreed-to monthly rent is already below market rent due to the condition of the premises, the landlord who has breached the warranty of habitability may receive only a minimal amount of rent for the premises.

The court-ordered rent properly may be so minimal as to result in a financial penalty to the landlord.

Note — While this penalizing rental amount actually may be unfair to the landlord until he repairs the premises, the courts are unconcerned. [Cazares, *dicta*]

The purpose of the warranty of habitability is to prevent illegal, substandard housing from having any market rental value and to encourage landlords to maintain their premises in a condition where market rents can be charged and actually enforced in a UD action.

The criteria used to determine the percentage of habitability or useability lost caused by the landlord's failure to maintain includes:

- the area of the rental unit affected;

- the duration of the tenant's exposure to the defect;

- the degree of discomfort the defect imposes on the tenant;

- whether the defect is health-threatening or intermittently annoying; and

- the extent to which the defect caused the tenant to find the premises uninhabitable. [Cazares, *supra*]

Landlord's breach on full disclosure

The mere existence of unsafe and unsanitary conditions, whether or not they are known to the tenant, establishes the landlord's breach of the implied warranty of habitability.

Consider a prospective tenant who contacts a property manager to rent a unit in an older apartment building. The tenant inspects the unit and notices wall cracks and broken windows.

Considering the condition of the unit and the tenant's financial condition, the tenant offers to rent the premises in exchange for a reduced rent. The landlord agrees, and the property manager rents the unit.

The tenant takes possession. Soon afterwards, the tenant notifies the property manager the unit has an inoperable heating system, electrical fixtures with exposed wiring, no hot water, and is infested with rodents and cockroaches.

The manager advises the landlord of the need for repairs and pest control. However, the landlord gives no authority to the property manager to correct the defective conditions in the unit.

The tenant remains in possession but refuses to pay any rent, claiming his unit has substandard living conditions which make the unit uninhabitable.

The tenant is served with a 3-day notice to pay or quit. The tenant still does not pay, and a UD action is filed.

The tenant claims he is not obligated to pay rent since the landlord breached the implied warranty of habitability by failing to put or bring his apartment unit into a habitable condition.

The landlord claims the tenant cannot assert he has breached the warranty of habitability since the tenant was fully aware of the extent of the defective conditions at the time he took possession.

Here, the landlord is not relieved of his duty under the implied warranty of habitability even though the tenant was **fully aware** of unsafe and unsanitary conditions when he took possession. It is the state of the premises which constitutes a breach of the implied warranty of habitability, not the state of the disclosures about the existence of defective conditions. [**Knight v. Hallsthammer** (1981) 29 C3d 46]

When a landlord fails to care for and maintain his residential property in a habitable condition, he cannot rent the property "as-disclosed" and escape liability.

Landlord has no time to respond

The warranty of habitability does not entitle a residential landlord to a reasonable period of time after a tenant takes possession in which he may repair unsafe and unsanitary living conditions before the tenant takes other action, such as withholding rent.

The landlord who breaches the habitability warranty is already well aware he is not maintaining his property.

When residential property contains unsafe and unsanitary living conditions, the landlord has either received complaints from tenants or the neglected state of the premises is visibly apparent on an inspection.

Since a residential tenant is not required to pay rent if the landlord fails to maintain the premises in a habitable condition, the landlord should not allow a tenant to take possession until the premises is repaired.

The warranty of habitability is breached when the need for repairs is:

- known by the landlord, either through notice from the tenant or by the physical state of the property at the time it is rented; and

- the landlord fails to immediately correct the defective conditions.

The purpose of the implied warranty of habitability is not to encourage tenants to use the need for repairs to avoid the payment of rent; it is to promote access for low-income tenants to living structures that provide safe and sanitary housing.

The "no notice" and "no reasonable time to repair" rules imposed on landlords by the warranty of habitability are based on the notion that landlords are or should be aware of the condition of the physical components of the premises at the time the unit is rented since landlords have a duty to inspect and maintain their property and improve or correct known substandard conditions before renting it. [CC §1714]

Now consider a tenant who rents a single-family residence which is in a safe and sanitary condition when he takes possession. The condition of the premises is documented.

During the tenant's occupancy, the toilet begins to leak and the linoleum floor does not repel the water.

On noticing the leak, the tenant has a duty to notify the landlord and give him a reasonable amount of time to make the repairs before taking other action. [CC §1942]

However, the tenant fails to notify the landlord of the need for repairs.

Eventually, the bathroom floor rots due to the plumbing leak, weakening the subfloor and eventually creating a hole.

Then, in lieu of paying rent before it becomes delinquent, the tenant notifies the landlord of the unsafe and unsanitary bathroom conditions.

The tenant is promptly served with a 3-day notice to pay rent or quit. Repairs are commenced by the landlord.

The 3-day notice expires and a UD action is filed and served on the tenant.

The repairs are completed by the landlord prior to the UD hearing.

At the UD hearing, the tenant claims the landlord breached the implied warranty of habitability and only a reduced rent is due since the rental was not in a safe and sanitary condition.

The landlord claims the warranty of habitability has not been breached, since he did not have notice of the need for repairs until the tenant complained and at the same time refused to pay rent.

Has the landlord breached the implied warranty of habitability?

No! The tenant brought about the unsafe and unsanitary condition by failing to promptly notify the landlord of the need for repairs. [CC §1942]

New landlord steps into the breach

Consider a landlord of an apartment building who is notified by his tenants of serious unsafe living conditions in the units.

The owner, being financially incapable of paying for the repairs needed, sells the complex. The new landlord inspects the building and is aware of the defective and substandard conditions in the units prior to taking title. The new landlord intends to correct the conditions by renovating the building.

The new landlord notifies the tenants of the change in ownership of the complex and an increase in their monthly rent to amortize the cost of renovation he is incurring.

A tenants' association is organized. The tenants refuse to pay rent due to the ongoing state of disrepair in the units.

The landlord serves 3-day notices on the tenants who fail to pay the agreed rent.

Unlawful detainer actions are filed, and the tenants raise the breach of the implied warranty of habitability as a defense to avoid eviction and reduce rents.

The landlord claims he is not breaching the warranty of habitability since the previous owner breached the warranty of habitability, not him.

The tenants claim the change in ownership did not terminate their right to raise the warranty-of-habitability defense since the breach was a condition of the property which continued after the new landlord took possession, whether or not he knew of the breach.

Can the tenants raise the warranty-of-habitability defense against a new owner who did not cause the existing unsafe conditions?

Yes! The tenants have a valid implied warranty-of-habitability defense which justifies their failure to pay rent since:

- the premises were uninhabitable during the new landlord's ownership; and

- the new landlord is attempting to evict the tenants for rental amounts due under his ownership. [Knight, *supra*]

Thus, even though the landlord did not cause the premises to become uninhabitable and intended to rehabilitate the property when he purchased it, the tenants can still refuse to pay the agreed-to rent and avoid eviction.

Duty to avoid foreseeable injury

A tenant can recover more than a rent adjustment when the landlord breaches the implied warranty of habitability.

For instance, a tenant inspects a rental unit and enters into a month-to-month rental agreement with the landlord.

On occupying the unit, the tenant discovers faulty electrical wiring, a clogged kitchen sink and a leak in the roof which later damages the tenant's personal property.

The tenant notifies the landlord (and the county health department) of the defective property conditions and asks the landlord to make the necessary repairs.

The landlord fails to make any repairs. The tenant continues to reside on the premises. Eventually, the county health department issues a notice condemning the building as unfit for occupancy. The tenant relocates.

The tenant makes a demand on the landlord for water damage to his personal property and the cost of relocating to a new residence since the landlord breached his duty of care to repair the defective conditions.

Here, the landlord owes a *duty of care* to the tenant, separate from the warranty the premises is up to minimum standards of habitability, to properly maintain the premises to avoid the risk of a foreseeable financial loss by the tenant caused by the failure to maintain the property.

Thus, the landlord is liable for the costs incurred by the tenant in replacing damaged personal property and relocating. The costs incurred by the tenant were due to the landlord's breach of his duty of care by failing to make the necessary repairs to eliminate unsafe and uninhabitable conditions. [**Stoiber** v. **Honeychuck** (1980) 101 CA3d 903]

In addition, the tenant can recover excessive rent paid for periods of occupancy during which the premises was uninhabitable.

Even if a residential tenant fails to raise the warranty-of-habitability defense in a UD action and is evicted or otherwise vacates, the tenant can later recover any excessive rent paid during the period the landlord failed to maintain the unit in a habitable condition. [**Landeros** v. **Pankey** (1995) 39 CA4th 1167]

Conditions creating a nuisance

Now consider a tenant of an apartment unit who is forced to relocate due to unsafe flooring and unsanitary conditions that caused the local health department to issue an order condemning the apartment complex.

The tenant makes a demand on the landlord to pay his relocation expenses, claiming the defective conditions in the rental unit constitute a *nuisance* since he is deprived of the safe and healthy use and enjoyment of the leased premises.

The tenant also seeks to recover *punitive damages* from the landlord. The tenant claims the landlord's failure to correct the defective conditions which created the nuisance was intentional and malicious.

The landlord claims the tenant cannot recover losses based on a nuisance, much less receive a punitive award for money, since his interference with the tenant's use and enjoyment of the premises is a breach of the contractual warranty of habitability implied in the lease agreement, not the tortious creation of a health nuisance.

However, besides breaching the habitability warranty, the landlord has, by the same conduct, also created a nuisance for the tenant. The landlord's failure to make repairs and properly maintain the rental unit *substantially interfered* with the tenant's continuing **use and enjoyment** of the premises. [Stoiber, *supra*]

A **nuisance** is any condition which:

- is injurious to health;

- obstructs the free use of property; or

- interferes with the comfortable enjoyment of property. [CC §3479]

Further, the landlord's continued failure to maintain and repair the premises in a safe condition throughout the health department's investigation and condemnation action indicates the landlord **intentionally maintained** a nuisance on the premises — an ongoing disregard for the safety and health of the tenant.

Besides recovering his out-of-pocket losses to relocate, the tenant is entitled to an award for an additional sum of money, called *punitive damages*, since the landlord maintained a nuisance due to his intentional failure to repair. [Stoiber, *supra*]

Further, the landlord's liability to the tenant for creating a nuisance is additional to any refunds of rent and rent reduction for breaching the warranty of habitability in the rental agreement.

The tenant can also recover from the landlord any medical expenses and personal injury due to an intentional infliction of **mental distress** if the landlord's failure to maintain the premises in a habitable condition is the result of the landlord's extreme and outrageous conduct. [Stoiber, *supra*]

Chapter 27

Fire safety programs

This chapter discusses fire safety requirements for landlords, including smoke detectors, posting fire safety information and security bars.

Smoke detectors, security bars and safety information

A residential apartment building contains state-approved smoke detectors in each individual unit and in the common areas.

Later, a tenant informs the landlord the smoke detector in his unit does not operate even with new batteries.

The landlord and his manager do not repair or replace the broken smoke detector. Later, a fire breaks out in the tenant's unit during the night.

The tenant is unaware of the fire until he is injured and his property is damaged due to the defective smoke detector.

The tenant claims the landlord is liable for his losses since the landlord has a duty to repair or replace the defective smoke detector on notice from the tenant.

Is the landlord liable for property damage and personal injuries caused by the defective smoke detector?

Yes! On receiving notice that the smoke detector is inoperable, the landlord is required to promptly repair or replace it. [Calif. Health and Safety Code §13113.7(e)]

Further, a landlord will be subject to a $200 penalty for each failure to:

- install a smoke detector in each unit and in common areas as required; and

- repair or replace a faulty smoke detector on notice from the tenant. [Health & S C §13113.7(f)]

Tenant's duty to notify

Smoke detectors are required to be installed and maintained in all dwelling units intended for human occupancy, including single-family residences, duplexes, apartment complexes, hotels, motels, condominiums and time share projects. [Health & S C §§13113.7(b); 13113.8]

The smoke detector must be in operable condition at the time the tenant takes possession. [Health & S C §13113.7(e)]

If a smoke detector does not work when tested by the tenant, the **tenant is responsible** for notifying the landlord or property manager. The landlord is not obligated to investigate whether detectors are operable during the occupancy.

If the tenant does not notify the landlord about an inoperable smoke detector and the landlord is unaware of the condition, the landlord is not responsible for injuries caused by the faulty smoke detector. [Health & S C §13113.7(e)]

To repair or replace a faulty smoke detector, the landlord may enter the unit 24 hours after serving a written notice on the tenant of his intent to enter, unless the tenant gives permission for a prior entry. [Health & S C §13113.7(e); see **first tuesday** Form 567; see Chapter 3]

Duty to install and maintain

An ordinary battery-operated smoke detector installed according to the manufacturer's instructions satisfies the requirement for both single- and multiple-unit dwellings, unless another type is required by local ordinances. [Health & S C §13113.7(a)]

For example, some local ordinances require the smoke detector to receive its power from the building's electrical system.

To determine the smoke detector requirements for a property, the landlord can contact the **local fire department** or the county fire planning department.

In apartment units and other multiple-unit dwellings, such as condominiums, smoke detectors must also be installed in the common stairwells. The apartment landlord and his property manager are responsible for **installing and maintaining** smoke detectors in both the common stairwells and the individual units. [Health & S C §13113.7(c)]

Posting fire safety information

The landlord of an apartment building must provide emergency fire safety information to all tenants if the building consists of:

- two or more stories;

- three or more units; and

- a front door which opens into an interior hallway or lobby area. [Health & S C §13220(c)]

The information must be on signs using **international symbols**. The signs must be located:

- at every stairway and elevator landing;

- at the intermediate point of any hallway exceeding 100 feet in length and all hallway intersections; and

- immediately inside all public entrances. [Health & S C §13220(c)(1)]

Further, the landlord must provide fire information to all tenants through brochures, pamphlets or videotapes, if available, or conform to regulations adopted by the State Fire Marshal. [Health & S C §13220(c)(2)]

If the landlord negotiates the lease or rental agreement in a language other than English, the required information provided to the tenant must be in English, international symbols and the four most common foreign languages in California. [Health & S C §13220(c)(3)]

Note — A consumer-oriented brochure in English, international symbols and the four most common foreign languages was to be available from the State Fire Marshal by July 1, 1996. [Health & S C §13220(d)]

However, this model brochure is still not available.

The State Fire Marshal has adopted California Code of Regulations Title 19 §3.09 concerning the dissemination of fire information to tenants in hotels, motels, office buildings and high-rises. Health and Safety Code §13220 addresses these issues for tenants in apartment complexes. However, information does not exist as to which four languages will be used to translate the fire information.

If a landlord has any questions about the enforcement or the requirements for posting and informing tenants of fire information, he should contact his local fire department or the county fire planning department.

The codes and regulations are enforced on a local level, and each county or city may have different requirements for complying with the fire information regulations.

Emergency procedures for office buildings

Emergency procedures and information for office buildings of two or more stories must be provided to the building's occupants. [Health & S C §13220(a)]

The **emergency procedures information** for an office building of two or more stories may be published in the form of **literature**, pamphlets, etc., and must be available to all persons entering the building as well as located immediately inside all entrances to the building. [19 California Code of Regulations §3.09(a)(1)]

In lieu of literature, a **floor plan** providing emergency procedures must be posted at every stairway landing, elevator landing, and immediately inside all public entrances. [19 CCR §3.09(a)(2)]

For **high-rise structures**, fire safety requirements include:

- posting emergency procedures on a floor plan at every stairway landing, elevator landing, and immediately inside all public entrances; and

- appointing a Fire Safety Director to coordinate fire safety activities, train employees in the building, develop an emergency plan, etc. (which is also required of operators of hotels, motels and lodging houses). [19 CCR §3.09(c), (d)]

A high-rise structure is a building rising more than 75 feet above the lowest floor level providing access to the building. [Health & S C §13210(b)]

Release mechanism in security bars

Security bars on residential property must have release mechanisms for fire safety reasons. The release mechanisms are not required if each bedroom with security bars contains a window or door to the exterior which opens for escape purposes. [Health & S C §13113.9]

Also, the owner of an apartment house must **install exit signs** that can be felt or seen near the floor of the exit. [Health & S C §17920.8]

Note — Any questions concerning fire safety requirements or whether an owner has properly complied with the requirements should be directed to the local fire department or the county fire planning department. Some departments provide checklists of requirements which must be met.

Chapter 28

Security to prevent crimes

This chapter focuses on the responsibility of the landlord to reduce crime through prevention when he has knowledge of criminal activity on the leased premises.

Security measures and warnings

A landlord of an apartment complex is aware assaults against tenants have recently occurred in the common areas of the property.

The landlord receives a composite drawing of the criminal, and a description of the criminal's mode of operation is released by the local police department.

The landlord undertakes none of the security steps available to reduce the risk of a recurrence of the same or similar criminal activities.

Later, the landlord rents a unit to a prospective tenant. The landlord does not disclose the recent criminal assaults or the criminal's mode of operation. The tenant is not given a copy of the composite drawing of the perpetrator developed by the police.

Further, the landlord represents the complex as safe and patrolled by security.

Later, the tenant is assaulted by the same perpetrator inside her apartment unit, not in the areas open to the public.

The tenant seeks to recover losses from the landlord. The tenant claims the landlord failed to disclose the prior assaults and misrepresented the safety of the apartment complex to induce her to rent and occupy.

The landlord claims he is not liable for the tenant's injuries since the assault occurred within the tenant's apartment unit, and not in the common areas where the prior attacks had occurred.

Here, the landlord is liable for the injuries suffered by the tenant inside the apartment unit.

The landlord had knowledge of criminal activity on the premises and thus owed a duty to protect the tenant by either:

- providing security measures in the common areas; or

- warning the tenant of the prior assaults. [**O'Hara** v. **Western Seven Trees Corporation Intercoast Management** (1977) 75 CA3d 798]

Based on the occurrence of prior similar criminal incidents, the likelihood of future assaults on tenants is *reasonably foreseeable*.

When criminal activity is reasonably foreseeable due to known prior criminal activity, the landlord has a duty to take reasonable measures **to prevent harm** to persons on the property from future similar criminal activities.

The landlord's conduct — failure to warn the new tenant about known criminal activity or provide adequate security — creates a risk in which a tenant may be injured. Due to his failure to put security measures in place to prevent harm, the landlord must compensate the injured person by the payment of money.

Alternatively, the landlord could be liable for the tenant's losses based on his intentional misrepresentation to the tenant regarding the safety of the apartment complex.

Note — A homeowners' association (HOA), like a landlord, has a duty to maintain the common areas since it has exclusive control over the maintenance of the common areas.

A HOA will be liable for any injury caused by a dangerous condition created or allowed to exist by the association when it or its agents knew or should have known of the dangerous condition and the injury suffered was reasonably foreseeable. [**Frances T.** v. **Village Green Owners Association** (1986) 42 CA3d 490]

Degree of foreseeability

Consider a landlord of a shopping center who has exclusive control over the maintenance and repair of the common areas.

Burglaries and purse snatchings have recently occurred on the premises. However, the landlord is unaware of the criminal activity in the shopping center.

At tenant association meetings, concerns about the lack of security in the center are addressed. The tenant association decides not to hire security guards on account of the expense.

The tenants do not discuss or bring their security concerns to the attention of the landlord.

Later, a tenant's employee is physically assaulted within the leased premises.

The employee claims the landlord is liable for her injuries since the landlord failed to provide security guards which would protect employees of tenants from an unreasonable risk of harm.

The landlord claims he is not liable since the assault on the tenant's employee was unforeseeable.

Here, the landlord has no duty to provide security guards in the common areas since the prior crimes (theft) were not of a similar nature which would have made a physical assault foreseeable. [**Ann M.** v. **Pacific Plaza Shopping Center** (1993) 6 CA4th 666]

The landlord's duty to provide protection is partly determined by balancing the foreseeability of harm against the **burden imposed** on the landlord by the duty to remove or prevent the harm. A high degree of foreseeability is required to impose a duty on a landlord or homeowners' association to hire security guards.

Without prior incidents of similar crimes being brought to the landlord's attention, the high degree of foreseeability required to impose a duty on the landlord to take steps to prevent or eliminate future injury does not exist.

However, **prior similar incidents** are not always required to find that a landlord has a duty to take measures to prevent future criminal activity.

The *foreseeability of an injury* is determined by the circumstances surrounding the injury and its occurrence, such as the nature, condition and location of the premises, and any prior incidents of similar or related activity in and around the premises. [Ann M., *supra*]

For example, consider a landlord of an office building and parking structure located in a neighborhood known to be a "high-crime" area.

Many petty thefts and acts of vandalism have occurred on the premises, but no assaults have taken place. The security system installed by the landlord to monitor the parking structure is in disrepair and does not function.

A visitor returning to his car enters the parking structure while an armed robbery is taking place. The visitor is shot and killed.

The visitor's spouse seeks to recover losses from the landlord, claiming her husband's death was reasonably foreseeable and could have been prevented by the landlord. The spouse also claims the landlord, who was aware of criminal activity on the premises, breached his duty to take measures to prevent further criminal activity.

The landlord claims the injury was not reasonably foreseeable since the prior criminal acts were not similar to the act causing the death of the visitor.

Is the landlord liable for failing to provide adequate security in the parking structure?

Yes! The landlord's failure to properly maintain existing security features in light of prior criminal activity and the nature of a public parking structure is a breach of the duty of care the landlord owes to persons who enter the structure.

Although the foreseeability of the type of criminal activity causing the death is low, the landlord is liable since the burden on him to maintain the existing security system is minimal.

Not only did the landlord know vandalism and thefts occurred often in the parking structure, the parking structure is located in a high-crime area. Further, parking structures by their dark and private nature tend to invite criminal activity.

Thus, death resulting from a visitor's accidental disruption of an armed robbery is reasonably foreseeable, if only to a low degree, even though no other armed assaults had previously occurred on the premises. [**Gomez v. Ticor** (1983) 145 CA3d 622]

No liability if not foreseeable

The extent of security measures the landlord is required to provide is dictated by the degree of foreseeability of any future harm to others. [Ann M., *supra*]

If an injury is not foreseeable since the *nature, condition and location* of the leased premises do not indicate a person entering or using the property is at risk, a landlord is not liable if an injury, which security measures may have prevented, occurs on the premises.

For example, consider an apartment complex where previous criminal activity has not occurred. However, the community where the complex is located is generally known as a "high-crime" area.

The light bulb installed at the entrance to a tenant's apartment unit burns out. The tenant asks the landlord to replace the light bulb.

The lighting in the common areas is functional.

Before the landlord replaces the bulb, the tenant is assaulted in his unit and suffers injuries.

The tenant claims the landlord is liable for his injuries since the landlord has a duty to provide adequate lighting as a security measure.

The landlord claims he is not liable since the light bulb outside the tenant's unit is for the tenant's convenience, and is not intended as a security measure to protect tenants.

Here, the landlord is not liable. Prior criminal activity had not occurred on the premises which would put the landlord on notice of foreseeable risks. Thus, the landlord has no duty to take security precautions against criminal activity. Further, lighting alone is not considered an adequate security measure for deterring crime. [**7735 Hollywood Boulevard Venture** v. **Superior Court** (1981) 116 CA3d 901]

On-site, not off-site prevention

Tenants occupying an apartment complex have been victimized by numerous assaults and robberies in the garage area and courtyard.

The landlord is aware of the criminal activity **on the premises**. In response to tenants' complaints, he promises to install additional lighting.

A tenant parks on the street instead of in the garage due to the inadequate lighting in the common areas. One night, while parking on the street, the tenant is attacked and injured.

The tenant claims the landlord is liable for his injuries since the landlord's failure to provide adequate on-site lighting created a dangerous condition which forced him to park on the street.

The landlord claims he is not liable since the tenant's injury occurred on a public street, not on the leased premises.

Is the landlord liable for the tenant's injuries which occurred on a public street?

No! The landlord does not have a duty to protect a tenant from criminal acts committed by others which injure the tenant when he is not on the leased premises. [**Rosenbaum** v. **Security Bank Corporation** (1996) 43 CA4th 1084]

While the landlord's conduct may have caused the tenant to park in the right of way, the tenant's decision to park on the public street imposes no duty on the landlord to also eliminate dangerous off-premises conditions.

A landlord's **duty of care** is to prevent harm to others in the maintenance and management of the leased premises, not adjoining properties. [Calif. Civil Code §1714]

Prevent dangers within your control

The landlord's duty of care is derived from his *ability to prevent* dangerous conditions from existing on the **property he controls**, not adjacent properties or public right of ways over which he has not taken control.

A duty of care toward tenants can be imposed on the landlord only when a **connection exists** between the harm suffered by the tenant and the landlord's care and maintenance of his property and any surrounding property over which he takes control.

The landlord's failure to remove or prevent injury from a dangerous condition over which the landlord has control must contribute to the injuries suffered by a tenant before liability for injuries will be imposed.

While the landlord in *Rosenbaum* failed to exercise care in the maintenance and repair of his premises, the landlord **exercised no control** over the public street, nor did he create or permit the dangerous condition in the street which caused the tenant's injury.

The purpose of providing adequate lighting in the common areas of a leased premises is to help protect tenants or others against the risk of criminal attacks **on the leased premises**, not on a public street where the responsibility for lighting and security lies with government agencies.

Thus, the lack of adequate lighting in the apartment complex was not the cause of the attack suffered by the tenant on the public street; it only caused the tenant to use the street. [Rosenbaum, *supra*]

Ability to control is not control

Now consider a landlord who is aware of criminal activity occurring on public property adjacent to the leased premises.

The client of a tenant leaves the leased premises at night by way of a public sidewalk adjacent to the premises. Lighting is not installed on the public side of the premises to illuminate the sidewalk.

While walking on the public sidewalk, the individual is assaulted and injured.

The client makes a demand on the landlord to recover losses incurred from his injuries. The client claims the landlord of the premises has a duty to protect patrons of tenants from criminal assaults on public sidewalks providing access to the premises.

The client contends the landlord knew criminal activity had occurred on the sidewalk and **had the power** to exert control over the sidewalk by installing lights on the outside of the building — the sidewalk was the means of ingress and egress to the building.

Is the landlord liable for the client's injuries due to a dangerous condition on adjacent property?

No! The landlord's duty of care does not require him to take control over adjoining property and remove or prevent injury from dangerous conditions known to exist on the adjoining property. Thus, the landlord is not liable for failing to take steps to prevent possible injuries from occurring on a public sidewalk adjacent to the leased premises. [**Donnell** v. **California Western School of Law** (1988) 200 CA3d 715]

The landlord's failure to provide lighting for a public sidewalk which the landlord **does not own or control** did not create the dangerous condition that caused the assault against the tenant's client. Control could have prevented the injuries, but the landlord has no duty to take control of property he does not own.

While the leased premises may be accessed by ingress and egress that is publicly owned, the landlord does not have a duty to provide lighting for public sidewalks. The landlord does not own, possess or control the public sidewalk.

The fact the landlord can influence or alter the condition of the public sidewalk by voluntarily adding lighting in no way indicates he has control over the sidewalk, which would impose liability for failure to provide off-site security. [Donnell, *supra*]

Chapter 29

Dangerous on-site and off-site activities

This chapter presents the duty of care a landlord has to others, on or off the property, for dangerous on-site and off-site activities.

Duty to all to remove on-site dangers

A landlord must exercise *reasonable care* in the management of his property to prevent *foreseeable injury* to all others who may, for whatever reason, be on the premises. [**Rowland** v. **Christian** (1968) 69 CA2d 108; Calif. Civil Code §1714]

If a person — a tenant, guest, invitee or trespasser — is injured due to the landlord's breach of his duty of care to remove or correct a known dangerous on-site condition, the landlord is liable. [CC §1714]

Note — The legal terms trespasser, invitee and licensee determine the rights of individuals who enter onto a parcel of real estate. Distinctions in the status of the person when on the property do not apply when determining a landlord's liability for injuries **suffered by others** *on the leased premises.* [Rowland, *supra*]

The duty of care for others owed by the landlord **applies to all persons** on the property whether they enter the premises with or without permission or are mere social guests, unless the person is committing a felony on the property.

Conditions imposing responsibility

To **impose liability** on a landlord for an injury suffered by any person on the leased premises, several factors must be considered, including:

- the *foreseeability* of the type of harm suffered by the individual;

- the closeness of the *connection* between the landlord's conduct and the injury suffered;

- the *moral blame* attached to the landlord's conduct;

- the *public policy* of preventing future harm;

- the extent of the *burden* on the landlord and the *consequences* to the community of imposing a duty to exercise care to prevent the harm suffered; and

- the availability, cost, and prevalence of *insurance* for the risk involved. [Rowland, *supra*]

For example, the landlord with knowledge of a dangerous situation created by the presence of a tenant's dog is liable for injuries inflicted on others by the dog based on several of these factors.

The landlord's failure to remove from his property the dangerous condition created by the dog is **closely connected** to injuries inflicted by the dog.

The landlord is sufficiently aware of the dangerous condition created by the presence of the dog to **reasonably foresee** the possibility of injury to others.

Also, the landlord has the **ability to eliminate** or reduce the dangerous condition and prevent future harm by serving a 3-day notice to remove the dog or vacate. [**Uccello** v. **Laudenslayer** (1975) 44 CA3d 504]

Landlord's duty to inspect

The landlord must use reasonable care in the repair and maintenance of the leased premises to **prevent harm** to others.

To accomplish this level of safety through prevention of harm, the property must be inspected by the landlord whenever **entry is available** to the landlord.

Thus, before a landlord enters into, renews or extends a lease or rental agreement, a *reasonable inspection* of the leased premises for dangerous conditions must be completed as part of his duty of care to prevent injury to others.

If the landlord fails to inspect when the opportunity exists, the landlord will be **charged with knowledge** of any dangerous condition he should have discovered had he undertaken an inspection.

Consider a landlord and tenant who enter into a nonresidential lease agreement.

The lease allows the landlord to enter the premises for **yearly inspections**. Also, the tenant is required to obtain the landlord's approval before making any improvements.

With the landlord's consent, the tenant builds a roadside marketing structure and operates a retail produce business. The structure's concrete floor is improperly constructed and unfinished. Produce is often littered on the floor.

More than a year after construction, a customer slips and falls on produce littered on the floor and is injured.

The customer claims the landlord is liable for his injuries since the landlord's right to inspect the property puts him on notice of the dangerous condition created by produce falling on the improperly constructed and finished concrete floor.

The landlord claims he is not liable for the customer's injuries since he had no actual notice of the dangerous condition created by the temporary deposit of produce on the floor.

However, the landlord is liable for the customer's injuries if the construction of the concrete floor:

- is a dangerous condition; or

- poses a dangerous condition when littered with produce from a permitted use. [**Lopez** v. **Superior Court** (1996) 45 CA4th 705]

A landlord is required to **conduct an inspection** of the leased premises for the purpose of making the premises safe from dangerous conditions when:

- a lease is executed, extended or renewed; and

- the landlord exercises any periodic right to re-enter or any other control over the property, such as an approval of construction. [**Mora** v. **Baker Commodities, Inc.** (1989) 210 CA3d 771]

Here, the landlord would have observed the condition of the floor had he conducted the yearly inspection of the premises called for in the lease. Thus, the landlord is liable for *slip and fall* injuries when the condition of the floor is determined to be dangerous. [Lopez, *supra*]

A reasonable inspection

A landlord has a duty to inspect the leased premises when he **enters the premises** for any single purpose, such as maintenance, water damage or some other exigency which causes him to make an emergency visit.

While a landlord may enter the premises during the lease term, he is not required to make a thorough inspection of the entire leased premises. However, the landlord who enters will be charged with the knowledge of a dangerous condition if the condition would have been observed by a reasonable person. [Mora, *supra*]

A landlord of a leased premises containing **areas open to the public** will be liable for injuries caused by a dangerous condition in the public area if the condition would be discovered during an inspection by the landlord.

However, unless the landlord is responsible under the lease agreement for repair and maintenance of **nonpublic areas**, a landlord will not be liable for failing to discover a dangerous condition occurring in nonpublic sections of a leased premises.

The landlord is not required to expend extraordinary amounts of time and money constantly conducting extensive searches for possible dangerous conditions. [Mora, *supra*]

For example, a triple-net lease usually transfers all responsibility for maintaining and repairing the property to the tenant.

Under a triple-net lease, the landlord will not be liable for injuries to persons on the leased premises caused by a dangerous condition if:

- the dangerous condition came about after the tenant takes possession; and

- the landlord has no actual knowledge of the dangerous condition.

Note — Often, landlords concerned about tenant maintenance of a leased premises will reserve the right to enter the premises every six months or once a year.

However, frequent inspections of a leased premises create a greater potential of liability for the landlord. Landlords often reserve the right to conduct frequent inspections to assure that the tenant is not damaging or wasting the premises and reducing its market value.

The right to enter brings with it the **obligation to inspect** *for dangerous conditions. Also, the landlord may tend to erroneously overlook possible dangerous conditions he can control which are connected to the tenant's use, not maintenance, of the property.*

Knowledge of dangerous conditions

Consider a landlord and tenant who enter into a residential rental agreement which gives the tenant permission to keep a German Shepherd on the premises.

After the tenant takes possession of the property, the landlord never visits the premises and never sees the dog.

Later, an employee from a utility company enters the yard and suffers injuries when he is attacked by the tenant's dog.

Licensed property managers

Often, landlords employ real estate licensees as property managers.

When acting as an agent for the landlord, the licensed property manager has a duty to notify the landlord of his activities regarding the maintenance and management of the landlord's property. [CC §2020]

However, the landlord is considered to have the same knowledge about the property's condition as does the property manager with regard to the landlord's property. [CC §2332]

Further, since the property manager is the landlord's representative, the landlord will be liable for the property manager's actions performed in the scope of his representation. [CC §2330]

However, the landlord is entitled to indemnity from the property manager should the landlord be liable for the property manager's failure to properly perform his duties.

The licensed property manager will be liable to the landlord for breach of his agency duty. [CC §3333]

The utility company employee seeks to recover money from the landlord as compensation for the injuries inflicted on him by the tenant's dog. The employee claims the landlord should have known the dog is dangerous since German Shepherds are a breed with the propensity for viciousness.

Is the landlord liable for the employee's injuries?

No! The landlord did not have knowledge the tenant's dog was vicious and presented a danger to others. [**Lundy** v. **California Realty** (1985) 170 CA3d 813]

A landlord's obligation to prevent harm to others arises only when the landlord is aware of or *should have known* about the dangerous condition and failed to take preemptive action.

For instance, the landlord receiving complaints from neighbors about the behavior of a tenant's dog may deduce the dog is a dangerous condition, even if the dog has not yet injured anyone.

Note — The landlord's duty to protect others from an injury inflicted by a dog does not yet include asking the tenant if his dog is dangerous.

However, it is feasible the legislature could enact a law or the courts could impose a duty of inquiry on landlords when authorizing the tenant to keep a dog on the premises.

Thus, the pet authorization provision in the lease or rental agreement could include a declaration that the authorized pet is not dangerous.

Further, the owner of a dog is neither civilly nor criminally liable for a dog bite suffered by a person who enters the dog owner's property, lawfully or otherwise, unless the person is invited onto the property by the owner of the dog, is an employee of a utility company, a police officer or a U.S. mailman. [CC §3342(a)]

Landlord should have known

Now consider a landlord who leases nonresidential property to a tenant who operates a retail sales business on the property.

The tenant keeps a dog on the premises and posts a "Beware of Dog" sign. A newspaper article written about the dog's vicious temperament is also posted on the premises.

The landlord visits the leased premises several times a year and knows the dog is kept in the public area of the premises.

After the lease is renewed, a delivery man is attacked and injured by the dog.

The delivery man claims the landlord must compensate him for his injuries since the landlord has a duty to inspect the property and ensure it is safe for members of the public to enter.

The landlord claims he is not liable since he was personally unaware the dog was dangerous.

Is the landlord liable for the delivery man's injuries?

Yes! The landlord owes a duty to the delivery man as a member of the public to:

- exercise reasonable care in the inspection of his property **to discover** dangerous conditions; and

- remove or otherwise **eliminate** the dangerous condition that may be created by the presence of a dog.

The injured person can recover when the landlord is **personally unaware** of the dog's vicious propensities since a reasonable inspection of the premises on renewal of the lease would have revealed to the landlord the newspaper article and the "Beware of Dog" sign. [**Portillo** v. **Aiassa** (1994) 27 CA4th 1128]

Also, it is foreseeable that a guard dog kept on a premises during business hours could injure someone.

Further, the landlord's failure to require the tenant to remove the dog from the premises on discovery that the dog constitutes a dangerous condition is closely connected to the delivery man's injuries.

The landlord had control over the condition, as he could serve a 3-day notice on the tenant requiring the tenant to remove the dog from the premises during business hours or vacate the premises.

Note — In Portillo, *the court held* moral blame *is attached to the landlord's conduct because of his failure to remove a condition he should have known was dangerous and over which he had control.*

Also, a landlord can often remove a dangerous condition by merely exercising his responsibility to make repairs which will eliminate the condition. However, a dangerous condition caused by a tenant's activity may require a 3-day notice ordering the tenant to correct or remove the dangerous condition, or vacate the premises. [See **first tuesday** Form 576]

On-site danger leads to off-site injury

Now consider a landlord and tenant who enter into a rental agreement for a residential dwelling.

The agreement allows the tenant to keep dogs on the premises.

After the tenant occupies the residence, the landlord visits the premises monthly to collect the rent payments. During his visits, the landlord observes the dogs. The landlord is aware of the dogs' vicious nature.

One day, a neighbor and his dog are attacked and injured by the dogs two blocks away from the leased premises.

The neighbor demands the landlord pay for losses resulting from the injuries. The neighbor claims the landlord owes him a duty of care to prevent injuries arising from dangerous ani-

mals the tenant keeps on the landlord's premises.

The landlord claims he is not liable since the injuries occurred off the leased premises.

Here, the landlord is liable for the off-site injuries since the landlord:

- was *aware* of the vicious propensities of dogs housed on his premises; and

- had the ability to remove the dangerous condition by serving a 3-day notice on the tenant to remove the dogs or vacate the premises. [**Donchin** v. **Guerrero** (1995) 34 CA4th 1832]

The landlord's liability for injuries inflicted by a tenant's dog off the premises is the same as his liability for injuries inflicted by the dog which occur on the premises.

While the landlord did not have control over the property where the injury occurred, the landlord did have control over the tenant's right to keep and maintain a known dangerous condition — the dogs — on the premises.

The landlord's failure to have dangerous dogs removed from the premises caused the injuries suffered by the neighbor.

The injury would not have occurred but for the landlord allowing the dogs, which he knew to be vicious, to remain on the premises he controlled. [Donchin, *supra*]

Tenant's dangerous on-site activity

Consider a landlord who is aware the tenant of his single-family rental occasionally discharges a firearm in the backyard.

One day, a bullet fired by the tenant enters the backyard of the neighboring residence and kills the neighbor.

The neighbor's spouse makes a demand on the landlord for her losses resulting from her husband's death. The spouse claims the landlord breached his duty to individuals located on neighboring property by failing to exercise care in the management of his property when he did not remove the known dangerous activity from the premises.

Is the landlord liable for the neighbor's death which occurred off the premises?

Yes! Even though the injury occurred off the leased premises, the landlord is liable since the landlord:

- knew of the dangerous on-site activity carried on by the tenant which inflicted the injury; and

- had the ability to eliminate the dangerous condition by serving a 3-day notice on the tenant to refrain from discharging the gun or quit the premises. [**Rosales** v. **Stewart** (1980) 113 CA3d 130]

Thus, the landlord had a duty to prevent the tenant from continuing to fire the gun on the premises.

The landlord is liable for an injury resulting from a known dangerous condition or activity maintained or occurring on his property which he has the ability to remove, regardless of whether the injury from the on-site activity is suffered on or off the leased premises.

However, had the tenant left the premises with his gun and then shot and killed an individual, the landlord would not be liable. [Medina, *supra*]

Failure to avoid obvious dangers

Some dangerous conditions are obvious to persons entering or using the premises which impose a duty of care on the person to avoid injury to themselves.

For example, a person wearing cleated shoes walks on a concrete path alongside of which is a rubber walkway for use to prevent slip and fall injuries. The person wearing cleated shoes walks on the concrete path and slips, injuring

himself in the fall. A sign does not exist to explain the danger of the person's activity.

Here, a landlord has no duty to warn or guard others against a dangerous condition that is obvious. [**Beauchamp** v. **Los Gatos Golf Course** (1969) 273 CA2d 20]

While a landlord must compensate others for injuries caused by his failure to use skill and ordinary care in the management of his property, the liability has its limits.

A person, who willfully or by his own **lack of ordinary care** brings an injury upon himself, exonerates the landlord, wholly or in part, from liability. [CC §1714]

Thus, a person has a duty of care to himself to be sufficiently observant and keep himself out of harm's way.

When the injured person's lack of care for himself contributes to his injury, recovery for his losses is limited to the percentage of the negligence attributed to him, called *comparative negligence*. The money losses recoverable by the injured person will be diminished in proportion to the percent of negligence attributable to the injured person for causing his own harm. [**Li** v. **Yellow Cab Company of California** (1975) 13 CA3d 804]

Further, consider a trespasser who enters into or onto property illegally and fails to conduct himself with care to avoid harming himself, called *negligence*.

When the trespasser is negligent in exercising care in his conduct to prevent harm to himself while entering or moving about the property, any losses recoverable by the injured trespasser will be reduced by the percentage amount of negligence attributed to his injury. [**Beard** v. **Atchison, Topeka and Santa Fe Railway Co.** (1970) 4 CA3d 129]

Further, the landlord's liability will be limited if the trespasser was in the process of committing a felony on the property when he was injured. [CC §847]

Not a dangerous condition

Now consider a person who enters leased nonresidential property and wants to look inside the building.

Next to the building, below a window, stands a vat of acid maintained by the business authorized to operate on the leased premises. The vat is covered with plywood for the purpose of keeping out dirt and dust.

In order to see through the window, the person climbs up and steps onto the plywood cover which immediately collapses. The person falls into the vat and suffers injuries.

The person attempts to recover money from the landlord for losses suffered from his injury.

Here, the landlord is not liable for the person's injuries since the vat is not a dangerous condition which presents a risk of harm. The vat of acid is an integral part of the business run on the leased premises and is not a danger to any person who conducts himself with care around the vat.

Thus, the injured person undertook the risk of harm to himself by climbing on top of the vat and creating the dangerous situation which led to his injuries. [**Bisetti** v. **United Refrigeration Corp.** (1985) 174 CA3d 643]

Note — In Bisetti, *the injured person happened to be a trespasser.*

Consider a landlord of an apartment complex used by gang members as a hangout and base from which they commit criminal offenses when off the premises. One of the gang members is a named tenant.

The tenants and law enforcement officials complain to the landlord about the gang. However, the gang members do not harm or pose a threat of danger to the tenants.

Later, a pedestrian walking past the complex in the public right of way is chased by the gang members. One of the gang members, who is not the tenant, shoots and kills the pedestrian on a street adjacent to the complex.

The spouse of the pedestrian claims the landlord is liable for the death since he failed to remove the dangerous condition, the presence of gang members, on his premises.

However, the landlord does not have a duty to protect members of the public who use adjacent public streets from assaults by gang members who congregate on his leased premises. [**Medina** v. **Hillshore Partners** (1995) 40 CA4th 477]

The congregation of gang members on the leased premises is not itself a dangerous condition. The gang members do not pose a physical threat to others of which the landlord is aware.

Thus, the landlord's failure to take steps to prevent the gang members from congregating on the leased premises is not the cause of the off-site shooting of a pedestrian by one of the gang members.

Again, the landlord is not liable for injuries that occur off the leased premises, since the landlord has **no control over the activities** of individuals or tenants while they are on public property, only when they are on his property. [Medina, *supra*]

Dangerous off-site conditions

Now consider a landlord who leases a residence to a tenant. The residents of the neighboring property own a dog the landlord knows to be vicious.

The neighbor brings his leashed dog onto the leased premises. The neighbor invites the tenant's child to pet the dog.

The dog breaks free from the leash and attacks the child, causing injuries.

The tenant claims the landlord is liable for the injuries since the landlord failed to warn him of the dangerous condition created by the neighbor's vicious dog.

Is the landlord liable for injuries inflicted on-site by the neighbor's dog, which he knew was vicious?

No! The dangerous condition was not maintained on the leased premises. Thus, the landlord has no control or authority himself to remove the dangerous condition from the neighbor's property. [**Wylie** v. **Gresch** (1987) 191 CA3d 412]

While a landlord owes a duty to others to remove a dog from his property which he knows to be dangerous, he does not have a duty to warn his tenants of the presence of vicious animals located on other properties in the neighborhood.

The landlord's failure to protect the tenant by warning him about the neighbor's dog did not create a dangerous condition on the leased premises which caused the tenant to be injured.

A landlord's duty to correct or prevent injury from dangerous conditions does not extend to the dangerous conditions which exist off the premises. [Wylie, *supra*]

While the landlord does have a duty to make the leased premises safe by removing dangerous on-site conditions and properly maintaining the premises, he is not the insurer of the tenant's safety from off-site hazards. [**7735 Hollywood Boulevard Venture** v. **Superior Court** (1981) 116 CA3d 901]

Off-site injuries under landlord control

The public right of way for a street fronting a leased premises includes part of the lawn in front of the premises, located between the street curb and the property line. The landlord maintains the entire lawn up to the curb.

A water meter is located on the lawn in the street right of way. Several tenants inform the landlord the water meter box is broken and needs repair.

A tenant trips on the broken water meter box and suffers injuries.

The tenant makes a demand on the landlord for losses caused by his injuries, claiming the landlord has a duty to eliminate dangerous conditions located in the public right of way within the lawn maintained by the landlord.

The landlord claims he is not liable since the water meter box is not located on his property and the landlord does not own or control the meter box.

However, the landlord is liable for the injuries suffered by the tenant caused by dangerous conditions — the broken water meter box — located in a public right of way surrounded by a lawn created and maintained by the landlord. [**Alcaraz** v. **Vece** (1997) 14 C4th 1149]

Also, a landlord or other property owner who installs and maintains trees adjacent to or in the lawn area between the public sidewalk and the street-side curb owes a duty of care to avoid injuring pedestrians by hazards created by the trees he maintains.

For example, trees planted and maintained by the property owner grow and eventually produce roots which extend under the sidewalk and crack and uplift it. The owner is aware of the hazard created but undertakes no steps to have the hazardous condition repaired or replaced.

Here, the owner has taken control over the off-site area containing the public sidewalk and will be liable to any pedestrian who is injured due to the hazard created by the roots of trees he maintains since the trunks of the trees are located on his property. [**Alpert** v. **Villa Romano Homeowners Association** (2000) 81 CA4th 1320]

SECTION F

Nonresidential Lease Provisions

Chapter 30

Nonresidential lease agreement

This chapter reviews a nonresidential lease agreement as the conveyance of a leasehold interest in real estate.

The conveyance of a leasehold

A lease agreement is **a contract** entered into by a landlord and tenant for payment of money and care of real estate. The lease also acts to **convey a possessory interest** in real estate, called a *leasehold estate*. [Calif. Civil Code §761(3)]

By entering into a lease agreement, the landlord conveys to the tenant the **exclusive right to occupy** a parcel of real estate, or space in a parcel, for a fixed period of time. The continued right to occupancy of the real estate *is conditioned* on the tenant's performance under the contractual provisions in the lease, such as the payment of rent and any maintenance of the property delegated to the tenant.

On **expiration** of the term of occupancy, the right of possession to the real estate reverts to the landlord. During the term of the leasehold, the landlord as the fee owner holds only a *reversionary interest* in the leased parcel or space.

Once the lease agreement has been entered into, the landlord's and tenant's **right to possession** of the leased real estate is controlled by landlord/tenant law, not contract law.

On the other hand, the rent provisions contracted for in the lease agreement **evidence the debt** owed by the tenant to the landlord over the term of the lease.

Also, the lease contains contractual provisions establishing the responsibilities of the tenant or landlord to pay the operating costs and provide for the **care and maintenance** of the property.

The landlord may regain possession of the real estate by forfeiting (terminating) the tenant's leasehold interest should the tenant fail to comply with — *breach* — the contracted terms of the lease, such as the failure after service of a 3-day notice to either pay rent, maintain the property, or fully perform under some other provision in the lease agreement.

The tenant's leasehold right to possession may be prematurely terminated and returned to the landlord on a forfeiture declared in a notice to quit or by eviction — an unlawful detainer (UD) action. However, on forfeiture of possession, the lease agreement **remains uncancelled** and in effect as a contract to pay rent and other amounts until it expires.

Conversely, the tenant's obligation to pay can be cancelled prior to expiration of the lease by the landlord's conduct or misunderstanding of the forfeiture provision in the notice to quit, called a *surrender*. [**Desert Plaza Partnership v. Waddell** (1986) 180 CA3d 805]

Validity of lease agreement form

A lease conveying a term of occupancy exceeding one year must be written to be enforceable, a requirement of the *statute of frauds*. [CC §1624(a)(3)]

The provisions of a written lease agreement fall into one of three categories of activities:

- **conveyance** of the leasehold interest;

- the **lease debt**, called *rent*; and

- responsibility for **care and maintenance** of the leased premises. [See Form 552 accompanying this chapter]

NONRESIDENTIAL LEASE AGREEMENT
Commercial, Industrial or Office

DATE:_____, 20_____, at _____, California

Items left blank or unchecked are not applicable.

1. FACTS:

1.1 The Landlord, _____,

leases to Tenant(s) _____,

and _____,

the real estate referred to as _____

_____.

1.2 The Landlord acknowledges receipt of $_____ to be applied as follows:

☐ Security deposit $_____   ☐ First month's rent $_____

☐ Last month's rent $_____

1.3 The following checked addendums are made a part of this nonresidential lease:

☐ Additional terms addendum [**first tuesday** Form 250]   ☐ Option to Renew/Extend [ft Form 565]

☐ Authority to Sublease/Assign   ☐ Property Description

☐ Brokerage Fee Addendum [ft Form 273]   ☐ Option to Buy [ft Form 161]

☐ Condition of Premises [ft Form 560]   ☐ Option to Lease Additional Space

☐ Building rules   ☐ Plat of leased space

☐ Operating Expense Sheet [ft Form 562]   ☐ Other: _____

2. TERM OF LEASE:

2.1 The lease commences _____, 20_____, and expires _____, 20_____, the month of commencement being the anniversary month.

2.2 The lease terminates on the last day of the term without further notice.

2.3 If Tenant holds over, Tenant to be liable for damages at the daily rate of $_____.

2.4 ☐ This lease agreement is a sublease of the premises which is limited in its terms by the terms and condition of the attached master lease.

3. RENT:

3.1 Tenant to pay rent monthly, in advance, on the first day of each month, including rent for any partial month prorated at 1/30th of the monthly rent per day.

3.2 ☐ Monthly rent for the entire term is fixed at the amount of $_____.

3.3 ☐ Monthly rent, from year to year, is adjusted on each anniversary month as follows:

Initial year's monthly rent:................ $_____, and

a. _____% increase in monthly rent over prior year's monthly rent; or

b. First anniversary monthly rent:.......... $_____

Second anniversary monthly rent:....... $_____

Third anniversary monthly rent:......... $_____

Fourth anniversary monthly rent:........ $_____

3.4 ☐ Monthly base rent for the initial 12 months of the term is the amount of $_____, adjusted annually on the first day of each anniversary month by increasing the initial monthly base rent by the percentage increase between the applicable CPI-U index figures published for the third month preceding the month of commencement and the third month preceding the anniversary month.

a. The applicable CPI-U Index (Consumer Price Index for All Urban Consumer)(1982-1984 = 100) is:

☐ Los Angeles-Anaheim-Riverside   ☐ SanFrancisco-Oakland-SanJose

☐ SanDiego ☐ National ☐ Other: _____.

b. Rent increases under CPI-U adjustments are limited for any one year to an increase of _____%.

c. On any anniversary adjustment, should the CPI-U have decreased below the CPI-U for the prior twelve-month period, the monthly rent for the ensuing 12 months shall remain the same as the rent during the prior 12 months.

d. If the CPI-U is ☐ changed or replaced by the United States Government, the conversion factor published by the Government on the new Index shall be used to compute annual adjustments.

3.5 ☐ Additional percentage rent equal to _____% of gross sales made from the premises during each calendar year, less credit for other rent, real estate taxes, insurance and common area maintenance (CAM) charges paid for the calendar year.

— — — — — — — — — — — PAGE ONE OF FOUR — FORM 552 — — — — — — — — — — — — — — —

a. The percentage rent shall be computed and paid for each month of the lease with a signed written statement of the gross income and percentage computation by the tenth day of the following month.

b. The additional percentage rent to be payable monthly shall be credited for other rent, taxes, insurance, and CAMs paid by Tenant for the month.

c. Within one month after each calendar year and on expiration of the lease, Tenant shall compute and deliver a written statement of sales and the percentage rent due for the calendar year, less credit for rent, taxes, insurance and CAMs paid for the calendar year, to annually adjust the percentage rent remaining due from Tenant or to be refunded to Tenant by Landlord, which difference will be paid on delivery of the annual statement.

d. Gross sales includes all money or equivalent received by Tenant, subtenant, licensees or concessionaires, in the ordinary course of business, whether wholesale or retail, cash or credit, less credit for goods returned by customer or merchandise returned by Tenant or transferred to tenant-affiliated stores.

e. Landlord has the right, on reasonable notice, to audit Tenant's books regarding sales information.

3.6 ☐ Every _____ years after commencement, including extensions/renewals, the monthly base rent will be adjusted, upward only, to current market rental rates for comparable premises, and computation of any future CPI-U adjustments will treat the year of each current market adjustment as a commencement year for selecting the Index figures.

a. The monthly rent during any year shall not be less than the previous year's monthly rent.

b. Landlord to reasonably determine and advise Tenant of the adjusted rental rates prior to three months before the adjustment becomes effective.

3.7 Rent to be paid by:

a. ☐ cash, ☐ check, or ☐ cashier's check, made payable to Landlord.
Personal delivery of rent to be at Landlord's address during the hours of _____ am to _____ pm on the following days: _____

b. ☐ credit card #_____/_____/_____/_____ issued by _____,
which Landlord is authorized to charge each month for rent due.

c. ☐ deposit into account number _____ at:
_____ (Financial Institution)
_____ (Address)

3.8 Tenant to pay a charge of $_____ as an additional amount of rent, due on demand, in the event rent is not received within five days of the due date.

3.9 If any rent or other amount due landlord is not received within five days after it's due date, interest will thereafter accrue on the amount at 12% per annum until paid. On receipt of any past due amount, landlord to promptly make a written demand for payment of the accrued interest which will be payable within 30 days of the demand.

3.10 Tenant to pay a charge of $_____ as an additional amount of rent, due on demand, for each rent check returned for insufficient funds, and thereafter to pay rent by cash or cashier's check.

4. OPERATING EXPENSES:

4.1 Tenant is responsible for payment of utility and service charge as follows: _____
_____

4.2 Landlord is responsible for payment of utility and service charges as follows: _____
_____

4.3 Tenant to pay all taxes levied on trade fixtures or other improvements Tenant installs on the premises.

4.4 Should Landlord pay any charge owed by Tenant, Tenant shall pay, within 10 days of written demand, the charge as additional rent.

4.5 As additional rent, Tenant to pay _____% of all real property taxes and assessments levied by governments, for whatever cause, against the land, trees and building containing the leased premises, within 30 days after written computation and demand from Landlord.

4.6 As additional monthly rent, Tenant to pay _____% of the common area maintenance (CAM) incurred each month, within 10 days of written statement and demand for payment.

a. Common area maintenance is the cost of maintaining and operating the "Common Areas," including all sidewalks, corridors, plazas, hallways, restrooms, parking areas, interior and exterior walls and all other open areas not occupied by tenants.

b. Common area maintenance includes "all charges" for garbage removal, janitorial services, gardening, landscaping, printing/decorating, repair and upkeep, utilities and other operating costs, including charges for property management of the common area maintenance.

5. POSSESSION:

5.1 Tenant may terminate the lease if Landlord does not deliver up possession within 10 days after commencement of the lease.

5.2 Landlord is to recover and deliver possession of the premises from the previous tenant. Tenant will not be liable for rent until possession is delivered.

5.3 If Landlord is unable to deliver possession of the premises, Landlord will not be liable for any damages.

6. USE OF THE PREMISES:

6.1 The Tenant's use of the premises shall be: _____

6.2 No other use of the premises is permitted. Tenant may not conduct any activity which increases Landlord's insurance premiums.

6.3 Tenant will not use the premises for any unlawful purpose, violate any government ordinance or building and tenant association rules, or create any nuisance.

6.4 Tenant shall deliver up the premises together with all keys to the premises on expiration of the lease in as good condition as when Tenant took possession, except for reasonable wear and tear.

7. APPURTENANCES:

7.1 Tenant shall have the right to use Landlord's access of ingress and egress.

7.2 Tenant shall also have the use of _____ parking spaces for the running of its business.

8. SIGNS AND ADVERTISING:

8.1 Tenant will not construct any sign or other advertising on the premises without the prior consent of Landlord.

8.2 Landlord will maintain a directory in the lobby of the premises displaying the name and suite number of Tenant. Landlord has the right to determine the size, shape, color, style and lettering of the directory.

8.3 Landlord will provide a sign to be placed on the primary door to Tenant's suite. The fees for the cost and installation will be paid by Tenant.

9. TENANT IMPROVEMENTS/ALTERATIONS:

9.1 Tenant may not alter or improve the real estate without Landlord's prior consent. Tenant will keep the real estate free of all claims for any improvements and will timely notify Landlord to permit posting of notices for nonresponsibility.

9.2 Any increases in Landlord's property taxes caused by improvements made by Tenant shall become additional rent due on demand.

10. REPAIR AND MAINTENANCE:

10.1 The premises are in good condition, except as noted in an addendum.

10.2 Tenant shall maintain and repair the premises, except for the following which are Landlord's responsibility:
☐ Plumbing and sewers ☐ Structural foundations ☐ Exterior walls ☐ Heating and air conditioning ☐ Store front ☐ Plate glass ☐ Roof ☐ Parking areas ☐ Lawns and shrubbery ☐ Sidewalks ☐ Driveways/right of ways ☐ Electrical ☐ Other: _____

11. RIGHT TO ENTER:

11.1 Tenant agrees to make the premises available on 24 hours notice for entry by Landlord for necessary repairs, alterations, or inspection of the premises.

12. WASTE:

12.1 Tenant will not destroy, damage, or remove any part of the premises or equipment, or commit waste, or permit any person to do so.

13. LIABILITY INSURANCE:

13.1 Tenant shall obtain and maintain commercial general liability and plate glass insurance covering both personal injury and property damage to cover Tenant's use of the premises insuring Tenant and Landlord.

13.2 Tenant shall obtain insurance for this purpose in the minimum amount of $_____.

13.3 Tenant shall provide Landlord with a Certificate of Insurance naming the Landlord as an additional insured. The Certificate shall provide for written notice to Landlord should a change or cancellation of the policy occur.

13.4 Each party waives all insurance subrogation rights it may have.

14. FIRE INSURANCE:

14.1 Tenant shall obtain and maintain a standard fire insurance policy with extended coverage for theft and vandalism to the extent of 100% of the replacement value of all personal property and the restoration of Tenant improvements.

15. HOLD HARMLESS:

15.1 Tenant shall hold Landlord harmless for all claims, damages or liability arising out of the premises caused by Tenant or its employees or patrons.

16. DESTRUCTION:

16.1 In the event the premises are totally or partially destroyed, Tenant agrees to repair the premises if the destruction is caused by Tenant or covered by its insurance.

16.2 The lease shall not be terminated due to any destruction.

16.3 Landlord shall repair the premises if the cause is not covered by the tenant's insurance and is covered by Landlord's policy.

16.4 Landlord may terminate the lease if the repairs cannot be completed within 30 days, the cost of restoration exceeds 70% of the replacement value of the premises, the insurance proceeds are insufficient to cover the actual cost of the repairs, or the premises may not be occupied by law.

17. SUBORDINATION:

17.1 Tenant agrees to subordinate to any new financing secured by the premises which does not exceed 80% loan-to-value ratio, interest of two percent over market and not less than a 15-year monthly amortization and five-year due date.

18. TENANT ESTOPPEL CERTIFICATES:

18.1 Within 10 days after notice, Tenant will execute a certificate stating the existing terms of the lease to be provided to prospective buyers or lenders.

18.2 Failure to deliver the certificate shall be conclusive evidence the information contained in it is correct.

19. ASSIGNMENT, SUBLETTING AND ENCUMBRANCE: [Check only one]

19.1 ☐ Tenant may not assign this lease or sublet any part of the premises, or further encumber the leasehold.

19.2 ☐ Tenant may not transfer any interest in the premises without the prior consent of Landlord.

a. ☐ Consent may not be unreasonably withheld.

b. ☐ Consent is subject to the attached conditions. [ft Form 250]

20. SURRENDER:

20.1 Tenant may surrender this lease only by a written cancellation and waiver agreement with Landlord.

21. EMINENT DOMAIN:

21.1 Should a portion or all of the premises be condemned for public use, Landlord may terminate the lease and Tenant's possession. If the lease is not terminated, Tenant shall receive a rent abatement for the actual reduction (if any) in the value of the lease.

21.2 Tenant waives the right to any compensation awarded from the condemning authority for the whole or partial taking of the premises.

21.3 Any Tenant's damages shall come solely from the condemning authority.

22. WAIVER:

22.1 Waiver of a breach of any provision in this lease shall not constitute a waiver of any subsequent breach. Landlord's receipt of rent with knowledge of Tenant's breach does not waive Landlord's right to enforce the breach.

23. DEFAULT REMEDIES:

23.1 If Tenant breaches any provision of this lease, Landlord may exercise its rights, including the right to collect future rental losses after forfeiture of possession.

24. BROKERAGE FEES:

24.1 ☐ Landlord and Tenant to pay Broker fees per the attached schedule of leasing agent's fee. [ft form 113]

25. MISCELLANEOUS:

25.1 ☐ See attached addendum for additional terms. [ft Form 250]

25.2 In any action to enforce this agreement, the prevailing party shall receive attorney fees.

25.3 This lease shall be binding on all heirs, assigns and successors except as provided in section 19.

25.4 This lease shall be enforced under California law.

25.5 This lease reflects the entire agreement between the parties.

25.6 ☐ This lease is secured by a trust deed. [ft Form 451]

25.7 ☐ The performance of this lease is assured by a guarantee agreement. [ft Form 439]

I agree to let on the terms stated above.	I agree to occupy on the terms stated above.
Date:_____, 20_____	Date:_____, 20_____
Landlord: _____	Tenant: _____
Agent: _____	Tenant: _____
Signature: _____	Signature: _____
Address: _____	Signature: _____
_____	Address: _____
Phone: _____	_____
Fax: _____	Phone: _____
E-mail: _____	Fax: _____
	E-mail: _____

To be valid, a lease agreement must:

- designate the **size and location** of the leased premises with *reasonable certainty*;

- set forth a **term** for the tenancy conveyed; and

- state the **rental amount**, and its time and manner of payment. [**Levin** v. **Saroff** (1921) 54 CA 285]

Offers to lease and lease agreements

A broker, whether he represents the landlord or the tenant, should use an **offer to lease** form to initiate and document lease negotiations prior to entering into the lease agreement itself. [See **first tuesday** Form 556]

An *offer to lease* entered into by both the tenant and the landlord is also referred to as an *agreement to lease*. The preparation and signing of the actual lease remains to be done after its terms and conditions have been agreed to in the offer to lease.

Consider a potential tenant who signs an offer to lease property which is submitted to the landlord.

The offer calls for the landlord to erect a building on the property for use in the tenant's business.

The landlord accepts the offer to lease. In the offer to lease, the landlord agrees to lease the premises to the tenant on the completion of the improvements by the landlord.

The offer to lease also states the tenant will lease the premises for five years, commencing on completion of the improvements, and then begin making the agreed-to monthly rental payments.

After construction of the building is completed, the tenant takes possession of the premises and makes monthly rental payments to the landlord.

A formal lease agreement is not prepared or entered into by the landlord and tenant. Both the landlord and the tenant perform according to the terms stated in the offer to lease, except for the failure to enter into the lease agreement.

Later, the property becomes the subject of an action for inverse condemnation. Persons with an interest in the property are entitled to money.

The landlord claims the tenant is not entitled to any part of the monies from the condemnation award since the tenant has no interest in the property. The tenant lacks a signed lease agreement **conveying** to him the agreed leasehold interest.

The tenant claims he has a leasehold interest in the property under the offer to lease and is entitled to recover his losses resulting from the condemnation of the property.

Here, the tenant owns a leasehold (estate) interest in the property. The written agreement entered into by the landlord and the tenant — an offer to lease on the terms stated — becomes the lease agreement when the tenant takes possession of the premises without entering into a formalized lease agreement. [**City of Santa Cruz** v. **MacGregor** (1960) 178 CA2d 45]

The offer to lease contains all the essential terms needed to create a lease, including:

- a *description of the premises* to be leased and its location — a building on the premises;

- a *lease term* — five years; and

- the *amount of periodic rent* and when it will be paid.

Since all the elements necessary to create a lease are agreed to in writing, the landlord's act of delivering possession to the tenant **conveys** the agreed leasehold interest to the tenant.

To record or not to record

A lease agreement need not be recorded. Between the landlord and the tenant, and all parties who have *knowledge* of the lease, the lease is enforceable whether or not it is recorded. [CC §1217]

Thus, an unrecorded lease which exceeds one year in length is only void as against a *bona fide purchaser* (BFP). [CC §1214]

However, a BFP is a person who, *without knowledge* the lease exists or that a tenant is in possession, purchases the leased real estate for valuable consideration or accepts the real estate as security for a debt.

Should a tenant actually occupy the property at the time it is purchased or encumbered, the purchaser or secured lender is *charged with knowledge* of the tenant's leasehold interest — whether or not the lease is recorded. Thus, the tenant's occupancy puts the purchaser and lender on *constructive notice* a lease (or some other arrangement with the occupant) exists. [**Manig** v. **Bachman** (1954) 127 CA2d 216]

However, when a lease is recorded, the content of the recorded lease may be relied on by a purchaser or lender as containing **all the rights** of the tenant. Thus, the need for a tenant estoppel certificate to establish the tenant's rights in the property is eliminated by the recording.

*Note — An unrecorded option to buy the leased property or extend the lease cannot be enforced against a buyer or lender acquiring an interest in the property when the **lease is recorded**, if:*

- *the option to extend the lease or buy the property itself is not recorded; or*

- *the unrecorded options are not referenced in the recorded lease.* [**Gates Rubber Company** v. **Ulman** (1989) 214 CA3d 356]

The contents of a lease agreement

A nonresidential lease agreement form has five main sections:

- *identification* of the parties and the premises, and the conveyance and term of the leasehold interest;

- the *rent* and terms of payment of any amounts owed;

- the *care and maintenance* of the leased property;

- *miscellaneous provisions* for circumstances peculiar to the transaction; and

- the *signatures* of the parties.

The **identification section** of a real estate lease agreement includes:

- the names of the landlord and the tenant;

- a description of the leased premises;

- words of conveyance which are a part of the lease agreement;

- a receipt for prepaid rents and the security deposit; and

- a list of the addenda which contain exhibits or additional terms. [See Form 552 §1]

The leasehold conveyance

The lease agreement includes words of transfer by which the landlord conveys a leasehold interest in the property to the tenant upon signing and delivery to the tenant. [See Form 552 §1.1]

The **conveyance** of a leasehold interest is typically achieved with the words "landlord . . . leases to . . . tenant the real estate referred to as . . . ." [See Form 552 §1.1]

However, consider an owner of a department store who enters into an agreement with a tenant to occupy space in the store for three years. The tenant will use the space to conduct his business.

The agreement states the space to be occupied by the tenant will be designated by the owner at the time of occupancy. The agreement also:

- outlines the formula for the monthly **rent** to be paid for the space;

- gives the tenant the sole and **exclusive right** to conduct his business in the store without competition;

- **restricts transfer** of the tenant's right to occupy the space without the owner's consent; and

- states the tenant will **surrender** the occupied premises on the last day of the rental term.

After the tenant takes possession, and before the term for occupancy expires, the owner notifies the tenant he is terminating the agreement and the tenant must vacate the premises.

The tenant does not comply with the owner's notice to vacate. The landlord removes the tenant's fixtures, equipment and inventory, and bars the tenant from entering the premises.

The tenant claims the owner cannot terminate the occupancy, much less remove his possessions, without first filing a UD action and obtaining a judgment to recover possession since the occupancy agreement constitutes a lease which conveyed a leasehold interest in the occupied space to the tenant.

The owner claims the agreement is a mere *license* to conduct business in the store and is not a lease since **no defined space** was described in the agreement to identify the location of the leased premises.

Here, the agreement to occupy the space is a lease. While the agreement itself does not identify the space to be acquired by the tenant or contain words of conveyance, the agreement becomes a lease on the tenant's occupancy of the **premises designated** by the landlord since the agreement states:

- possession of the premises is to be delivered to the tenant for his exclusive use in exchange for monthly rent;

- the lease cannot be assigned without the consent of the landlord; and

- the premises need not be delivered up to the landlord until the end of the rental term. [**Beckett** v. **City of Paris Dry Goods Co.** (1939) 14 C2d 633]

The agreement entered into by the landlord does not contain the words "landlord . . . leases to . . . tenant" as words of conveyance.

However, the contents of the agreement indicate the landlord intended to convey a leasehold interest to the tenant, and the act of **delivering possession** to the tenant of space designated by the store owner is the conveyance.

Conversely, an agreement is not automatically a lease just because it uses words of leasehold conveyance. The *economic function* of a "lease transaction" may actually be that of a sale which has been recharacterized by the parties under the guise of a lease.

For instance, a lease-option agreement which allocates option money or a portion of each rental payment, or both, toward the purchase price or down payment to be made on the purchase of the property is not a lease at all. The lease-option agreement is a *disguised security device* that evidences a credit sale by a carryback seller and the reporting of taxable profits on the down payment undeferred by option rules. [**Oesterreich** v. **Commissioner of Internal Revenue** (9th Cir. 1955) 226 F2d 798]

Proper identification of the parties

Each party to a lease must be properly identified.

On the lease agreement form, the tenant should indicate how the leasehold interests conveyed will be vested, such as community property, joint tenancy, tenancy-in-common, sole ownership, as a trustee for someone or as a business entity.

When the vested interest of the landlord is also community property, both spouses must consent to agreements leasing the community property for a fixed term exceeding one year. If not, the community is not bound by the lease, and the tenant cannot enforce the leasehold conveyance if challenged within one year after commencement by the nonconsenting spouse. [Calif. Family Code §1102]

Business entities, which excludes individuals, their trusts and DBAs, that own or lease property include:

- corporations and out-of-state entities qualifying as a corporation;

- limited liability companies (LLCs);

- partnerships;

- real estate investment trusts (REITs);

- nonprofit organizations; and

- governmental agencies.

When the landlord or tenant is a partnership, the lease should indicate:

- whether the partnership is a limited, general or limited liability partnership;

- the partnership's state of formation, and if out of state, whether it is qualified to do business in California; and

- the name of the partner authorized to bind the partnership.

With information on the partnership, the landlord and any title company insuring the leasehold can confirm in recorded documents the authority of the general or managing partner to bind the partnership.

Whether a corporation is the landlord or tenant, the full corporate name and the state of incorporation should be disclosed, as well as the name and title of the officer who will be signing the lease.

The corporate information, along with a *resolution* from the board of directors authorizing corporate officers to enter into the lease in the name of the corporation, will allow for confirmation of the corporation's good standing to operate in the state, the officers registered with the state, and whether the officers are authorized by resolution to execute the lease on behalf of the corporation.

Premises identification with certainty

The nonresidential lease agreement must describe the premises to be leased so the premises can be identified with *reasonable certainty*. While the description may not itself be "definite and certain" as worded, to be *reasonably certain* an imperfectly worded description need only furnish a "means or key" for a surveyor to identify the parcel's location on the earth's surface or within a building. [**Beverage** v. **Canton Placer Mining Co.** (1955) 43 C2d 769]

If the premises is a building or a space in a building, the common street address, including the unit number, is a sufficient description to identify the premises.

If the premises is not easily identified by its common address, a plot map or floor plan should be included as an addendum to the lease, with the space to be rented highlighted or otherwise identified.

A plot map or floor plan eliminates confusion over the location of the leased parcel or space in the building, and initially establishes the parameters of the space being leased.

An attached plan noting square footage is also useful if the calculation of any part of the rent is based on square footage occupied by the tenant, or on the percentage of square footage within a project leased to the tenant.

Also, an inaccurate or incomplete description of the leased premises will not preclude a landlord from conveying, and the tenant from accepting, a leasehold interest in a parcel of real estate for lack of certainty.

A sufficient description

A tenant signs and hands the landlord an **offer to lease** together with the proposed lease agreement for space in a retail commercial center.

Attached to the proposed lease is a plot plan outlining the dimensions of the leased premises.

The lease contains a provision stating the exact legal description of the premises will be prepared as an addendum to the lease no sooner than 30 days after the leased premises is occupied by the tenant.

After submitting the offer to lease, the tenant decides he would rather lease space at another location. The tenant mails a revocation letter to the landlord for the withdrawal of his offer.

However, the tenant receives the signed offer and lease agreement from the landlord before the landlord receives the tenant's revocation letter. The lease agreement fails to include a copy of the plot plan addendum attached to the offer and lease.

The tenant refuses to perform under the lease agreement claiming the lease agreement is unenforceable since the landlord failed to deliver the plot plan addendum which designated the size of the leased premises.

The landlord seeks to enforce the tenant's performance of the lease agreement.

Here, a lease has been entered into which is enforceable.

The precise size of the leased premises is not crucial to the lease transaction since the location of the premises is known and the lease agreement states the exact size of the premises identified in the lease will be determined at a later date. [**Mabee** v. **Nurseryland Garden Centers, Inc.** (1978) 84 CA3d 968]

Also, when the premises described in a lease is incomplete or inaccurate, the tenant's actual possession of the premises will set the boundaries. [Beckett, *supra*]

Further, an incomplete or inaccurate description of the leased premises occupied by the tenant does not release a tenant from liability under the lease. [City of Santa Cruz, *supra*]

Security deposit and prepaid rent

After identifying the landlord, tenant and the property leased, a nonresidential lease acknowledges the landlord's receipt of the tenant's security deposit and any prepaid rent. [See Form 552 §1.2]

The receipt states the total amount of funds paid up front by the tenant, and the allocation of the funds between security deposit and prepaid rent.

Addenda to the lease agreement

The terms common to all nonresidential leases are contained in the provisions of a standard lease form.

However, the terms and conditions peculiar to the leasing of a particular type of nonresidential tenancy, such as commercial, industrial, office, farming operation or hotel, or provisions unique to the parties and their advisors, should be handled in an addendum.

The use of an addendum to house extraordinary and atypical provisions not in common use avoids the element of a later unpleasant (and litigious) surprise. Extraordinary provisions occasionally go unnoticed at the time the lease agreement is entered into because they are buried in preprinted copy.

Also, any handwritten or typewritten provisions added to an agreement control over conflicting pre-printed or boilerplate provisions. [**Gutzi Associates** v. **Switzer** (1989) 215 CA3d 1636]

Thus, should inconsistencies arise between provisions in the pre-printed lease agreement and an attached addendum, the provisions in the addendum control.

The use of addenda for making changes or additions to lease provisions allows parties to tailor the lease transaction to meet their needs, while retaining the integrity of the contents of the lease form.

Standard addenda typically attached to a nonresidential lease include:

- terms unique to the type of property leased [See **first tuesday** Form 250];

- a property description addendum, such as a plot map or site plan;

- a structural or tenant improvement agreement;

- a condition of premises addendum [See **first tuesday** Form 560];

- a building rules addendum;

- an option to renew or extend [See **first tuesday** Form 566];

- a brokerage fee addendum [See **first tuesday** Form 273];

- a tenant leasehold subordination agreement regarding a future loan;

- a non-disturbance and attornment provision;

- a signage or tenant association agreement;

- an option to lease additional space;

- authority to sublease or assign; and

- an option to buy. [See **first tuesday** Form 161]

If the lease agreement is for a sublease of the premises, a copy of the master lease should be attached.

The lease term

A nonresidential lease agreement is an agreement to rent real estate for a fixed term, a type of leasehold estate called a *tenancy for years*. [CC §761(3)]

The lease should clearly indicate the dates on which the lease term commences and expires. [See Form 552 §2.1]

Delivery and acceptance of possession are addressed separately since the transfer of possession is independent of the commencement date for the lease agreement. [See Form 552 §5]

On expiration of the lease term on the date stated in the lease, the lease automatically terminates and the tenant must have vacated without further notice to either the landlord or tenant. [CC §1933]

However, a tenant who breaches a provision in a lease must be served with the appropriate 3-day notice before the landlord can terminate the lease by a declaration of forfeiture in the notice or by a UD trial. [Calif. Code of Civil Procedure §1161]

On expiration of a lease, a holdover tenancy, called a *tenancy-at-sufferance*, is created when:

- the tenant remains in possession after the lease term expires; and

- the landlord refuses to accept further rent payments.

The holdover tenancy ends when the tenant vacates or is evicted, or the landlord starts accepting rent.

The lease contains a holdover rent provision calling for a set dollar amount of rent due for each day the tenant holds over. The rent is due and payable after the tenant vacates or is evicted. The daily rent should be significantly higher than the fair market rate, although the amount might be unenforceable as unreasonable. [See Form 552 §2.3]

If the amount of holdover rent is not set in the lease, a fair market rate will be recoverable during the holdover (which is also the ceiling for rent awarded in a UD action for the holdover).

The landlord can initiate UD proceedings immediately after the lease expires to evict the holdover tenant. [CCP §1161(1)]

However, the landlord who accepts rent for any period of occupancy falling after the lease expires and before the tenant vacates creates a periodic tenancy. To terminate the resulting periodic tenancy, the landlord must serve the tenant with the appropriate notice to vacate the premises before he can evict the tenant. [**Palmer** v. **Zeis** (1944) 65 CA2d Supp 859; see **first tuesday** Form 571]

Delivery and acceptance of possession

Lease provisions pertaining to the date for delivery of the leased premises to the tenant address the landlord's failure to deliver up the premises to the tenant. [See Form 552 §5]

The tenant is given the opportunity to terminate the lease if possession is not delivered within an agreed-to number of days after commencement of the lease. [See Form 552 §5.1]

Sometimes a landlord fails to deliver possession to the tenant due to his inability to recover the premises from a previous tenant.

The lease agreement should state the tenant will not be liable for rent payments until possession is delivered. [See Form 552 §5.2]

Further, the lease should state the landlord will not be liable for damages if he is unable to deliver possession. [See Form 552 §5.3]

Eminent domain

A tenant can contract away his right to receive any compensation awarded to the landlord in a condemnation action. [**New Haven Unified School District** v. **Taco Bell Corporation** (1994) 24 CA4th 1473]

Thus, nonresidential leases typically reserve for the landlord all rights to any condemnation award for the real estate of a condemning authority under the *eminent domain provision*. [See Form 552 §21]

Also, the landlord may reserve his right to terminate the lease in the event of a partial condemnation. If the landlord does not choose to terminate the lease when a **partial taking** occurs, the tenant is entitled to a rent abatement for the reduction in value of the leasehold interest.

A tenant under a lease has a right to receive compensation for his leasehold interest if his lease is terminated due to a condemnation proceeding. [CCP §1265.150]

Since the lease provisions divest the tenant of any rights in the compensation awarded to the landlord, the tenant must look to the condemning authority to recover any losses, such as:

- relocation costs;

- loss of goodwill;

- bonus value of the lease (due to below market rent); or

- severance damages if a partial taking occurred.

Brokerage fees

Initially, the responsibility for paying any brokerage fees for leasing services is controlled and enforceable under separate leasing agent authority or property management agreements between the tenant or the landlord and their respective brokers.

Second, and of equal effect as a separate underlying fee agreement, is the placement of a brokerage fee provision within the tenant's offer to lease.

Lastly, a provision for payment of the broker's fee is included in the lease to allow enforcement in case of the broker's failure to obtain a prior written commitment from either the tenant or the landlord to pay the fee. [See Form 552 §24.1]

Miscellaneous provisions

An *attorney fee provision* is essential in a lease if the landlord is to recover the costs he incurs to enforce payment of rent or evict the tenant.

Regardless of how an attorney fee provision is written, the prevailing party, if any, is entitled to his fee. [CC §1717(a); see Form 552 §25.2]

The *heirs, assigns and successors clause* binds those who later take the position of the landlord or tenant by grant or assignment (privity of estate) or by an assumption (privity of contract). [**Saucedo v. Mercury Savings and Loan Association** (1980) 111 CA3d 309; see Form 552 §25.3]

A *choice-of-law provision* assures application of California rules of law should a dispute arise with a tenant over the lease. [See Form 552 §25.4]

Application of California rules in disputes over property located in California adds stability to the legal expectations of the landlord and tenant under the lease, produces greater commercial certainty to real estate transactions and stabilizes property values.

Also, the lease must reflect the entire agreement between the parties and should be modified only in writing.

An *entire agreement clause* serves two key purposes. An entire agreement clause limits:

- the tenant's ability to imply terms into the lease based on oral statements **made before entering** into the lease; and

- the **later oral modification** of lease terms and the attendant disputes over "just what are" the terms of the oral modification.

The tenant's performance of lease obligations may also be *secured* by a trust deed encumbering other real estate owned by the tenant (or others). [See **first tuesday** Form 451; see Form 552 §25.6]

If the tenant fails to pay rent or otherwise breaches the lease, the landlord can evict the tenant and foreclose under the performance trust deed to recover rent due under the lease, attorney fees and costs of the trustee's sale. [**Willys of Marin Company** v. **Pierce** (1956) 140 CA2d 826]

Signatures on behalf of the parties

Individuals who sign a lease on behalf of the landlord or the tenant must have the capacity and the authority to act on behalf of and bind the landlord or tenant. [CC §§2304; 2307]

When a corporation enters into a lease, the person signing the lease is given authority to bind the corporation by a *corporate resolution* from the board of directors of the corporation. [Calif. Corporations Code §300]

Unless the landlord actually knows that the person signing has no authority to enter into a lease on behalf of the corporation, the lease entered into by a corporate tenant is valid if it is signed by:

- the president;

- the chief executive officer;

- the vice president;

- secretary;

- chief financial officer; or

- treasurer. [Corp C §313]

However, a corporate resolution is the best evidence of the corporate officer's authority to act on behalf of the corporate tenant.

When a limited liability company (LLC) or limited liability partnership (LLP) enters into a lease agreement, the **manager** signing on behalf of the LLC or LLP to bind the entity to the lease must be the person named as the manager in the LLC-1 or LLP-1 certificate filed with the Secretary of State and recorded with the local county recorder.

However, an LLP or an LLC will be bound to a lease agreement if a partner or member, other than the general partner or manager, signs the lease and the landlord believes the partner or member is acting with the authority of the entity due to their title as chairman or president. [Corp C §17154(c)]

The economics of nonresidential leases

Nonresidential lease agreements are used in transactions involving industrial, commercial, office and other types of nonresidential income-producing property.

A tenant who acquires a leasehold interest in nonresidential real estate agrees to be obligated for none, some or all of the operating costs of the real estate, as rent in addition to payment of the base rent and adjustments.

Note — A residential lease agreement usually provides for the tenant to assume no care and maintenance responsibilities for the property except for excess wear and tear which may occur during his occupancy.

Typically, the longer the term of the nonresidential lease, the more extensive the shift of ownership costs and responsibilities to the tenant, including:

- property operating expenses;

- all or future increases in real estate taxes, called *ad valorem taxes*;

- hazard insurance premiums;

- repair and maintenance; and

- the risk of an increase in interest payments on an adjustable rate loan encumbering the property.

When a long-term lease obligates the tenant to pay for all expenses incurred in the ownership and operation of the property, the tenant incurs the expenses in one of two ways:

- directly, where the tenant contracts for services and pays the cost, including taxes and insurance premiums; or

- indirectly, when the landlord incurs the expenses and bills the tenant for payment, such as common area maintenance charges (CAMs).

The responsibility for the payment of operating costs is reflected in the reference to nonresidential leases as **gross** or **net**, with variations on each.

Leasing agents have no universally accepted definitions or guidelines for titles they use to identify the economics of a lease, and the classifications for leases are forever changing. Often agents must clarify with each other the type of lease their clients intend to enter.

A nonresidential lease is typically called a *gross lease* if the tenant pays for his utilities and janitorial fees, but is not responsible for any other care, maintenance or carrying costs of the property.

In a lease for space in an office building, when the landlord retains the responsibility for payment of all costs of care and maintenance, including the tenant's utilities and janitorial services, the lease used is referred to as a *full service gross lease.*

Conversely, a nonresidential lease which transfers to the tenant the obligation to pay some or all of the costs and responsibilities of ownership, in addition to utilities and janitorial services, is referred to as a *modified gross lease* or *net lease.*

A lease becomes more *net* (and less gross) for the landlord as more ownership responsibilities and operating costs are shifted to the tenant.

The modified gross or net lease is the most commonly used lease agreement in nonresidential properties, other than for multiple tenant office buildings or large industrial structures.

If a lease passes on the responsibility for all costs and maintenance of the property to the tenant, either directly or through CAMs, leaving the landlord responsible for capital improvements only, such as structural repairs or replacement, the lease is referred to as *net-net-net* or *triple-net* lease in the industry.

When a tenant assumes absolutely all ownership duties under a lease agreement, and the landlord merely collects rent payments without concern for his management of the property, the lease is called a *pure net lease*.

Reformation of the lease agreement

During lease negotiations, a landlord orally assures a tenant he will enter into a lease for an initial term of five years with two five-year options to renew. Written offers to lease are not prepared.

However, the lease the landlord prepares and hands to the tenant sets the lease term at 15 years.

Without reviewing the lease agreement and actually discovering the term written into the lease, the tenant signs the lease and takes possession of the premises.

The business operated by the tenant on the leased premises later fails, and the tenant defaults on the rent payments. The tenant then discovers for the first time the length of the lease term is 15 years.

The landlord seeks to collect the unpaid rent for the 15-year period under the lease agreement (subject to any mitigation and discounting).

The tenant seeks to *rescind* the lease agreement due to the landlord's oral misrepresentation about the length of the lease term.

The tenant claims the lease provisions contradict the oral agreement made by him and the landlord before the lease was entered into.

Can the tenant rescind the lease agreement?

No! The landlord's oral representations regarding the lease term prior to execution of the lease do not invalidate or render the lease unenforceable. The terms of the lease set forth in the written lease agreement control. [**West** v. **Henderson** (1991) 227 CA3d 1578]

Rescission of lease agreements is rare since intentional misrepresentation or other fraud in the inducement must be shown.

Now consider a landlord who accepts a tenant's written **offer to lease**. A lease agreement called for in the tenant's offer is prepared by the landlord. However, the lease term stated in the lease agreement differs from the term set forth in the written offer to lease. The tenant accepts the lease without review.

Later, the tenant discovers the discrepancy between the two documents. Instead of attempting to *rescind* the lease, the tenant *reforms* the lease by court order to conform it to the underlying written offer to lease on which the lease was based, called a *reformation action*.

Another reason for *reformation* of lease provisions arises when a significant difference exists between the square footage contained in the leased space and the square footage given in the lease for calculating rent.

Chapter 31

Rent provisions in nonresidential leases

This chapter examines the principles and formulas for various nonresidential rent provisions, inflation and market appreciation adjustments, and reimbursement of operating expenses.

The landlord's future return

By entering into a lease, a landlord conveys to the tenant a possessory interest in real estate for a period of time **in exchange for** a tenant's promise to make dollar payments, called *rent*.

Residential leases usually are for one year and provide for a **fixed amount** of monthly rent paid in dollars during the term of the lease. In contrast, nonresidential leases are for longer periods and contain rent adjustment clauses to ensure the landlord will receive the maximum future return available for his income property in the rental market, even if the lease is negotiated during an economic downturn.

The economic function of a long-term nonresidential lease for the landlord is similar to that of a note and trust deed carried back by a seller of real estate or held by a lender. The documentation in both cases is almost exclusively concerned with the debt owed and the maintenance of the real estate.

Just as a trust deed note evidences the debt owed a carryback seller or a lender, rent provisions in a lease evidence the debt owed to the landlord. Both are creditors of the person who holds the right to possession of the real estate. The lender holds a security interest in the property; the landlord holds a right of reversion.

The lender's trust deed outlines the responsibilities of the borrower for the care and maintenance of the secured real estate, as the care and maintenance provisions in a landlord's lease do for the tenant.

If the owner of the real estate encumbered by the trust deed fails to pay on the trust deed note or breaches the care and maintenance provisions in the trust deed, the creditor forecloses. The owner loses his interest in the real estate due of his uncured default.

Likewise, if the tenant fails to pay rent or breaches the care and maintenance provisions in the lease, the landlord forfeits the tenant's right to possession of the property, and the tenant loses his interest in the property if the default is not cured.

The termination of these possessory rights in nonresidential real estate can be accomplished without extinguishing or cancelling the debtor's obligation to pay any loss incurred under the lease agreement or the trust deed note. [Calif. Civil Code §1951.2; Calif. Code of Civil Procedure §725a]

Setting the rent

Various rent formulas exist to meet the economics of the marketplace and the financial needs of the landlord and tenant.

In all nonresidential leases, a minimum amount of monthly rent is agreed to for payment, called *base rent*. [See **first tuesday** Form 552 §3.4]

Typically, the base rent is the monthly amount paid during the first year of the lease. However, in many short-term leases — two to five years — the base rent is paid monthly during the entire term of the lease, without an adjustment.

A lease which sets monthly rent payments at a specific dollar amount over the entire life of the lease is called a *fixed-rent lease*.

Rent provisions and the NOI

The rent payments a landlord receives from all tenants constitute his *actual gross income* from the property.

The current rent and the terms for setting future rents contained in the rent provisions of a lease greatly influence:

- the *market value* of the real estate;

- the amount of *long-term financing*;

- the property's attractiveness to *potential buyers*; and

- the landlord's *future return* on his investment.

The *market value* of nonresidential income property is based primarily on its anticipated net operating income (NOI). A property's NOI is composed of the property's gross income less operating expenses. Without a future flow of NOI, improved real estate has little value since no income exists to capitalize.

The present and projected NOI is relied on extensively by buyers and lenders when evaluating a property's current fair market value.

The NOI is capitalized at the current yield obtained on comparable investments. The capitalization rate sets the property's fair market value for the price (present worth) a buyer will pay, and the amounts a lender will lend.

Lenders limit loan amounts lent on property based on, among other conditions:

- the real estate's NOI; and

- the financial strength of the tenants to meet their lease obligations.

Likewise, buyers determine what purchase price will be offered based on, among other things:

- the property's NOI;

- a review of the tenants' financial track records; and

- the landlord's control over operating costs.

Thus, the leasing agent or property manager negotiating a nonresidential lease on behalf of the landlord must make certain the landlord has considered whether the *economics of the lease* will produce rents and control costs effectively to produce a maximum return, now and in the future.

In a rising local economy or period of general price inflation, a fixed rate of rent on a long-term lease will prove to be a financial disaster for the landlord. Fixed rent shifts the inflation hedge against price increases and appreciation in the property's rental value to the tenant.

However, a landlord may be forced to accept fixed-rent provisions in leases negotiated during an economic downturn or static rental market. To avoid a potential loss of return during an ensuing economic recovery, a short-term lease or month-to-month tenancy should be negotiated by the landlord.

When leasing retail space, landlords often include a rent provision in the lease agreement which calculates the amount of rent the tenant will pay as a percentage of the tenant's gross sales, called a *percentage lease*. [See **first tuesday** Form 552 §3.5]

The tenant under a **percentage lease** pays the greater of the base rent or the percentage rent.

Most nonresidential leases contain provisions under which the base rent is **adjusted periodically**, usually on each anniversary of the commencement of the lease or every three years, to reflect changes in:

- price inflation in the property's rental value due to conditions affecting the U.S. dollar, called a *Consumer Price Index (CPI) clause*; and

- *property appreciation* due to changes in the local market conditions, such as population density, age demographics, traffic count, visitors or spending habits, called an *appreciation clause*. [See **first tuesday** Form 552 §§3.4 and 3.6]

Additionally, or as an alternative to the CPI, the base rent can be adjusted annually based on an agreed percentage or dollar amount over the prior year's rent, called *graduated rent*. [See **first tuesday** Form 552 §3.3]

The lease must precisely state the formula for rent adjustments for the landlord to enforce them.

Setting the grace period and late charge

The nonresidential lease must, as the minimum rental terms for enforcement, indicate:

- the **time** for payment;

- the **place** for payment; and

- the **manner** of payment. [**Levin** v. **Saroff** (1921) 54 CA 285]

For the landlord to receive rent in advance, namely prepaid before it *accrues*, the lease must include a provision stating the tenant will pay rent in advance. [CC §1947; see **first tuesday** Form 552 §3.1]

Due rent payments are not yet delinquent until time has passed for a late charge to be incurred, called a *grace period*. In nonresidential leases, the grace period is negotiable by the landlord and the tenant without legal restriction. When a late fee is not charged, and thus no grace period exists, rent is delinquent if not paid on or before the due date. [See **first tuesday** Form 552 §3.8]

Having agreed to a grace period, the landlord cannot serve a 3-day notice to pay until the grace period expires.

The grace period can be:

- the time period stated in the lease; or

- a time period set by the landlord's conduct of consistently accepting rent on a date later than the expiration date for the grace period without demanding payment of a late charge. [**Baypoint Mortgage** v. **Crest Premium Real Estate Investments Retirement Trust** (1985) 168 CA3d 818]

The landlord may provide for a late charge to reimburse himself for his collection efforts due to the delinquency of rent. The charge must be reasonably related to the landlord's out-of-pocket money losses incurred during collection efforts or the delay in receipt of the untimely payment.

However, the late charge provision will be unenforceable if the amount charged:

- is so onerous as to penalize the tenant for late payment (in an effort to induce timely payment of rent); and

- does not serve solely to reimburse the landlord for its late receipt. [**Garrett** v. **Coast and Southern Federal Savings and Loan Association** (1973) 9 CA3d 731; see Chapter 25]

Late charges are typically assessed in leases as either a percentage of the rent due or a flat rate charge. The flat rate charge should approximate the costs incurred to enforce collection and the loss of use of the rent money.

In addition to amounts equivalent to reimbursement of collection costs, annual interest accrual on any delinquent amount is often included to cover the loss of use of the rent. [See **first tuesday** Form 552 §3.9]

Place and manner of payment

Rent is paid in United States dollars at a set location, such as at the landlord's or leasing agent's office, either personally or by mail. [See **first tuesday** Form 552 §3.7]

However, rent does not have to be paid with money. Rent can be paid by the delivery of crops, precious metals, services, or currencies or assets other than those denominated in United States dollars. [**Clarke** v. **Cobb** (1898) 121 C 595]

The manner of payment also is set forth, typically cash, check, credit card, electronic transfer or other means of transmitting funds.

For checks returned for insufficient or unavailable funds, the lease must include a flat rate charge in order for the landlord to shift this expense item to the tenant, such as $25 to $35 (and rising). [See **first tuesday** Form 552 §3.10]

If the tenant develops a history of writing checks on insufficient funds, the landlord can require, on a written 30-day notice, payment of rent in cash or by money order. [See **first tuesday** Form 552 §3.10]

Square footage sets the rent

In nonresidential leases for industrial, commercial, office and retail space, the amount of the base rent is generally agreed to as a result of multiplying the total number of square feet rented by a per-square-foot rate.

For example, a tenant leases 4,000 square feet at $2 per square foot. The base rent is set in the lease as $8,000 payable monthly.

The per-square-foot rent formula is used to negotiate the specific dollar amount of rent stated in the lease.

The per-square-foot formula used in negotiations usually is not mentioned in the lease agreement unless the footage is uncertain at the time the lease is entered into.

When either the base rent or additional rent, such as common area maintenance (CAMs) expenses, is based on square footage stated in the lease, the space attributable to the leased premises should be clearly defined and accurately measured. Per-square-foot rents exist in many office, commercial and industrial projects.

To avoid disputes, the landlord and tenant must agree on how the square footage will be measured:

- from the interior walls;

- from the middle of the walls;

- from the exterior of the walls; or

- to include a portion of the common hallways, lobby, restrooms or other interior areas of the structure.

Lease audits undertaken by existing tenants often establish a lesser square footage amount than the footage represented by the owner and relied on by the tenant to set the rent and share of operating costs.

The standard for determining how the square footage will be measured is negotiated through the offers and counteroffers to lease, and the competitive availability of space.

Additional rent and other sums due

As additional rent to the base rent or as future periodic adjustments in the base rent, the tenant may agree to pay some or all of the operating expenses of the leased property.

The objective for the landlord is to provide a constant monthly **net income flow** on his investment in the property, a flow of income which will not vary with fluctuations in the cost of operating the property.

Property operating expenses typically include:

- utilities;

- property management;

- repairs and maintenance;

Fig. 1   *Excerpt from* **first tuesday** *Form 552*
Nonresidential Lease Agreement

4.   **OPERATING EXPENSES:**

4.1   Tenant is responsible for payment of utility and service charge as follows:
_____

4.2   Landlord is responsible for payment of utility and service charges as follows:_____

4.3   Tenant to pay all taxes levied on trade fixtures or other improvements Tenant installs on the premises.

4.4   Should Landlord pay any charge owed by Tenant, Tenant shall pay, within 10 days of written demand, the charge as additional rent.

4.5   As additional rent, Tenant to pay _____% of all real property taxes and assessments levied by governments, for whatever cause, against the land, trees and building containing the leased premises, within 30 days after written computation and demand from Landlord.

4.6   As additional monthly rent, Tenant to pay _____% of the common area maintenance (CAM) incurred each month, within 10 days of written statement and demand for payment.

   a.   Common area maintenance is the cost of maintaining and operating the "Common Areas," including all sidewalks, corridors, plazas, hallways, restrooms, parking areas, interior and exterior walls and all other open areas not occupied by tenants.

   b.   Common area maintenance includes "all charges" for garbage removal, janitorial services, gardening, landscaping, printing/decorating, repair and upkeep, utilities and other operating costs, including charges for property management of the common area maintenance.

- hazard insurance premiums; and

- real estate taxes and assessments. [See **first tuesday** Form 352]

The allocation of the responsibility for operating expenses depends on:

- the type of property and its use;

- the relative bargaining positions of the landlord and tenant in the current real estate market;

- the financial objectives of the landlord and tenant; and

- the length of the lease term.

The landlord and tenant can agree the property operating expenses will be paid by the tenant directly to the provider or creditor, or indirectly to the landlord as a reimbursement.

Taxes and assessments

Tenants with long-term leases often agree to pay some or all of the real estate taxes, insurance premiums and special assessments when the leased premises is an industrial or single-use building.

Property is reassessed by the county assessor when the landlord sells his interest, even if the tenant remains in possession. [Calif. Revenue and Taxation Code §60]

Should the landlord sell the leased property and cause the tenant to face higher real estate taxes due to reassessment, the increase is caused by the owner's conduct, not by the tenant's use of the property. [See Fig. 1 §4.5, *ante*]

A savvy tenant will demand a **cap on any rent** increases due to reassessment caused by the landlord.

When a cap is agreed to in the lease, such as a 2% annual increase, the landlord is responsible for any property tax increases exceeding the ceiling.

However, the tenant should always be held responsible for the payment of assessments and taxes caused by his own improvements and trade fixtures. [See Fig. 1 §4.3]

Common area maintenance

The landlord and tenant can also agree to allocate some or all of the landlord's cost of maintaining the common areas to the tenant for reimbursement to the landlord. [See Fig. 1 §4.6]

The cost of maintaining the common areas when paid by the tenant is **additional rent**, called *common area maintenance (CAM) charges*.

Customarily, CAM charges are based on the ratio between the space leased by the tenant and the total rentable space in the project.

The term "common areas" is broadly defined to include sidewalks, corridors, plazas, halls, restrooms, parking facilities, grounds, etc.

The term "maintenance" should also be defined to include garbage removal, janitorial services, gardening and landscaping, repairs and upkeep, utilities and other specified operating costs.

Utility charges

The utilities provision covers the cost of utilities used in the space leased by the tenant, as opposed to the utilities required to operate the common areas. [See Fig. 1 §§4.1 and 4.2]

To protect against the increased cost of utilities consumed by the tenant, the landlord who pays for utilities can negotiate to pass the responsibility on to the tenant. The landlord can determine the tenant's pro rata share, or have each leased premises privately metered to determine the charge for the tenant's consumption.

Tenants who use a lot of energy and utilities should be required to contract with the utility companies themselves.

As a practical matter, the landlord should avoid paying the utilities whenever possible, except, perhaps, for water. However, if the landlord pays the utilities and charges the tenant, the charge is additional rent to all other rent agreed to be paid.

Chapter 32

Adjustable rent provisions

This chapter discusses the various adjustable rent clauses used in nonresidential leases.

Economic goals of nonresidential landlords

Rent works, like interest, to provide a yield on an investment.

A lender receives *interest* for the use of money lent for a specific period of time.

Likewise, a landlord receives *rent* for the use of property let for a specific period of time.

At the end of the respective right-to-use periods, both the money and the real estate are returned.

Like interest provisions in a note, rent provisions in a nonresidential lease should anticipate market changes which will affect the investment (value, income, expenses and debt) and provide for the changes to be reflected in the income received by the landlord.

Types of adjustable rent

The three basic types of rent adjustment provisions found in nonresidential leases, sometimes called *rent escalation clauses*, are:

- *graduated rent* provisions;

- *inflation adjusted rent* provisions based on a price index; and

- *appreciation adjusted rent* provisions.

Further, the economic goals a leasing **agent must review** with his nonresidential landlord-client when negotiating rent provisions for future rents include:

- adjustments for the lost purchasing power of the dollar due to future *price inflation*;

- adjustments in rent to reflect the *rate of appreciation* on comparable properties (beyond the rate of inflation); and

- the absorption of increased expenditures for operating expenses and interest adjustments on mortgage debt.

To protect the property's income, and in turn its value, against loss of the **dollar's purchasing power** due to inflation, rent can be periodically adjusted based on a price inflation provision in the lease. The provision calls for periodic rent increases based on figures from an inflation index, such as the Consumer Price Index (CPI) or the Cost of Funds Index.

Further, and to attain rents which will reflect as an increase in the property's dollar value due to **local appreciation**, rent can also be adjusted periodically (for example, every three years) to rent amounts received by comparable properties.

Also, increased **operating and ownership costs** can be absorbed directly or indirectly by the tenant.

The nonresidential lease can pass on to the tenant the responsibilities for either all the operating expenses or only future increases in the expenses by including a provision calling for the tenant to pay specified expenses or his pro rata share of common area maintenance expenses (CAMs), property taxes and hazard insurance premiums. [See Chapter 31]

Future increases in the cost of carrying debt on the property due to **variable interest rate** mortgage financing can be passed on to the tenant as increases in rent to provide the landlord with a triple-net or pure-net lease.

With knowledge and understanding about the economic and financial consequences of the terms submitted by a tenant in an **offer to lease**, the landlord can make an informed decision whether to accept, counter or reject the tenant's offer to lease based on financial objectives.

Graduated rents from year to year

Rents bargained for during the initial years of a lease are often below market, comparable in purpose (and timing) to the initial *teaser* or *qualifying* rates for adjustable rate loans (ARMs) and graduated payment loans (GPMs).

Likewise, **graduated rent** provisions periodically increase the base monthly rent semi-annually or annually, usually in pre-set increments.

The amount of the periodic upward adjustment is set at a specific dollar amount or a percentage of the base rent or rent paid during the prior period. [See Fig. 1]

Graduated rent adjustments are not determined by use of index figures or formulas dependent on data from other sources at the time of the adjustment.

Also, any below-market rents paid in the early years are often picked up in future rents which will exceed market rents as though the lease had a negative amortization feature.

For example, the base monthly rent might be increased each year on the anniversary of the lease by:

- $1,000 per month; or

- 5% of the base rent set forth in the lease for the first year.

A graduated payment provision with annual rent increases can also be structured based on a *percentage* increase over the prior year's monthly rent, a *compounding of rents*.

For example, the monthly payment during the last year of a graduated payment plan would become the base rent for annual CPI inflation adjustments to set rates annually for the remainder of the lease.

Typically, in the fourth or fifth year of long-term nonresidential leases with graduated rents, future rent increases will be set under a price inflation clause.

Fig. 1　　　*Excerpt from first tuesday Form 552 —*
Nonresidential Lease Agreement

3.3 ☐ Monthly rent, from year to year, is adjusted on each anniversary month as follows:

Initial year's monthly rent:$_____, and

a. _____% increase in monthly rent over prior year's monthly rent; or

b. First anniversary monthly rent:................... $_____

Second anniversary monthly rent:................ $_____

Third anniversary monthly rent: .... $_____

Fourth anniversary monthly rent: .... $_____

Percentage rents and the base rent

Now consider a tenant who operates his business under a **percentage lease**.

The **base rent** is set at a specific monthly dollar amount during the first 12 months of the lease.

The percentage rent rate is set at 7% of the tenant's gross sales. The tenant pays a total rent equal to the **greater amount** of the base rent or percentage rate.

However, the landlord and tenant also agree the base rent for each year will be increased by 2% of the base rent for the previous year, called a *compounded base rent*. Alternatively, the base could (and likely would) be increased by agreement at the rate of inflation during the prior period.

Thus, the adjustment to the base rent provides a *floor rent* for a fair rate of return on the landlord's investment throughout the lease term should the tenant's business suffer a downturn or a drop in annual gross receipts.

A **price inflation adjustment** to the base rent would also increase the base rent floor.

Price inflation adjustments

To annually adjust the base rent to compensate for price inflation due to the dollar's continuing loss of purchasing power, a *price inflation clause* or *CPI clause* can be included in the lease. [See Fig. 2]

Inflation adjustments are usually made annually on each anniversary of the commencement of the lease. Adjustments are based on the annual percentage change in figures from the CPI for the region in which the real estate is located.

The CPI clause can be used to establish the annual rent adjustment in one of two ways:

- a base year-to-current year increase; or

- a year-to-year increase for a compounding effect.

The unpredictable and cyclical movement of price inflation both lulls and infuriates landlords. Thus, for landlords, the rent inflation clause should be boilerplate in every lease — if the competitiveness of the marketplace allows for its inclusion.

Occasionally, landlords will ignore the CPI as a basis for inflation adjustments and use a set annual percentage increase of 3% or 4% in its place, which of course is back to graduated rent schedules.

Periodic appreciation adjustments

If the CPI is the only rent adjustment provision used by the landlord over the life of a long-term lease, the landlord risks loss of any increase in rents in excess of the CPI which is enjoyed by comparable properties, called *appreciation*. The same risk exists when exclusively using graduated rent provisions.

To reflect rent increases brought about by **local rental market** conditions, the landlord should consider a provision calling for periodic rent adjustments to increase rents to meet current market rates, called an *appreciation* or *fair market rent clause*. [See Fig. 3]

To make the rent adjustment, the base monthly rent is, as agreed-to in the lease, *reasonably adjusted* by the landlord every three to five years to reflect local market trends in comparable properties, or as otherwise agreed for adjustment in the appreciation clause.

Thus, a lease containing both an inflation clause and an appreciation clause assures the landlord will receive:

- an annual inflation adjustment to retain for the term of the lease the **purchasing power** of the rent amount he receives at the inception of the lease; and

- a periodic adjustment to reflect any future increases in rents for comparable properties exceeding inflation.

A provision can be included in the lease for an appraisal process to set the appreciated rent if the tenant is concerned about his remedies should the amount set by the landlord as the appreciation adjustment be unacceptable.

Setting fair market rents

Consider a nonresidential lease agreement with a **use clause** calling for the tenant to operate a movie theater on the premises for ten years.

The lease agreement contains a rent appreciation clause stating the landlord will adjust the base rent in five years to reflect the then current *fair market rent*.

At the time for the appreciation adjustments five years later, the landlord determines the fair market rent for the property by using rent amounts received by comparable properties put to uses other than a movie theater.

The tenant disputes the amount of the adjusted rent demanded by the landlord.

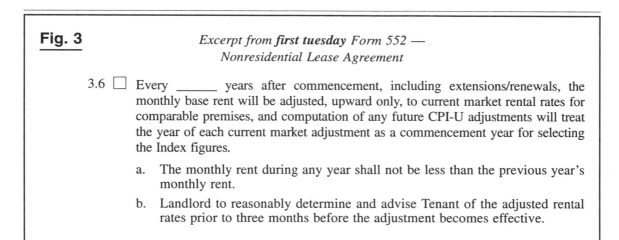

Fig. 3

Excerpt from first tuesday Form 552 —
Nonresidential Lease Agreement

3.6 ☐ Every _____ years after commencement, including extensions/renewals, the monthly base rent will be adjusted, upward only, to current market rental rates for comparable premises, and computation of any future CPI-U adjustments will treat the year of each current market adjustment as a commencement year for selecting the Index figures.

    a. The monthly rent during any year shall not be less than the previous year's monthly rent.

    b. Landlord to reasonably determine and advise Tenant of the adjusted rental rates prior to three months before the adjustment becomes effective.

The tenant claims the fair market rental value of the premises should be based on the present use of the property as intended by the lease, since the lease agreement does not provide for the landlord to adjust the rent to reflect a return on the fair market value of comparable properties that have been put to a higher and better use.

Here, the lease states the tenant will use the property to operate a movie theater for the term of the lease. Thus, the rent can only be adjusted to reflect the fair market value of the property based on its use as a movie theater. [**Wu** v. **Interstate Consolidated Industries** (1991) 226 CA3d 1511]

Chapter 33

Nonresidential use-maintenance provisions

This chapter examines the provisions in nonresidential leases that establish the landlord's and tenant's rights and obligations regarding the use and care of the leased premises.

Shifting ownership obligations

A nonresidential lease contains two basic categories of provisions that place obligations on the tenant:

- rent provisions for the payment of amounts owed; and

- use-maintenance provisions for the use, care and preservation of the grounds and improvements.

Rent provisions evidence any money obligations owed the landlord by the tenant in exchange for the possession of the leased premises over a specific period of time.

Use-maintenance provisions in a nonresidential lease establish the rights and obligations between the landlord and tenant regarding who is responsible for performing the care and maintenance of the premises during the lease term. [See **first tuesday** Form 552 accompanying Chapter 30]

Use-maintenance obligations do not include the payment of monies (rents), but define who bears the burden of entering into or contracting for the repairs and maintenance of the leased premises — the landlord or the tenant.

If the landlord retains the majority of the maintenance obligations, the base rent the tenant will pay will be higher. If it is the tenant who assumes the majority of the maintenance obligations, the base rent the tenant will pays will be lower.

Just as when a tenant breaches a lease when he fails to pay rent, he also breaches the lease when he fails to perform or acts in violation of a use-maintenance provision in the lease.

The tenant's breach of an essential use-maintenance obligation is followed by either a 3-day notice to **perform or quit** that states precisely what must be done by the tenant within three days, or a 3-day notice to **quit** if the breach is incurable, such as a use violation, the maintenance of a nuisance or waste to the property.

If the noticed breach **can be cured** and the tenant fails to cure it after notice, he loses the right to possession by a declaration of forfeiture in the notice.

If the breach is **incurable**, as under a notice to quit, the tenant automatically loses any right to continue in possession and must vacate the premises within three days after notice.

Likewise, a landlord who fails to meet his use-maintenance obligations to care for the property breaches the lease.

A breach of the use-maintenance provisions by the landlord or the tenant, and the remedies available for the breach, can be litigated under contract law since the lease is a contract.

However, when the landlord involves the tenant's possessory rights in the property as part of his remedy on a breach, landlord/tenant law controls, as evidenced by the use of a forfeiture election to terminate the tenancy. [**Kendall** v. **Ernest Pestana, Inc.** (1985) 40 C3d 488]

Which use-maintenance provisions to include

The contents of each provision in a nonresidential lease are fully negotiable when agreeing to enter into a lease transaction. The results of negotiations depend on the respective bargaining power of the landlord and the tenant.

Also, lease provisions vary due to the type of property involved, the intended use of the property, delegation of operating costs and responsibility for the property's physical conditions, as well as the length of the lease term.

Occasionally, the landlord or the tenant will use a lease form especially prepared by their respective attorneys for their repetitive use, i.e., when the landlord has many properties to let or the tenant leases many locations (such as franchisors).

However, landlords more frequently use standard forms that contain provisions basic to nonresidential leases, and then attaching addendums for any provisions not included in the form or contrary to the contents of the form. [See **first tuesday** Form 552 §1.3]

Note — The following discussion of use-maintenance clauses refers to provisions in **first tuesday** *Form 552 —* Nonresidential Lease Agreement *accompanying Chapter 30.*

Use of the premises

On entering into a nonresidential lease agreement, a landlord and tenant agree the premises will be used by the tenant for a single, **specified purpose**, such as a retail clothing store or an auto mechanics shop, called a *use-of-premises provision*.

If a lease provision does not restrict the tenant's use of the leased premises, the premises may be used for any lawful purpose. [Calif. Civil Code §1997.210(b)]

Conversely, a lease may absolutely prohibit any change in use or set *standards* or *conditions* to be met before a change from the use specified in the use-of-premises provision may be implemented. [CC §1997.230]

If the use provision requires the landlord's consent to a change in use, but gives no *standard* or *condition* to be applied or met for the consent, the landlord must have a commercially reasonable basis for withholding his consent to the new proposed use sought by the tenant. [CC §1997.250]

The standard of reasonableness applied to the landlord's consent is the same as applied to assignment restrictions.

In the use-of-premises provision, the tenant agrees to deliver up the premises on expiration of the lease in as good condition as it was when he took possession, except for reasonable wear and tear.

Even if the tenant's use of the leased premises is unrestricted, the tenant cannot impair the premises by damaging it, creating a nuisance, engaging in illegal activities or subjecting the premises to greater wear and tear than the use contemplated when the lease was entered into.

In addition to the use allowed, the tenant agrees not to conduct any activities on the property which would:

- increase the landlord's liability or hazard insurance premiums; or

- violate any laws, building ordinances or tenant association rules, called a *compliance-with-laws clause*.

Appurtenances

Any use incidental to the leased premises for the benefit of the tenant's leasehold interest, i.e., reasonably necessary for the use and enjoyment of the leased premises, is called an *appurtenance*. [CC §662]

Leasehold **appurtenances** include rights in real estate owned by the landlord which are located outside the leased premises, such as:

- a right of way for vehicular travel through an industrial or office complex;

- parking for employees and customers;

- storage space, lobbies and restrooms; and

- access of ingress and egress from public roads to the leased premises, such as a road or driveway.

Signs and advertising

A landlord maintains the integrity of the building's physical and aesthetic appearance, and is assured all signs, advertising and addresses placed about the premises will comply with local ordinances and the landlord's policies by including a *signage provision* in the lease.

Under the **signage provision**, the landlord retains control over the size, style, content and location of signs constructed or installed on the premises to advertise the location or existence of the tenant's business.

The cost of sign installation can be charged to either the landlord or tenant by the terms of the lease.

Tenant improvements and alterations

A tenant's right to make alterations or further improve the premises **during the tenancy** is governed by the lease provision called a *tenant improvements and alterations clause*, or more simply a *TI clause*.

To ensure the landlord retains control over the structures on or about the leased premises, the tenant agrees not to alter or further improve any part of the building without first obtaining the landlord's written consent.

Should the landlord later consent to alterations or further improvements by the tenant, the tenant will pay all costs incurred in the construction unless agreed to the contrary in an addendum or later modification of the lease.

A lease for retail space, especially in malls, should include provisions which require the tenant to renovate his storefront and interior every number of years. Renovations by tenants every five to seven years will help maintain a fresh appearance which is vital to the overall success of retail shopping centers.

Once the landlord consents to alterations by the tenant, the tenant must promptly notify the landlord of the commencement of construction so the landlord can post and record a notice of nonresponsibility. [See Chapter 4]

The **notice of nonresponsibility** is a form, the contents of which state the landlord is not responsible for any claims made by contractors for improvements they construct on the leased premises under contract with the tenant. [CC §3094; see **first tuesday** Form 597]

The notice bars mechanic's liens on the fee simple in the real estate and denies recovery from the landlord by unpaid contractors employed by the tenant.

Any increase in property taxes due to alterations made by the tenant are the responsibility of the tenant and will be paid to the landlord on demand.

Unless otherwise agreed, the tenant's improvements become the property of the landlord at the end of the lease term and cannot be removed by the tenant, with the exception of the tenant's trade fixtures. [**Wolfen** v. **Clinical Data, Inc.** (1993) 16 CA4th 171]

Further, when the tenant alters or improves the premises resulting in a new and different use of the premises, the tenant must, separate from the contractual duty imposed by a compliance-with-laws clause, comply with all building code requirements.

If the tenant's installation of improvements violate building codes and ordinances, the tenant will be liable for the landlord's cost of conforming the new improvements to codes and ordinances. [Wolfen, *supra*]

Repair and maintenance

Of equal financial importance and effect as the amount of rent to be paid under a nonresidential lease are the responsibilities for the payment of the cost of maintenance and repair of the premises. Ultimately, the tenant must bear them, either directly by incurring the costs himself or indirectly by reimbursing the landlord through the payment of basic rent or additional rent in the form of common area maintenance charges (CAMs).

The extent of the maintenance and repair obligations assumed by the tenant typically depends on the type of space leased and the length of the lease term.

The longer the lease term, including renewal options, the more likely the obligations for maintenance will be shifted to the tenant, with the exception of multi-tenant commercial and office space. The shift will be even more likely if the premises is a single-user building, such as a warehouse or bank building as opposed to a multi-tenant building.

During the leasing period, the nonresidential tenant has a duty to notify the landlord of those repairs which are needed and are the responsibility of the landlord.

Some net leases contain a *compliance-with-laws provision* requiring the tenant to make any government-ordered repairs, such as asbestos removal or seismic retrofitting.

However, if the lease containing the compliance clause is short term and the landlord will be the primary beneficiary of the government-ordered repairs, the landlord may be responsible for making the repairs in spite of the wording in the lease. [**Hadian** v. **Schwartz** (1994) 8 C4th 836]

Right to enter

Once a tenant acquires a leasehold interest in a nonresidential premises, the landlord no longer has the right to enter the premises for any reason, unless agreed to the contrary or an emergency exists.

In a lease, the landlord **reserves the right** to enter to make any necessary repairs, alterations or inspections of the premises, called a *right-to-enter* provision.

A landlord may need to enter the premises when:

- the landlord makes necessary or agreed-to repairs or alterations, or is supplying necessary services to the tenant;

- the landlord shows the premises to a prospective tenant;

- the tenant has abandoned or surrendered the premises;

- the tenant requests a pre-termination inspection [See Chapter 13];

- a court order was issued allowing the landlord to enter; or

- an emergency exists which endangers the property. [See Chapter 3]

Waste

As would be expected in a lease, the tenant agrees not to destroy, damage or remove any part of the premises or equipment, or commit waste on the premises or permit anyone else to do so, called a *waste provision*.

If the tenant or a person permitted on the premises by the tenant commits waste on the property, the tenant commits an *incurable breach* of the lease and automatically forfeits his right to possession. [See Chapter 19]

The landlord can serve the tenant who has committed or permitted waste to the property with a 3-day notice to quit, and initiate a UD action to evict the tenant if he does not vacate. [Calif. Code of Civil Procedure §1161(4)]

Liability insurance

A landlord and tenant may agree the tenant will purchase a liability insurance policy to cover losses which might occur on the premises, including:

- property damage; and

- bodily injury.

The lease should set the policy limits or minimum amount of liability insurance the tenant must obtain. These limits should be set as a result of the landlord's discussion and analysis with an insurance agent.

Typically, a tenant's obligation to maintain liability insurance under a lease is covered under the tenant's commercial general liability insurance policy which the tenant purchases to insure the business he will operate on the premises.

To protect the landlord from any dissipation of insurance proceeds by the tenant, the landlord should be **named** as an additional insured on liability and hazard insurance policies obtained by the tenant to cover the leased premises.

To be assured the landlord is named, the lease should require the tenant to provide the landlord with a certificate of insurance from the carrier naming the landlord as an additional insured.

Note — When an insurance agent reviews a lease that requires the landlord to be named as an additional insured on a liability policy and fails to name the landlord, the landlord can recover losses from the insurance company if damage or an injury occurs which subjects him to personal liability. [**Jackson** v. **Aetna Life and Casualty Company** (1979) 93 CA3d 838]

Under the insurance provision, both the landlord and the tenant waive any insurance subrogation rights each might have against the other. Thus, an insurance carrier cannot seek to recover from the landlord or tenant who was the cause of the injury or property damage. [**Gordon** v. **J.C. Penney Company** (1970) 7 CA3d 280]

Hazard insurance

In a multi-tenant building, a landlord obtains a hazard insurance policy and passes the cost of the premiums through to the tenant, generally by way of the monthly base rent or common area maintenance (CAM) expenses.

The landlord and tenant can agree the tenant will purchase a standard hazard insurance policy for fire losses, which also covers theft and vandalism of all personal property and the restoration of tenant improvements, including the destruction of plate glass windows.

Requiring the tenant to maintain a hazard insurance policy assures the landlord the tenant will be in the financial position necessary to

continue to operate his business should fire, theft or vandalism occur during the term of the lease.

When the tenant is required to maintain an insurance policy for property damage resulting from fire, theft or vandalism, the landlord must be named by the carrier as an additional insured so the landlord can control the use of any insurance proceeds.

In a long-term, triple-net lease where the tenant has assumed all obligations and duties of ownership, the lease shifts to the tenant:

- the obligation to maintain hazard insurance; and

- the burden of repairing any destruction of the real estate, regardless of the cause.

Hold harmless

The hold harmless provision covers the landlord for liability from injuries occurring on the premises which:

- arise out of the tenant's negligent use of the premises; and

- are caused by the tenant, his employees or customers due to the tenant's negligence.

However, nonresidential leases often favor the landlord by including a hold harmless provision through which the tenant holds the landlord harmless for all claims, damages or liability arising from any cause, including the landlord's negligence.

When a hold harmless clause is included in a lease, the tenant needs to purchase liability insurance coverage for the risk of loss he has agreed is his — his *contractual liability* under the lease.

Contractual liability insurance is separate from general liability insurance which covers bodily injury and property damage.

Government-ordered repairs

When determining whether the landlord or the tenant is responsible for **government-ordered repairs**, the terms of the lease agreement do not always control.

Six factors are applied to the lease transaction to determine if the burden of complying with any government-ordered curative actions to correct or eliminate deficiencies in the leased premise are to be the tenant's or the landlord's responsibility.

The six **burden-of-compliance** factors are:

- the ratio of the cost of repairs to the amount of rent due over the life of the lease;

- the length of the lease, including renewal options;

- whether the landlord or the tenant will benefit more from the repairs in terms of the useful life of the building and the remaining term of the lease;

- whether the repairs are structural or nonstructural;

- whether or not the repairs will substantially interfere with the tenant's enjoyment of the premises; and

- whether or not the government-ordered repairs were foreseeable at the time the lease agreement was entered into by the landlord and the tenant.

Each burden-of-compliance factor is weighed based on the circumstances surrounding the execution of the lease, the text of the lease provisions and the **economic realities** of the lease transaction.

For example, a landlord and tenant enter into a 15-year nonresidential net lease agreement.

Boilerplate use-maintenance provisions transfer to the tenant all ownership duties, including structural repairs.

Less than two years into the 15-year lease, the county discovers friable asbestos on the premises and issues an abatement order to the tenant. Neither the landlord nor the tenant had previous knowledge asbestos existed on the premises as it was a pre-existing condition of the building.

On receiving the compliance order, the tenant seals off the contaminated area and conducts business out of another section of the building.

The costs of repairing the building is a sum roughly equal to 5% of the aggregate amount of rent due over the entire life of the lease.

Here, the provisions in the lease agreement and the circumstances under which the lease was entered into imply the duty to comply with the government order was transferred to the tenant since:

- the cost of repairs amounted to less than 5% of the aggregate amount of rent due over the life of the lease;

- the lease was for 15 years, thus the cost of repairs could easily be amortized by the tenant during the remaining tenancy;

- the asbestos removal would most benefit the tenant since the contamination was discovered less than two years into the lease;

- the repairs are structural and the lease clearly transfers structural repairs to the tenant;

- the tenant's use of the premises would not be greatly interfered with during the abatement; and

- neither the tenant nor the landlord had reason to believe asbestos existed on the premises, yet the tenant was experienced in retail leasing and elected not to investigate the premises. [**Brown** v. **Green** (1994) 8 C4th 812]

Now consider a landlord and tenant who enter into the same nonresidential net lease agreement but for a term of three years with an option to renew for five additional years.

The net lease contains boilerplate compliance with laws and maintenance and repairs provisions which shift all the duties of ownership to the tenant, including structural repairs.

After the tenant exercises his option to renew the lease for five years, the landlord receives a compliance order from the city requiring the leased premises to be earthquake-proofed.

The cost of quake-proofing the building roughly equals 50% of the aggregate amount of the rent due over the entire life of the lease, which is now in its fourth of eight years.

Here, even though the lease shifted the major burdens of ownership from the landlord to the tenant, an application of the six-factor test determines the landlord must bear the burden of the quake-proofing costs since:

- the cost of quake-proofing the premises was roughly equal to 50% of the aggregate rent due over the total eight-year term of the lease;

- the eight-year lease was short-term with little time remaining for the tenant to amortize the cost or the repairs; and

- the quake-proofing primarily benefits the landlord due to the short term remaining on the lease. [Hadian, *supra*]

Thus, when entering into a nonresidential net lease agreement, a landlord should consider including a provision calling for the tenant to assume the cost of compliance orders that do not regulate the tenant's use of the premises — government-ordered retrofitting or renovation.

Yet the landlord must be aware, if the economic realities of the lease agreement are not in accord with the text of the lease agreement, the landlord may still be liable for government-issued

Regardless of the type of hold harmless provision used, the landlord cannot shift to the tenant responsibility for any liability arising from the landlord's *intentional misconduct* or violation of law. [CC §1668]

For example, a landlord cannot escape liability to others for injuries occurring on the leased premises due to the landlord's failure to maintain the premises as obligated by the lease, including abatement of any known dangerous conditions. [See Chapter 29]

Destruction

Initially, the responsibility for the costs of making repairs to nonresidential property when the leased premises is partially or totally destroyed lies with the landlord.

However, some or all of the responsibilities can be shifted to the tenant or allocated between the landlord and the tenant by a clause in the lease, called a *destruction provision*.

In the **destruction clause**, the tenant agrees to repair and pay for any destruction to the premises:

- caused by the tenant;

- covered by insurance policies held by the tenant; or

- required by other lease provisions, such as the repair and maintenance clause.

When the tenant is obligated to carry insurance to pay for the cost of repairs, the landlord is assured the disbursement of any insurance proceeds under the tenant's policy will be used to pay for the repairs if he is named as an additional insured on the tenant's policy. [See **first tuesday** Form 552 §14]

On the other hand, the landlord agrees to repair and pay for any damage to the premises which:

- is not caused or covered by the tenant's insurance policies;

- is insured only by the landlord's policy; or

- is not insured by any policy. [See **first tuesday** Form 552 §16.3]

Typically, a destruction clause states the lease will not terminate due to any destruction of the premises, unless the landlord chooses to terminate it under specified conditions, such as:

- the repairs cannot be completed within 30 days;

- the cost of restoration exceeds 70% of the replacement value of the premises;

- the insurance proceeds are insufficient to cover the actual cost of the repairs; or

- the premises may not be occupied by law.

Thus, the landlord may opt to terminate the lease if the casualty is underinsured.

However, if the landlord fails to begin repairs which are his responsibility or, alternatively, terminates the lease within a reasonable time, the tenant can:

- abandon the premises due to a *constructive eviction* and be excused from further performance under the lease [CC §1942]; or

- pay rent and recover from the landlord any losses suffered due to the landlord's failure to repair. [**Ng** v. **Warren** (1947) 79 CA2d 54]

Chapter 34

Lease assignments and subleases

This chapter presents the standards and conditions for a landlord's consent and compensation under lease alienation provisions restricting leasehold assignments and subletting by tenants.

Consent conditioned on exactions

A landlord and tenant enter into a nonresidential lease. The lease contains an assignment and subletting provision, called a *restriction-on-transfer* or a *restraint-on-alienation* provision.

The provision does not prohibit transfers, but requires the tenant to obtain the landlord's consent prior to assigning the lease or subletting (or further encumbering) the tenant's leasehold interest. The provision either:

- states the landlord's consent will not be unreasonably withheld; or

- fails to state any standards for objecting and withholding consent. [See Fig. 1]

The lease also contains a *cancellation provision* allowing the landlord to cancel the lease agreement on the landlord's receipt of the tenant's written request seeking consent under the assignment or subletting provision.

The tenant vacates the premises and relocates his operations to another property with no intention of returning to the leased premises. The tenant finds a user who will pay rent at current market rates for the space, an amount which exceeds the rent owed the landlord on the lease, called *overriding rent*.

The tenant makes a request for the landlord's consent to sublease to the user. The landlord responds by cancelling the lease agreement under the cancellation provision.

The landlord, having terminated the tenant's leasehold by cancellation of the lease agreement, negotiates directly with the user. The landlord enters into a lease of the premises with the user at current rental rates.

The tenant makes a demand on the landlord for the overriding rent he lost due to the landlord's refusal to consent to the sublease, claiming the landlord's consent was unreasonably withheld since no *conditions* for the consent were agreed to which would entitle the landlord to the overriding rent.

The landlord claims his cancellation of the lease is valid, even though cancellation is an absolute restraint on the proposed transfer of the tenant's leasehold interest, since the tenant and landlord freely bargained for the cancellation provision which the landlord exercised when the provision was triggered by the tenant's request for the landlord's consent to an assignment.

May the landlord cancel the lease agreement even though the landlord agreed not to unreasonably withhold his consent or condition consent on the exaction of the excess rents?

Yes! The two provisions in the lease, the consent-to-assignment provision and the cancellation provision, are mutually exclusive alternatives authorizing the landlord to take either of two completely separate courses of action when confronted with a request for consent to an assignment.

On receipt of the tenant's request for consent, the landlord exercised the cancellation provision, relieving the tenant of any further obligation under the lease — as well as his tenancy in the premises and any potential profit from the property's appreciated rental value.

Thus, the issue as to whether the landlord refused his consent never arises. The landlord cancelled the lease as agreed, thus nullifying any need to consider the request for consent.

However, should the landlord choose not to cancel the tenant's leasehold interest on the tenant's request for consent to an assignment, the landlord is then **left to analyze** whether or not to consent. As a result, he is required to be **reasonable** about any objection he may have to the assignment since no other standard was set in the lease.

Also, the cancellation provision in the lease is bargained for and not the unconscionable result of an advantage held by the landlord. The prospective tenant did not have to enter into this lease or lease this premises.

Thus, the landlord did not unreasonably interfere with the tenant's right to assign or sublet by cancelling the lease agreement since the tenant's real estate interest in obtaining higher rent had been contracted away by inclusion of the cancellation provision. [**Carma Developers, Inc.** v. **Marathon Development California, Inc.** (1992) 2 C4th 342]

Transfer of any interest

An assignment or subletting provision in a lease typically calls for the tenant to acquire consent from the landlord before the tenant may *transfer* any interest in the leasehold. [Calif. Civil Code §1995.250]

A **transfer** by the tenant includes an *assignment, sublease* or *further encumbrance* of the leasehold. [CC §1995.020(e); see Fig. 1]

An **assignment** of the lease transfers the original tenant's entire interest in the lease to a successor tenant, leaving no interest held by the original tenant. However, the original tenant named on the lease agreement remains liable for the successor tenant's performance on the lease, even though the landlord consents to the assignment and the successor tenant assumes (i.e., becomes primarily responsible for) the lease obligations.

For the original tenant to be **released of his liability** under the lease on an assignment, a *novation* must be negotiated and entered into by the landlord and both tenants, sometimes called a *substitution of liability*. [**Samuels** v. **Ottinger** (1915) 169 C 209]

On the other hand, when entering into a **sublease** with a subtenant, the original (master) tenant transfers to the subtenant less than all of the master tenant's interest in the property. Also, **possession reverts** back to the master tenant on expiration of the sublease.

The master tenant granting the sublease remains solely obligated to perform on the master lease. The subtenant does not assume liability of the master lease. However, the subtenant may do no acts which would constitute a breach of the master lease, a copy of which is attached to the sublease.

Fig.1　　　　　*Excerpt from* **first tuesday** *Form 552 —*
Nonresidential Lease Agreement

19.　ASSIGNMENT, SUBLETTING AND ENCUMBRANCE: [Check only one]

　19.1　☐　Tenant may not assign this lease or sublet any part of the premises, or further encumber the leasehold.

　19.2　☐　Tenant may not transfer any interest in the premises without the prior consent of Landlord.

　　　a.　☐　Consent may not be unreasonably withheld.

　　　b.　☐　Consent is subject to the attached conditions. [**ft** Form 250]

The **further encumbrance** of a tenant's leasehold interest occurs when the tenant places a lien on his leasehold to secure a loan, such as a trust deed or the delivery of a collateral assignment.

Note — For simplicity's sake, the following discussion will only refer to an assignment of a lease. However, the discussion fully applies to any sublease or further encumbrance transaction.

Various alienation provisions

Leases include various types of assignment provisions, also called *alienation clauses*, which may:

- entirely prohibit any assignment of the lease [CC §1995.230];

- require the landlord's consent prior to an assignment without containing approved standards or place any monetary conditions for the withholding of the landlord's consent [CC §1995.260];

- require the landlord's consent prior to an assignment, stating consent will not be unreasonably withheld [CC 1995.250(a)];

- require the landlord's consent, subject to *conditions* first being met by the tenant, e.g., payment to the landlord of all or part of the tenant's gains on the assignment, a higher rental rate and an assignment fee, and an assumption by the tenant of maintenance and utility expenses [CC §1995.250(b)]; or

- contain *conditions* for a valid assignment without requiring any consent at all, such as the landlord is entitled to all or part of the consideration the tenant receives for the assignment in excess of rent due on the lease. [CC §1995.240; see Fig. 1]

Standards lay out the analytical process imposed on the landlord which he must apply when making a judgment whether or not to withhold consent.

Conditions are sums of money or leasing terms that must be met by the tenant as a requisite to consent should the landlord consent to the assignment.

No standards for withholding consent

Consider a lease with an assignment provision calling for the landlord's consent prior to the tenant's assignment, but devoid of any standard or condition for consent, such as consent "will not be unreasonably withheld" or fees must be paid.

Thus, the assignment provision does not set a standard for consent or exactions to be paid as a condition for granting or withholding consent. Here, for lack of agreement to the contrary, the standards and conditions for the landlord's consent are set by law.

A lease entered into on or after September 23, 1983, with **no standard** agreed to for the landlord to consent to an assignment, requires the landlord to have a commercially reasonable basis for his denial should he choose to withhold consent. The landlord cannot deny consent arbitrarily.

Also, **no conditions** for an exaction can be attached to granting the consent, such as a higher rental rate, unless bargained for as a condition for consent and included in the lease agreement. [**Kendall** v. **Ernest Pestana, Inc.** (1985) 40 C3d 488]

Commercial reasonability standard

Commercial reasonability standards relate to the landlord's ability to:

- **protect his ownership interest** from property waste and financial deterioration due to the successor tenants' propensity to care for and make suitable use of the property under the use-maintenance provisions in the lease; and

- **ensure the future performance** of the lease by an assignment to a creditworthy tenant.

Commercially reasonable objections for withholding consent to an assignment include:

- the successor tenant's financial responsibility (net worth), prior operating history and creditworthiness;

- the successor tenant's intended use, care and maintenance of the property;

- the suitability of the successor tenant's use, product marketing and management style for the property; and

- the need for tenant alterations to the premises. [Kendall, *supra*]

For example, a lease use provision gives a tenant the right to operate a service business in a shopping center in which the landlord operates a retail business outlet. The lease restricts the tenant's use to "office use related to the business" of the tenant.

The lease alienation provision in the lease agreement requires the tenant to obtain the landlord's prior consent to an assignment of the lease. The alienation provision sets **no standard** for withholding consent and provides for **no conditions** to be met (paid) by the tenant for the consent if it is granted.

Later, the tenant seeks to transfer the lease to a successor who will operate a retail business from the premises. The successor tenant's retail business will be in direct competition with the landlord's retail outlet.

The landlord refuses to consent to the assignment since it calls for a change in use of the premises.

The tenant claims the landlord's refusal is commercially unreasonable since it amounts to *economic protectionism* unrelated to the landlord's ownership and operation of the rental property.

Here, the landlord's refusal is a commercially reasonable application of the use restriction in the lease. He sought only to retain the use originally intended by the lease. The refusal is not due to improper economic protectionism in the management and operation of the real estate since the landlord did not seek an increase in rent or other economic benefits to enhance himself as a *condition* for his consent to the assignment of the lease. [**Pay 'N Pak Stores, Inc.** v. **Superior Court of Santa Clara County** (1989) 210 CA3d 1404]

Also, the landlord can reasonably refuse his consent to a trust deed lien the tenant seeks to place on the leasehold interest when the proceeds of the loan are not used to improve the property. [**Airport Plaza, Inc.** v. **Blanchard** (1987) 188 CA3d 1594]

Reasonable increases in rent

Consider a nonresidential tenant who agrees to pay rent in an amount equal to a percentage of the tenant's gross sales, but not less than a base monthly amount, called a *percentage lease*.

An alienation provision in the lease requires the tenant to obtain the landlord's consent before assigning the lease. The provision does not include standards or conditions for the landlord's consent to an assignment.

The tenant enters into an agreement to sell his business and assign the lease to a new operator. The operator buying the lease (and the business) is to pay the tenant a monthly premium over the remaining life of the lease, called *overriding rent*.

The tenant requests consent from the landlord for the assignment of the lease. On investigation, the landlord determines the operator will manage the business in a manner which will not generate gross sales at the same level as the current tenant. Thus, under the percentage lease, the new operator will not become obligated to pay the amount of rent currently being paid by the tenant seeking consent.

However, the landlord agrees to consent to the assignment **conditioned** on the landlord receiving the overriding rent premium the tenant is to be paid for the assignment.

The tenant claims the landlord cannot condition consent on exacting the rent premium since no standards or conditions for consent exist in the lease and thus cannot now be imposed.

Here, the landlord can **condition** his consent to the tenant's assignment of the lease on the landlord's receipt of the monthly rent premium to be paid by the new tenant in spite of the fact he did not contract in the lease agreement for the premium.

The landlord's conditional consent to the assignment is **commercially reasonable**. The landlord when granting consent is entitled to preserve the rental income he currently receives from the existing tenant. The landlord does not need to accept the certain risk of a lower monthly percentage rent from the assignee while the original tenant receives a monthly premium. [**John Hogan Enterprises, Inc.** v. **Kellogg** (1986) 187 CA3d 589]

Proceeds from assignment demanded

Now consider a nonresidential lease that contains an assignment provision authorizing the landlord to demand all the consideration the tenant will receive for an assignment of the lease as a *condition* for his consent to the assignment.

The landlord using the lease does not bargain for any other exaction, such as a portion of the purchase price the tenant will receive on a sale of the business that the tenant operates from the premises.

Later, the tenant agrees to assign the lease to a new operator as part of the sale of his business. The operator will pay the tenant a lump sum payment for the lease as part of the purchase price since rent due on the lease is below market rates.

The landlord demands the tenant pass on the price paid for the lease as a condition for his consent to the assignment, which the tenant rejects.

The tenant claims the landlord's demand in exchange for consent is commercially unreasonable, and thus unenforceable, since the landlord has no lawful justification for the premium or additional rent they agreed to in the lease.

Here, the landlord may condition consent on his receipt of the payment made for the assignment of the lease.

Nonresidential leases granting the landlord the right to receive any consideration the tenant is to receive related (and limited) to the *value of the lease* to be assigned are enforceable. [CC §1995.240]

Absent unconscionable or discriminatory provisions, nonresidential landlords and tenants are free to place *commercially reasonable* restrictions limited to the value of the leasehold on any assignment of the lease. [Carma Developers, Inc., *supra*]

More than rental value demanded

Again, a nonresidential lease may provide for the landlord to receive all consideration the tenant receives for the assignment of the lease in exchange for his consent since these amounts are considered commercially reasonable. [CC §1995.240]

However, the consideration the landlord may receive for his consent to an assignment is limited to financial benefits directly related to the **value of the lease** assigned.

For example, a tenant occupies nonresidential property under a lease.

The lease includes a *profit-shifting clause* calling for the tenant to pay the landlord, in exchange for his consent to an assignment, 25% of the consideration the tenant receives for goodwill on the sale of the tenant's business. Both agree it is the location of the leased property which will give the tenant's business its goodwill value.

The tenant's business is a success and the tenant locates a buyer for the business and the remaining term on the lease. The tenant seeks the landlord's consent for an assignment of the lease.

As agreed, the landlord demands 25% of the consideration the tenant will receive for his business goodwill. The tenant refuses to meet the demand and the landlord refuses to consent to the assignment.

As a result, the sales transaction fails to close. The tenant makes a demand on the landlord for 100% of his lost profits on the sale.

The tenant claims the landlord's demand for a share of the profits on the sale of the business as agreed to in the lease was a commercially unreasonable and unenforceable condition for granting consent to the assignment.

The landlord claims the profit-shifting provision is enforceable since all consideration received by the tenant on a transfer of the lease, even in excess of the value of the lease, can be agreed to and taken in exchange for consent.

Here, the landlord's right to receive consideration the tenant receives for the sale of a business and an assignment of the lease is limited to consideration the tenant receives for the **increased value** of the lease — and even then the condition of payment for consent must be agreed to in the lease alienation provision to be enforceable. [**Ilkhchooyi** v. **Best** (1995) 37 CA4th 395]

Unconscionable advantage situations

Now consider a subtenant who must negotiate a new lease with the landlord or be evicted. The master tenant's lease has been terminated by the landlord due to no fault of the subtenant.

The landlord submits a proposed lease to the subtenant which differs significantly in its terms and conditions from the wiped out sublease the subtenant held with the master tenant. When the subtenant attempts to negotiate a reasonable rent based on "comps" and eliminate unacceptable provisions, the landlord tells the subtenant to "take it or leave it." The subtenant is told he will be evicted if the proposed lease is not signed.

The proposed lease includes an alienation clause calling for a 200% increase in rent as a condition to be met before the landlord will consent to an assignment of the lease.

The subtenant signs the lease. Later, the subtenant seeks the landlord's consent to an assignment of the lease on his sale of the business. The landlord demands a modification of the lease rent provision to reflect the 200% increase in monthly rent as agreed, which the subtenant's buyer refuses to sign.

The landlord claims the alienation clause is enforceable since the clause was freely bargained for.

The tenant claims the provision was the result of an *unconscionable advantage* held by the landlord when they negotiated the terms of the lease since the tenant was in no position to bargain with the landlord. When the lease was negotiated, the tenant could not refuse to rent due to the goodwill he had built up for his business at this location through a heavy investment in advertising, and the landlord was unconscionable in his negotiation in light of his advantage.

Can the tenant avoid enforcement of the profit-shifting clause?

Yes! The alienation clause agreed to was the result of the landlord taking *unconscionable advantage* of the subtenant's situation. The subtenant was in possession under a wiped out sublease without any power to freely bargain. He was already in possession and operating a business that had developed goodwill that would be lost if he vacated.

Collection of future rents so hugely excessive as to **effectively shift profits** from the sale of the business to the landlord for his consent to an assignment of a lease was overreaching on the landlord's part. Thus, the profit-shifting assignment provision was unenforceable as the product of unconscionable demands resulting from the advantage held by the landlord over the subtenant. [Ilkhchooyi, *supra*]

Also, any consideration the landlord seeks which is beyond the **value of the leasehold interest** or the landlord's interest in the real estate is not reasonable, whenever or however bargained for.

Proceeds from the sale of a business, or a rent amount so large in its increase as to reduce the goodwill value of the business occupying the premises, reach beyond the economics (rental value) of the lease.

Thus, the demands agreed to unlawfully shift profits that are unrelated to the value of the leasehold. The right to freely bargain is not intended to give the landlord the right to freely fleece a tenant in the name of freedom of contract. [Ilkhchooyi, *supra*]

Tenant-mitigation provisions

When a nonresidential lease contains a tenant-mitigation provision and the tenant breaches the lease, the landlord may treat the lease as continuing and recover rent for the life of the lease. The provision shifts to the tenant the responsibility for leasing the property to **mitigate losses** when the tenant vacates and breaches the lease.

Under the tenant-mitigation provision, the landlord and tenant agree the tenant has a duty to find a replacement tenant, pay for any tenant improvements (TIs) and collect rent when the tenant breaches the lease and vacates the premises. [CC §1951.4]

Thus, on the tenant's breach of a lease with a tenant-mitigation provision, the landlord does not have the duty to mitigate his rental losses by **repossessing and reletting** the space himself before enforcing collection of future rents due under the lease from the tenant.

However, if the lease also provides for the landlord's prior consent to a transfer, the tenant-mitigation provision is enforceable only if the landlord's consent to an assignment is not unreasonably withheld. [CC §1951.4(b)(3)]

A landlord who prohibits assignments or unreasonably withholds consent retains the duty to mitigate his loss of rents on the tenant's breach.

Broker's role

Assignment (alienation) provisions restricting the transfer (assignment) of the leasehold interest held by a tenant become a concern of the bus-op or industrial broker when:

- negotiating the assignment of a lease in a bus-op sale (or negotiating a sublease or a further encumbrance);

- relocating a tenant whose current lease has not yet expired; or

- negotiating the origination of any lease.

A broker handling a **bus-op sale** or **relocation** of a business or industrial tenant must determine the tenant's ability and under what standards or conditions the tenant is allowed to assign the existing lease to a buyer of the business operation or other successor tenant.

The broker starts the analysis by ascertaining the type of assignment clause the landlord's proposed lease contains. The broker can then determine the tenant's assignment rights under the lease.

Now consider a leasing agent who is **negotiating a lease** on behalf of a prospective tenant. The tenant's agent should limit the wording of an assignment provision to include:

- the landlord's consent "will not be unreasonably withheld"; and

- any exaction to be paid for the consent is limited to any increased rental value of the premises received by the tenant.

Any prohibition against assignment should be eliminated by including the "with consent" provision.

Conversely, the landlord's leasing agent who arranges a lease should review the assignment provision in the proposed lease and include any consideration the tenant is to pay the landlord as a condition for his consent to an assignment.

For example, as compensation for consent to an assignment, the landlord may want to:

- adjust rents to current market rates;

- receive fees and costs incurred to investigate the successor tenant's credit and business conduct so he can analyze his risk of loss should he consent to the assignment;

- receive any overriding rent or lump sum payment the tenant receives which is attributable to the value of the lease;

- require the successor tenant to pay operating expenses as additional rent such as maintenance, utilities, insurance and taxes; or

- alter the terms of the lease and any options to extend/renew the lease or buy the property.

However, any exactions the landlord may expect or later seek for his consent must be agreed to and set forth in the lease, and be related to the value of the lease to be enforceable.

SECTION G

Residential Leases and
Rental Agreements

Chapter 35

Residential leases and rental agreements

This chapter distinguishes residential lease agreements from month-to-month rental agreements.

Fixed-term or periodic tenancy

Residential landlords and tenants enter into either a lease agreement or a periodic rental agreement when the landlord transfers the right to occupy property to the tenant, called *letting* or *renting* property. Periodic rental agreements are nearly always structured as month-to-month rental agreements.

Other than the **expiration** of the tenancy conveyed by each agreement, residential leases and rental agreements grant and impose on the landlords and tenants the same rights and obligations. It is the expectation of continued occupancy which differs.

Provisions agreed to which are not included as boilerplate provisions in the pre-printed form used by the landlord are included in an addendum to the lease or rental agreement. The provisions are entered on the addendum, and the addendum is referenced in the body of the lease or rental agreement to which it is attached.

Additional terms and conditions placed in addendums include authorization for the tenant to maintain such items on the premises as a pet, fish tank or liquid-filled furniture, or the landlord's grant to the tenant of an option to buy the property or to renew or extend the term of the lease.

Month-to-month vs. lease

A month-to-month **rental agreement** renews monthly, automatically and on the same terms, until modified or terminated by notice. [See **first tuesday** Form 551 §2]

Month-to-month tenancies, a type of *periodic tenancy*, can be terminated by either the landlord or the tenant on 30 days written notice, except for the landlord's use of a 60-day notice to vacate when the tenant has occupied residential property for one year or more. [Calif. Civil Code §1946; see Chapter 21]

On the other hand, a **lease agreement** creates a tenancy that continues for a fixed period, called its *term*, such as six months or one year, at the end of which the tenant's right to occupy expires. [See Form 550 §2 accompanying this chapter]

Also, a lease terminates at the end of its fixed term without further notice, called *expiration* of the lease. Unlike a periodic rental agreement, no renewal of a lease occurs on expiration of its term unless agreed to in a renewal/extension option.

Unlike the required use of a notice to vacate to bring a month-to-month tenancy to termination, a lease contains the only notice of termination of the leasehold the tenant or the landlord is entitled to receive. The expiration provision in the lease sets forth the day the leasehold tenancy expires, reverting the right to occupancy to the landlord.

Rental market influences

The availability of tenants and the number of properties competing for these tenants, as well as a property's location and its amenities as compared to competing properties, create the **rental market**. It is the rental market which sets the amount of rent a residential landlord is able to charge on any given day.

Generally, tenants on month-to-month rental agreements pay higher amounts of rent for a unit than do tenants with lease agreements.

Month-to-month tenants pay a premium for the privilege of being able to vacate the premises on 30 days notice, without liability for future rents. This privilege contributes to the landlord's uncertainty about his income and costs of tenant turnover, hence the premium rent.

Tenants typically pay lower rents when they enter into a lease. In stable rental markets, the longer the lease, the lower the rent. Rent is, however, subject to adjustments for inflation.

The landlord offers lower rents on leases to induce tenants to commit themselves to longer periods of tenancy.

The landlord entices tenants to enter into lease agreements as part of a strategy to stabilize income, reduce the vacancy rate and minimize turnover costs.

However, during a market in which rents have been rising significantly, residential landlords favor using month-to-month rental agreements rather than leases.

Just as a month-to-month rental agreement can be terminated on 30 days notice (except for the landlord's 60-day notice to vacate when a residential tenant has occupied a unit for one year or more), the amount of rent can be increased to current market rates on 30 days written notice (except for a 60-day notice on increases of 10% or more within a 12-month period, and for rent control properties). [CC §827]

Lease negotiations on expiration

Conversely, a landlord cannot alter the terms of a lease agreement during the life of the lease without the tenant's consent.

When a tenant holds a lease, the landlord desiring to keep the tenant should contact the tenant prior to the lease's expiration and offer to enter into another lease or a month-to-month

rental agreement. Unless contacted (and the lease is renewed or extended), the tenant knows he is expected to have vacated the premises on expiration of the lease.

Should the tenant desire to remain in possession when his lease expires, the amount of rent a landlord can demand is limited only by negotiations and the availability of other rentals and tenants.

On expiration of a lease, the tenant has no lawful right to possession of the unit. If the tenant remains and refuses to pay the amount of rent demanded by the landlord, he may be evicted immediately. [Calif. Code Civil Procedures §1161(1)]

As a better plan for retaining tenants, the landlord on entering into a lease might give the tenant an option to renew or extend the lease for a set period of months at the **prevailing rent** as determined by the landlord at the time of renewal.

Requisites to accepting tenants

On locating a prospective tenant for a residential unit, the landlord requires the prospect to complete a credit application and establish he is creditworthy before entering into either a lease or rental agreement. [See **first tuesday** Form 302]

The credit application should be referenced and attached as an addendum to any rental or lease agreement entered into by the landlord and tenant. The application is part of the leasing process which induces the landlord to accept the applicant as a tenant and sign a lease.

Initially, the landlord uses the authorization provided by the tenant on the application to verify the tenant's rental history, employment, credit standing and check writing history.

If a prospective tenant has a poor credit rating or no credit rating at all, but meets the landlord's income requirements, the landlord might seek assurances in addition to the maximum security deposit allowed, such as:

RESIDENTIAL LEASE AGREEMENT

DATE:_____, 20_____, at _____, California

Items left blank or unchecked are not applicable.

FACTS:

This lease agreement is entered into by _____ , Landlord,

and Tenant(s) _____, and

_____ , regarding residential

real estate referred to as:_____

_____

Including the following:

☐ Garage/parking space #_____

☐ Storage space #_____

☐ Furnishings: _____

The following checked attachments are part of this agreement:

☐ Condition of premises [**first tuesday** Form 560]

☐ Tenant's credit application [ft Form 302]

☐ Condition/Inventory of furnishings [ft Form 561]

☐ Rent control disclosures

☐ Brokerage fee addendum [ft Form 273]

☐ House/Building rules

1. **DEPOSIT:**

   1.1 Landlord acknowledges receipt of $_____ as a security deposit.

   1.2 The deposit is security for the diligent performance of Tenant's obligations, including payment of rent, repair of damages, reasonable repair and cleaning of premises on termination, and any loss, damages or excess wear and tear on furnishings provided to Tenant.

   1.3 No interest will be paid on the deposit, and Landlord may place the deposit with his own funds, except where controlled by law.

   1.4 Within 21 days after Tenant vacates, Landlord to furnish Tenant with a security deposit statement itemizing any deductions, with a refund of the remaining amount.

2. **TERM OF LEASE:**

   2.1 This lease will begin on _____, 20_____, and continue until _____, 20_____.

   2.2 The lease terminates on the last day of the term without further notice.

   2.3 If Tenant holds over, Tenant to be liable for rent at the daily rate of $_____.

3. **RENT:**

   3.1 Tenant to pay, in advance, $_____ rent monthly, on the _____ day of each month.

   3.2 Rent to be paid by:

   a. ☐ cash, ☐ check, or ☐ cashier's check made payable to Landlord or his agent and delivered to:

   _____ (Name)

   _____ (Address)

   _____

   _____ (Phone)

   Personal delivery of rent to be accepted at Landlord's address during the hours of _____ am to _____ pm on the following days: _____

   — — — — — — — — — — — — — *PAGE ONE OF THREE — FORM 550* — — — — — — — — — — — — —

    b. ☐ credit card #_____/_____/_____/_____ issued by _____,
        which Landlord is authorized to charge each month for rent due.

    c. ☐ deposit into account number _____ at:
        _____ (Financial Institution)
        _____ (Address)
        _____

3.3 Tenant to pay a charge of $_____ as an additional amount of rent, due on demand, in the event rent is not received within five days after the due date.

3.4 If any rent or other amount due Landlord is not received within five days after its due date, interest will thereafter accrue on the amount at 12% per annum until paid. On receipt of any past due amount, Landlord to promptly make a written demand for payment of the accrued interest which will be payable within 30 days of the demand.

3.5 Tenant to pay a change of $_____ as an additional amount of rent, due on demand, for each rent check returned for insufficient funds, and thereafter pay rent by cash or cashier's check.

4. POSSESSION:

4.1 Tenant will not be liable for any rent until the date possession is delivered.

4.2 If Landlord is unable to deliver possession, Landlord will not be liable for any damage, nor will this lease terminate.

4.3 Tenant may terminate this lease if Landlord fails to deliver possession within five days of commencement.

4.4 Only the above-named Tenant(s) to occupy the premises.

4.5 Tenant will not assign this lease agreement or sublet, or have boarders or lodgers.

4.6 Tenant(s) will have no more than _____ guests staying no more than 10 consecutive days, or 20 days in a year.

4.7 Except as noted in an addendum, Tenant agrees the premises, fixtures, appliances and furnishings are in satisfactory and sanitary condition. [ft Form 561]

4.8 Landlord to make any necessary repairs as soon as possible after notification by Tenant. If Landlord does not timely make necessary repairs, Tenant may have the repairs made and deduct the cost, not to exceed one month's rent.

5. TENANT AGREES:

5.1 To comply with all building rules and regulations and later amendments or modifications.

5.2 To pay for the following utilities and services:_____
_____
_____

    a. Landlord to pay for: _____

5.3 To keep the premises clean and sanitary and to properly dispose of all garbage and waste.
☐ Yard maintenance included.

5.4 To properly operate all electrical, gas and plumbing fixtures and pipes, and keep them clean and sanitary.

5.5 To make the premises available on 24 hours notice for entry by Landlord to make necessary repairs, alterations or services, or to exhibit the premises to prospective purchasers, tenants, employees or contractors. In case of emergency or Tenant's abandonment of premises, Landlord may enter the premises at any time.

5.6 Not to disturb, annoy, endanger or interfere with other occupants of the building or neighboring buildings.

5.7 Not to use the premises for any unlawful purpose, violate any government ordinance, or create a nuisance.

5.8 Not to destroy, damage or remove any part of the premises, equipment or fixtures or commit waste, or permit any person to do so.

5.9 Not to keep pets or a waterbed on the premises without Landlord's written consent.
See attached ☐ pet addendum [ft Form 563], ☐ waterbed addendum. [ft Form 564]

5.10 Not to make any repairs, alterations or additions to the premises without Landlord's written consent. Any repairs or alterations shall become part of the premises.

5.11 Not to change or add a lock without written consent.

6. GENERAL PROVISIONS:

6.1 Tenant agrees to hold Landlord harmless from claims, demands, damages or liability arising out of the premises caused by or permitted by Tenant, Tenant's family, agents employees and guests.
☐ Tenant to obtain insurance for this purpose naming Landlord as an additional insured.

6.2 Landlord to maintain the premises and common areas in a safe and sanitary condition and comply with all applicable ordinances and regulations.

6.3 Waiver of a breach of any provision shall not constitute a waiver of any subsequent breach. Landlord's receipt of rent with knowledge of Tenant's breach does not waive Landlord's right to enforce the breached provision.

6.4 In any action to enforce this agreement, the prevailing party shall receive attorney fees.

6.5 **Notice:** The California Department of Justice, sheriff's departments, police departments serving jurisdictions of 200,000 or more and many other local law enforcement authorities maintain for public access a data base of the locations of persons required to register pursuant to paragraph (1) of subdivision (a) of Section 290.4 of the Penal Code. The database is updated on a quarterly basis and a source of information about the presence of these individuals in any neighborhood. The Department of Justice also maintains a Sex Offender Identification Line through which inquires about individuals may be made. This is a "900" telephone service. Callers must have specific information about individuals they are checking. Information regarding neighborhoods is not available through the "900" telephone service.

6.6 ☐ See attached addendum for additional terms and conditions. [ft Form 250]

6.7 ☐ See attached Notice of Illegal Controlled Substance. [ft Form 583]

7. _____

_____

_____

_____

_____

_____

_____

_____

_____

_____

I agree to let on the terms stated above.	**I agree to occupy on the terms stated above.**
Date:_____, 20_____	Date:_____, 20_____
Landlord: _____	Tenant: _____
Agent: _____	Tenant: _____
Signature: _____	Signature: _____
Address: _____	Signature: _____
_____	Address: _____
Phone: _____	_____
Fax: _____	Phone: _____
E-mail: _____	Fax: _____
	E-mail: _____

- a co-signer on the lease; or

- a guarantee agreement executed by a creditworthy individual. [See **first tuesday** Form 439-L]

Then, if the tenant defaults in rent payments or damages the premises, the landlord can hold the co-signer liable or collect his losses from the guarantor should the security deposit prove insufficient to cover lost rents and maintenance charges.

Condition of premises addendum

Residential landlords and tenants have a statutory duty to, respectively, maintain the property and refrain from damaging the premises. [CC §§1941; 1941.2]

To avoid disputes over who is responsible for any damage to the premises, the residential landlord and tenant should complete and sign a *condition of premises addendum* **before** the tenant is given possession and **after** the tenant has vacated. [See **first tuesday** Form 560; see Chapter 14]

Before a tenant takes possession, the landlord or his manager needs to inspect the unit with the tenant, called a walk-through. Together, the landlord (or resident manager) and the tenant will use a condition of premises addendum to confirm:

- the premises is in satisfactory condition;

- if there is any existing damage to the premises; and

- if there are any repairs the landlord must make to the premises.

If the unit is furnished, the landlord and tenant will complete and sign an additional form on their walk-through called a *condition of furnishings addendum.* [See **first tuesday** Form 561]

The condition of furnishings addendum confirms:

- the inventory of furnishings located in the unit;

- the current condition of the furnishings; and

- the tenant's acceptance of the furnishings.

On review of the premises **after** the tenant has vacated, the condition of premises addendum (and any furnishings addendum) completed when the tenant took possession is referenced to determine if the physical condition of the premises (and furnishings) at the time the tenant vacates is the result of only reasonable wear and tear.

Pet addendum

Generally, a lease or month-to-month rental agreement prohibits a tenant from keeping pets on the premises.

Some landlords do allow pets, but often:

- impose restrictions on the type or size of the pet; and

- require the landlord's written consent to keep the pet on the premises. [See Form 550 §5.9 and **first tuesday** Form 551 §5.9]

Note — A landlord cannot prohibit a disabled person from keeping a dog on the premises which is specially trained to assist the person. [CC §54.1(b)(5); see Chapter 37]

The landlord and tenant can sign and attach a pet addendum that states:

- the type of pet and its name;

- the security deposit to be charged for the pet; and

- the tenant's agreement to hold the landlord harmless for any damage caused by the pet. [See **first tuesday** Form 563]

Waterbed addendum

Leases and month-to-month rental agreements also prohibit a tenant from keeping a waterbed or other liquid-filled furnishings on the premises without the landlord's written consent. [See Form 550 §5.9 and **first tuesday** Form 551 §5.9]

When a tenant has a waterbed, the landlord should require the tenant to sign a *waterbed addendum*. [See **first tuesday** Form 564]

The waterbed addendum indicates:

- the additional security deposit the tenant will be required to provide for keeping a waterbed on the premises; and

- the tenant's agreement to maintain an insurance policy to cover potential property damage should the waterbed leak or burst. [See Chapter 13]

Brokerage fee addendum

A broker who is retained under an exclusive authorization to lease property must be paid a fee should the landlord rent to a tenant during the listing period. [See **first tuesday** Form 110; see Chapter 9]

Likewise, a broker is entitled to a fee from a tenant who has retained the broker under an exclusive authorization to locate space and the tenant rents space during the listing period. [See **first tuesday** Form 111; see Chapter 10]

However, brokers too often fail to insist on a written fee agreement from either the landlord or the tenant before rendering services.

To be assured a fee when a prior written fee agreement does not exist, the broker will typically attempt to include a fee agreement as part of an offer to lease or as an addendum to the proposed lease or rental agreement prepared for the tenant to sign. [See **first tuesday** Form 273]

Other addenda

Other information handed to a residential tenant which is made a part of a lease or rental agreement includes:

- house or building rules; and

- any rent control disclosures required by local rent control ordinances.

Also, a tenant entering into a lease agreement may have negotiated for an option to renew or extend the lease at its expiration. Provisions for the option to renew or extend would be included in an addendum attached to the lease. [See **first tuesday** Form 565]

A residential landlord seeking to sell the property may grant the tenant an option to purchase the property. [See **first tuesday** Form 161; see Chapter 5]

However, no credit for option money or rent should ever be applied to the purchase price.

By the terms of the lease or option agreement, any credit applied toward the purchase price, or to a down payment on the purchase price establishes the tenant has acquired an *equitable ownership* interest in the property.

A transaction involving a lease and a purchase option calling for rent or option money payments to be applied toward the purchase price is called a *lease-option sale*, and is a sale of the property for all purposes, and not a leasing arrangement at all.

Terms of residential occupancy

On executing a residential lease or month-to-month rental agreement, a landlord conveys the right to possession of the unit to a tenant, called a *leasehold estate*.

Also, a lease or month-to-month rental agreement sets forth the respective rights and obligations of the landlord and tenant for the use, care and maintenance of the property during the tenant's occupancy.

A **security deposit** is usually received from the tenant to cover any damage caused to the unit by the tenant beyond reasonable wear and tear. [See Form 550 §1 and **first tuesday** Form 551 §1; see Chapter 13]

In return for the use and possession of the premises, the tenant pays the landlord **rent** until expiration of the lease or rental agreement and possession is returned to the landlord.

The tenant agrees to pay a **late charge** if rent is not paid within a fixed period of time after it is due, called a *grace period*. [See Form 550 §3 and **first tuesday** Form 551 §3]

Also, the number of **guests** the tenant may have in his unit and the period of time over which his guests may visit is limited. [See Form 550 §4.6 and **first tuesday** Form 551 §4.6]

The tenant agrees to comply with all building or project **rules** and **regulations** established by CC&Rs or the landlord. [See Form 550 §5.1 and **first tuesday** Form 551 §5.1]

The landlord and tenant agree who will pay for or how they will share in the financial responsibility for the unit's **utilities**.

Landlords of apartment buildings or complexes often retain the responsibility of providing water to the units. [See Form 550 §5.2 and **first tuesday** Form 551 §5.2]

In a lease and rental agreement, the tenant agrees to hold the landlord harmless from all liability for damages caused by the tenant or his guests. [See Form 550 §6.1 and **first tuesday** Form 551 §6.1]

Statutory rights and duties

Residential leases and month-to-month rental agreements often contain provisions that restate the landlord's and tenant's statutory rights and duties.

For example, the rental agreement reiterates the landlord's statutory obligation to furnish a tenant with:

- a security deposit refund; and

- a statement of security deposit accounting within 21 days after the tenant vacates which itemizes any deductions. [CC §1950.5(f); see Form 550 §1.4 and **first tuesday** Form 551 §1.4; see Chapter 13]

Also, rental agreements often advise tenants of their limited statutory right to make necessary repairs to the premises and deduct the cost from the rent should the landlord fail to make the repairs that were noticed by the tenant. [CC §1942; see Form 550 §6.2 and **first tuesday** Form 551 §6.2; see Chapter 25]

A lease or rental agreement may prohibit a tenant from:

- using the premises for an unlawful purpose;

- creating a nuisance; and

- committing waste. [See Form 550 §§5.7, 5.8 and **first tuesday** Form 551 §§5.7, 5.8]

More importantly, a tenant who either uses the premises for an unlawful purpose, creates a nuisance or commits waste — even if these activities are not prohibited by the tenant's lease or rental agreement — may be evicted with a 3-day written notice to quit. [CCP §1161(4); see Chapter 19]

Chapter 36

Lead-based paint disclosures

This chapter discusses the federal lead-based paint disclosure and the duty of landlords renting pre-1978 residential property to disclose their knowledge of any lead-based paint to tenants.

Pre-contract disclosure for pre-1978 housing

A landlord retains a broker to locate a tenant to lease residential property built before 1978. The property is not a vacation rental, hotel, motel or elderly (senior citizen) housing, and it is not certified as lead-based paint free.

The broker informs the landlord that leasing residential property built before 1978 requires disclosure to the tenant regarding lead-based paint hazards which may exist on the property or are known to the landlord or the broker before the tenant enters into a lease of the premises.

The broker prepares a lead-based paint disclosure form to be reviewed and signed by the landlord. The disclosure is attached to the authorization to lease or to the property management agreement entered into by the broker and the landlord. The disclosure will be handed to prospective tenants who are interested in renting the property.

Here, the broker has properly informed the residential landlord of the lead-based paint disclosures mandated by federal regulations. Lead-based paint disclosures must be provided to prospective tenants of any residential property built before 1978, other than transient and elderly housing. [24 Code of Federal Regulations §35.82; 40 CFR §745.101]

Thus, **before a tenant** enters into an agreement to rent or lease a pre-1978 residential unit, unless it is exempt housing, the landlord of the property must provide the tenant with the following:

- a **lead-based paint disclosure statement** attached to the lease or rental agreement disclosing the presence of any known lead-based paint or related hazards on the property [See Form 557 accompanying this chapter];

- any **information available** concerning lead-based paint hazards known to the landlord or the broker, such as any reports that determine lead-based paint exists on the property, including common areas and other residential dwellings in multi-family housing if the other housing units were part of an evaluation or reduction of lead-based paint in the multi-family housing as a whole; and

- an EPA-approved lead hazard information **pamphlet** entitled, *Protect Your Family From Lead in Your Home*, or an equivalent pamphlet approved for use in California by the EPA. [24 CFR §35.88(a); 40 CFR §745.107(a)]

If the disclosure occurs after an application to rent or lease has been received from a tenant, the landlord must provide the disclosures to the tenant **prior to accepting** the lease application.

The tenant must be given an opportunity to either abandon the application or further negotiate in light of the newly disclosed information on the property's lead-based paint condition. [24 CFR §35.88(b); 40 CFR §745.107(b)]

However, the mandated lead-based paint disclosure laws **do not obligate** the landlord:

- to conduct an inspection to determine whether any lead-based paint exists; or

- to abate or remove any lead-based paint. [24 CFR §35.88(a); 40 CFR §745.107(a)]

Brokers involved in residential leasing transactions are obligated as agents to ensure the landlord complies with the **pre-contract disclosure** regulations. Thus, it is incumbent on brokers to know the rules, prepare the disclosures and inform everyone involved of the known or possible existence of lead-based paint and their rights and obligations under federal law — all done before rental applications are prepared or accepted.

Lead-based paint hazards

Lead-based paint was **banned** by the Federal Consumer Product Safety Commission in 1978.

Lead-based paint is defined as paint or other *surface coating* that contains lead equal to at least 1.0 milligram per square centimeter or 0.5% by weight. [24 CFR §35.86; 40 CFR §745.103]

A **lead-based paint hazard** is any condition that causes *exposure to lead* from lead-contaminated dust, soil or paint which has deteriorated to the point of causing adverse human health effects. [24 CFR §35.86; 40 CFR §745.103]

Exempt residential rentals

Now consider an owner, broker or vacation rental operator who provides lodging on a **vacation property** for a stay of less than 100 days by a guest, called a *transient occupancy*.

Further, the occupancy agreement provides for no extension or renewal. At the end of the stay, the guest must depart.

The owner is concerned about the disclosure requirements of lead-based paint since the vacation property is residential real estate built before 1978.

Is the vacation owner, operator or broker required to provide the occupant of the vacation rental with the lead-based paint disclosure?

No! The lead-based paint disclosure requirements do not apply to any occupancy agreement for a period of 100 days or less, where renewal or extension of the occupancy has not been provided for. [24 CFR §35.82(c); 40 CFR §745.101(c)]

By definition, a transient occupancy by a guest automatically terminates on the expiration (departure) date and time of day stated in the occupancy agreement.

Thus, the regulations **exempt** all vacation rentals, hotels and motels due to their short-term transient lodging arrangements.

Federal Pamphlets

A copy of *Protect Your Family From Lead in Your Home* can be obtained from the National Lead Information Center and Clearinghouse (NLIC) at http://www.epa.gov/opptintr/lead/nlic.htm or by calling (800) 424-LEAD. Requests may also be sent by fax to (301) 588-8495 or by e-mail to ech@cais.com.

Bulk copies of the pamphlet are available from the Government Printing Office (GPO) at http://bookstore.gpo.gov/ or by calling (202) 512-1800. Refer to the complete title or GPO stock number 055-000-00632-6. The price is $50.50 for a pack of 50 copies.

Alternatively, the pamphlet may be reproduced for use or distribution if the text and graphics are reproduced in full. Camera-ready copies of the pamphlet are available from the NLIC.

LEAD-BASED PAINT DISCLOSURE
For Renting and Leasing Residential Property

1. Lead Warning:

Housing built before 1978 may contain lead-based paint. Lead from paint, paint chips, and dust can pose health hazards if not managed properly. Lead exposure is especially harmful to young children and pregnant women. Before renting pre-1978 housing, landlords must disclose the presence of lead-based paint and/or lead-based painthazards in the dwelling. Tenants may also receive a federally approved pamphlet on lead poisoning.

> **NOTE:**
> For use on the lease or rental of residential property which was constructed pre-1978.

Items left blank or unchecked are not applicable.

2. Landlord's Certification:

2.1 Presence of lead-based paint and/or lead-based paint hazards:

☐ a. Are known to Landlord to be present in the housing as explained: _____

_____

_____

☐ b. Are not known to Landlord to be present in the housing.

2.2 Records and reports available to Tenant:

☐ a. Landlord has provided Tenant with all available records and reports listed below pertaining to lead-based paint and/or lead-based paint hazards in the housing: _____

_____

_____

☐ b. Landlord has no reports or records pertaining to lead-based paint and/or lead-based paint hazards in the housing.

Date: _____, 20_____ Landlord: _____

3. Tenant's Acknowledgement:

3.1 Tenant has received:

☐ a. Copies of all information listed above.

☐ b. The pamphlet *Protect Your Family From Lead in Your Home.*

Date: _____, 20_____ Tenant: _____

Date: _____, 20_____ Tenant: _____

4. Broker's Certification: (When Applicable)

4.1 Broker certifies to have informed the landlord of his/her obligation under 42 USC §4852(d) to disclose to the tenant and agent all information known to the landlord regarding the presence of lead-based paint and lead-based paint hazards within this target housing and that all information known to the agent regarding the presence of lead-based paint and lead-based paint hazards within this target housing has been disclosed to the tenant.

4.2 Broker further certifies that the tenant received the lead hazard information pamphlet *Protect Your Family From Lead in Your Home.*

Date:_____, 20_____ Broker: _____

FORM 557   10-00   ©2003 **first tuesday**, P.O. BOX 20069 RIVERSIDE, CA 92516 (800) 794-0494

However, if the stay in the vacation rental is intended to extend beyond 100 days, then the lead-based paint disclosure requirements must be complied with by the owner and his broker.

Further, all landlords entering into month-to-month **rental agreements** for non-exempt residential property must comply with the lead-based paint disclosure requirements.

Month-to-month rental agreements, being automatically renewable, open-ended tenancies, do not limit the time period before the tenant must vacate to less than 100 days. Unless terminated by a later notice, a month-to-month rental agreement will automatically continue beyond the 100-day period.

Also exempt from the lead-based paint disclosures are housing for the elderly or disabled where no child under the age of six is expected to live. **Elderly housing** includes retirement communities or other housing that is required to be occupied by one or more individuals over the age of 62. [24 CFR §35.86; 40 CFR §745.103]

Also exempt is any **zero-bedroom dwelling** defined as a residential dwelling in which the living room is not separated from the sleeping area, such as occurs in studio apartments, dormitories or the rental of an individual room in residential housing. [24 CFR §35.86; 40 CFR §745.103]

Broker compliance

All brokers who represent the landlord of a non-exempt pre-1978 residential structure must ensure the landlord complies with the lead-based paint requirements. [24 CFR §35.94(a); 40 CFR §745.115(a)]

However, landlords who are not represented by brokers are themselves required to make the disclosures.

A landlord's broker should begin by preparing the lead-based paint disclosures for the landlord's signature when the property management or leasing agent authorization is entered into.

Further, a landlord owes a duty to the broker to disclose any known lead-based paint hazards to the broker. Thus, a broker will not be held liable for failing to disclose lead-based paint hazards if:

- the landlord knows of the hazards and fails to inform the broker by an entry in the disclosure statement; and

- the broker has no independent knowledge of the hazardous condition, such as the structure being a pre-1978 construction. [24 CFR §35.94(b); 40 CFR §745.115(b)]

Use of the disclosure statement

All leases or month-to-month rental agreements for non-exempt pre-1978 residential property must include the lead-based paint disclosure form as an attachment. [24 CFR §35.92(b); 40 CFR §745.113(b); see Form 557]

The disclosure form must be in the **same language** as the lease or rental agreement. [24 CFR §35.92(b); 40 CFR §745.113(b)]

The disclosure form must include:

- the Lead Warning Statement [See Form 557 §1];

- the landlord's disclosure of any known lead-based paint hazards or the fact the landlord is unaware of any hazards [See Form 557 §2.1];

- a list of all records or reports available to the landlord concerning lead-based paint on the property, the location of the lead-based paint and the condition of the painted surfaces [See Form 557 §2.2];

- a statement by the tenant affirming receipt of the lead-based paint information and pamphlet [See Form 557 §3];

- a statement by the landlord's broker indicating the broker is aware of his duty to comply with the disclosure requirements [See Form 557 §4]; and

- the signatures of the landlord, tenant and broker. [24 CFR §35.92(b); 40 CFR §745.113(b)]

The landlord and the landlord's broker are required to keep a copy of the disclosure statement for a period of no less than three years from the commencement of the lease or rental agreement. [24 CFR §35.92(c); 40 CFR §745.113(c)]

Rentals certified as lead-based paint free

A landlord may take steps to have his pre-1978 property certified as lead-based paint free.

Pre-1978 residential property is considered lead-based paint free housing if no lead-based paint exists on the property. [24 CFR §35.86; 40 CFR §745.103]

The landlord of pre-1978 property does not need to provide lead-based paint disclosures with the leases or rental agreements when:

- the property is inspected by an inspector certified under the federal certification program or a federally accredited state or tribal certification program; and

- the inspector has determined the property to be lead-based paint free. [24 CFR §35.82(b); 40 CFR §745.101(b)]

Note — A list of statewide laboratories certified for analyzing lead in hazardous material, including paint, is available from the California Department of Health Services Environmental Lab Accreditation Program at (510) 540-2800, or from the National Lead Information Center and Clearinghouse at (800) 424-LEAD. Lists are also available on the web at http://www.leadlisting.org and http://www.dhs.ca.gov/childlead.

Lease renewal triggers disclosure

If an existing lease is **extended or renewed** and the lead-based paint disclosures were not previously handed to the tenant, the landlord must then make the disclosure to the tenant at the time of the extension or renewal.

The landlord does not need to provide new disclosures when existing leases are renewed or extended if:

- the landlord previously supplied the lead-based paint disclosures; and

- the landlord has not received any new information concerning lead-based paint on the property. [24 CFR §35.82(d); 40 CFR §745.101(d)]

When a lease expires and the tenant remains in possession under a month-to-month tenancy, the lease is not considered to have been extended or renewed and a new tenancy is not established. However, if the landlord and tenant change some aspect of the tenancy other than the extension of the occupancy, such as a rental rate, then the disclosure must be made. [61 Federal Register 9068]

Once a change in the terms of a lease occurs, other than the right to remain in occupancy, the lead-based paint disclosure rules require the landlord to then disclose any new information he may have obtained on the hazard since the original disclosure was handed to the tenant.

Failure to disclose

While a failure of the landlord or the broker to comply with the pre-contract disclosure requirements does not affect the enforceability of the lease or rental agreement, an **intentional violation** by the landlord or the broker will subject the violator to:

- liability to the tenant for three times the amount of the tenant's actual money losses caused by the existence of the hazard, called *trebled damages*;

- civil penalties;

- court costs and attorney fees; and

- civil and criminal sanctions. [24 CFR §35.96; 40 CFR §745.118]

Chapter 37

Permitting pets and waterbeds

This chapter reviews the handling of rent applications received from tenants with pets or liquid-filled furniture.

Role of the security deposit

Landlords and their property managers are frequently confronted with acceptable, prospective tenants who own pets or liquid-filled furniture.

Landlords cannot automatically refuse to rent to a prospective tenant whose furnishings include liquid-filled furniture or deny an existing tenant the use of liquid-filled furniture, such as a waterbed, on the premises.

However, landlords can automatically, as a matter of policy, refuse to accept all tenants who want to occupy a unit with their pet, unless the tenant is **disabled and uses:**

- a *guide dog,* which is a seeing-eye dog trained by a licensed person to aid a blind person;

- a *signal dog,* trained to alert a deaf or hearing-impaired person to intruders or sounds; or

- a *service dog,* trained to aid a physically disabled person by protection work, pulling a wheelchair or fetching dropped items. [Calif. Civil Code §54.1(b)(6)]

Disabled persons accompanied by a specially trained dog must keep the dog **leashed and tagged** as a specially trained dog by an identification tag issued by the county clerk, animal control department or some other authorized agency.

The disabled tenant accompanied by a tagged guide/signal/service dog cannot be required by the landlord to **pay any extra** rent, charge or security deposit for the dog to be kept on the premises.

However, the owner of a guide, signal or service dog is liable for the cost to repair any damages brought about by the dog's activities. [CC §54.2(a)]

Also, any public agency owning and operating rental accommodations must permit any person over 60 years of age to keep two pets or less (i.e., dog, cat, bird or fish). The **elderly pet owner** is responsible for any damages caused by the pets. [Calif. Health and Safety Code §19901]

Pet addendum

A property manager who allows a tenant to occupy a unit with a pet should reduce the arrangement to a writing in the form of a Pet Addendum and attach it to the lease or rental agreement. [See Form 563 accompanying this chapter]

The pet addendum establishes the responsibilities of the pet owner and the acceptable behavior standards for the pet.

To avoid misunderstandings as to size, type and number of pets allowed on the premises, a careful description of the pet should be given on the form.

The property manager can charge an **additional security deposit** for the pet to offset any expenses or losses caused by the pet, unless the rules for disabled persons and their trained dog apply or the security deposit ceiling would be exceeded.

A typical deposit for a pet is one-third of the first month's rent, with an extra $100 to $200 for each additional pet, limited to the ceiling amount for residential security deposits. [See Chapter 13]

Thus, the **total security deposit** for an unfurnished residential unit, including the pet deposit, cannot exceed an amount equal to two months' rent (in addition to the first month's rent).

For a furnished unit, the security deposit, including the pet deposit, cannot exceed three months' rent (in addition to the first month's rent). [CC §1950.5(c)]

Also, if a pet's behavior is not in keeping with the terms of the pet addendum, the lease or rental agreement has been breached by the tenant.

The property manager can serve a 3-day notice to the tenant to correct the activity or vacate the premises, called a *3-day notice to perform or quit*. [Calif. Code of Civil Procedure §1161(3); see Chapter 19]

Landlord liability for pets

A landlord permits a residential tenant to keep a dog on the premises. The landlord is not informed about and does not know the dog is vicious.

No "Beware of Dog" notice is posted by the tenant.

A utility serviceman properly enters the backyard to check the meter. The dog attacks and injures the serviceman.

The serviceman attempts to recover his losses due to the injury from the landlord.

Can the serviceman recover his losses from the landlord since the landlord allowed the tenant to keep a pet that was actually dangerous?

No! The landlord is not responsible for injury caused by dangerous domestic pets when he has no *actual knowledge* of their ferocity. Also, the landlord has no *duty to investigate* or inspect the rental unit to determine if the pet is dangerous. [**Lundy** v. **California Realty** (1985) 170 CA3d 813; see Chapters 28 and 29]

However, if the landlord has actual knowledge of the dangerousness of a tenant's pet and fails to serve the tenant with a 3-day notice to remove the pet or to vacate the unit, then the landlord is liable for injuries inflicted by the dangerous pet. [**Uccello** v. **Laudenslayer** (1975) 44 CA3d 504]

Also, a landlord has no responsibility to warn a prospective tenant of a dangerous pet located on a **neighboring property**, even when the landlord has knowledge of the ferocity of the neighbor's pet. [**Wylie** v. **Gresch** (1987) 191 CA3d 412]

Qualifying to maintain a waterbed

The use of waterbeds or other liquid-filled bedding in a rental unit cannot be grounds for refusal to rent to a prospective tenant. [CC §1940.5]

If the prospective tenant is otherwise qualified to rent, the landlord must rent to the tenant if the waterbed is qualified to be placed in the unit.

For a waterbed to qualify, the landlord may establish conditions for the use of the waterbed on the premises so long as the conditions meet the standards set by the waterbed law.

These requirements are itemized in the waterbed addendum which is attached to the lease or rental agreement. [See Form 564 accompanying this chapter]

The **waterbed conditions** a landlord can impose on the tenant to qualify his waterbed include:

- an insurance policy against property damage;

- a special waterbed frame;

- specific methods of installation and maintenance;

- a written receipt of installation by the manufacturer, retailer or movers;

PET ADDENDUM

DATE:_____, 20_____, at _____, California

Items left blank or unchecked are not applicable.

FACTS:

This is an addendum to the following:

☐ Residential lease agreement

☐ Residential rental agreement

☐ Other:_____

Dated _____, 20_____

Regarding real estate referred to as: _____

The above referenced agreement prohibits pets without Landlord's prior written consent.

AGREEMENT:

1. Landlord agrees the Tenant may keep the following pet:

   _____

2. Landlord hereby acknowledges receipt of $_____ as a security deposit, from which the Landlord may offset any expenses or losses caused by the pet. On termination of the above referenced agreement, the security deposit shall be refunded to Tenant with an itemization of its disposition.

3. Tenant agrees:

   3.1 Pet will not damage premises or annoy, endanger or inconvenience other tenants.

   3.2 The Tenant shall hold the Landlord harmless for any damages caused by the pet.

   3.3 To comply with all laws pertaining to the keeping and leashing of the pet.

   3.4 _____

   _____

   _____

   _____

   _____

   _____

I agree to the terms stated above.	I agree to the terms stated above .
Date:_____, 20_____	Date:_____, 20_____
Landlord/Agent: _____	Tenant: _____
Signature: _____	Signature:_____

FORM 563   10-01   ©2003 **first tuesday**, P.O. BOX 20069 RIVERSIDE, CA 92516 (800) 794-0494

- an increase in the maximum security deposit permitted; and

- requiring the tenant to comply with specific methods of installation or to remove the bed on 3-day written notice to perform (remove it) or quit. [CC §1940.5]

The floor of any residence has a limited capacity for weight centralized in one area.

Since a waterbed is considerably heavier than a regular bed, the weight of the waterbed must not exceed the weight limitation of the floor, especially if it is on an upper level.

Also, to ensure proper distribution of the weight, the tenant is required to provide an adequate bed frame specially designed to support and distribute the weight of a waterbed. [CC §1940.5(b)]

Waterbed addendum

When a tenant qualifies to maintain a waterbed on the premises, the landlord may increase the tenant's security deposit up to an additional one-half month's rent. The waterbed deposit is **in addition to** the maximum security deposit otherwise allowed. [See Chapter 13]

He may also charge a reasonable **administrative fee** to cover the time, effort and money expenditures necessary to process the waterbed paperwork, such as $50 to $100. [CC §1940.5(g)]

The amounts of both the additional security deposit and administrative charges are set forth in the waterbed addendum. [See Form 564 §§2; 3]

The tenant can be required to provide the landlord with a waterbed insurance policy or certificate of insurance for property damage caused by the waterbed.

The policy should name the landlord as an additional insured to eliminate any question over the disbursement of funds from a claim.

The waterbed insurance policy must be accepted by the landlord if several conditions are met, including:

- the policy is issued by a company licensed in California;

- the company possesses a Best Insurance Report rating of B or better; and

- the policy offers coverage of no less than $100,000. [CC §1940.5(a)]

The tenant must ensure the policy remains valid and enforceable throughout the period the waterbed is located on the premises. The landlord has the right to demand proof of insurance from the tenant at any time.

If the tenant fails to provide proof of insurance when requested, a 3-day notice to perform or quit should be served on the tenant to deliver up the policy, remove the furniture or vacate.

Consider the insurance policy a tenant holds on his waterbed which expires two months before he vacates. The tenant does not renew the policy as he will soon be moving. The landlord fails to purchase coverage and charge the tenant for the premium or serve the tenant with a 3-day notice to get insurance, remove the bed or vacate.

Sometime after the policy expires, a liner patch from a prior leak fails. The liner ruptures, releasing its water contents.

The whole apartment is flooded causing hundreds of dollars in damages as well as causing damage to the units and personal property on lower floors.

The landlord repairs the damages and demands payment from the tenant for all of his losses caused by the waterbed. The tenant claims the landlord had the responsibility to obtain coverage if the tenant did not.

Can the landlord collect the losses from the tenant?

WATERBED ADDENDUM

DATE:_____, 20_____, at _____, California

Items left blank or unchecked are not applicable.

FACTS:

This is an addendum to the following:

☐ Residential lease agreement

☐ Residential rental agreement

☐ Other:_____

Dated:_____, 20_____.

Prohibiting waterbeds and other liquid-filled furniture without the written consent of Landlord.

Regarding a residential unit referred to as: _____

> Possession in a rental of liquid-filled furniture is controlled by law. A tenant may keep and use liquid-filled furniture on the premises by complying with statutory conditions demanded by the landlord. [Calif. Civil Code §1940.5]

AGREEMENT:

1. Tenant may keep and use on the premises the following liquid-filled furniture:

    ☐ Waterbed described as:_____

    _____

    ☐ Other:_____

2. Landlord acknowledges receipt of $_____ as an additional security deposit, to be used to offset any expenses or losses caused to the landlord by the furniture.

    2.1 Within 21 days after removal of the furniture the security deposit shall be refunded to Tenant with an itemization of its disposition.

3. Landlord acknowledges receipt of $_____ as an additional fee to cover administrative costs incurred due to this agreement.

4. Tenant agrees:

    4.1 To maintain an insurance policy on the furniture for no less than $100,000 to cover property damage, naming landlord as an additional insured.

    a. To cause Landlord to receive at least 10 days prior written notice of cancellation or non-renewal of the insurance policy.

    b. To accept responsibility for property damage caused by the furniture should the policy expire unrenewed.

    4.2 To install the furniture according to manufacturer specifications, to operate properly all heaters and safety items, and to dispose of the liquid in a safe and sanitary manner.

    a. To give Landlord 24 hours notice of intent to install, move or remove the furniture.

    b. To provide Landlord with a written installation receipt stating the installer's name, address, and place of business when the furniture is installed, moved or removed by anyone other than Tenant.

    4.3 To strictly abide by the maintenance and safety precautions specified in the owner's manual supplied by the manufacturer of the furniture.

    4.4 Landlord may enter Tenant's residence on 24 hours notice to inspect the furniture to ensure it is being properly maintained.

    a. On lack of tenant's reasonable care and maintenance of the furniture Landlord may serve Tenant with a Three-day Notice to Perform or Quit regarding correction of the deficient care and maintenance or the removal of the furniture.

5. Other conditions: _____

6. Landlord's failure to enforce these conditions does not waive his right to an insurance claim.

I agree to the terms stated above.	I agree to the terms stated above.
Date:_____, 20_____	Date:_____, 20_____
Landlord: _____	Tenant: _____
Signature: _____	Signature: _____

FORM 564   10-00   ©2003 **first tuesday**, P.O. BOX 20069 RIVERSIDE, CA 92516 (800) 794-0494

Yes! Any damage resulting from the waterbed which is not covered by an insurance policy is the responsibility of the tenant. The landlord has no obligation to procure coverage even though he has authority to do so on the tenant's failure to provide coverage.

Further, if for some reason the tenant's waterbed liability policy is cancelled, expires or is not renewed, the tenant is obligated to give the landlord a ten-day notice of cancellation or nonrenewal of the insurance policy. [CC §1940.5(a)]

The notice is automatically given to the landlord by the insurer if the landlord is an additional named insured on the waterbed policy — as the landlord should be.

Installation and care of the waterbed

It is the tenant's responsibility to ensure the waterbed is properly installed and maintained.

The tenant must give the property manager 24 hours' notice if he intends to move, install or remove a waterbed.

If anyone other than the tenant installs the bed, specifically the manufacturer, a retailer or a moving company, the tenant must provide the landlord with a written receipt that contains the installer's name, address and place of business. [CC §1940.5(c)]

To ensure safety at all times, the tenant must comply with the manufacturer's specifications for proper use of the bed. [CC §1940.5(e)]

When a landlord suspects the tenant is not meeting the provisions in the waterbed addendum, he has the right to enter the residence to inspect the waterbed and ensure it is being maintained properly.

However, he must give the tenant a 24-hour notice of entry before his inspection. [CC §§1940.5(f); 1954; see **first tuesday** Form 567; see Chapter 3]

The landlord may give the tenant a 3-day notice to either comply with installation and maintenance standards or remove the bed from the premises (or vacate) if:

- the landlord finds the waterbed is not being properly maintained; or

- the waterbed has not been properly installed. [CC §1940.5(f)]

The landlord may serve a 3-day notice to perform or quit on the tenant, as long as the tenant is **given the option** of either curing the installation defects or removing the bed as performance in lieu of vacating. If the tenant fails to perform either alternative within three days, he must vacate the premises. [See Chapter 19]

In lieu of the notice to perform or quit, the landlord could serve an "advisory" letter giving notice to perform.

However, the landlord would have to later serve a 3-day notice to perform or quit should the tenant fail to either repair or remove the bed.

Finally, the landlord does not lose his right to make an insurance claim if he fails to exercise any of his rights to police the tenant's care and maintenance of the waterbed. [CC §1940.5(h)]

Chapter 38

Adults-only policies prohibited in housing

This chapter discusses unfair discriminatory practices in renting residential units based on familial status, and the tenant's remedies.

Familial status is protected

The landlord of a residential property cannot adopt an "adults-only" or "no children" policy no matter the number of units located on the property.

To comply with state and federal anti-discrimination laws, a landlord's screening policies must not serve to prevent children from living in his rentals, called *familial status*. A screening policy must be children neutral, as it must also be for race, religion, nationality, etc.

Rental policies or conduct that work to exclude pregnant women or families that contain one or more children under the age of 18 discriminate against a tenant based on *familial status*. Thus, residential "adults-only" policies are unlawful.

An individual submitting an application to rent cannot be discriminated against if the individual is the parent, legal custodian or a person authorized by written permission to take care of a child. [Calif. Government Code §12955.2; 42 United States Code §3602(k); see **first tuesday** Form 302]

Also, the *Federal Fair Housing Act (FFHA)* prohibits a landlord from using rental policies that discriminate against a tenant based on his familial status. [42 USC §3602]

Also, the *California Fair Employment and Housing Act (FEHA)* prohibits landlords from using discriminatory rental policies to avoid renting to a tenant based on familial status. [Gov C §12955(k)]

Additionally, the California *Unruh Civil Rights Act* prohibits a *business establishment* from discriminating in the rental of housing based on a tenant's age, unless the property is qualified for senior housing. [Calif. Civil Code §51.2(a)]

Each of these schemes provides a variety of remedies and recoveries for a tenant who, since he resides with a child, has been discriminated against by a landlord.

Discrimination in the rental of housing based on familial status violates all three acts, and, for a landlord, property manager or resident manager, can result in civil liability and civil penalties.

Discrimination prohibited

Consider a landlord who owns a two-bedroom residential unit which he rents. The unit is vacant and is advertised for rent in the local newspaper.

A prospective tenant contacts the landlord regarding the rental unit.

Before agreeing to show the tenant the property, the landlord asks the tenant how many people in his family will occupy the unit (an inquiry which may or may not be made for discriminatory reasons).

The prospective tenant informs the landlord his spouse and child will occupy the unit with him.

The landlord informs the tenant he does not qualify. The landlord explains families with children increase his maintenance costs by causing excessive wear and tear to the property.

The tenant is forced to look elsewhere for housing.

Has the landlord unlawfully discriminated against the tenant by refusing to rent the tenant a single-family residence based on his familial status as including a child?

Yes! A residential landlord unlawfully discriminates against a potential tenant when he refuses to rent a residential unit to a tenant based solely on the fact a child will occupy the unit — a violation of FEHA. [Gov C §12955(a), (k)]

Also, FEHA prohibits a residential landlord from inquiring, as part of the screening process, whether a prospective tenant even has children, if the reason is to exclude families. [Gov C §12955(b)]

However, a landlord who targets families with children is not necessarily acting in a prohibited discriminatory manner when he inquires about children. He may be intending to push advantages his property offers to tenants who have children, such as playground facilities or day care.

Thus, an inquiry about children can be made if a discriminatory intent does not exist to exclude children.

Whether or not an inquiry into familial status was made with discriminatory intent is shown by the landlord's subsequent behavior, i.e., refusal to rent, a higher security deposit, an increase in rent to anyone with children or the "steering" of families to other units or facilities.

The Unruh Act and the FFHA

The Unruh Act prohibits a *business establishment* from discriminating in the rental of housing based on an occupant's age. [CC §51.2(a)]

Owners of apartment complexes and condominium associations fall under the definition of a business establishment for purposes of unlawful discrimination. [CC §51.2(b)]

Note — Landlords of one-to-four units fall under FEHA and are likely to fall under the Unruh Act since the term business establishment as used by the Unruh Act is meant to be applied in the broadest reasonable manner. [**O'Connor** v. **Village Green Owners Association** (1983) 33 C3d 790]

However, California's Unruh Act does not control mobilehome park owners. [**Schmidt** v. **Superior Court** (1989) 48 C3d 370]

However, a mobilehome park owner who discriminates against tenants based on familial status violates federal law and California's FEHA, unless the mobilehome park is operated as qualified senior citizen housing. [CC §798.76; Gov C §12955.9; 42 USC §3607(b)]

Discrimination based on familial status does not occur under any law when the housing qualifies as senior citizen housing. [CC §§51.2; 51.10; Gov C §12955.9; 42 USC §3607(b)(1)]

Rental discrimination under the FFHA

Landlords, property managers and resident managers regularly and properly engage in discrimination for **legitimate purposes** when screening potential tenants for their rental units.

For example, a potential tenant's income, credit rating and rental and employment history are carefully considered for creditworthiness and an analysis of the landlord's risk of lost rent before a unit is rented to the tenant.

In economic downturns, landlords tend to be more lenient in their rental practices by lowering rental deposits and rates, and relaxing credit requirements to keep their rental units full. They tend to accept less-qualified tenants than they would accept in better economic times. In other words, landlords become less (or more) discriminatory when analyzing creditworthiness and risk from time to time.

However, when the real estate rental market turns up, landlords become more selective in the screening process as to the extent of risk they will take with a tenant.

Landlords raise rental rates and tighten up credit standards during a strong demand for units. Standards must be equally applied to all prospects. However, some landlords may overstep the law by cultivating an exclusive living atmosphere desired by older, more wealthy tenants, such as criteria that tend to prevent families with children from renting.

Prohibited discriminatory rental practices toward families include not only the refusal to rent, but the use of different rental or credit analyses or qualification criteria between competing tenants, such as:

using different income standards;

applying a different credit analysis;

using different rental approval procedures; or

- imposing different rental charges. [24 Code of Federal Regulations §100.60]

Thus, a landlord cannot require tenants with children to have a higher family income or a better credit rating than tenants without children.

Also, a landlord who rents to a tenant with children cannot include different terms in the lease or rental agreements, such as requiring higher security deposits or rental rates. [24 CFR §100.65(b)]

Any rental practice or policy that has the effect of *discouraging* or *preventing* families with children from renting a dwelling violates federal and state discrimination laws. [**Marina Point, Ltd.** v. **Wolfson** (1982) 30 C3d 721]

Discriminatory intent not required

A landlord cannot refuse to rent to families with children or adopt rental policies that **result in discrimination** against families with children. [24 CFR §100.60(b)]

Consider a landlord of an apartment complex who has a policy that limits occupancy of units to two persons. Each unit has two bedrooms.

A prospective tenant contacts the property manager of the apartment complex. The tenant intends to rent a unit for himself, his spouse and child.

The property manager advises the prospective tenant an application will not be processed even though units are available, since the complex has a policy that limits occupancy of each unit to two persons.

The prospective tenant is not shown any of the units in the complex.

The tenant files an action against the landlord to recover money losses incurred in his extended search for housing, claiming the landlord violated the Fair Housing Act since he refused to rent a two-bedroom apartment to a family of three.

The landlord claims his two-or-less occupancy restriction was not discriminatory since the restriction was even-handedly applied to all rental applicants with the intent of preventing excessive wear to the units in order to reduce maintenance costs and increase the property's value.

Is the landlord liable for the costs incurred by the tenant to find new housing since the landlord's refusal to rent was based on a two-tenant occupancy restriction?

Yes! The landlord's occupancy restriction limiting use of a two-bedroom residential unit to two persons automatically results in discrimination against families with children.

An intent on the part of the landlord to discriminate against children is not necessary for the landlord to violate the Fair Housing Act if the application of an **occupancy restriction** discriminates against families with children. [**Fair Housing Council of Orange County, Inc.** v. **Ayres** (1994) 855 F.Supp. 315]

While an occupancy restriction limiting the number of persons who may reside in the unit is enforceable if applied equally to all tenants, the restriction becomes an unlawful discriminatory housing practice when it has a *negative effect* on the availability of suitable rental units for families with children. [**United States** v. **Badgett** (8th Cir. 1992) 976 F2d 1176]

Number-of-occupants restriction

Now consider a landlord who owns several single-family residences which he operates as rentals.

The landlord imposes a five-person occupancy restriction on some of his rentals.

On one rental unit he has a four-person restriction since it has a small yard and 1,200 square feet of living space which includes two small bedrooms, a den opening onto the living room, a large kitchen and one bathroom.

The unit becomes vacant and is advertised for rent by the landlord's property manager.

A prospective tenant is shown the rental. The tenant completes a rental application, makes a deposit and passes the credit screening.

The property manager informs the landlord he has located a tenant for the unit consisting of a family of five.

The landlord advises the property manager he will only rent this unit to a family of four and rejects the application since the family is too large to occupy the property.

The tenant files a complaint with the Secretary of HUD claiming the landlord discriminated against him since he had children.

The landlord claims the occupancy restriction is not intended to discriminate against families with children, but is a business decision necessary to prevent excessive wear and tear to property not designed to accommodate a family larger than three or four members.

Is the landlord liable for the tenant's losses and the civil penalty because of his occupancy restriction?

No! The landlord must only show his occupancy restriction does not unreasonably limit or exclude families with children.

The landlord's occupancy restriction based on the size of the residence is a reasonable means of preventing the dilapidation of the property. [**Pfaff** v. **U.S. Department of Housing and Urban Development** (1996) 88 F3d 739]

The landlord can properly impose a reasonable numerical occupancy restriction since the purpose of limiting the number of occupants is to preserve the economic value of a property designed to house fewer occupants, occupants which may include families with children.

Chapter 39

Residential rent control

This chapter describes the nature of local rent control and the state phase-out rules.

Police power and rent control

A city's or county's ability to establish rent control comes from its "police power."

Police power is the basis for enacting local ordinances such as zoning, traffic, health and safety regulations, and rent control, as long as the ordinances enacted are for the public's benefit. [Calif. Constitution Article XI §7]

To be valid, rent control ordinances must be reasonably related to the purpose of preventing excessive rents and maintaining the availability of existing housing. No case has yet found an ordinance lacking in purpose. [**Santa Monica Beach, Ltd.** v. **Superior Court** (1999) 19 C4th 952]

Application for rent increases

Before increasing rent on residential rentals that are located within rent control communities, a prudent property manager must determine:

- Is this rental unit subject to any rent control ordinances?

- Does the unit fall within an exemption?

- What type of rent adjustment does the ordinance allow?

Units covered by controls

Frequently rent control ordinances do not cover all the rental units in the city. Examples of the types of property which may be exempt from a rent control ordinance in a particular city are:

- owner-occupied buildings;

- single-family residences and duplexes;

- luxury apartments;

- condominiums; or

- substantially rehabilitated buildings.

Rent control ordinances may also exempt newly constructed units from regulations to stimulate construction of additional housing.

Types of rent control

Despite the complexity and variety of rent control ordinances, two main types exist:

- strict rent control; and

- vacancy decontrol.

Under **strict rent control**, rent increases are limited across the board. The restrictions on rent amounts apply to landlords renting to either new or existing tenants. Even when a tenant vacates and a new one moves in, the rent restrictions apply to the unit.

The more common type of rent regulation is **vacancy decontrol**. Under vacancy decontrol, the rent ceilings apply only to existing tenants as long as they choose to remain in occupancy of the unit. When the tenant vacates, the landlord may raise the rent and charge the new tenant market level rents.

Rent adjustment standards

Once the manager determines a unit is governed by a rent control ordinance, the manager must then determine the type of rent adjustments allowed, *general* or *individual*.

Under a **general adjustment**, rents in all rental units in the city are adjusted using:

- an amount tied to an economic index, such as the Consumer Price Index (CPI);

- a maximum annual percentage rate increase; or

- an amount determined by the rent control board itself.

However, in most rent control cities, a landlord or property manager may also seek an **individual adjustment** from the rent control board. Usually, the individual adjustment is determined at a hearing before a rent control board.

The adjustments are sought when the general adjustment fails to provide a fair return on the residential property.

Rent increases may be based on:

- cash flow requirements to cover mortgage payments and operating expenses;

- a percentage of the net operating income; or

- a set return on value.

Also, almost all rent control cities allow individual adjustments for capital improvements made to upgrade the units.

Reasonable expenses recovered is rent

When a rent control ordinance bases rent increases for existing tenants on net operating income, the owner's operating expenses include fees and costs incurred by the owner for professional services he used to seek the rent increases. [Calif. Civil Code §1947.15(b)]

Also, reasonable fees incurred by the owner in successfully obtaining a **judicial reversal** of an adverse administrative rent control decision on a petition for upward adjustment in rents will be paid by the public agency that issued the adverse decision, not by the tenant. Unrecovered fees cannot be used to calculate the net operating income on the property. [CC §1947.15(c)]

If the owner's appeal of an adverse administrative decision is frivolous, the public agency will be awarded its reasonable expenses, including attorney fees, incurred to defend against the owner's action. [CC §1947.15(h)(2)]

When an owner's petition for a rent increase is without merit and the owner is assisted by attorneys or consultants, the tenant will be awarded a reduction in the rent to compensate for the costs incurred by the tenant to defend against the owner's petition. [CC §1947.15(h)(1)]

Eviction restrictions

In addition to restricting rent increases, rent control ordinances also restrict the landlord's **ability to evict** existing tenants.

In communities free of rent control, the landlord does not need to give a reason for serving a notice on a month-to-month tenant. [CC §827]

Conversely, in rent control communities, the landlord may only evict a tenant for just cause. Valid reasons for terminating a lease or rental agreement are set forth in the rent control ordinances.

Common situations that justify termination include:

- breach of the lease or rental agreement by the tenant;

- failure to pay rent;

- creating a nuisance; or

- owner occupancy of the unit.

Most other reasons (or no reason) for termination are prohibited or severely limited.

Phase-out of rent control

When a city's rent control laws conflict with state law, state law controls.

The Legislature enacted rent control phase-out measures to provide a more economically efficient statewide housing policy than provided by local rent control.

The economics of local rent control have generally debilitated investment in new and existing apartments, depriving local markets of necessary housing.

Thus, because state law overrides local rent control ordinances, landlords of residential rental property may establish rent for each unit which:

- was a newly constructed unit exempt from rent control on or **before** February 1, 1995;

- was issued a certificate of occupancy **after** February 1, 1995; or

- is a separately described parcel of real estate (single-family residence or condominium unit) or a unit in a community apartment project, stock operative or limited-equity housing cooperative. [CC §1954.52(a)]

However, consider a landlord of a residential rental unit that has a separate legal description from the title to any other lot or unit and was subject to a rent control ordinance on January 1, 1995.

The unit is now occupied by a tenant who was an occupant on January 1, 1999 under a lease or rental agreement entered into on or after January 1, 1996. Here, the landlord may establish rental rates for the existing tenant without concern for rent control. [CC §1954.52(a)(3)(C)(i)]

Also, the landlord of a single-family residence (SFR) or condominium unit can set rental rates for all new tenancies if the **prior tenant's occupancy** was entered into on or **before** December 31, 1995. [CC §1954.52(a)(3)(C)(ii)]

However, the landlord of a SFR or condo unit may not set the rental rates even though the previous tenant occupied before 1996, if:

- the previous tenancy was terminated by a notice to vacate or a 30-day notice of change of rental terms; or

- if it is a condominium unit that has not yet been sold by the subdivider. [CC §1954.52(a)(3)(B)]

Further, when any residential tenant vacates (other than on a notice to vacate from the landlord), abandons or is evicted, the landlord may establish the rental rate without concern for rent control.

A landlord who maintains a unit that has been previously cited for violations of health, fire or building codes, may not increase the rent charged to new tenants if the violation is not corrected at least six months before the unit is vacated. [CC §§1954.52(d); 1954.53(f)]

Further, the landlord may not set new rental rates if the landlord has contracted with a local agency to establish low income housing. [CC §1954.52(b)]

State law allowing landlords to set rental rates in rent control communities does not apply to rental units that were sublet under a rental agreement entered into before January 1, 1996. [CC §1954.53(d)]

Demolition of residential rentals

A landlord who wants to demolish a rental building, whether or not it is under rent control, must apply to a local governmental agency for a demolition permit.

A landlord is entitled to demolish his unit since he cannot be compelled to continue to provide residential rentals if he chooses to *withdraw* his property from the market. [Calif. Government Code §7060(a)]

However, before applying for a demolition permit, the residential landlord must first give a written notice of his intent to apply for a permit to all tenants in the structure he desires to demolish. [CC §1940.6(a)(2)]

A residential landlord who has applied for a demolition permit must give a written notice to prospective tenants of his application for a demolition permit before he accepts an application to rent, a screening or other fee, or enters into a lease or rental agreement, whichever comes first. [CC §1940.6(a)(1)]

The notice of intent to demolish the residential rental structure to be given to the existing and prospective tenants includes the *earliest possible approximation* of the date the demolition is to occur and the *approximate date* the tenants' occupancy will be terminated by the landlord. [CC §1940.6(b)]

SECTION H

Lender
Considerations

Chapter 40

Attornment clauses in nonresidential leases

This chapter discusses attornment, subordination and nondisturbance clauses in nonresidential leases, and the use of these clauses by landlords, tenants and lenders to later alter the priorities of leases and trust deeds.

Altering priorities for lenders

A lender holds a recorded trust deed lien on the fee ownership interest in nonresidential income-producing real estate.

The trust deed contains a due-on provision that states the owner may not sell, lease or encumber the secured property without the prior written consent of the lender, also called a *transfer clause* or an *alienation clause*.

The lender has advised the owner he will consent to new leases (as required by the due-on clause) on the condition the leases contain an *attornment clause* and a *lender subordination clause*.

A tenant enters into a lease with the landlord which contains an attornment clause. The lease is approved by the lender.

The **attornment clause** states the tenant will recognize a third party purchaser of the property at a foreclosure sale as the new landlord under the lease if the purchaser exercises his right under the attornment clause to enforce the lease. [See Fig. 1]

Later, the owner defaults on the first trust deed. The lender notices a foreclosure sale and acquires the property with a credit bid.

After the lender acquires the property, the lender mails a written notice to the tenant which states:

- the lender is the new landlord **under the lease**; and

- the tenant is to pay rent to the lender.

The tenant does not pay rent and vacates the premises.

The lender claims the tenant is required to accept the lender as the new landlord under the attornment clause in the tenant's lease since the lender purchased the property at the foreclosure sale and declared himself to be the landlord under the lease.

The tenant claims the attornment clause is unenforceable since the lease that contained the clause was eliminated by the lender's foreclosure sale.

Is the tenant required to accept the lender as the new landlord and perform under the lease?

Yes! While the leasehold interest held by the tenant was eliminated from title by the foreclosure sale, the lease agreement remains enforceable and the tenant is required to recognize — attorn to — the lender as the **substitute landlord** under the lease.

The lease is *restored and reattached* to title after the foreclosure sale when the lender (or other purchaser at the foreclosure sale) exercises the right given under the attornment clause to enforce the lease as the new substitute landlord. [**Miscione** v. **Barton Development Company** (1997) 52 CA4th 1320]

Fig. 1

Attornment clause

In the event Tenant's estate is exhausted by a disposition of Landlord's estate, Tenant will recognize the new owner who acquires Landlord's estate as Landlord under this lease should the new owner, within 30 days of acquisition, notify Tenant in writing of the new owner's election to be substituted as Landlord under this lease.

The attornment clause contracts around the permanent elimination of a junior leasehold interest on completion of a foreclosure sale by a senior trust deed lender. The clause allows the purchaser at the lender's foreclosure sale to restore the *extinguished* lease as though it were unaffected by the foreclosure sale.

Priority on foreclosure

A tenant's lease, whether or not recorded, has **priority on title** over an interest in the property held by a third party, such as a trust deed lien or abstract of judgment, when:

- the lease is **recorded** before the other interest (a trust deed) is recorded or, if unrecorded, is actually known to the third party holding the other interest [Calif. Civil Code §1214]; or

- the tenant takes **possession** before the other interest (a trust deed) is recorded or the tenant's right to possession is actually known to the third party holding the other interest. [**Gates Rubber Company** v. **Ulman** (1989) 214 CA3d 356]

For example, a trust deed recorded junior in time to a tenant's occupancy of the secured real estate is foreclosed upon. The tenant's leasehold interest, being senior in time, is undisturbed by the foreclosure — the tenancy held by the tenant under the lease remains in full effect.

Thus, the buyer at the foreclosure sale of a junior trust deed acquires title "subject to" the lease. Since the lease has priority, the buyer must perform the landlord's obligations under the lease if the tenant seeks to enforce them.

Now consider a lease which is entered into after a trust deed or judgment lien is recorded on the property.

Later, the trust deed or judgment lien is foreclosed.

Since the nonresidential tenant's leasehold interest in title is junior in time, and thus subordinate to the lien, the tenant's leasehold is wiped out by the foreclosure of the trust deed lien.

On elimination of a junior lease by a foreclosure sale of the premises, the tenant loses his right to possession of the premises. [**Hohn** v. **Riverside County Flood Control and Water Conservation District** (1964) 228 CA2d 605]

After foreclosure by the senior lienholder, the tenant's continued use and possession of the property is an unlawful detainer (UD) and the tenant can be evicted. A 3-day notice to quit due to foreclosure is required to be served (and to expire) before a UD action can be filed and the occupant, should he remain in possession, be evicted. [See **first tuesday** Form 578]

Altering the priorities

A tenant can agree in a lease agreement to allow the landlord or the secured lender to **act unilaterally** in the future to alter the priority of the tenant's lease and the lender's trust deed liens on the property. [**Dover Mobile Estates** v. **Fiber Form Products, Inc.** (1990) 220 CA3d 1494]

Nonresidential leases often contain boilerplate provisions, such as an attornment clause, a lender subordination clause, a future subordination clause and a nondisturbance clause, all of which relate to the priority of the lease as against trust deeds, present and future.

The *attornment clause* allows an owner-by-foreclosure to unilaterally avoid the automatic elimination and thus the unenforceability of a junior lease eliminated by the foreclosure sale.

The *lender subordination clause* gives a trust deed lender the right to unilaterally subordinate the lender's trust deed to a junior lease by written notice to the tenant. Thus, the lease would not be wiped out by the later foreclosure sale of the lender's subordinated trust deed since the lease would then have priority.

Under a *future subordination clause*, the tenant agrees to subordinate his leasehold interest to a trust deed to be recorded in the future. Here, the tenant remains involved since he must sign a *specific subordination agreement* to give the trust deed recording priority to his leasehold.

The *nondisturbance clause* is coupled with the future subordination clause. It entitles the tenant to a signed writing from the new trust deed lender stating the lease will remain in effect for its full term in spite of the fact the tenant is signing a specific subordination agreement.

Thus, the tenant will be restored with the rights it would lose by a subordination and be able to enforce the lease against the new lender.

By exercising the lender's rights under the *due-on clause* in its trust deed, a lender is able to control the terms of all future leasing of the property, except for those leases with a term of three years or less.

As a condition for the lender to give consent to each lease entered into by the landlord, a knowledgeable lender will require the landlord's leases to include both a lender subordination clause and an attornment clause.

The attornment clause and foreclosure

Attornment is the tenant's acknowledgement of the purchaser at a foreclosure sale under a senior trust deed as a *substitute landlord* who may elect to enforce the tenant's lease.

To enforce a wiped-out lease, the owner-by-foreclosure notifies the tenant he has elected to be the substitute landlord under the tenant's lease. The new owner need not do so, which then leaves the tenant with no interest in the property.

A nonresidential landlord has good financial justification to include an attornment clause in a lease.

Should a senior trust deed lender foreclose, it is essential for the landlord to maintain the property's value and reduce the potential of a deficiency judgment. [See Fig. 1]

A financially advantageous lease, enforceable by new owners after a foreclosure, will help maintain the value of the property.

On the other hand, if a financially advantageous lease does not contain an attornment clause, the property's market value will be lower than it would be had the owner-by-foreclosure been able to enforce the lease.

If an owner-by-foreclosure elects to enforce a lease containing an attornment clause, the lease remains in full effect for the remainder of its term.

Thus, the owner-by-foreclosure who makes the attornment election becomes the substitute landlord and must perform the obligations of the landlord under the lease. [Miscione, *supra*]

Before the foreclosing lender or other purchaser at a foreclosure sale substitutes himself as the successor landlord, he must consider which leases will generate rents at or above market rates. To help make the attornment decision, the new owner should first:

- obtain the equivalent of a Tenant Estoppel Certificate (TEC) from each tenant to discover any breach of their lease by the prior landlord [See Chapter 41]; and

- inspect the property to be assured its physical condition is acceptable to the new owner.

Subleases and attornment

Leases used by landlords to lease properties to a master tenant who will in turn sublet portions of the property to occupants of separate spaces, called subtenants, contain restraint-on-alienation clauses, called transfer restrictions or assignment and subletting prohibitions.

Thus, the landlord has control over the content of the sublease agreement because the landlord's consent is needed by the tenant in order to sublet. When consenting, the landlord should require an attornment provision in the sublease. Should the landlord ever terminate the master or ground lease on the property and, in the process, eliminate the sublease and the subtenant's right to possession, the landlord may retain the sublease under the attornment clause.

As the fee owner of the subleased premises (and the third party who may become the subtenant's landlord under the sublease by attornment), the landlord electing to enforce the sublease is acknowledged by the subtenant as the substitute landlord (sublessor) on the sublease; namely, the subtenant will continue paying rent as agreed, but to the new landlord.

No assurance of continued occupancy

Conversely, an attornment clause does not also give the tenant the election to enforce the lease against the owner-by-foreclosure. The attornment agreed to by the tenant to recognize a third party as his landlord under the lease is not initiated until an election to enforce the clause is made by the owner-by-foreclosure.

Thus, a tenant who enters into a lease containing an attornment clause, which is junior to a lender's trust deed, has no assurance the lease will be restored after a foreclosure sale.

Yet, tenants agree to an attornment clause as a provision in their lease, believing the clause states the obvious — the tenant will perform on the lease for anyone who becomes the new owner of the property. The tenant views it as a nondisturbance agreement with the (third party) lender, but it is not. The lender is not a party to the lease agreement.

However, when a junior lease is eliminated at a foreclosure sale, the new owner is unlikely to elect to enforce the lease if:

- the new owner acquired the property to occupy it as a user; or

- the rents due under the lease are significantly less than the rents available in the market.

Further, a tenant will regret the inclusion of an attornment clause if rents called for in the lease exceed market rates at the time of foreclosure, or if the location or premises are no longer desirable for the tenant when a foreclosure sale occurs and the attornment clause is enforced restoring the lease.

All these events typically come together during economically depressed times for all involved.

For a tenant to avoid the unilateral adverse economic impact of an attornment clause, the tenant, on entering into a long-term lease containing the clause, should:

- obtain an abstract of title or lessee's policy of title insurance to ascertain the trust deeds and other liens of record and their effect on the tenant;

- obtain a beneficiaries statement on the loans/liens of record;

- record a Request for Notice of Default; and

- record a Request for Notice of Delinquency on the lender. [See **first tuesday** Form 412]

With the information from these documents, the tenant can take steps to protect his interest should a default occur on senior liens or the ground lease obligations of his landlord, long before any foreclosure sale occurs.

Notifying the tenant

A lender or other purchaser who acquires a property at a foreclosure sale **elects to enforce** a lease under its attornment clause by giving the tenant a written notice which:

- states the owner-by-foreclosure is exercising his right to enforce the lease under the attornment clause; and

- instructs the tenant to make all future rent payments due under the lease to the purchaser. [Miscione, *supra*]

A specific time period should be stated in the attornment clause within which the owner-by-foreclosure must notify the tenant of his election to enforce the attornment agreement, such as within 30 days after the foreclosure sale. [See Fig. 1]

The new owner loses the right to enforce the attornment clause if:

- no time period for enforcing recognition of the new owner as landlord is specified in the clause; and

- the new owner does not elect to enforce the lease within a *reasonable period of time*.

No right to occupy

Should the owner-by-foreclosure choose not to enforce a nonresidential lease containing an attornment clause, a 3-day notice to quit due to foreclosure must be served on the tenant if the new owner intends to evict the occupant based on an unlawful detainer of the premises. [Calif. Code of Civil Procedure §1161a(b); see **first tuesday** Form 578]

The 3-day notice should be served as soon as possible to avoid intervention from the landlord or property manager, which could be construed as an enforcement of the lease (by attornment) or the establishment of an unintended periodic tenancy.

For example, a new owner who elects not to enforce the lease should not accept any advance rent payments from the tenant unless a new written rental agreement or lease is entered into with the tenant.

Accepting rent payments called for in the eliminated lease indicates the new owner intends to accept the lease under its attornment clause, regardless of the new owner's actual intent. [**Rubin** v. **Los Angeles Federal Savings and Loan Association** (1984) 159 CA3d 292]

Should the owner-by-foreclosure accept rent payments from a tenant when an attornment clause does not exist in the eliminated lease, a periodic tenancy is created. Neither the tenant nor the new owner can enforce the lease. [**Colyear** v. **Tobriner** (1936) 7 C2d 735]

Lender subordination clauses

In addition to requiring an attornment clause in leases entered into by the owner after a trust deed is recorded, knowledgeable lenders holding trust deeds on nonresidential income property require the leases to include a *lender subordination clause*. The lender subordination clause allows the lender to elect, at any time during the life of its trust deed, to subordinate his trust deed lien to leases the landlord enters into with tenants after the trust deed recorded. [See Fig. 2]

A lease that contains both a lender subordination clause and a tenant attornment clause allows the lender the maximum flexibility for preserving an advantageous lease by either:

- electing to subordinate his trust deed to the lease **before the foreclosure sale**; or

- **completing a foreclosure sale** and electing to enforce the lease.

Some attornment clauses are worded to state the lender must acquire the premises "subject to" the lease at the time of the foreclosure sale.

However, while an attornment clause in a lease may literally state the lender is to acquire the property "subject to" the lease, the lender cannot be required by the attornment clause wording to automatically elect to subordinate his trust deed to the lease after the foreclosure sale. The lender did not agree to the terms of the junior lease, even if the lender reviews it and waives his due-on clause by consenting to the lease.

When the lender notifies the tenant before foreclosure of his election to subordinate his trust deed lien to the tenant's lease, the election **need not be recorded** to be enforced. The change in priority only affects the lender, the tenant and their successors, not third parties. [CC §1217]

A trust deed that becomes senior to a lease by the lender's election to subordinate prior to foreclosure gives the lease priority over the trust deed. Thus, the lease is **not eliminated from title** by the foreclosure sale.

If the lease is not wiped out at the foreclosure sale because of the lender's prior election to subordinate, a later election under the attornment clause after foreclosure becomes unnecessary. Thus, the owner-by-foreclosure acquires the property "subject to" the lease which had priority over the trust deed.

After the foreclosure sale, by either a prior election by the lender to subordinate or a later election to have the tenant attorn to the new owner, the lease becomes enforceable by both the tenant and the new landlord. [Miscione, *supra*]

Electing to subordinate

Now consider a lender who holds a first trust deed on nonresidential real estate.

The owner then leases the property. The lease contains a lender subordination clause since the lender required it as a condition for waiver of the due-on clause in his trust deed.

During the term of the lease, the owner defaults on the lender's trust deed. The lender records a notice of default (NOD), initiating a trustee's foreclosure sale.

The lender has the property appraised and discovers the rent due under the tenant's lease exceeds current prevailing market rental rates.

The lender hears of negotiations between the owner and the tenant to modify the lease. The lender does not want the lease to be altered by the landlord prior to foreclosure and an attornment.

The lender serves written notice on the tenant of his election to subordinate his trust deed to the tenant's lease, thus altering priorities.

Fig. 2

Lender subordination clause

Any master lessor or holder of a lien on the leased premises may elect to subordinate its interest in the premises to this lease by service of written notice on the tenant of the election, and thereafter the lease shall have priority regardless of the priorities set by law.

For the same economic reasons which cause the lender to preserve the lease, the tenant wants out of the lease.

After notice of the subordination, the tenant and the landlord modify the lease to permit the tenant to terminate the lease at any time on 30 days written notice.

The trustee's sale is held and the lender acquires the property.

The lender notifies the tenant the lender is now the owner of the property and all rent payments under the lease are to be made to the lender.

The tenant notifies the lender in writing of his election to terminate the lease.

The lender claims the tenant cannot terminate the lease since the modification agreement, but not the lease, was eliminated by the foreclosure sale.

Can the tenant terminate the lease under the conditions stated in the lease modification entered into prior to the owner's loss of the property?

No! The original lease agreement remained unaffected by the foreclosure sale since the lender elected to subordinate the trust deed to the lease prior to the modification. However, the agreement modifying the lease became unenforceable by the tenant as against the owner-by-foreclosure since the modification agreement was junior in time to the subordination of the trust deed to the lease.

Thus, the modification, but not the lease, was eliminated by the lender's foreclosure. [**In re 240 North Brand Partners, Ltd.** (9th Cir. BAP 1996) 200 BR 653]

By subordination of the lender's trust deed to the lease, the lender acted to maintain the property's value based on rents under the lease. By subordinating, the lender was able to avoid the effect of any later modification of the lease prior to foreclosing and acquiring ownership at the trustee's sale.

Also, as with the lender, the landlord would prefer the property to remain encumbered by a financially advantageous lease after a **judicial foreclosure** to avoid a deficiency in the value needed to cover the loan.

The value of the property is maintained by a long-term lease during general declines in property values brought about by the effects of a depressed real estate market and a foreclosure sale.

Thus, the chance of a deficiency remaining after a judicial foreclosure is reduced for both the lender and the landlord, but the tenant must pay.

Future subordination clauses

A **landlord's ability** to further encumber or refinance property during the term of a lease is greatly diminished unless the lease contains a *future subordination clause*. [See Fig. 3]

Like the attornment clause and lender subordination clause, a future subordination clause is an agreement to alter priorities on title.

Under a future subordination clause, the tenant agrees he will subordinate his leasehold interest and the lease agreement to a trust deed to be recorded by the landlord sometime in the future.

In other words, the tenant agrees to place his leasehold interest in a lesser or worse position on title — whether or not his lease is recorded — than he enjoys at the time he enters into the lease. The tenant's leasehold will be subordinated to a new trust deed loan based on the terms of a new loan agreed to in the future subordination clause.

For a future subordination clause to be enforceable at the time the landlord arranges a new trust deed loan, the clause must state:

- the use of the loan proceeds, such as refinancing existing encumbrances or improving the property;

- the loan amount or loan-to-value ratio of the financing;

- the payment schedule;

- the interest rate; and

- the due date. [**Handy** v. **Gordon** (1967) 65 C2d 578]

Further, the clause must contain any other terms that might be unique to the future financing that would, if agreed to by the tenant, further impair the tenant's leasehold interest.

When the landlord later arranges financing for the property on terms within the parameters agreed to in the subordination clause, the tenant is obligated to sign a *specific subordination agreement*, a document required before a title company will insure the priority of the new trust deed over the tenant's leasehold interest.

However, the tenant may refuse to sign a subordination agreement if the financing terms are not substantially the same or within the parameters stated in the subordination clause.

The tenant has not agreed to accept a greater risk of loss for his leasehold interest than the risks established by the terms of the subordination clause in the lease.

Note — When the landlord wants to record a new trust deed to secure a loan and the tenant refuses to sign a specific subordination agreement, the landlord's primary recourse is to serve a 3-day notice to perform or quit. If *performance is not forthcoming, rather than evict, file an action against the tenant for declaratory relief and specific performance of the future subordination clause in the tenant's lease.*

Nondisturbance clauses

A nondisturbance clause gives the tenant the right to require the lender, as a condition for subordinating his lease to a new loan, to enter into a written agreement with the tenant. The clause states the lease will remain in effect for its full term after the subordination occurs, called a *nondisturbance agreement*.

A nondisturbance clause is only included in a lease if the lease also contains a future subordination clause. The tenant is the primary beneficiary of the nondisturbance clause.

A nondisturbance clause, when coupled with a poorly structured future subordination clause, is typically used by the landlord and leasing agents to avoid negotiating the terms of subordination with the tenant while hammering out the terms of the lease.

If the nondisturbance clause is included in a lease containing an enforceable future subordination clause, the tenant can refuse to sign a subordination agreement if the lender refuses to provide the tenant with a nondisturbance agreement, a serious problem for the landlord attempting to arrange financing.

Informed lenders are not likely to provide a tenant with a written nondisturbance agreement when making a loan to be secured by a first trust deed on property.

Fig. 3   *Excerpt from* **first tuesday** *Form 552 — Nonresidential Lease Agreement*

17. SUBORDINATION

    17.1 The Tenant agrees to subordinate to any new financing secured by the premises which does not exceed 80% loan-to-value ratio, interest of two percent over market with not less than a 15 year monthly amortization and five year due date.

A nondisturbance agreement **negates** the effect of the subordination agreement by reversing the priorities agreed to by subordinating the lease to the trust deed, sometimes referred to as a *self-destruct clause*.

The lease will not be truly subordinate to the lender's trust deed since the lender has agreed to recognize the continued existence of the lease after a foreclosure of the trust deed.

A knowledgeable landlord does not want a nondisturbance clause in his lease; he wants an enforceable future subordination clause.

Unlike the purpose of an attornment clause, the lease will not be eliminated by foreclosure and then restored by election of the owner-by-fore-closure; the nondisturbance agreement states the lease will remain in effect for its full term without regard to foreclosure.

Since the lease by agreement with the lender cannot be eliminated by foreclosure, it cannot also be junior to the trust deed.

Thus, a subordination of the lease to the trust deed never truly occurs because of the concurrent nondisturbance agreement.

Also, when a lender executes a nondisturbance agreement, an attornment clause serves no purpose, and like many clauses in a lease, becomes superfluous.

The tenant's leasehold interest when subject to a nondisturbance agreement remains undis-turbed and continuously enforceable by both the tenant and the new owner after the lender's foreclosure.

By entering into a nondisturbance agreement, the lender is **forced to become** the landlord under the lease should the lender foreclose and acquire the property.

However, a knowledgeable lender wants the choice afforded him by the lender's loan subordination and attornment clauses to accept or reject the lease either prior to or after the foreclosure.

Here, the landlord eliminates the need for a nondisturbance clause in a lease by negotiating an enforceable future subordination clause and outlining the parameters of a loan acceptable to both the landlord and the tenant when entering into the lease.

Chapter 41

Tenant Estoppel Certificates

This chapter explains the benefits landlords receive by including and using a Tenant Estoppel Certificate clause in lease agreements.

Protection for buyers and lenders

A real estate broker representing a landlord who wants to sell or refinance his income-producing property customarily prepares an annual property operating data (APOD) form. The completed APOD will be handed to prospective buyers and lenders to induce them to enter into a transaction with the landlord. [See **first tuesday** Form 352]

A thoughtfully prepared APOD provides buyers and lenders with a summary of financial information on the operating income and expenses generated by a property, as well as loans encumbering the property.

Buyers and lenders who rely on APOD figures should confirm the income and other leasing arrangements by conditioning the closing on their receipt and further approval of a signed *Tenant Estoppel Certificate* (TEC) from each occupant of the property. [See Form 598 accompanying this chapter]

The TEC details the **financial and possessory terms** of the lease, and whether the landlord and tenant have fully performed their obligations.

However, before the landlord can require a TEC to be signed and returned by the tenants to confirm the leasing arrangements, the lease must contain a Tenant Estoppel Certificate clause. [See Fig. 1; see **first tuesday** Form 552 §18]

The TEC clause calls for the tenant to:

- *sign and return* a TEC within a specific period of time after its receipt; or

- *waive his right* to contest its contents should the tenant fail to sign and return the TEC submitted for his signature.

The objective of the TEC is to confirm the current status of:

- rent schedules;

- security deposits;

- possessory and acquisition rights; and

- the responsibility for maintenance and other operating or carrying costs.

Fig. 1

Excerpt from **first tuesday** *Form 552 —*
Nonresidential Lease Agreement

18. TENANT ESTOPPEL CERTIFICATES:

    18.1   Within 10 days after notice, the Tenant will execute a certificate stating the existing terms of the lease to be provided to prospective buyers or lenders.

    18.2   Failure to deliver the certificate shall be conclusive evidence the information contained in it is correct.

Also, the TEC will reveal any option or first refusal rights held by the tenant to:

- extend or renew the lease;

- buy the property;

- lease other or additional space; or

- cancel the lease prematurely on payment of a fee.

Tenant response to a TEC

In addition to information regarding the rent schedule and the rights and responsibilities of the tenant, a TEC includes a statement indicating a lender or buyer will rely on the information provided by the TEC when making a decision to lend or purchase. [See Form 598 §10]

The tenant's *acknowledgment* of the TEC contents by his signed response, or *waiver* of the right to contest the contents of the TEC by nonresponse, can be relied on by a lender or buyer as establishing the contents of the TEC as complete and correct statements on the condition of the lease. [Calif. Evidence Code §623]

Should a dispute arise between the buyer (or a lender) and the tenant regarding conditions covered in a TEC, the properly submitted TEC bars any later claims made by the tenant which are in conflict with the contents of the TEC.

A buyer or lender asserts his right to rely on and enforce the conditions stated in the TEC by presenting the tenant's TEC as a defense to contrary claims made by the tenant, called *estoppel*.

The tenant would be *estopped from denying* the truth of the information in the TEC or *claiming* conflicting rights.

Security deposits confirmed

When leases are assigned to a buyer on closing a sale, the buyer requires the seller to account for any security deposits collected from the tenants and credit the amount of the remaining security deposits to the buyer, called *adjustments*.

With a TEC, the tenant confirms the correct accounting and amount of security remaining on deposit with the seller. Thus, the TEC avoids the transfer of insufficient security deposits on closing and establishes the buyer's liability for refund amounts.

If the buyer does not require a TEC to confirm the current amount of the security deposits claimed to be held by the seller for transfer to the buyer, the buyer may find himself paying tenants more than the security deposit amounts transferred by the seller on closing. [Calif. Civil Code §1950.5(i)]

To recover any deficiency in the credit received by the buyer on closing for security deposits held by the seller, the buyer would be required to pursue the seller.

TEC confirms prior representation

Use of an APOD form to present a summary of the operating data on a property's income and expenses confirms the income flow and operating expenses the buyer can immediately expect the property to generate.

To establish, **prior to closing**, the income and expenses the buyer can reasonably expect the tenants to pay, the buyer must:

- review all the leasing agreements the owner has with the tenants;

- compare the results of the lease examination to the figures in the APOD received before the offer was submitted; and

- confirm the rent schedules, rent adjustments and the expiration of the leases by serving TECs on the tenants and reviewing their responses.

Close on receipt of TEC

When received from the tenant, the TEC statement reflects only what has occurred at the time the tenant signed and returned the TEC.

TENANT ESTOPPEL CERTIFICATE

DATE:_____, 20_____, at _____, California

Items left blank or unchecked are not applicable.

FACTS:

This certificate pertains to conditions under the following agreement:

☐ Lease

☐ Month-to-month rental agreement

☐ Other:_____

Dated:_____, 20_____, at _____, California

Entered into by:

Landlord: _____

Tenant: _____

Recorded as document No. _____, _____, in _____ County records, California

Regarding real estate premises referred to as: _____

_____

STATEMENT:

Tenant certifies as follows:

1. The lease or rental agreement is:

   ☐ Unmodified and in effect.

   ☐ Modified and in effect under a modification agreement dated_____

   _____

2. Tenant is in possession of the premises, and has not assigned or sublet any portion of the premises.

3. If the agreement is a lease, the current term is for _____ years, ending _____, 20_____.

   3.1   Lease renewal/extension option term(s) run until _____, 20_____.

   3.2   The Tenant holds no privilege to terminate the lease prior to it's expiration.

4. The amount of monthly rent is $_____.

   4.1   No incentives, bonuses, free rent, discounts or refunds on the rental amount were given Tenant, except:

   _____

   4.2   Rent is paid through the period ending _____, 20_____.

   4.3   Tenant has not prepaid future rent, except the amount of $_____ for the rental period.

   4.4   No Tenant liens, claims, offsets or charges exist against Landlord, except _____

   _____

5. A security deposit of $_____ is held by Landlord to cover any expenses or losses caused by Tenant's breach of the agreement.

6. Any improvements required to have been made by Landlord or Tenant have been satisfactorily completed.

7. No breach of the agreement by Landlord or Tenant presently exists.

8. Tenant holds no contract, option or right to buy any interest in the real estate.

   8.1   Tenant holds no right to lease additional or substitute space in the real estate.

9. Tenant has caused no lien or encumbrance to attach to the leasehold interest in the property.

10. Tenant understands this certificate will be relied on by a buyer of the property or a lender secured by the real estate.

| TENANT: |
| I certify the above is true and correct. |
| Date:_____, 20_____ |
| Name: _____ |
| Phone: _____ |
| Fax: _____ |
| Signature: _____ |

Consider a tenant who signs and returns a TEC which is reviewed and approved by the buyer.

Before escrow closes, the seller breaches, modifies or enters into some other leasing arrangement with the tenant.

The seller's activities will not be noted on the TEC, and will also be unknown to the buyer when escrow closes unless somehow brought to the buyer's attention.

Thus, after receiving the TECs, a buyer or lender should review them and close the transaction as soon as possible.

Consequence of no TEC

A lender or buyer may be confronted at the time of closing with a tenant who has not signed and returned a TEC. Before closing, it is good practice to investigate whether differences actually exist between the owner's representations and the tenant's expectations under the lease agreement.

Even though the lender or buyer can legally rely on the contents of an unreturned TEC when the tenant's lease contains a TEC clause, an inquiry by the buyer or his agent is practical as a measure of prevention against future surprises.

Consider an owner of income-producing real estate who needs to generate cash and will do so by borrowing funds using the equity in his property as security for repayment of the loan.

Tenants occupy the property under lease agreements which include options to renew at fixed rental rates.

The lender does not condition the origination of the loan on the lender's receipt and approval of TECs from each tenant.

The lender makes the loan based on the value of comparable properties without regard for a schedule of the tenants' rent. [See **first tuesday** Form 380]

The owner defaults. The lender forecloses and is the successful bidder at the trustee's sale.

As the new owner, the lender (or anyone else who purchases the property at the trustee's sale) reviews the rent paid by the tenants.

The new owner decides to increase the rents to current market rates in order to bring the property's market value up to prices recently received on the sale of comparable properties.

However, the tenants who occupied the premises before the recording of the lender's trust deed claim their leases, which provide options to renew at old rental rates, are enforceable.

The lender claims his foreclosure sale establishes him as a new title holder with priority over the leases, and further, the leases are not recorded.

Can the tenants who occupied the property prior to the recording of the lender's trust deed enforce their renewal options even though the leases are not recorded?

Yes! The lender originating the loan on income-producing property, which was fore-closed and created the new ownership-by-fore-closure, recorded the trust deed *knowing* the tenants were in possession of the property. Thus:

- the leases *held by pre-existing tenants*, recorded or not, retain priority over the trust deed lien; and

- the lender is bound by the rent schedules in the pre-existing leases and renewal/extension options because of the seniority of the leases. [CC §1214]

The tenants' occupancy of the premises prior to originating the loan puts the lender on *constructive notice*, i.e., the lender is charged with knowledge of the lease agreements, renewal options and rent schedules. [**Evans** v. **Faught** (1965) 231 CA2d 698]

The requirement for lender approval of a TEC on each tenant would have informed the lender of the tenants' right and obligation to occupy and pay rent under their leases.

Thus, to be assured the owner's scheduled future income represents amounts the tenants expect to pay, every buyer or lender acquiring an interest in income-producing real estate should require tenant approval of TECs based on lease arrangements the owner/seller purports to hold with each tenant.

Signing an erroneous TEC

Consider a tenant who signs a tenant estoppel certificate (TEC) on the landlord's sale of nonresidential property. The TEC is erroneously prepared, stating an expiration date earlier than the date for termination provided in the lease.

The buyer relies on the TEC and purchases the property. The tenant remains in possession of the premises after the expiration date stated in the TEC.

Status of the lease

The TEC verifies the following:

- whether possession is held under a lease or rental agreement;

- the current monthly amount of rent and the basis for rent increases;

- the date rent is paid each month;

- the date to which rent has been paid;

- any incentives given to obtain the tenant;

- whether the tenant has prepaid any rents;

- the term of the lease and whether an early cancellation privilege exists;

- whether and in what manner the lease/rental agreement has been modified;

- whether the tenant holds any options to renew or extend, acquire additional or substitute space, or a right of first refusal to rent vacated space;

- whether the tenant holds any options to buy the real estate;

- the amount and status of any security deposit;

- any improvements the tenant must or can remove on vacating the premises;

- any landlord commitments to further improve the premises;

- whether the landlord or tenant is in breach of the lease or the rental agreement; and

- whether the tenant has assigned or sublet the premises, or liened his leasehold interest.

The buyer seeks to enforce the expiration date in the TEC by filing an unlawful detainer (UD) action to evict the tenant.

The tenant claims the buyer cannot enforce the expiration date in the TEC by a UD action since the TEC was not a written agreement which modified the lease, binding him to a different expiration date than actually stated in the lease.

The buyer claims the tenant is barred from contradicting the expiration date stated in the TEC.

Here, the new landlord can enforce the expiration date in the TEC and evict the tenant by a UD action. The TEC was a statement signed by the tenant certifying facts with respect to the lease which were relied on by the lender. Thus, the tenant was barred from later using the lease provision to contradict the TEC, called *estoppel*. [**Plaza Freeway Limited Partnership** v. **First Mountain Bank** (2000) 81 CA4th 616]

The erroneous, unsigned TEC

Now consider a purchase agreement for nonresidential rental property which requires the seller to provide the buyer with TECs for the buyer's further approval or cancellation of the purchase agreement.

One tenant's lease does not state the rent amounts but gives a formula for calculating rent. The seller instructs the buyer on how to calculate the rent due from the tenant based on the provisions in the tenant's lease.

The seller enters the rent amounts on the TEC based on the same calculations given the buyer and sends it to the tenant to be signed and returned to the buyer.

The tenant refuses to sign the TEC since the tenant is not obligated under his lease to provide a TEC.

The seller hands the buyer a copy of the tenant's unsigned TEC to satisfy the purchase agreement condition, which the buyer accepts.

After escrow closes, the buyer discovers the tenant's actual rent is significantly lower than the seller's estimate.

The buyer makes a demand on the seller for the difference between the actual rent paid by the tenant under the lease and the rent amounts calculated by the seller as the rent to be paid by the tenant.

Is the seller liable for the difference in the rent?

Yes! The buyer recovers lost rent from the seller in the amount of the difference between the seller's calculated estimate of rent and the actual amount owed by the tenant. The seller is obligated under the purchase agreement to provide the buyer with an accurate TEC, and the buyer based his decision to purchase the property on the information provided by the seller, not on the lease provisions for rent. [**Linden Partners** v. **Wilshire Linden Associates** (1998) 62 CA4th 508]

A seller avoids liability for errors in the TEC prepared and sent to tenants by including a TEC clause in the tenant's lease, calling for the tenant to sign and return a TEC on request. The failure of the tenant to provide the TEC called for in the lease is conclusive evidence any information contained in the TEC is correct. [See Fig. 1]

Thus, a tenant's refusal to sign a TEC when a TEC clause exists in the lease agreement results in the tenant, not the seller, being liable for the erroneous rent amount stated in the TEC prepared by the seller.

Chapter 42

Due-on-lease regulations

This chapter explains the rights of a trust deed lender under a due-on clause when the landlord leases the secured property to a tenant.

Rising interest rates bring lender interference

Real estate subject to a loan secured by a first trust deed containing a *due-on clause* is offered for sale or lease.

A user of the property is located who enters into a two-year lease of the property with an option to purchase the property.

Does the lease and option to buy trigger due-on enforcement by the lender?

Yes! A lease agreement that gives the tenant the option to purchase the leased property, which is encumbered by a trust deed containing a due-on clause, has triggered the due-on clause. Thus, the trust deed lender can call the loan **on discovery** of the transaction and foreclose if not paid in full. [12 Code of Federal Regulations §591.2(b)]

Interference under federal mortgage law

The **transfer** of any real estate interest that is encumbered by a trust deed containing a due-on clause allows the lender to enforce the clause under federal mortgage law. Thus, by *preemption*, Californians are deprived of their state law right to lease, sell or further encumber real estate without unreasonable lender interference. [12 United States Code §1701j-3; Calif. Civil Code §711]

For the landlord of property encumbered by a trust deed, leasing the property for a period of more than three years or entering into a lease for any period of time which is coupled with an option to buy, **triggers due-on enforcement**.

On discovery of the lease by the trust deed lender, the lender may either:

call the loan, demanding payment in full of all sums remaining unpaid, also known as *acceleration*; or

recast the loan, requiring a modification of the terms of the loan and payment of fees as a condition for the lender's consent to the triggering event, called a waiver.

Economics of the due-on clause

In times of rising rates, lenders seize on any event that legally triggers the due-on clause as an opportunity to increase the interest yield on their portfolio. Federal policy favors lender solvency.

As a condition for a trust deed lender to waive his due-on enforcement and allow the owner to enter into lease agreements, the lender may require the loan to be recast at current interest rates or pay a fee.

Thus, real estate interests, be they the owner's fee simple or simply the tenant's leasehold, when encumbered by a due-on trust deed, become increasingly difficult to transfer to new owners and tenants when interest rates are on the rise. Lender interference is then virtually guaranteed in their relentless pursuit to increase their portfolio yield and remain solvent during prolonged periods of rising rates.

However, the inability of landlords to lease their properties and at the same time retain existing financing has an adverse economic effect on real estate sales, equity financing and long-term leasing. Ultimately, as rates and therefore lender interference rise, many buyers, equity lenders and long-term tenants are driven out of the market. The result is depressed property values due to the reduced ability to sell, lease, assign a lease or encumber real estate interests.

Unless the lender's consent is obtained before closing a lease on encumbered real estate, the possibility of due-on enforcement and a call creates a high degree of risk for the landlord leasing property for more than a three-year period.

To best represent tenants, it is important for leasing agents to understand which events trigger the lender's due-on clause, which do not, and how to avoid or handle the lender's consent.

Due-on-lease clauses

The due-on clause, better known as a due-on-sale clause, is triggered when the owner of property secured by a due-on trust deed enters into:

- a lease with a term over three years; or

- a lease for any term with an option to purchase. [12 CFR §591.2(b)]

For example, an owner with a short-term interim construction loan on nonresidential rental property obtains a conditional loan commitment from a different lender for long-term "take-out" financing. The refinancing will pay off the construction loan once the construction is completed, providing permanent financing for the owner.

Funding of the take-out loan is conditioned on the property being 80% occupied by tenants with initial lease terms of at least five years.

The owner locates tenants for 80% of the newly constructed property, all with lease terms of five years or more, and the lender funds the loan. The loan is secured by a first trust deed on the property. The trust deed contains a due-on clause.

The five-year leases entered into to qualify for the refinancing pre-exist the refinancing and thus do not trigger the due-on clause in the new lender's trust deed.

However, after recording the trust deed, the owner continues to lease out space on his property for terms exceeding three years. None of the new leases are submitted to the lender for approval, and thus there is no waiver of the due-on clause.

Later, after interest rates rise, an officer of the lender visits the property and discovers new tenants. On inquiry, the officer learns the new tenants have leases with terms of more than three years.

The lender sends the owner a letter informing him the lender is calling the loan since "it has recently come to our attention" the owner has entered into lease agreements with terms over three years without first obtaining the lender's consent, an incurable violation of trust deed provisions.

The owner claims the lender cannot call the loan due since long-term leases were required by the lender as a condition for funding the loan, and thus the lender is estopped from invoking the due-on clause when five-year leases are later entered into.

Can the lender call the loan due or demand a recast of its terms?

Yes! By requiring leases with terms over three years as a condition for funding the loan, the lender did not waive his right to later call or recast the loan under its due-on clause when leases with a term over three years were entered into after the trust deed was recorded.

The landlord should have either obtained consent before leasing, leased for a three-year period with options to renew for three-year periods, or negotiated the elimination of the due-on clause from the trust deed when borrowing the funds.

Assignment/modification of the lease

An **assignment** or **modification** of an existing lease does not trigger the due-on clause in a trust deed encumbering the landlord's fee simple, unless the lease is modified to extend the term beyond three years from the date of modification or a purchase option is added.

For example, consider an owner of real estate who enters into a lease with a tenant.

Later, the owner takes out a loan secured by a trust deed containing a due-on clause.

After the trust deed is recorded, the tenant assigns the lease with the owner's approval, as provided for in the lease agreement.

Here, the lender's due-on clause is not triggered by the lease assignment. The lender's trust deed only encumbers the landlord's fee, not the leasehold interest held by the tenant. Thus, the tenant's assignment of his unencumbered leasehold does not trigger the lender's due-on clause since the leasehold assignment was not a transfer of an interest in the fee which is the lender's security and the lease provided for the assignment.

However, consider a landlord who releases the original tenant from all liability under the lease as part of an assumption of the lease by a new tenant. A trust deed with a due-on clause encumbers the landlord's ownership interest, whether junior or senior to the lease.

Here, the release of the original tenant creates a **novation** of the lease. Thus a new lease agreement has been entered into which conveys an interest in the secured property to the new tenant. [**Wells Fargo Bank, N.A.** v. **Bank of America NT & SA** (1995) 32 CA4th 424]

Thus, an *assumption* of the lease by the new tenant and the *release* of the former tenant from liability constitutes the present transfer of an ownership interest in the encumbered real estate. As a lease novation, the transaction triggers the due-on clause if the lease has a remaining term of over three years or includes an option to purchase.

Negotiations and conduct as waiver

Under federal regulations, lenders have the power to dictate the fate of most long-term real estate leasing transactions since most real estate is encumbered by trust deeds containing due-on clauses.

However, a landlord intending to lease his real estate without lender interference may be able to negotiate a *waiver* of the lender's due-on rights when originating a trust deed loan, if not the entire elimination of the clause or some limitation of its use.

Waiver agreements are basically trade-offs. The lender will demand some consideration in return for waiving or agreeing to an elimination or limitation of its future due-on rights, such as increased points on origination, additional security, increased interest, a shorter due date or an assumption fee on each consent.

The lender's waiver of his due-on rights would apply only to the current lease transaction under review for consent. Unless additionally agreed, any later leasing of the property will again trigger the due-on clause, allowing the lender to call or recast the loan again (due in part to the nonwaiver provision in the trust deed).

Besides obtaining a written waiver agreement, waiver of the lender's due-on rights may occur **by conduct**. By failing to promptly enforce his due-on rights when he has knowledge of the transaction, the lender may lose his right to enforce the clause on past leasing arrangements.

For example, a landlord enters into a long-term lease on property encumbered by a loan secured by a trust deed containing a due-on clause. The lender is informed of the leasing arrangements by letter or annual audit, but does not call the loan or make demands on the landlord.

Instead, the lender accepts payments from the landlord for over a year after being informed (unilaterally claiming he has been reserving his due-.on rights). The lender then calls the loan under its due-on clause based on the lease transaction disclosed to him over a year earlier.

However, the lender **by his conduct waived** the right to enforce his due-on clause. The lender accepted payments from the owner for over a year after learning of the lease. [**Rubin** v. **Los Angeles Federal Savings and Loan Association** (1984) 159 CA3d 292]

Broker liability for due-on avoidance

A lender can only call the loan when he discovers a lease of more than three years in duration or a lease with an option to buy.

If the tenant's option to purchase is not recorded, and the lease agreement is for a term under three years, the lender might not discover any transfer of an interest in the real estate has taken place which triggers its due-on clause.

However, when the lender later discovers the lease is coupled with an option to purchase, his only remedy against the landlord is to call the loan due, or agree to recast the loan as a condition for waiving his right to call. The lender cannot recover any retroactive interest differential (RID) from the landlord for the period beginning on commencement of the lease and ending on discovery of the lease transaction. When the lender calls the loan, it cannot add additional back interest to the loan payoff amount.

However, an adviser, such as a leasing agent or attorney, assisting the landlord or the tenant to mask the lease and option to purchase from the lender for the purpose of avoiding due-on enforcement, has wrongfully interfered with the lender's legal right to call or recast the loan and can be held liable for the lender's losses, called tortious interference with *prospective economic advantage*.

The adviser's liability arises based on the extent to which the adviser's actions were specifically intended to conceal the lease and prevent a call by the lender, and on the foresight that the lender would incur losses due to the concealment. [**J'Aire Corporation** v. **Gregory** (1979) 24 C3d 799]

The **lender's losses** caused by the adviser's wrongful interference are calculated based on the interest differential between the note rate and the market rate at the commencement of the lease, retroactive to the date of the lease.

Cases

California Codes

Code of Civil Procedure

Federal Codes

Topical index

L

W